The Politics and Power of Tourism in Palestine

Tourism in Palestine has been receiving an increasingly important profile given its economic and religious importance and the significant role it plays in Israeli-Palestinian relations, representation of Palestinian statehood and identity, and wider Middle Eastern politics. Nevertheless, Palestine, like much of the Middle East as a whole, remains extremely underrepresented in tourism literature. This title aims to fill this void by being the first book dedicated to exploring the significance of tourism in relationship to Palestine.

The book examines the role of tourism in Palestine at three main levels. First, it provides an overview of destination management and marketing issues for the tourism industry in Palestine and addresses not only the visitor markets and the economic significance of tourism but also the realities of the difficulties of destination management, marketing and promotion of the Palestinian state. Second, it provides chapters and case studies that interrogate not only the various forms of tourism in Palestine but also its economic, social, environmental and spiritual importance. This part also conveys a dimension to tourism in Palestine that is not usually appreciated in the Western mainstream media. The third part indicates the way in which tourism in Palestine highlights broader questions and debates in tourism studies and the way in which travel in the region is framed in wider discourses. A significant dimension of the book is the attention it gives to the different voices of stakeholders in Palestinian tourism at varying levels of scale.

This timely volume will offer the reader significant insight into the challenges and issues of tourism in this area now and in the future. It will benefit those interested in tourism, Middle East studies, politics, economics, development studies and geography.

Rami K. Isaac is currently a Senior Lecturer in tourism teaching at the NHTV Breda University of Applied Sciences in the Netherlands. His research interests in the area of tourism development and management, cultural heritage and political aspects of tourism. He has published numerous articles and book chapters on critical theory and tourism and political (in)stability, occupation, tourism and war, violence and transformational tourism.

C. Michael Hall is a Professor in the Department of Management, Marketing and Entrepreneurship at the University of Canterbury, New Zealand and is also Docent, Department of Geography, University of Oulu, Finland. He holds visiting positions in Finland, Sweden and South Africa. As co-editor of *Current Issues in Tourism* he has a long legacy of publications on tourism politics and policy as well as its role in regional development.

Freya Higgins-Desbiolles is a Senior Lecturer with the School of Management of the University of South Australia. She has published numerous articles and book chapters on justice and human rights issues in tourism, indigenous tourism and policy, planning and management of tourism.

Contemporary geographies of leisure, tourism and mobility
Series Editor: C. Michael Hall
Professor at the Department of Management, College of Business and Economics, University of Canterbury, Christchurch, New Zealand

For a complete list of titles in this series, please visit www.routledge.com.

The aim of this series is to explore and communicate the intersections and relationships between leisure, tourism and human mobility within the social sciences.

It will incorporate both traditional and new perspectives on leisure and tourism from contemporary geography, e.g. notions of identity, representation and culture, while also providing for perspectives from cognate areas such as anthropology, cultural studies, gastronomy and food studies, marketing, policy studies and political economy, regional and urban planning, and sociology, within the development of an integrated field of leisure and tourism studies.

Also, increasingly, tourism and leisure are regarded as steps in a continuum of human mobility. Inclusion of mobility in the series offers the prospect to examine the relationship between tourism and migration, the sojourner, educational travel, and second home and retirement travel phenomena.

The series comprises two strands:

Contemporary geographies of leisure, tourism and mobility aims to address the needs of students and academics, and the titles will be published in hardback and paperback. Titles include:

1 **The Moralisation of Tourism**
Sun, sand....and saving the world?
Jim Butcher

2 **The Ethics of Tourism Development**
Mick Smith and Rosaleen Duffy

3 **Tourism in the Caribbean**
Trends, development, prospects
Edited by David Timothy Duval

4 **Qualitative Research in Tourism**
Ontologies, epistemologies and methodologies
Edited by Jenny Phillimore and Lisa Goodson

5 **The Media and the Tourist Imagination**
Converging cultures
Edited by David Crouch, Rhona Jackson and Felix Thompson

6 **Tourism and Global Environmental Change**
Ecological, social, economic and political interrelationships
Edited by Stefan Gössling and C. Michael Hall

7 **Cultural Heritage of Tourism in the Developing World**
Edited by Dallen J. Timothy and Gyan Nyaupane

Routledge studies in contemporary geographies of leisure, tourism and mobility is a forum for innovative new research intended for research students and academics, and the titles will be available in hardback only. Titles include:

The Politics and Power of Tourism in Palestine

Edited by
Rami K. Isaac, C. Michael Hall
and Freya Higgins-Desbiolles

Routledge
Taylor & Francis Group

LONDON AND NEW YORK

First published 2016 by Routledge

2 Park Square, Milton Park, Abingdon, Oxfordshire OX14 4RN
711 Third Avenue, New York, NY 10017

Routledge is an imprint of the Taylor & Francis Group, an informa business

First issued in paperback 2018

British Library Cataloguing in Publication Data
A catalogue record for this book is available from the British Library

Library of Congress Cataloging in Publication Data
A catalog record for this book has been requested

ISBN: 978-1-138-82470-6 (hbk)
ISBN: 978-1-138-59228-5 (pbk)

Typeset in Times New Roman
by Saxon Graphics Ltd, Derby

Contents

Figures

Tables

Contributors

Jamil Alfaleet, Gaza University, Palestine.

Rania Filfil Almbaid, Pocket Theatre, Palestine.

Nada Atrash, Centre for Cultural Heritage Preservation, Palestine.

Michel Awad, Siraj Centre for Holy Land Studies, Palestine.

Ryvka Barnard, New York University, USA.

Erdinç Çakmak, NHTV Breda University of Applied Sciences, the Netherlands.

Freya Higgins-Desbiolles, University of South Australia, Australia.

C. Michael Hall, University of Canterbury, Christchurch, New Zealand.

Waleed Hazbun, American University of Beirut, Lebanon.

Rami K. Isaac, NHTV Breda University of Applied Sciences, the Netherlands.

Rami Kassis, Alternative Tourism Group, Palestine.

Suhail Khalilieh, Applied Research Institute, Palestine.

Yiota Kutulas, Siraj Centre for Holy Land Studies, Palestine.

Ian S. McIntosh, Indiana University–Purdue University at Indianapolis, USA.

Bisan Mitri, Occupied Palestine and Syrian Golan Heights Advocacy Initiative, Palestine.

Hassan Muamer, Battir Resident, Palestine.

Vincent Platenkamp, NHTV Breda University of Applied Sciences, the Netherlands.

Raed Saadeh, Rozana Association, Palestine.

Tom Selwyn, School of Oriental and African Studies, University of London, UK.

Ranjan Solomon, Alternative Tourism Group, Palestine.

Acknowledgements

There are few regions where the subject of tourism has come as fraught as in what is usually termed the Middle East. In this area tourism has been inseparable from broader issues of self-determination, occupation, openness, power, representation, terrorism, transparency, mobility and, of course, peace. Arguably the location in which these concerns have been brought into sharpest focus is Palestine. A state to and in which mobility is potentially one of the most constrained in the world, yet is simultaneously an extremely attractive destination not only for pilgrimage, for which it is most recognized, but a range of other tourism activities as well. To further complicate any study of tourism in Palestine the politics of the region are also deeply enmeshed with its study. To pretend otherwise would be naïve. Yet, despite what some observers may perceive, this is not a book with an intended political position at the outset. Instead, the aim of the book is to bring together a number of different Palestinian tourism focused voices in a single English-language volume so as to allow greater discussion and insight into the past, current and future role of tourism in Palestine. This is regarded as an essential first step to better understand not only the possibilities that exist in Palestinian tourism development but also the implications of different positions that exist with respect to policy formulation and marketing strategies in Palestine and the wider region, especially in relations with Israel and other countries and the determination of Palestinian sovereignty. This book therefore does not include Israeli voices with respect to Palestine or, just as significantly in some instances, Egyptian, Jordanian and those of international institutions. Hopefully, these voices, along with those of Palestinians, will be assembled in a future volume as part of a broader discussion as to the role of tourism in the sustainable development and promotion of the region and how tourist mobilities can be better encouraged and enabled as part of community-based tourism strategies.

The editors have a number of acknowledgements they would like to make that have contributed to the development of the book. We would like first to thank all the contributors to this volume. We very much appreciate their chapters and particularly their assistance, understanding and patience at times with our request for details and adjustments. Their breadth of viewpoint, thought-provoking and detailed knowledge of their very different subject matter has provided us with a unique and wide ranging themes of the subject of the volume.

We also wish to thank the staff at Routledge for their patience and support throughout the preparation of the book proposal and submission of the manuscript, and in particular Emma Travis and Philippa Mullins for their continued encouragement and support. Jody Cowper-James also provided invaluable assistance with respect to checking referencing and formatting. There are also numerous individuals, businesses and institutions in Palestine, Jordan, Israel and elsewhere that have supported the editors' research in Palestine which has greatly helped in the development and reading of the present volume. Finally, we thank our families, who inevitably have had to put up with disappearances, frustrations and the usual range of emotions and problems that are part of completing an edited book.

1 Introduction

*Rami K. Isaac, C. Michael Hall and
Freya Higgins-Desbiolles*

An academic text on tourism in Palestine has been long overdue. There are numerous reasons as to why this is the case, but not least of which is the interminable wait for a 'peace process' to offer some sort of settlement to ease the political and strategic tensions that feature in this region. Writing in 2015, we can wait no longer for this elusive settlement and we write in a contingent way to explore what contemporary tourism in Palestine looks like and to examine what it may reveal about tourism and indeed our wider world.

Tourism is now a complex global phenomenon with political, economic, social, cultural, environmental and educational dimensions. Robinson (2001: 31) considers tourism to be the 'largest of multi-national activities'. When Lanfant (1995: 26) described the omnipresence of tourism, she noted that tourism on a world scale makes itself felt at geographical, ecological and technological levels – as well as in the less visible domain of symbolic processes. AlSayyed (2001: 1) considers the twentieth century to have 'been the century of travel and tourism'. Indeed, the number of international journeys has increased dramatically in recent decades and the source of travellers is shifting, such that travel and tourism is changing the very nature of the global community (Cohen and Kennedy 2000). As travel around the world has risen to unprecedented levels, the number of tourists visiting certain countries and cities in given year often exceeds the numbers of those place's native populations. Additionally, many countries have become dependent on tourism as a source of their economic prosperity, and numerous countries see tourism serve as their top source of foreign exchange. As a result, tourism is a force of global significance and all countries wish to access its benefits.

Understanding the development of tourism in Palestine requires some insight into the region in which Palestine is located. The Eastern Mediterranean holds a long tradition with tourism attracting visitors for business, cultural, leisure and religious purposes. The region occupies a unique geographical location, at the crossroads between Europe, Asia and Africa. As the cradle of cultures it has much to offer with respect to history and antiquities, such as the ancient civilizations of Egypt and Mesopotamia and the numerous Greek and Roman ruins along the Mediterranean coast. The region is also where the most important Jewish, Christian and Muslim sites are located. With respect to natural attractions, the

Middle East includes spectacular desert landscapes, the Nile, the Red Sea beaches and coral reefs, and the Dead Sea (Kester and Carvo 2004).

However, the term the 'Middle East' can also be understood as a politically charged Western European, colonial construct (Daher 2007). This region of the eastern Mediterranean has been known by several names through the centuries, including: Bilad al Sham, Masreq, Levant, Orient, Near East, Middle East, Near East and North Africa (NENA), and Middle East and North Africa (MENA). It is clear that the Middle East has been viewed in relation to others because of its strategic location between continents and more recently its value in terms of vital oil and gas resources which has seen the political-strategic power plays that have created such instability and strife. In terms of tourism, locating the region by reference to some orientation to the Western powers indicates that the destination image of the region is rendered through a particular cultural lens that undermines local agency and self-determination.

The topic of tourism in the Middle East has been receiving greater recognition in the English language academic literature (e.g., Daher 2007; Kliot and Collins-Kreiner 2003; Mansfeld 1996; Wahab 2000), especially with respect to its political and economic dimensions but, until recently, work on tourism in Palestine has been relatively limited (e.g., Al-Rimmawi 2003; Clarke 2000; Shoval and Cohen-Hattab 2001; Brin 2006; Isaac 2008, 2009, 2010a, 2010b, 2010c, 2011, 2013, 2014; Isaac and Hodge 2011; Cakmak and Isaac 2012; Isaac and Ashworth 2012; Isaac and Platenkamp 2012, Isaac *et al.* 2012; Blanchard and Higgins-Desbiolles 2013; Cohen-Hattab and Shoval 2014). However, tourism in Palestine has been receiving an increasingly important profile given its economic and religious importance and the significant role it plays in Israeli–Palestinian relations, representation of Palestinian statehood and identity, and wider Middle Eastern politics. Nevertheless, Palestine, like much of the Middle East as a whole, remains extremely underrepresented in tourism research and, to date, there is no book dedicated to exploring the significance of tourism in relationship to Palestine.

Hannam (2008), for example, commented on the book edited by Daher (2007) entitled *Tourism in the Middle East*:

> the collection on the whole is somewhat biased to a relatively small number of countries in the Middle East ... I would certainly look forward to a second volume of chapters that would give us a wider geographical coverage, including perhaps some critical insights and contrasts with the contemporary research that has been published on Israel too.

This indeed also includes Palestine and we are offering this work to contribute to filling this gap.

The roots of Palestine's tourism particularly rest in religious pilgrimages undertaken by the three great monotheistic religions which were born in the region. A great example of how the West came to know Palestine as a pilgrimage site is the travel book *Cook's tourists' handbook for Palestine and Syria* (1876), which indicates how mass tourism was developed around the pilgrimage sector in that era.

Following on from the break-up of the Ottoman Empire after World War I, the British took over administration of Palestine under a 'mandate' of the League of Nations. During colonization, traditional religious pilgrimage used to be mainstream tourism prior to the British Mandate in Palestine. During the British Mandate, Palestine became more westernized, more democratic and attracted more secular western tourists and also more politically oriented tourists (Bar and Cohen-Hattab 2003; Cohen-Hattab 2004a, 2004b; Cohen-Hattab and Katz 2001). On the one hand, infrastructure was improved, hotels and resorts were built, and historical, religious as well as cultural sites and monuments were preserved and even restored. However, simultaneously the ideological battle between Zionists and Arab Palestinians started to be articulated. 'Jewish tourism to Palestine' (Cohen-Hattab and Katz 2001: 170) started off under the British Mandate with Tel Aviv being promoted as 'the first Hebrew city' and the setting up of guest houses in new Jewish settlements. Therefore, this 'Jewish tourism' was 'mainly brought about and developed by Zionist publicity following the flowering of Jewish nationalism' (Cohen-Hattab and Katz 2001: 171).

The Arab–Palestinian population opposed the institution of a Jewish/Israeli state in their own Palestinian homeland. This opposition was taken onto the streets as well as in the political and economic arena culminating in the Arab Revolt of the 1930s. At this time, tourism began to be employed as an ideological tool to present tourists with their own vision of Palestine (Cohen-Hattab and Katz, 2001). Political tourism, as it is practiced today in the Occupied Territories of Palestine, therefore has its roots in this shift from traditional mainstream pilgrimage to politically and ideologically infused tourism during and after the British Mandate.

During the British Mandate in Palestine, tourism became the battleground for economic and political superiority between Jews and local Arabs (Bar and Cohen-Hattab 2003). Tourists in Jerusalem had at that time more interactions with local Arabs since 'Arabs made detailed preparations to prevent anyone but themselves from profiting economically [from tourism]' (Bar and Cohen-Hattab 2003: 65). Due to historical events, most notably the dispossession caused by the establishment of the state of Israel in 1948 and the occupation that followed the 1967 War, Israel was in the position to make their narrative the mainstream tourism discourse and to direct the benefits of tourism to the Israeli economy. As a result the Palestinian narrative was suppressed by depictions of Palestine and Palestinians as 'dangerous and dirty' (Kassis 2006) and Palestinian sites were appropriated and presented as Jewish heritage (see for instance Noy 2014).

This book examines the role of tourism in Palestine at three main levels. First, it provides an overview of destination management and marketing issues for the tourism industry in Palestine and addresses not only the visitor markets and the economic significance of tourism but also the realities of the difficulties of destination management, marketing and promotion of the Palestinian state. Second, it provides a series of chapters and case studies that interrogate not only the various forms of tourism in Palestine but also its economic, social, environmental and spiritual importance. This section also conveys a dimension to tourism in Palestine that is not usually appreciated in the Western mainstream media. The third section indicates the way in which tourism in Palestine highlights broader questions and debates in tourism studies and the way in which travel in the region is framed in wider discourses.

A significant dimension of the book is the attention it gives to the different voices of stakeholders in Palestinian tourism. Appropriately, this aspect of the book reflects Edward Saïd's (1974) notion of silenced voices. Silenced voices are voices that have been silenced or that are unable to express themselves. They are not observed in official, academic or professional discussions. This is mostly due to the reality of the predominant hegemonic power relations – they have been filtered out of the focus of interest in these discussions. While there may be also a number of reasons that this is the case, it results in an important research gap which this edited volume in part seeks to fill in the tourism context and involves a variety of stakeholders to gain as rich and vibrant a text as possible.

Palestine is a unique faith tourist destination – its long history, religious significance and natural beauty make it an amazing place to visit. Palestine's importance derives partly from the fact that it is home to the three monotheistic and Abrahamic religions of Judaism, Christianity and Islam. Every year it attracts many pilgrims, people of faith and scholars who visit the holy places. Secular tourists come to explore the historical sites, Palestine's vibrant cities, rural life and natural reserves. However since the beginning of the twentieth century Palestine has seen complicated changes in its political circumstances. These have included the creation of Israel in 1948 and the 1967 war. Consequently of the latter, Israel occupied the West bank including East Jerusalem and the Gaza strip. These events have created catastrophic political, economic and social facts which have deeply affected the life of the Palestinian people, many of whom became refugees dislocated to neighbouring states and indeed the world as a Palestinian diaspora. In many ways Palestine itself was simply wiped off the map, historic Palestine coming to be known as Israel. In this context tourism became a political tool in the supremacy and domination of the Israel establishment over land and people, and an instrument for preventing the Palestinians from enjoying the benefits of the fruits of the cultural and human interaction on which tourism thrives.

Despite the fact that Israel signed the Oslo Agreements with the PLO in the 1990s and recognized the establishment of the Palestinian Authority to administer some of the Palestinian territories, namely the West Bank and the Gaza Strip, many years of life in those areas are still under Israeli control. For example, Israel controls all access to Palestine (land and sea borders as well as access from the airport), most of the Palestinian water resources, and all movement of people and goods from, to and within Palestine. These facts have significant impacts on the development of tourism in the Palestinian territories and the dissemination of information. Jerusalem – the heart of tourism in the region – has been illegally annexed to Israel, filled with illegal settlements, besieged, surrounded by checkpoints, and encircled by the Apartheid Wall, (Alternative Tourism Group 2014) all of which has resulted in the city's distancing from its social and geographical surroundings.

For the first two and half decades of the Occupation, from 1967 through the first Intifada and until the economic closure following the Gulf War, Israel's economic policy towards the Occupied Territories of Palestine (OTP) was one of controlled development – 'asymmetric containment' (United Nations Conference on Trade and Development (UNCTAD) 2006). Israel wanted to incorporate the territories' economy into Israel. The Palestinian population thus became one of Israel's major agricultural export markets. The Old City of Jerusalem became its most important tourist venue and Palestinian themselves provided cheap produce and labour. However, the economy of the territories had to be kept under strict control for fear that their cheap products and labour could undermine or compete with Israel's own market – and in case of economic strength and independence create demands for political independence (Halper 2008). Through the years, economic development in the Occupied Territories of Palestine fell under ever greater limitations. Palestinians were not allowed to open a bank of their own or open a hotel; tariffs and subsidies for Israeli produce, and import controls prevented the Palestinian economy from seriously competing with the Israeli one; and economic ties between the Palestinians and Arab countries were severely curtailed (Hever 2007). Simultaneously, Israel actively de-developed the Palestinian economy. It invested almost nothing in infrastructure, housing or services. In the agricultural sector, a pillar of the Palestinian economy, farm land continued to be expropriated at a rapid pace. The closure policy prevented Palestinian produce from reaching Israeli markets and the steadily tightening internal closure closed access even to Palestinian markets within the Occupied Territories of Palestine.

Israel maintains control over utilities such as water, electricity and phone services in the Occupied Territories, even though Israel charges very high prices for these utilities, in spite of low income of the Palestinians. In fact, they actually pay more for electricity than Israelis. And so, in 2004, Israel confiscated US$ 15.8 million from humanitarian aid sent to the Palestinians for utility bills owed by Palestinian municipalities (Hever 2007).

Key sectors of the Palestinian economy are under Israeli control: 98 per cent of Palestinian National Authority (PNA) electricity comes from the Israel Eclectic Corporation; the Palestinian natural gas and oil market is monopolised by Dor Alon and other Israeli companies. Israeli companies' share of the Palestinian mobile line market is as much as 45 per cent. Nowadays, the West Bank and Gaza function as captive markets. Overall, Israeli exports to the West Bank and Gaza have risen from US$0.8 billion in 1988 to US$2.6 billion in 2007, solidifying the Palestinian economy's dependence on Israel.

Nevertheless, as the Oslo peace process began, the Israeli government took an almost unexplainable decision to impose an economic closure on the West Bank. 'Closure', writes Amira Hass (2002: 6, cited in Halper, 2008: 180) – one of the Israel's most respected journalists, a close observer of the peace process, and a resident of the occupied Territories of Palestine for many years – 'had a very immediate advantage in the [Oslo] negotiating process underway'. Particularly under Rabin and Peres, the use of closure as an instrument of economic leverage over the PNA was blatant: 'You arrest this one or that one, and we'll give you 500 more work permits and if you behave yourselves and agree to our (slow) implementation timetables, we'll allow you to export more vegetables and release from Israeli customs the heavy machinery you imported' were the unexpressed but widely understood premises underlying negotiations.

Following the Oslo Accords, it was expected that the Palestinian economy would enter a period of sustained rapid growth. By 1999 real GDP had grown to US$4,512 million. However, since 2000, when Israel instituted a strict closure regime in response to the second Intifada, the Palestinian economy has been on downward trend. GDP fell to US$3,557 million at the height of fighting in 2002 and the recovered slightly in 2004 and 2005. But, with the continuing growth in settlements, closures and the cut off in direct aid, GDP fell again in 2006 (World Bank 2007).

The most important geographic factors to have stemmed from the 1993 and 1995 Oslo Accords were the breakdown of Palestinian lands under Areas A, B, and C, denoting the extent of Israeli or Palestinian jurisdiction, and the policy of closures. Closure is meant to deny Palestinians their right to free movement, stemming from a 'pass system' first introduced in 1991, which required that every Palestinian had to obtain a colour coded identification card and apply for a permit to move between and within what would eventually become Areas A, B and C (Tawil-Souri 2011). Currently, in the West Bank, Area A, under direct Palestinian control, includes the major populated cities but constitutes no more than 3 per cent of those areas; Area B encompasses 450 Palestinian towns and villages representing 27 per cent of the West Bank, jointly-controlled territory in which the Palestinians would exercise civil authority but Israel would retain security control; and Area C, in which Israel has exclusive control, constitutes the rest of the West Bank (70 per cent), including agricultural land, the Jordan Valley, natural reserves, areas with lower population density, Israeli settlements and military areas (Hanafi 2009).

Because of the hostile economic policies, the almost complete denial to Palestinians workers of access to the Israeli labour market, and the effects of the Segregation Wall (Isaac 2009), the economic situation of the Occupied Territories of Palestine reached emergency proportions. Unemployment runs to 67 per cent in Gaza, 48 per cent in the West Bank, and 75 per cent of Palestinians including two thirds of the children, live in poverty, on less than US$2 a day, defined by the UN as 'deep poverty'. More than 100,000 Palestinians out of the 125,000 who used to work in Israel, have lost their jobs (UNCTAD 2006).

In recent years, these efforts at de-development have been seemingly facilitated by agents such as the World Bank, the British Department for International Development (DFID) and the Japan International Cooperation Agency (JICA). All these actors work together with the Palestinian National Authority (PNA) to implement 'development' schemes that treat the Occupation as a partner rather than an occupier, thus normalizing the existing patterns of domination, rather than enhancing Palestinian capacity to develop independently. For instance, Murad (2014) examines aid through the lens of 'complicity' and exposes shortcomings in current legal frameworks. She argues that regardless of the limitations of applicable law, international aid actors are fundamentally responsible to those they seek to assist and must be held accountable for the harm they cause or enable.

She identifies the areas in which questions need to be asked and concludes with some of the steps that Palestinian civil society and the international solidarity movement should take. Palestinians have a right to request international aid, and donors have an obligation to provide it. The manner in which this aid has been provided, however, may actually facilitate violations of Palestinian rights under international humanitarian law (IHL). The failure of international actors to act in line with their obligations as third-state and non-state actors enables the status quo to continue, incriminating aid actors in on-going violations. In fact, several factors that are actually under the control of the international aid system serve to reinforce a regime that facilitates violations of Palestinian rights. These include: (1) donor categorization of the situation of Palestinians living under the Israeli occupation as an 'emergency' year after year that leads to short-term interventions that perpetuate need by focusing on symptoms rather than causes; (2) the policy of non-confrontation with Israel regardless of its actions conveys international acquiescence and contributes to Israeli impunity; and (3) the lack of accountability of the aid system itself has enabled it to marginalize Palestinians and become self-serving.

We have highlighted only briefly here the circumstances and context of current Palestinian tourism. It is a most unusual case and detailed study of it will yield useful insights into this special tourism destination, into tourism politics and tourism dynamics and into our world. We will leave it to the chapter authors to flesh out these issues and help theorize their significance.

Structure of the book

The next chapter in this introductory section provides an overview of destination management and marketing issues for the tourism industry in Palestine and addresses not only the visitor markets and the economic significance of tourism but also the realities of the difficulties of destination management, marketing and promotion of the Palestinian state. The subsequent chapters in this volume are organized into two parts.

Part II examines the ways in which tourism matters to Palestine, beginning with eight chapters that explore the ways in which tourism is so important to Palestine in every way, including economically, socially, politically, environmentally and spiritually. The section analyses how tourism is being hampered and constrained and the impacts of this on Palestinian lives, and the political-economic difficulties in developing tourism. In Chapter 3 Kassis, Solomon and Higgins-Desbiolles provide a case study of justice and solidarity tourism. These are forms of tourism that counter dominant trends and are based on the desire of travellers to learn and engage rather than to gain a mere glimpse and leave with even greater prejudices. Solidarity and justice tourism starts from a comprehensive analysis of what tourism means, not just for those engaged in it but also for the local populations in tourist destinations. This sort of tourism is planned with a prime regard for the needs of the local people and challenges the monopoly imposed by Israel in the tourism industry. It also aims to raise the awareness of travellers about the political realities 'see it for yourself' experience and advocate for Palestine and the Palestinian. It is followed in Chapter 4 by Kutulas and Awad who present bike and hike in Palestine, a new form of tourism and the implications of it for the Palestinian people. The visitor experiences warm hospitality by staying with Palestinian families – learning firsthand about the rich culture, traditions and cuisine. Experiential tourism is regarded as paving the way for sustainable tourism in Palestine, enabling local communities to benefit directly, enhancing their standard of living and rural development overall.

Chapter 5 examines the story of Battir as a case study in which tourism development, colonialism and resistance are all at play. Battir's story represents an example of the many challenges facing Palestinian villages suffering under Israeli colonial rule. In the summer of 2014, the small West Bank village of Battir made international news headlines when it was declared a World Heritage Site (WHS). For many tourism host communities, a UNESCO designation is key to putting them on the tourism map, and a potential boost to the tourism economy. For the village of Battir, the expectations were more modest, but simultaneously represented extremely high stakes. The UNESCO designation process for Battir was less about potential for tourism, than the village's larger struggle for survival, a struggle that has reached and is waged far beyond the scope of UNESCO and tourism. Chapter 6 focuses on Bethlehem which aims to present a view of the potential impacts that a WHS should offer to tourism in the town, taking into consideration the current situation and the future expectations based on the outputs of the conservation and management plan. Experiential community-based rural tourism is further explored in Chapter 7 and provides a description of the key sustainability elements that are necessary to develop not only tourism but also provide the environment needed to create the local readiness and the differentiation to improve the competitive advantage of the national Palestinian product. Chapter 8 explores the potential of Palestinian diaspora and VFR, followed by the history and different periods of forced displacement of the Palestinian people during the last 60 years and presents an example of the Palestinian birth rights that are starting to gain ground in Palestine. Pilgrimage tourism in Palestine, which is still the backbone of the Palestinian tourism economy, is examined in Chapter 9. The chapter also touches the difficulties and challenges dealing with this form of tourism, in which Israel has a stranglehold on the flow of international market. Chapter 10 investigates the potential of tourism through identification of the archaeological and cultural sites that are of interest for tourism, as well as the social and cultural assets of Gaza.

Part III deals with the ways in which Palestine matters to tourism. This section provides a macro-level perspective and communicates the ways in which engaging with Palestinian issues has relevance to the worlds of tourism. Chapter 11 briefly examines how tourism's relationship to academic and cultural boycott fits into the struggle for liberation and self-determination of the Palestinian people. It provides a historical overview of the history of the Palestinian Campaign for the Academic and Cultural Boycott of Israel (PACBI) as part of the global Boycott, Divestment and Sanctions (BDS) Movement, its objectives and goals and how they coincide with the general objectives (and pillars) of the BDS Movement. Chapter 12 examines and revisits questions of travel in Israel/Palestine and explores how travel can offer a more complex experience of place. Although a journey may take place in one moment in time, the 'place' visited can be viewed and experienced as reflecting multiple moments. The establishment of Israel in 1948 and the occupation of the reminder of the Palestinian Territories from 1967 have resulted in a regime of restrictions on mobility. Chapter 13 shows that they are worthy of study not only for the extreme negative impacts on Palestinian people but also for what they show us about the privilege of mobility in our world.

The concluding part explores possible futures that imagine what tourism could be in a sovereign, viable, self-determining and peaceful Palestine. In Chapter 14 Selwyn and Isaac discuss the future of tourism and pilgrimage in Palestine and examine how tourism/pilgrimage could be re-shaped in Palestine in order to meet the needs of the widest cross section of Palestinians. Chapter 15 reports on an initiative which demonstrates the potentials and limitations of such assertions in places of 'hot conflict' such as Palestine. McIntosh and Alfaleet's work was instrumental in setting up a peace incubator through a virtual classroom by linking students from Gaza with students from the United States. As a result of these efforts, students of Gaza University developed a profound vision for the Gaza Strip in 2050 that identified tourism as the key to a renewed and thriving economy. In Chapter 16 Çakmak and Isaac discuss the State of Palestine as a new country, but probably the oldest nation brand in the world. The chapter aims to serve as an early step of developing the Palestine's state branding strategy and concludes with some key suggestions for state branding management. Chapter 17, the final chapter, is a closing piece by Isaac, Platenkamp, Higgins-Desbiolles and Hall who endeavour to give Palestinian tourism(s) a voice in academic as well as professional discussions that have emerged from the volume. It also discusses the potential of future research and dialogue and provides a call for a revitalization of a critical and humanistic intellectual position, in terms of giving a voice to the excluded, in the tourism academy.

References

Al-Rimmawi, H.A. (2003) 'Palestinian tourism: a period of transition', *International Journal of Contemporary Hospitality Management*, 15(2): 76–85.

Al-Sayyed, N. (2001) 'Global norms and urban forms in the age of tourism: Manufacturing heritage, consuming tradition', in N. Al-Sayyed (ed.) *Consuming tradition, manufacturing heritage: global norms and urban forms in the age of tourism*, New York: Routledge.

Alternative Tourism Group (ATG) (2014) *Palestine and Palestinians*, Beitsahoutrr: ATG.

Bar, D. and Cohen-Hattab, K. (2003) 'A new kind of pilgrimage: the modern tourist pilgrim of nineteenth century and early twentieth century Palestine', *Middle Eastern Studies*, 39(2): 131–148.

Blanchard, L.B. and Higgins-Desbiolles, F. (eds) (2013) *Peace through tourism: promoting human security through international citizenship*, London: Routledge.

Brin, E. (2006) 'Politically-oriented tourism in Jerusalem', *Tourist Studies*, 6(3), 215–243.

Cakmak, E. and Isaac, R.K. (2012) 'Image analysis of Bethlehem: what can destination marketers learn from their visitors' blogs?', *Journal of Marketing & Destination Management*, 1(1–2): 124–133.

Clarke, R. (2000) 'Self-presentation in a contested city, Palestinian and Israeli political tourism in Hebron', *Anthropological Today*, 16(5): 12–18.

Cohen, R. and Kennedy, P. (2000) *Global sociology*, Houndsmills: Macmillan Press.

Cohen-Hattab, K. (2004a) 'Zionism, tourism, and the battle for Palestine: tourism as a political-propaganda tool', *Israel Studies*, 9(1): 61–85.

Cohen-Hattab, K. (2004b) 'Historical research and tourism analysis: the case of the tourist-historic city of Jerusalem', *Tourism Geographies*, 6(3): 279-302.

Cohen-Hattab, K. and Katz, Y. (2001) 'The attraction of Palestine: tourism in the years 1850-1948', *Journal of Historical Geography*, 27(2): 166–177.

Cohen-Hattab, K. and Shoval, N. (2014) *Tourism, religion and pilgrimage in Jerusalem*, Abingdon: Routledge.

Cook's Travel Agency (1876) *Cook's tourists' handbook for Palestine and Syria.* Available at https://archive.org/details/cookstouristsha04ltdgoog [Accessed 24 February 2015].

Daher, R. (ed.) (2007) *Tourism in the Middle East*, Clevedon: Channel View Publications.

Halper, J. (2008) *An Israeli in Palestine: resisting dispossession, redeeming Israel*, London: Pluto.

Hanafi, S. (2009) 'Spacio-cide: colonial politics, invisibility and rezoning in Palestinian Territory', *Contemporary Arab Affairs*, 2(1): 106–121.

Hannam, K. (2008) 'Book review', *Tourism Review International*, 11: 407–414.

Hever, S. (2007) *The economy of the occupation: the Separation Wall in East Jerusalem: economic consequences*, Jeruslaem and BeitSahour: Alternative Information Centre.

Isaac, R.K. (2008) 'Master of arts in pilgrimage and tourism', *Tourism and Hospitality Planning & Development*, 5(1): 73–76.

Isaac, R.K. (2009) 'Can the Segregation Wall in Bethlehem be a tourist attraction?' *Tourism and Hospitality Planning & Development*, 6(3): 247–254.

Isaac, R.K. (2010a) 'Alternative tourism: new forms of tourism in Bethlehem for the Palestinian tourism industry', *Current Issues in Tourism*, 13(1): 21–36.

Isaac, R.K. (2010b) 'Moving from pilgrimage to responsible tourism', *Current Issues in Tourism*, 13(6): 579–590.

Isaac, R.K. (2010c) 'Palestinian tourism in transition: hope, aspiration, or reality?', *Journal of Tourism and Peace Research*, 1(1): 23–42.

Isaac, R.K. (2011) 'Steadfastness and the Wall conference in Bethlehem, Palestine', *Tourism Geographies*, 13(1): 166–171.

Isaac, R.K. (2013) 'Palestine: tourism under occupation: the ramifications of tourism in Palestine', in R. Butler and S. Wantanee (eds.) *War and tourism: a complex relationship*, London: Routledge.

Isaac, R.K. (2014) 'A wail of horror: empathic atrocities tourism in Palestine', in H. Andrews (ed.) *Tourism and violence*, Surrey: Ashgate.

Isaac, R.K. and Ashworth G.J. (2012) 'Moving from pilgrimage to dark tourism: leveraging tourism in Palestine', *Tourism, Culture and Communication*, 11(3): 149–164.

Isaac, R.K. and Hodge D. (2011) 'An exploratory study: justice tourism in controversial areas the case of Palestine', *Tourism Planning & Development*, 8(1): 101–108.

Isaac, R.K. and Platenkamp V. (2012) 'Ethnography of hope in extreme places: Arendt's agora in controversial destinations', *Tourism, Culture and Communication*, 12(2): 173–186.

Isaac, R.K., Platenkamp V. and Cakmak E. (2012) 'Message from paradise: critical reflection on the tourism academy in Jerusalem', *Tourism, Culture and Communication*, 12(2): 159–171.

Kassis, R. (2006) 'The Palestinians and justice tourism: another tourism is possible', paper prepared for the Masters of Pilgrimage, Tourism and Cultural Heritage, Bethlehem TEMPUS Programme, viewed 11 June 2007, from <http://www.atg.ps/index.php?page=1177263149.1199956205>.

Kester, J.G.C. and Carvo, S. (2004) 'International tourism in the Middle East and outbound tourism from Saudia Arabia', *Tourism Economics,* 10(12): 220–240.

Kliot, N. and Collins-Kreiner, N. (2003) 'Wait for us – we're not ready yet: Holy Land preparations for the new Millennium the Year 2000', *Current Issues in Tourism*, 6(2): 119–149.

Lanfant, M.F. (1995) 'International tourism, internationalisation and the challenge to Identity', in M.F. Lanfant, J.B. Allock and E.M. Bruner (eds.) *International tourism, identity and change: Sage studies in international sociology*, London: Sage.

Mansfeld, Y. (1996) 'Wars, tourism and the "Middle East factor"', in A. Pizam and Y. Mansfeld (eds.) *Tourism, crime and international security issues*, New York: Wiley.

Murad, N. (2014) 'Donor complicity in Israel's violations of Palestinian Rights'. http://www.al-shabaka.org/policy-brief/politics/donor-complicity-israels-violations [accessed 24 October].

Noy, C. (2014). Peace activism in tourism: two case studies (and a few reflections) in Jerusalem. In L. Blanchard and F. Higgins-Desbiolles (eds.), *Peace through tourism: promoting human security through international citizenship*. Abingdon: Routledge.

Robinson, M. (2001) Tourism encounters: inter-and intra-cultural conflicts and the world's largest industry. In N. Alsayyed (ed.) *Consuming tradition, manufacturing heritage*. London: Routledge.

Saïd, E. (1974) *Orientalism*, London: Penguin Books.

Saïd, E. (2004) *Humanism and democratic criticism: Columbia themes in philosophy*, New York: Columbia University Press.

Shoval, N. and Cohen-Hattab, K. (2001) 'Urban hotel development patterns in the face of political shifts', *Annals of Tourism Research*, 28(4), 908–925.

Tawil-Souri, H. (2011) 'Qalandia Checkpoint as space and nonplace', *Space and Culture*, 14(1): 4–26.

United Nations Conference on Trade and Development (UNCTAD) (2006) *The Palestinian war-torn economy: aid, development and state formation*, New York: United Nations.

Wahab, S. (2000) 'Terrorism: a challenge to tourism in risks in travel and tourism'. *Proceedings of the Talk at the Top Conference*, Ostersund: Mid-Sweden University.

World Bank (2007) *Investing in Palestinian economic reform and development*, Paris: World Bank.

Part I

An overview of tourism in Palestine

2 Palestine as a tourism destination

Rami K. Isaac, C. Michael Hall and
Freya Higgins-Desbiolles

Palestine is a region that is difficult to define and delimit as it has changed its geographical borders, social composition and political status over that last three millennia. The geo-historical area of Palestine is almost 27,000 km², while the area governed by the Palestinian National Authority (PNA) is currently 6,000 km² including the West Bank and Gaza Strip. Located in the southwest of the Asian continent and on the east of the Mediterranean basin, the region has strategic links with Asia, Africa and the Mediterranean Sea. With four seasons throughout the year, climate in the area is pleasant and attracts increasing numbers of tourists. Palestine is often associated with the Holy Land, as the main destination for pilgrimage, religious and cultural tourism for pilgrims of the three monotheistic or Abrahamic religions: Christianity, Islam and Judaism.

Until the establishment of the Israeli state in 1948, tourism in Palestine was a marginal and undeveloped sector, not-with-standing visits by pilgrims and others to holy places, especially in the cities of Jerusalem, Bethlehem, Hebron and Nazareth. Although tourism has developed in many countries of the region since the 1950s, the prolonged Middle East conflict has prevented this in Palestine. The division of Palestine in 1948 into three entities (Israel, the Gaza Strip and the West Bank, including East Jerusalem), completely transformed the structure and market orientation of tourism. Some important tourist attractions, both of a natural beauty, historical and religious, remained within the borders of Israel, and as a consequence, were inaccessible to tourists from Arab and Islamic countries (Bethlehem University 1995).

After 1967, the Palestinian tourism sector in general and the hotel industry in particular suffered a significant decline in the volume and quality of business. There was an increasing competition from the Israeli tourism industry and physical, institutional and financial restrictions were imposed on Palestinian tourism. On the whole, the tourism industry has suffered greatly since the occupation and remained underdeveloped. Strong pressures and profound changes have resulted in the effective separation of the Israeli and Palestinian tourism sectors and the marginalization of Palestinian facilities.

The private organization structure was under the Israeli strict control and has weakened since 1976 (Isaac 2010c). Throughout the years of occupation, the Arab private sector has managed to undertake limited tourism related activities in spite of the difficulties due to occupation. Between 1976 and 1994, the number of Palestinian hotels remained unchanged. Barely any permits to build hotels, or convert to hotels were granted by the Israeli occupation to any investor in the Palestinian sector.

The State of Palestine's unique history is often what attracts tourists but at the same time this history has been the cause of the unrest and perceived insecurity that has hindered the growth of the tourism sector. Although visitors that come for pilgrimages (which have been the industry's traditional focus and represent the vast majority of tourism services exports) are relatively less sensitive to security concerns, historical events have inhibited the sector's growth. Thus, in spite of the fact that the State of Palestine enjoys tourist assets that provide it with a rich tourism offering (including holy and cultural/historical sites), this offering has not been fully leveraged and the tourism sector makes less of a direct contribution to GDP and to Palestinian employment when compared with other economies in the immediate region: only 4 per cent and 2 per cent, respectively, whereas for its neighbors, tourism contributes between 6 per cent to 37 per cent to GDP, and 8 per cent to 19 per cent to employment (International Trade Center 2013).

The relationship between Israeli–Palestinian relations and the success of the State of Palestine's tourism services exports was clear following the Arab–Israeli War of 1967 and until 1993, when growth of the State of Palestine's tourism sector was minimal. The second intifada that began in September 2000 and lasted until 2005 or 2006 (the end date is disputed) also affected the State of Palestine's tourism sector negatively. For example, the number of guest night stays dropped from 1,016,683 in 2000 to 184,857 in 2001. After hitting a low in 2003 figures began to rise, most dramatically in 2006 (to 383,603). By 2008 the number of guest night stays exceeded the figure for the year 2000 (at 1,127,286 in 2008). Despite a small dip in 2009, the number has continued to rise to the present day.

On the other hand, the State of Palestine's history has also borne certain benefits for its tourism sector – a perception that the State of Palestine (together with Israel) is more closely connected with Europe than its neighbors means that during periods of unrest in surrounding countries the Holy Land has continued to receive moderate numbers of arrivals while its neighbours experienced sharp drops in tourism. For example, Jordan and Egypt experienced sharp drops in 2011 due to unrest (International Trade Center 2013).

Other challenges that have inhibited the growth of the State of Palestine's tourism sector have been a lack of investment in the sector and the lack of a national strategy. There appears to have been a correlation between the degree of investment and security concerns and the desirability of the State of Palestine as a tourist destination. For example, there was increased investment in the sector prior to 2000 (in preparation for the millennium celebrations 'Bethlehem 2000 Project') (see Isaac 2010a) and from 2008, as evidenced by the opening of new hotels. The lack of a national strategy may have been originally a consequence of the State of Palestine's history and its lack of control over its territory. However, in recent years, it appears to reflect the fact that the Palestinian authorities do not consider tourism to be a priority sector (reflected in the current underfunding of the ministry dedicated to tourism). For the tourism sector, perhaps the most significant event in recent history was the establishment of the Palestinian National Authority (PNA) in 1993 and the resulting establishment of MOTA. Prior to 1993 the State of Palestine did not have control over its tourism policy. During Mandatory Palestine (1920–1948), there was a Department of Antiquities, mandated with the excavation and preservation the State of Palestine's cultural (i.e. tourist) sites (International Trade Center 2013).

After the establishment of the Palestinian National Authority in 1993, several necessary steps were carried out to promote and encourage tourism. First, an economic agreement was signed between the Palestinian National Authority and Israel on 4 May 1994. Secondly, the Palestinian Ministry of Tourism and Antiquities was established and took responsibility for recognising the tourism sector in the West Bank and Gaza Strip. But due to the political unrest and the Palestinians' limited resources, the ministry was unsuccessful in its mission. Nonetheless, the Palestinian ministry has its own plan to develop basic infrastructure. For example, it succeeded in re-organizing the internal transportation, restaurants, tourism agencies and other segments; and rehabilitating of religious sites and cultural centres (Al-Khawaja 1997).

Nevertheless, the tourism industry in Palestine is characterized by a high amount of unskilled labourers. Those who are formerly educated in tourism and hospitality in this country are very few, with the exception of TEMPUS Programme developed at Bethlehem University (Isaac 2008). Consequently, as a result of the low levels of training and education the Palestinian tourism sector requires significant human resource initiatives to improve service and management levels (Al-Rimmawi 2003).

The tourism sector has always been a primary sector in the Palestinian economy and an essential income generating industry accounting for 15.2 per cent of GDP in 2014, and approximately 14 per cent in 2013 (International Trade Centre 2013), and an employment generator either through direct employment in the tourism field or indirect employment in other related fields accounting for 19.9 per cent in 2004 (Isaac and Ashworth 2012). Though, in spite of the essential part that pilgrimage has played in the tourism industry in Palestine, most of money earned in the Palestine finds its way into the Israeli economy. As a result, it is very important to stress the importance of the Palestinian tourism industry and propose solutions for its reactivation and further development.

The resources and the assets of the Palestinian areas are located in Bethlehem, Jericho, and East Jerusalem, mostly Christian sacred sites. Bethlehem is located 10 km south of Jerusalem. Christian sites in Bethlehem are the Basilica and Grotto of the Nativity, which are sacred for Catholics, Orthodox, and Armenians, and all have ownership rights in the church. In addition, sacred sites in Bethlehem include the Church of St. Catherine, St. Jerome Church, Milk Grotto, and the pilgrimage site of Shepherds' Field. Bethlehem is the only important pilgrimage site ruled by the Palestinian National Authority (Kliot and Collins-Kreiner 2003). The Biblical name for Jericho 'city of palm trees' (Ariha in Arabic) indicates the striking contrast the oasis makes to the surrounding desert; luxuriant greenery and fragrant flowers flourish here; its subtropical climate makes it an extraordinary garden, ideal for winter vacation, when wealthy families from Jerusalem, Ramallah and Bethlehem come to enjoy the warmth. Situated on the west bank of the Jordan valley, 8 km north of the Dead Sea, Jericho owes its fertility to cool, abundant springs. Dating back more than 10,000 years, Jericho is the oldest city and the oldest continuously inhabited site in the world. Its walls and towers were built 4,000 years before the pyramids of Egypt. Some of the world's most important historical sites are concentrated in a 15-km² area, in and around the city. There are at least four different historical Jerichos: Ancient Jericho, 'Tel al-Sultan', Hellenistic-Roman Jericho Herod's winter Palace 'Tulul Abu al-Alaieq', Byzantine-Moslem Jericho, and modern Jericho. Another interesting site is the Monastery of the Qurantul (the Forty). The monastery, perched on the side of Temptation, offers a stunning panorama of the Dead Sea, Jordan Valley and Jericho. Tradition has it that this mountain was where Jesus fasted for 40 days and was tempted by the devil. Hisham's Palace, in the heart of hunting and farmland, was one of the most impressive country residences of the Omayyad period, so archaeologists call it 'the Versailles of the Middle East' (Alternative Tourism Group 2014).

The Palestinian tourism industry is yet to fully capitalize on its potential and to develop across the value chain to prevent major leakages of tourism revenue thus becoming a viable, independent destination. More than two million foreign tourists visited Palestine (The West Bank and the Gaza Strip) in 2010 and that number increased in 2011 and 2012. Total overnight stays in Palestinian hotels increased by 40 per cent in 2010 reaching a record high of 1,400,000 (including both foreign and domestic overnight stays including in East Jerusalem). Overnight stays in the West Bank increased by 51 per cent, however, about 76 per cent of overnight stays were in the Bethlehem area and not geographically spread throughout Palestinian National Authority (International Trade Center 2013).

Approximately 90 per cent of inbound tourists to Palestine visit Bethlehem. While many of these tourists are day visitors, the number of overnight stays in the city has been on the rise since early 2005. Poland, Italy and Russia are the top three countries of origin for foreign visitors to Palestine with 103,398, 84,438 and 68,933 overnight stays respectively. Markets such as Germany, Spain, France and United Kingdom remain among the top 10 generating countries. Palestine has also seen an increase in visitors from emerging and growing markets such as Indonesia, India and Brazil. Palestinians living inside Israel also account for a substantial portion of visitors across the West Bank with over 600,000 visits recorded in 2012 (International Trade Center 2013).

Looking at recent available figures more than half a million guests have spent 1.5 million nights in Palestine in 2013. Of these 38 per cent Europeans, 9 per cent Palestinians as well as 9 per cent Americans and Canadians have stayed in hotels in the West Bank (see Palestinian Central Bureau of Statistics (PCBS) 2014a). According to a survey where 113 hotels in the West bank have been responded an increase of number of guests as well as of spent guest nights is visible. Nevertheless hotel occupancy rates have been always quite low (Table 2.1).

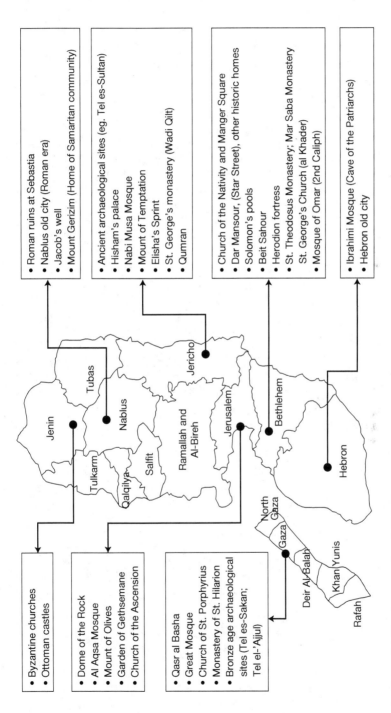

- Byzantine churches
- Ottoman castles

- Dome of the Rock
- Al Aqsa Mosque
- Mount of Olives
- Garden of Gethsemane
- Church of the Ascension

- Qasr al Basha
- Great Mosque
- Church of St. Porphyrius
- Monastery of St. Hilarion
- Bronze age archaeological sites (Tel es-Sakan; Tel el-'Ajjul)

- Roman ruins at Sebastia
- Nablus old city (Roman era)
- Jacob's well
- Mount Gerizim (Home of Samaritan community)

- Ancient archaeological sites (eg. Tel es-Sultan)
- Hisham's palace
- Nabi Musa Mosque
- Mount of Temptation
- Elisha's Sprint
- St. George's monastery (Wadi Qilt)
- Qumran

- Church of the Nativity and Manger Square
- Dar Mansour, (Star Street), other historic homes
- Solomon's pools
- Beit Sahour
- Herodion fortress
- St. Theodosus Monastery; Mar Saba Monastery
- St. George's Church (al Khader)
- Mosque of Omar (2nd Caliph)

- Ibrahimi Mosque (Cave of the Patriarchs)
- Hebron old city

Figure 2.1 Tourism attractions in Palestine.

Source: Portland Trust (2013).

Hotels in the West Bank have to bear high overhead expenses, especially when visitors stay away because of political troubles, whereas guest houses have much greater flexibility with respect to cost structures. Overall, at times of instability international arrivals have decreased whereas after the Oslo peace process and the second intifada the numbers have grown (Figure 2.2). That reinforces the extent to which tourism development in Palestine is highly dependent on political security.

Due to the limitations in free movement of people and control of the resources by the Israeli occupation, the scale of tourism development in Palestine is relatively small. Swarbrooke (1999: 228) suggested that sustainable tourism development in Palestine is a challenging matter and that 'there is a great need for sustainable forms of tourism which can in turn sustain the host population'. He observed that Palestinians 'rely on Tel Aviv Airport which can be closed at any time to Palestinians and Palestinian-based tourists by the Israeli Government (1999: 228)'. Additionally Isaac (2013) noted that because of the control of all ports of entries as well as the issuance of visa by Israel, the free flow of people can be hindered whenever needed (see Chapter 13). In several cases tourists who wanted to travel to Palestine have been bullied at border controls. Mobility and accessibility for Palestinians as well as for international visitors are limited owing

Table 2.1 Value of variables in main hotel indicators 2011–2013

Indicator	2011	2012	2013
No. of guests	507,372	575,495	600,363
No. of guest nights	1,245,509	1,336,860	1,467,709
Room occupancy	28.4%	29.1%	24.8%

Source: PCBS (2014a).

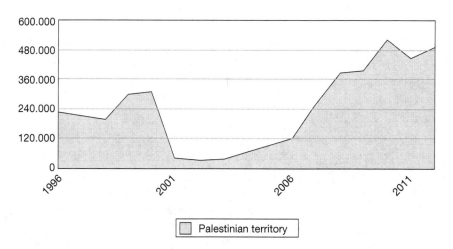

Figure 2.2 International tourist arrivals to Palestine.

Source: World Bank 2014 (cited from Fact Fish, 2015).

to border control. Furthermore, there is a difficulty in getting proper statistics about numbers of international or domestic visitors to Palestine as there is no effective border control by the Palestinians (Isaac 2013). According to Swarbrooke (1999: 228) the 'years of military occupation and underinvestment have resulted in a poorly developed tourism infrastructure', where 'new hotels are being built... often with little evidence of real demand [and] relatively few visitor attractions, restaurants and events encourage tourists to spend more money in Palestine'. The main visitors are pilgrims who 'spend little money in Palestine'. Ten years later this theme was revisited by White (2009: 1) who noted 'the vast majority of tourists in the "Holy Land" only see Palestinians through the window of a tour bus, as they dash in and out of Bethlehem for a couple of hours'. Itineraries are designed for primarily presenting the Jewish history and sites without consideration to Palestinian cultural heritage and narrative (see Chapter 5). The situation is further complicated by the fact that licensing for Palestinian tour guides is restricted by Israel and tourism is controlled by Israeli tour operators, therefore further contributing to a reduction of 'economic benefits to the host community' (White 2009: 1). As Isaac (2013: 144) suggests 'Israel has continued to maintain a virtual monopoly over the tourism industry in the region, by exploiting Palestinian resources and heritage at the same time as excluding Palestinians from tourism's economic, political and social benefits'.

The year 2014 started off with tremendous energy given that 2013 was the best year yet for Palestine tourism (MOTA 2014). The number of visits and overnight stay reached an historic high, and the sector led by the MOTA was thriving as new projects helped to build momentum. Right from the start of 2014, the ministry focused on various tracks to preserve and showcase the Palestinian national heritage and to raise service quality and standards in the tourism and hospitality sector. The listing of Battir on the World Heritage List so as to preserve the historical and natural riches of the Valley and defend the site in the face of the Israeli Segregation Wall (MOTA 2014; see Chapter 5) was also an extremely significant political and heritage events. The major tourism event of the year was the visit of his Holiness Pop Francis to Palestine, who celebrated mass on Bethlehem's Manger Square and his stop at the northern entrance of the city, in front of the Segregation Wall for a moment of prayer for peace and an end of the occupation.

On the occasion of World Tourism Day on September 27, the Palestinian Central Bureau of Statistics (PCBS) (2014b) in collaboration with the Ministry of Tourism and Antiquities (MOTA), presented the following facts on tourism in Palestine. During the first half of 2014, around 3.16 million visits were made to tourist and leisure sites in the West Bank. These included 1.69 million visits by domestic visitors and 1.47 million visits by inbound visitors. The number of domestic and inbound visits grew by 26 per cent and 19 per cent respectively compared with the same period in 2013. Most inbound visits were to Bethlehem governorate with 42 per cent, followed by Jericho and Al-Aghwar governorate with 28 per cent, and Jenin and Hebron with 11 per cent each.

A third of inbound visits were by residents from 1948 Occupied Palestine (Israel). Palestinians residing in areas occupied in 1948 accounted for the largest proportion of inbound visitors with 34 per cent, followed by 16 per cent from

Russia, 7 per cent from the United States, 4 per cent each from Italy and Germany, and 3 per cent each from Poland and Indonesia (see Table 2.2). Nablus Governorate had the largest proportion of domestic visits (22 per cent), followed by Qalqilya and Tulkarm governorates with 17 per cent each, Jenin governorate with 14 per cent, while Ramallah and Al-Bireh governorate has the lowest share of domestic visits at 2 per cent. It should be noted that inbound and domestic visitor data do not include Jerusalem governorate and the Gaza Strip. With an average just under 2.4 nights stay, 357,000 hotel guests spent 855,000 nights during the first half of 2014 in the West Bank hotels. The number of hotel guests in the West Bank grew during the first half of 2014 to 356,609 hotel guests spending 854,815 nights, an increase of 30 per cent compared with the first half of 2013 (MOTA 2014). However, there are substantial differences between markets with respect to overnight stays (Table 2.2). Guests were also distributed by region as follows: 51 per cent in the south of the West Bank, 31 per cent in Jerusalem hotels, 14 per cent in the middle of the West Bank, and 4 per cent in the north of the West Bank. In June 2014, there were 113 hotels in the West Bank comprising 6,621 available rooms with a total of 14,675 beds.

There were 6,593 establishments working in the tourism sector in Palestine. The main operations included 3,490 restaurants, 965 outlets in beverage serving, 283 shops selling souvenirs and handicrafts, 229 working in antiques and wooden handcrafts, 270 car rental services, 126 providing services organizing trips to Haj and Umrah, 117 in short-term accommodation (hotels), 151 travel and tourism agencies, and a further 962 establishments engaged in related tourism activities such as creative, arts and entertainment activities, and other recreational activities (PCBS 2014b).

The total value added of establishments working in tourism activities was USD 326.2 million: this was made up of 33 per cent by accommodation activities, 29 per cent by restaurants, 10 per cent by other amusement and recreation activities, 9 per cent by beverage serving activities, 6 per cent by renting and operational leasing of passenger cars (without drivers), 3 per cent by retail sale of souvenirs, craftwork and religious articles, and 10 per cent distributed on the remaining tourism activities (PCBS, 2014b).

Table 2.2 Number of guests by nationality during the first half of 2013 and 2014

Nationality	2013	2014
Palestine	25,773	28,063
Israel	29,168	28,286
Asia	33,187	26,983
USA & Canada	21,922	35,680
European Union	110,610	126,177
Other European States	29,203	74,696
Other countries	23,663	26,724

Source: PCBS (2014b).

Palestinian tourism has all the necessary infrastructure, facilities and attractions to become a viable and independent destination. However, the industry has had a turbulent past and indeed is faced with an uncertain future. The basic infrastructure and support services are intact in the town and cities with high tourist traffic such as Bethlehem, Jericho, Ramallah and Nablus. There are a number of private sector associations and NGOs operating in tourism, hospitality and cultural related activities. However, there is a need for improvement and collaboration among various stakeholders to have a more focused and consensus vision for the tourism industry for the future.

The institutional development and regulatory environment in the tourism industry began to take shape in the mid-1990s following the establishment of the Palestinian Authority. The Ministry of Tourism and Antiquities (MOTA) was established to safeguard the historical, archaeological, cultural and religious sites under its jurisdiction as well as to regulate tourism entities and promote Palestine regionally and internationally as a viable tourism destination. In 1993 The Higher Council for Arab Tourism Industry (HCAT) was also established. The council is an umbrella organization comprising the tourism organizations belonging to the Palestinian industry. It is a private sector organization freely elected from the executive committees of various Palestinian organizations. The HCAT's main aims are to safeguard the interests of the Palestinian tourism community, to strengthen and build a strong, well organized sector to meet internationally accepted standards and to coordinate efforts between the private and public sector. In 2003, the offices of the HCAT in Jerusalem were closed down by the Israeli government during a crackdown of Palestinian institutions in East Jerusalem. Following the closing of the HCAT offices in Jerusalem, the structure of Private Sector association and representation took several new forms. The following institutions are key players for the development of the tourism sector.

Arab Hotel Association (AHA)

Established in Jerusalem in 1962, AHA is a non-profit organization representing Palestinian hotels throughout the Holy Land and assisting other Palestinian tourism associations. AHA has 56 members, which altogether offer about 3,700 guest rooms, and AHA anticipates further expansion. AHA sees itself as the leading partner in developing a competitive tourism industry. Indeed, AHA has partnered with numerous actors relevant to the tourism services sector, including MOTA, Holy Land Incoming Tour Operators Association (HLITOA) and Bethlehem University (BU).

Holy Land Incoming Tour Operators Association (HLITOA)

Established in 2005, HLITOA has 43 member tour operators working in incoming tourism. Of that membership, 80 per cent have their head offices in East Jerusalem. HLITOA members are the main actors in the tourism industry, especially for pilgrimage tourism. The Association sees itself as a key player and a major catalyst in the development of the industry by supporting and enhancing Palestinian incoming tour operators in the Holy Land. PUM Netherlands is developing a strategy for HLITOA 2014–2020 (Personal communication, 5 January 2015).

Arab Tourist Guides Union (ATGU)

With its headquarters in Jerusalem, ATGU covers membership of tourist guides from East Jerusalem licensed by the Israeli authorities as well as guides from the West Bank licensed by MOTA. Forty of them have the right to guide within Israel as per special agreements following the Paris Accords.

Ministry of Tourism and Antiquities (MOTA)

MOTA is the major public actor in charge of supporting the tourism industry, both as a regulator and through its marketing department. Thanks to its support, the State of Palestine is represented almost every year at the major trade fairs on tourism in Europe (Milan, London, Berlin, Madrid, and Warsaw as well as Istanbul). The 2013 Diagnostic Study (The International Trade Centre, 2013) considers that 'MOTA has led the industry since the establishment of the PNA. It has been to some extent positively responsive to the existing market and the private sector and NGO initiatives but it is not innovative or proactive' (2013: 27).

Palestinian Central Bureau of Statistics (PCBS)

Tourism data are currently insufficient to conduct reliable planning. In fact, one of the major deficiencies in this sector is the lack of proper information and statistics. PCBS is not a reliable source since its data are not accurate for areas such as Jerusalem. Tourism stakeholders express the view that PCBS does not have sufficiently frequent dialogue with the private sector and does not have an accurate sense of private sector needs. Therefore, in many ways it is impossible to measure the trends of the sector.

Municipalities, Chambers of Commerce, and cultural and religious institutions also support the industry. Other actors include publishing agencies such as This Week in Palestine and Alternative Business Solutions (ABS) Tourism and its tourism portal VisitPalestine.ps

Current political, legal, regulatory and development framework

Tourism law

The tourism sector is currently regulated through a main Tourism Law and five regulations (on travel agents, tourist guides, hotel and restaurants, tourist shops and parks). As tourism regulations are perceived as being outdated given that many date back to Jordanian rule, a new draft law is being discussed with different stakeholders (private sector, government and neighboring countries experts). The new tourism law aims to:

- Cover shortcomings in the current law, especially those relevant to punitive measures and enforcement, which are poorly covered in the current law.
- Increase the availability of protection in the sector by granting the Ministry's inspectors the mandates and authorities of judicial officers.
- Facilitate investment in the sector, most importantly by allowing investment in ancient and historic sites, while maintaining a good level of protection for such sites (which is a major impediment to investment in the current law).
- Expand the licensing of tourism activities to include several new activities in addition to the four currently regulated. For instance, the new law will include car rentals, resorts, tourism media, tourism marketing, festivals, activities and transportation as licensable activities, organized / supervised by MOTA.
- Create tourism schools and institutes, set curricula to teach tourism, and create a tourism stream for high school students who wish to specialize in tourism at university. Moreover, a new specialized tourism university will be established (currently in the proposal phase – funded by the United States Agency for International Development (USAID), the second of its kind in the region.
- Introduce a different method in licensing tourist guides. Guides will also be licensed according to routes (a certain street routes, hiking and biking).

Tourism policy

MOTA has led the industry since the establishment of the PNA. It has been to some extent positively responsive to the existing market and the private sector and NGO initiatives, but it is debatably not innovative or proactive (International Trade Center 2013: 27). The 'Bethlehem 2000 Project' was one of the major initiatives for Bethlehem. With the cooperation of both the private and public sectors, it managed to lead a rather successful series of measures at that time. Other planning and initiatives at MOTA level, such as the Kendel study in 2005 (International Trade Center 2013), reflected on the nature of the regulatory system and proposed some initiatives, not all of which, however, were taken on board. In addition to the new law there are currently various policy initiatives under way, including with respect to tourism signage and the rehabilitation of sites.

The 2013 Diagnostic Study (International Trade Centre 2013) recommends that there is a lack of a clear national tourism development strategy and urban planning (tourism-supportive zoning). Government support to this sector is limited and appears not to be considered a priority for economic development and growth. However, there are several initiatives were made by various bodies, such as the Portland Trust (2013), Quartet (2013), PUM Netherlands senior experts and the International Trade Centre (2013).

The National Tourism Strategy is to have Palestine successfully compete and get its share of regional tourism arrivals, through developing and diversifying the tourism offer and promoting the richness in cultural, historical and natural resources. While pilgrimage and religious tourism will remain the backbone of any tourism offer in the region, the Palestinian Ministry of Tourism and Antiquities (MOTA) together with stakeholders create experiential programmes and non-traditional itineraries to be able to attract more visitors and encourage them to spend more resources such as time and money in Palestine. However, there is a need for developing the infrastructure and make these alternative attractions and sites more visible to the global market. Together with stakeholders from the public as well as the private sector, such as Alternative Tourism Group, Arab Tourism Guide Union, Holy Land Incoming Tour Operators and Arab Hotel Associations, alternative tourism ventures through experiential programmes and non-traditional itineraries are developed. There is a strong focus on developing alternative tourism to Palestine since it offers a suitable platform to showcase Palestine's diverse range of religious, historical, cultural and natural sites. Biking, hiking and bird-watching activities are only a few of the initiatives underway. Cultural celebrations are another key component of enriching the visitor experience. There are regular cultural festivals that attract both local and international visitors. From olive harvest and the Taybeh Oktoberfest to the Sebastiya Festival, the Artas Lettuce Festival. Christmas activities in Bethlehem, work is underway to promote and integrate these activities and festivals into the overall visitor experience. In addition, MOTA identified strategic approaches, which are: building on the comparative advantage the pilgrimage market; developing the competitive edge and gradually integrating into the region tourism offer; diversifying and repackaging the tourism offer and targeting new/existing markets from new/existing source markets (Abukumail 2013).

While Christian pilgrimage will remain the core of Palestine's tourism offer, the industry has identified the following other segments as potential opportunities to target: religious pilgrimage (Christian and Muslim); cultural heritage tourism; eco-tourism; business tourism; domestic tourism; Palestinian diaspora; alternative/solidarity and political tourism and foreign individual travellers. The following four strategic pillars have been identified in achieving this strategy: product development and enhancing the overall tourism offer; policy reforms and industry regulations; private sector support and capacity building and marketing and promotion of Palestine as a tourism destination (Travel Palestine 2011).

New development initiatives

Palestine Tourism Board (PTB)

One of the main recent policy initiatives was the 2010 decision to establish PTB in the form of a public–private partnership aiming to lead the marketing and promotion of 'Destination Palestine'. PTB, however, has so far not been operationalized. The responsibility is arguably shared by both the public and the private sector.

PTB was and is meant to become the marketing arm, the development stimulator, and the tourism think tank of the State of Palestine. It should include a marketing department, a development and planning department and an advocacy department, in addition to other administrative functions. There is a clear need for such a body in the State of Palestine, given the current state of very limited strategic and day-to-day coordination.

Advisory board

In 2012 MOTA announced the re-establishment of an advisory board by Presidential decree, a development awaiting further evaluation by stakeholders (International Trade Centre 2013). Stakeholders are concerned that the much weaker, less representative body may de facto replace PTB.

Hotel classification rating system

A hotel classification effort is under way, with the first hotels having been classified according to a rating system closely aligned with international standards. Other tourism subsectors/professions, such as restaurants, may equally benefit from classification soon. Positive experiences were gathered in the recent hotel classification efforts that were seamlessly led and implemented by an ad hoc public-private sector committee. Stakeholders suggest that this provides a near-perfect example for how PTB should be operationalized, albeit on a permanent basis (International Trade Centre 2013).

Constraints facing the Palestinian tourism industry

Israeli occupation impact on Palestinian tourism

Israeli measures in Holy places and throughout occupied Palestine explicitly target religious and cultural heritage, including damaging and demolition of mosques and ancient sites. Constant military incursions and unilateral measures taken in occupied Palestine, severely damage tourism by not only affecting destination image but also creating an unstable business environment for any developments or investments in the sector (see Isaac 2010a).

Threats to the development of the tourism sector

The development of the tourism sector is the responsibility of the Palestinian private and public sectors, however, the Israeli limitations affect the sovereignty of the Palestinian government in many areas and therefore the governmental performance regarding improving and supervising the sector. Road closure, use of random checkpoints and overt use of military power by the Israeli government prevent many Palestinians from accessing certain areas that have potential for development and tourism growth. This situation is particularly clear in the significant number of the locations and sites in Palestine that are in areas which are controlled by the Israeli military (area C), according to Oslo II – (Article XI). Area C is supposed to be transferred to be under Palestinian authority control in the redeployment phase, but since the peace agreement was frozen, the transformation never happened and hence a permit is required from the Israeli military administration to the Palestinian government for the implementation of any development activities in the area. This situation clearly limits the development progress and weakens the tourism management and development ability of Palestinian government (International Chamber of Commerce 2013).

The State of Palestine has no borders yet: points of entry/exit or visa delivery

Israel and Jordan are the main entry points to the State of Palestine, but all borders are under Israeli control. Israel also controls the delivery of visas and can at any time deny visitors (Isaac *et al.* 2012) entry into the country. This means that the State of Palestine remains dependent on Israeli goodwill to a very significant extent. The Muslim world, and especially the Arab world, would potentially represent a major potential market for tourism and Foreign Direct Investment (FDI) inflows if the State of Palestine were in full control of its borders. Many other types of tourism would also potentially find a market much more easily.

Many nationalities with a potential interest in visiting the State of Palestine, in particular Arab states, have no means of obtaining visas. Tourists from other potential markets such as India, Indonesia or Cuba also have difficulties in obtaining visas, with only group visas providing an (insecure) access, with delays and visa denials being a regular occurrence (International Trade Centre 2013). Even in the context of organized group travel there are, in many cases, long delays for permits or travellers are eventually not authorized to enter Israel, which causes losses to tour operators (International Trade Center 2013). The Muslim world, and especially the Arab world, has significant potential for tourism and capital inflows into the State of Palestine if it was in full control of its borders. This would potentially permit a significant improvement in the development and marketing of the different tourism subsectors. The State of Palestine's lack of control in this regard is a serious obstacle to the development of services exports.

Circulation between Palestinian territories is restricted

Israel controls visitors' physical movement between the different parts of the Palestinian territory. Travel between Jerusalem and Bethlehem is often complicated, with the effect that Bethlehem is sometimes perceived as difficult to reach. As Israel does not allow Israelis (e.g., guides and drivers) inside Area A, Israeli tour operators often try to skip this destination if at all possible. Moreover, since 2000 the traditional road from the Galilee to Jerusalem passing through Jericho is closed to through traffic as Jericho forms part of Area A – a bypass road now services passing traffic. This has reduced traffic through Jericho by almost 75 per cent. Gaza is entirely off limits for tourists coming directly from the West

Bank or from inside Israel. All these constraints on the movement of persons render the business environment very difficult and the development of tourism a challenge. It can also explain to some extent the low levels of foreign direct investment inflows into the State of Palestine's tourism sector. These restrictions on movements, such as checkpoints, closed roads, and closures enforced, must be seen in relation to the relative mobility that they create for Israeli settlers living illegally on Palestinian land (Isaac and Ashworth 2012) as well as, perhaps somewhat ironically, for Palestinians to enter Israel.

The Segregation Wall

In 2002, the State of Israel decided to erect a Segregation Wall separating Israel from Palestine. The Israeli authorities use concrete and metal walls to segregate, displace and apply domination and control over Palestinians living in the occupied territories of Palestine. This Segregation Wall is a series of walls, razor wire, electrified fences, trenches and many watchtowers flanked by a 27.5 meters (Isaac 2009). As of the time of writing the total length of the Wall is 707 km long – Almost 75 per cent of its total length is inside the West Bank, rather than along the Green Line, the internationally recognised border between the state of Israel and Palestine. The length of the Wall is the distance between London and Zürich and more than four times as long as the Berlin Wall, (154.5 km), many of these sections have armed sniper towers every 300 meters (Isaac 2014). The route of the Wall has been built so that it encircles more than 80 illegal Israeli settlements suggesting that its primary purpose is to incorporate these communities into future Israeli state (Shehadeh 2008). About 30,000 Palestinians are trapped between Israel and the Wall, cut off from families and friends and isolated from the economic and urban hubs and services of the West Bank. Almost 28,000 more Palestinians are completely imprisoned by the Segregation Wall, linked to the rest of the West Bank only by a tunnel or a gate controlled by the Israeli military. An additional 126,000 Palestinians are surrounded by the Wall on three sides, their freedom of movement greatly curtailed (Affouneh 2010). The construction of the Wall severely affects Palestinian domestic tourism and Palestinian life in general (Harker 2009). For example 22 local Palestinian communities have been separated from their schools as a result of the Wall (Affouneh 2010).

The image of Palestine

The overall instability in the region and the growth of radicalism, even though minimally relevant in the West Bank in general and for tourists in particular, create perceptions of insecurity. Even if they are often exaggerated, these perceptions obviously affect the marketability of the State of Palestine as a tourist destination.

At the present time, Israel has a stranglehold and monopoly on the flow of international tourists, starting from visa issuing, flights, lodging, (Israeli) guides and tours within the country (Al-Rimmawi 2003). This is often reflected in the half-empty hotels in major Palestinian cities, while in Israel it has been difficult to make a reservation during the summer. It seems evident that the situation will not improve unless the closures are lifted to allow freer flow of people (domestic and international visitors) between Israel and Palestinian cities, and between cities in the West Bank. In addition, negative Israeli branding of Palestine as an unsafe place to visit also potentially reduces the number of visitors to Palestine.

The State of Palestine thus still suffers from a partly tarnished international image because of the permanent conflict with Israel. To improve the State of Palestine's international image the country, among other measures, needs to improve communication about its cultural and natural assets. The State of Palestine's membership in the United Nations Educational, Scientific and Cultural Organization (UNESCO) provides the opportunity to obtain recognition of its key ancient sites as the common heritage of mankind (see Chapter 6). Participation in all major international trade fairs and use of UNESCO as a channel to advertise the wonders of the State of Palestine are promising avenues. Although counter-marketing negative media stories and an Israel dominated news discourse is costly, the organization of familiarization trips to raise the awareness of international tour operators of the State of Palestine's assets and actual (as opposed to perceived) situation could help increase the volume of visitors.

Palestinian tourist guides

The Israeli Ministry of Tourism deliberately downplays the occupation as an inconvenience to ignore (Isaac 2010a, 2010b) and discourages tourists from entering Palestine, while broadcasting propaganda that travel to Palestine is unsafe. Such destructive policies are highlighted by the unsurprisingly fact that while there are more than 6,000 Israeli tour guides, there are only 300 Palestinian tour guides, with a mere 42 Palestinian guides who are permitted by Israel to work beyond the West Bank in Israel. Without having stated it explicitly, such a situation confirms the asymmetrical relationship between Israel and Palestine.

The Palestinian territory: Area C

Area C, which makes up 70 per cent of the West Bank and contains all the major Jewish 'settlement blocs', is under full Israeli civil and security control. Slowly but surely, Israel has been moving Palestinians into these disconnected islands while strengthening its settlement regime over Area C and is rapidly blurring the distinction between Area C and Israel proper. Israeli-only highways now lead from Israel into the heart of the West Bank, connecting the Jewish settlements to each other while bypassing Palestinian communities. Jewish communities are also connected through their common use of electrical and water resources that are denied non-Jewish communities (Pundak 2012). Israel has invested billions of shekels in Area C while deliberately preventing the development of Palestinian infrastructure there. The B'tselem (2013) report now offers a detailed and devastating picture of the sophisticated bureaucratic process by which Israel has been able to create these facts on the ground.

Tour operators and lack of structured marketing efforts

Incoming tour operators, mostly based in East Jerusalem, are currently the main influencers in the construction of group programmes. For legitimate reasons they tend to focus almost entirely on standard packages for pilgrims as the main market segment. However, a more diversified marketing of 'Destination Palestine' and the breadth of sites and activities available for visitors would likely lead to an increase in overall visitor numbers, more visits to more sites, and an increase in nights spent by existing visitors.

At the time of writing there was a lack of mapping of sites and activities for tourists, as are 'off the beaten track' campaigns and general awareness-raising campaigns regarding the State of Palestine's tourism offers. The future PTB may remedy this lack of structured marketing efforts and has the potential to increase entry to a broader array of sites when it starts leading the promotion of 'Destination Palestine'.

Tapping the Leisure market and other complementary markets

A first step towards realizing the potential of leisure, solidarity, political and nature tourism might be the completion of a study that examines the programmes of current (traditional/pilgrim) packages and identifies gaps for add-ons and plug-ins of these alternative tourism offers, and that proposes strategies for the marketing of these types of tourism services. Legal reforms, the establishment of an NPA and (importantly) the operationalization of PTB should also encourage development. Such steps would appear to be particularly important in light of the focus of private tour operators on traditional pilgrim packages.

High unemployment, migration and 'brain drain'

Due to the limited investment in the tourism sector, the rate of job creation in comparison to the supply of labour in the market has resulted in a high rate of unemployment and hence Palestinian society is witnessing 'brain drain' with many youth seeking work abroad. The brain drain can be also attributed to the Palestinian workers being easily tempted by the high income that can be earned in the same job level in other countries. According to the head of the Tourism department in Bethlehem University, 50 per cent of the graduates travel to work abroad every year (International Chamber of Commerce 2013). The establishment of a Palestinian state with control over secure borders might potential attract a number of these skilled workers back to Palestine and enable greater use of their international skills and networks.

The Israeli policies have resulted in a significant migration of Palestinians to Europe, US and Latin America in search of better living conditions. However, in addition to the loss of human capital another implication of this process is the potential loss of Christian and other communities and the museumification of a country that contains religious sites without the context of an existing culture.

Conclusion

Naturally, at the time of writing, the biggest challenge or obstacle facing the tourism industry in Palestine is the on-going Israeli occupation in all its facets. The lack of control over borders, the vulnerability to regular incursion and subsequent physical damage to tourism infrastructure, the restrictions of freedom of movement for Palestinians and even tourists, the regular closures of Palestinian areas, and the Segregation Wall, which cuts deep into Palestinian areas, are only some of the challenges or problems associated directly with the Israeli Occupation. In addition to or as a consequence of this occupation, Palestinians have been unable to fully develop their tourism offer and more importantly have been unable to plan for future development without a clear indication of when the conflicts will end and how Palestine will look once a final status agreement is reached.

Mobility, accessibility and borders control are closely related and interlinked, each of these challenges pose a direct threat to any development for tourism to Palestine. The freedom of movement (mobility and accessibility) between Palestinian towns and cities (whether for Palestinian, Israelis or tourists) is a major concern for Palestinian tourism planners. In fact referring to the Paris Protocol, the most striking feature of the agreement is that related to accessibility of both parties to the tourist sites as stated in article 10 sections 6 and 7, and this is yet to be realized. As for Border Control, while very closely connected to mobility and accessibility, has far reaching implications for Palestinian planners.

Whether on the private or public sector levels, the resources available to overcome these challenges are very limited. This weakness is evident across the board. From the institutional reforms, and financial level to the human resource level, Palestinian tourism planners need to develop their institutional, legal framework, effective co-ordination among various stakeholders, joint marketing campaign and private sector capacities as well as their human capital in order to develop their tourism industry. Developing these aspects will require massive investment in capacity building and training.

References

Abukumail, A. (2013) Experiential tourism in Palestinian rural communities: Abraham Path. Online http://siteresources.worldbank.org/INTMENA/Resources/QN82.pdf [Accessed July 1, 2015].

Affouneh, S. (2010) 'The Wall is a snake: the impact of the Wall on Palestinian children's education: facts and photo', a paper presented at the Sumud and the Wall Conference in Bethlehem 30 April–1 May, 2010.

Al-Khawaja, H. (1997) *The current status of Palestinian tourism sector and range of its response to the requirements of regional cooperation* (in Arabic), (pp. 41–92). Al-Bireh:

Palestinian Centre for Regional Studies and Conrad Adenauer Association, Regional Tourism in a Regional Frame.

Al-Rimmawi, H.A. (2003) 'Palestinian tourism: a period of transition', *International Journal of Contemporary Hospitality Management,* 15(2): 76–85.

Alternative Tourism Group (ATG) (2014) *Towards theological explorations of Kairos Pilgrimage for Justice,* Beitsahour: ATG.

B'tselem (2013) Acting the landlord: Israel's policy in Area C, the West Bank. Online http://www.btselem.org/publications/summaries/201306_acting_the_landlord [accessed 28 June, 2015].

Bethlehem University (1995) *Tourism, culture and development, the case of Palestine,* Bethlehem: Bethlehem University.

Fact Fish (2015) http://www.factfish.com/statistic-country/palestinian+territory/internatio nal+tourism,+number+of+arrivals [Accessed 1 July].

Harker, C. (2009) 'Student im/mobility in Birzeit, Palestine', *Mobilities,* 4(1): 11–35.

International Chamber of Commerce Palestine (2013) The tourism sector in Palestine. Online http://www.iccpalestine.com/resources/file/publications/WTO%20&%20the% 20Palestinian%20Tourism%20Sector.pdf [Accessed 1 July, 2015].

International Trade Centre (2013) The state of Palestine: tourism sector export strategy, 2014–2018, Switzerland: The International Trade Centre. Online. https://www.paltrade. org/upload/multimedia/admin/2014/10/5448e8c6d8011.pdf [Accessed 12 March, 2015].

Isaac, R.K. (2008) 'Master of Arts in pilgrimage and tourism', *Tourism and Hospitality Planning and Development,* 5(1): 73–76.

Isaac, R.K. (2009) 'Can the Segregation Wall in Bethlehem be a tourist attraction?' *Tourism and Hospitality Planning & Development* 6 (3), 247–254.

Isaac, R.K. (2010a) 'Alternative tourism: new forms of tourism in Bethlehem for the Palestinian tourism industry', *Current Issues in Tourism,* 13(1): 21–36.

Isaac, R.K. (2010b) 'Moving from pilgrimage to responsible tourism', *Current Issues in Tourism,* 13(6): 579–590.

Isaac, R.K. (2010c) 'Palestinian tourism in transition: hope, aspiration, or reality?', *Journal of Tourism and Peace Research,* 1(1): 23–42.

Isaac, R.K. (2013) 'Palestine – tourism under occupation', in R. Butler and W. Suntikul (eds.) *Tourism and war,* London: Routledge.

Isaac, R.K. (2014) 'A wail of horror: empathic atrocities tourism in Palestine, in H. Andrews (ed.) *Tourism and violence,* Surrey, Ashgate.

Isaac, R.K. and G.J. Ashworth (2012) Moving from pilgrimage to dark tourism: leveraging tourism in Palestine. *Tourism, Culture and Communication* 11(3): 149–164.

Isaac, R.K., E. Cakmak and V. Platenkamp (2012) Message from paradise: critical reflection on the tourism academy in Jerusalem. *Tourism, Culture and Communication,* 12(2), 159–171.

Kliot, N. and Collins-Kreiner, N. (2003) 'Wait for us – we're not ready yet: Holy Land preparations for the new Millennium the Year 2000', *Current Issues in Tourism,* 6(2): 119–149.

Ministry of Tourism and Antiquities (MOTA) (2014) 'Destination overview 2014: all I want for Christmas is justice', Bethlehem: MOTA.

Office of the Quartet Representative (OQR) Tony Blair (2013) *Initiative for the Palestinian economy: tourism.* Bethlehem, Office of the Quartet Representative.

Palestine Central Bureau of Statistics (PCBS) (2014a) 'Press release on hotel activity survey 2013', 28 April. http://pcbs.gov.ps/portals/_pcbs/PressRelease/Press_En_hotelActiv2013E.doc [accessed 7 September 2014].

Palestine Central Bureau of Statistics (PCBS) (2014b) 'On the occasion of the World Tourism Day', 27 September. http://www.pcbs.gov.ps/site/512/default.aspx?tabID=51 2&lang=en&ItemID=1218&mid=317 2&wversion=Staging [accessed 12 December 2014].

Portland Trust (2013) Beyond aid: a Palestinian private sector initiative for investment, growth and employment, Ramallah, Portland Trust. Online. http://www.portlandtrust. org/publications/beyond-aid-palestinian-private-sector-initiative-investment-growth-and-employment [Accessed March 1, 2015].

Pundak, R. (2012) Decoding Bibi's West Bank agenda Netanyahu's plot to leave the Palestinians with the Oslo Accords' scraps would be a disaster for everyone. Haaretz, 1 August. Online http://www.haaretz.com/opinion/decoding-bibi-s-west-bank-agenda -1.455265 [Accessed 1 July, 2015].

Shehadeh, R. (2008) *Palestinian walks*, London: Profile Books.

Swarbrooke, J. (1999) *Sustainable tourism management*, CAB International.

Travel Palestine (2011) Destination Palestine overview (2011). Online https:// travelpalestine.files.wordpress.com/2012/01/2011-tourism-industry-overview-final.pdf [Accessed July 1, 2015].

White, B. (2009) 'Visit Palestine says West Bank's growing alternative tourism industry', *The Electronic Intifada,* 16 July. http://electronicintifada.net/content/visit-palestine-says-west-banks-growingalternative-tourism-industry/8343 [Accessed 7 September 2014].

Part II

The ways in which tourism matters to Palestine

3 Solidarity tourism in Palestine

The alternative tourism group of Palestine as a catalyzing instrument of resistance

Rami Kassis, Ranjan Solomon and Freya Higgins-Desbiolles

Introduction: the broad contours of modern-day tourism

We write this chapter based on a view that is derived from our positioning of being grounded in the communities negatively impacted by tourism, which has honed a sharply critical view of tourism and its power dynamics. We are aware that it diverges radically from those in mainstream tourism and its associated academic institutions. Therefore to contextualize our case study of the Alternative Tourism Group of Palestine (ATG), we will briefly outline our perspective on contemporary tourism.

In our view, tourism is too often associated with leisure and recreation with its emphasis on fun and hedonism. This has allowed for a strong emphasis on the individual and their self-indulgence and self-gratification. Indeed, modern day tourism has become predicated on the conspicuous consumption of the wealthy and we have noted that the gross wealth disparities condemned within nations and between nations in recent political debates (e.g., that generated by Piketty 2013) plays out with great perversity in tourism. We therefore strongly disagree with arguments made in tourism academe that tourism is getting more equitable and democratic, such as that made by Franklin and Crang when they noted 'mobility remains a relative privilege but one that is getting more widespread' (2001: 11). A plethora of niche sectors of tourism have proliferated to cater to every whim but the most obvious displays of ostentatious wealth and attendant damages include the bespoke tours of the world's richest, the extravagance and waste of Dubai and the voyeuristic slum tours (McLaren 2003; Mowforth and Munt 2003; Higgins-Desbiolles 2008). While those regimented to the market fundamentalism of neoliberalism will argue wealth is earned and individuals are free to spend the bounties of their hard work as they wish (perhaps within legal boundaries), we by contrast see an unjust accumulation of wealth through the structural exploitation of the developing world, marginalized communities in the developed world, precarious workers and a ravaged environment (Higgins-Desbiolles 2008). Through such a critical lens, taking holidays, being waited on by the 'host' community, playing in an appropriated paradise and 'finding oneself' amidst the poverty of others (as embodied in slum tours and some volunteer tourism or depicted in movies like *Eat, Pray, Love* (Pitt *et al.* 2010), is predicated on an ideology of tourism that needs to be exposed and then resisted.

In point of fact, with the onslaught of globalization and the universalization of free market fundamentalism, these dynamics have worsened and wealth has concentrated in the hands of fewer people. Tourism becomes a tool of perpetuating the system and exploiting the assets of others for the profit-making of a corporate elite (Higgins-Desbiolles 2009a). The outcomes are: developing communities must sell themselves in the global tourism marketplace as their niche of competitive advantage; luxury tourism products are developed for the global rich; big corporations and multinationals develop prestige developments such as golf courses, all-inclusive luxury resorts and lodges which dispossess local people and harm environments; and cheaper mass tourism offerings are developed to placate the lower classes and serve as an opiate to dissipate opposition to the ravages of capitalism (Pleumarom 1994; Higgins-Desbiolles 2009a).

Such a system exposes a stark contrast between classes of people which are generated by this activity. The consumers of luxury experiences are the beneficiaries of the pleasures of tourism and are greeted as an economic blessing in the constant striving for economic growth, which is the linchpin to the neoliberal system. On the other hand, we find the workers who provide the services which underpin the pleasures of the holiday and which are integral to them, are usually underpaid, overworked, seasonal, precarious and generally exploited (see Chok 2013, for instance). What is quite invisible, and in fact 'disappeared' from view, is the local community resident in the 'destination'; what some call the 'host' community.

The intent of briefly exposing this critical description of tourism is not merely to analyse what happens in mainstream tourism, but to underscore how mainstream tourism acts as a diversionary tool that blinds people to the reality of the impacts of their choices (Higgins-Desbiolles 2010) and encourages a culture of indifference to societies which are more often than not characterized by injustice, inequality and oppression. In fact, the tourism industry would tell the tourists they are doing their bit to alleviate poverty in their chosen destination by deciding to enjoy their holiday there, even if it is an all-inclusive package which in fact often delivers very little benefit to the place and usually wreaks a good deal of negative impacts instead (Wheatcroft and Francis n.d.). It is for such reasons that a number of critical voices have spoken out against tourism and its negative impacts and drawn attention to its exploitative practices.

We note we have witnessed in our lifetimes a partial dismantling of the social capacities of tourism which were promised by such phenomena as grassroots initiated tourism ventures through the promotion of community-based tourism and the inclusive and just vision of social tourism (McCabe, Minnaert and Diekmann 2012; Higgins-Desbiolles 2006), which have been effectively disappeared with the hegemony of corporatized tourism. This is why justice tourism activists argue that until tourism becomes an encounter with the dominant injustices of this world, it will remain exploitative (Kassis n.d.; Higgins-Desbiolles 2008). The challenge is to bring to the tourism agenda alternative paradigms that have as their base values of justice, development, respect for cultures and ecological sensitivity (Higgins-Desbiolles 2008). When these things occur, tourism will become the theatre of opportunity for solidarity, sharing and caring, of desiring to return to the place visited not just because it was exciting and good fun but because it was challenging, uplifting and ethical to return to continue to support the people and develop ongoing relationships rather than collect tourism sites in a 'been there, done that', narcissistic mindset. Indeed, tourism as a means of solidarity can be the path to justice and understanding. Tourism could thus be a vehicle for building human community, for understanding and for recognizing the many sided gifts of humanity.

Defining justice tourism and solidarity tourism

In this chapter, we are exploring one form of justice tourism which is known as solidarity tourism. Scheyvens (2002: 104) describes justice tourism as 'both ethical and equitable' and states it has the following attributes:

- builds solidarity between visitors and those visited;
- promotes mutual understanding and relationships based on equity, sharing and respect;
- supports self-sufficiency and self-determination of local communities;
- maximizes local economic, cultural and social benefits.

Scheyvens (2002) outlines five forms of justice tourism which include the 'hosts' telling their stories of past oppression, tourists learning about poverty issues, tourists undertaking voluntary conservation work, tourists undertaking voluntary development work and revolutionary tourism. Kassis (n.d.) adds that at the global level 'justice tourism is a social and cultural response to the policy of cultural domination as reflected in the globalization of tourism'. The definition of solidarity tourism offered by a Steering Committee of *Union Nationale des Associations de Tourisme* (UNAT) in 2004 serves as a useful starting point. This definition was created by tourism associations and their partners to suggest that solidarity tourism is a form of alternative tourism that offers 'an innovative and sustainable way of traveling that combines volunteering and tourism' (UNAT 2004). The basis for this type of tourism strongly affirms the 'involvement of local people in the different phases of the tourism project, the respect for people, cultures and nature and a more equitable distribution of resources generated' (UNAT 2004). With this understanding, tourism includes the host communities as the active subjects of tourism; they are not merely commodities or artifacts who visitors come to have a glimpse of as if they are an object in a museum.

This definition, in itself, is somewhat restricted because it may suggest that the only transformation required in tourism is a change in ownership of the tourism enterprise. For one thing, such a transfer will not happen willingly at the level of the corporatized tourism industry that sees the sector as a cash cow whose aim is to exploit all factors of production for their profit-making. So, ownership transfer, will in itself, require a huge struggle and paradigm shift. After all, the rich and privileged are not identified by their willingness to part with power or privilege voluntarily. Only pressure from below can alter the power and ownership equation.

But the issue of solidarity tourism surpasses even the thorny ownership question. There are political factors that must be contended with. The tourist should not only have access to the host but also understand what impacts tourism creates for the communities and spaces that receive the visitor. More importantly, what are the political conditions that prevail in the country visited? Who are the winners and losers from the maneuverings of the political structures? Does tourism camouflage these hard facts or does it work to address them?

The Palestinian condition

The case of Palestine is notable in the global community for injustices that remain unaddressed since the United Nations Partition Plan of 1947 allowed for the dispossession of Palestinians and led to the establishment of the state of Israel. The plan proposed a Jewish State covering 56.47 per cent of Mandatory Palestine (excluding Jerusalem) with a population of 498,000 Jews and 325,000 Arabs and an Arab State covering 43.53 per cent of Mandatory Palestine (excluding Jerusalem), with 807,000 Arab inhabitants and 10,000 Jewish inhabitants to be created side by side (Bennis 2007).

For the Palestinians and Arabs this was a deep injustice because it overlooked the rights of the Palestinians. The Arab League and Palestinian institutions rejected the partition plan. The wars that followed by Arab armies resulted in a superior Israeli army crushing the rebellion, expelling at least 750,000 Palestinian men, women and children from their homes. This massive humanitarian disaster now known as 'The Catastrophe', or *Al-Nakbah* in Arabic, saw Zionist forces committing a terror campaign of massacres and destruction of innumerable Palestinian towns in an effort to expel as many Palestinians as possible and claim territory (Pappe 2007).

The 1948 Al-Nakbah is a pivotal experience in Palestinian history and indeed human history as it has come to stand as a 'reference point for justice and freedom' in the twentieth century (Khoury 2012; Said 1979). It was followed by the six-day war of 1967 which resulted in Israel capturing huge territories from the Arabs and creating what we now call the Occupied Palestinian Territories (OPT). Israel acquired total control of all Palestinian territories as a result. Repeated UN resolutions have not deterred Israel from holding on to these lands illegally. Instead, they have gained a stranglehold by expropriating more lands through settlement activity and confiscation of lands for Israeli military infrastructure and, thus, complete Israeli control. The Al-Nakbah is ongoing (Khoury 2012) and struggle has featured in the lives of Palestinians living in the OPT, living as citizens in Israel as well as living in diaspora in the region and beyond. This ongoing struggle is particularly visible in the intifadas that erupted as resistance to oppression and occupation.

The First Intifada exploded in late 1987 when an Israeli truck smashed into a line of Palestinian workers waiting to return to the Gaza Strip. This incident sparked a spontaneous eruption of resistance and protests that spread throughout the West Bank releasing the frustrations of people too long oppressed (Smith

2010: 399). With Israel instigating forcible land acquisitions across the West Bank and confiscating areas through their military supremacy, Palestinians quickly found themselves like prisoners in their own land, subject to multiple abuses including harassments, arrests and beatings (Smith 2010).

The Intifada was a civil disobedience movement against Israeli rule. Its appeal was powerful because of the simplicity of its message. It acquired mass appeal and used tax avoidance, boycott of Israeli products and political graffiti as some of the methods of resistance. It emerged as a logical enlistment of the Palestinian people that had formed themselves into small organizations to stand up for their rights. It was notable for the symbolism of a people confronting a hugely superior military force, with children and youth throwing stones at army tanks and soldiers stationed as street patrols on many street corners; the world increasingly recognized the lie of the propaganda that Israel was confronted by an existential threat from terrorist organizations and Israel itself was revealed as the oppressor (May 2010: 64). As Halper (2012) has stated, 'the significance of the first Intifada... is that it initiated this process of revelation and table-turning. The success of Israel in portraying itself as an innocent victim rather than an oppressing power has run its course'.

The movement which lasted till 1993 did not win the Palestinians freedom from occupation, but it did bring Palestine back to the attention of the world. Media images were instrumental in exposing the brutality of the Israeli army while also exposing the aspirations of the Palestinians and their intent to achieve their goals through relatively, if not wholly, peaceful means (May 2010). Not only did influential countries begin to recognize the gravity of the situation, they also grew vocal in their criticism of Israeli attacks on peaceful and legitimate protest. Suddenly, the Palestinian struggle acquired a new profile and raised hopes that an end to their suffering could be imminent.

What commenced as micro-level protests escalated into a sweeping popular uprising that refused to disappear despite the suppression. The First Intifada marked one of the most significant points in the history of the Israeli–Palestinian conflict; in its four years, the impact of the intifada was felt and it led to the Madrid peace conference at the end of 1991 to be followed by the Oslo Accords of 1993 (Sela 2012). Political changes arose as even the PLO found rejuvenation and evolved into the creation of the Palestinian Authority. But as we know, the promise of these negotiations was never fulfilled as the commitment to accepting two sovereign and independent states was not there; Israel wanted to keep control of Palestinian territory, resources and economy (preferably with as few Palestinian people as possible) (Pappe 2013b).

The Intifada also had an impact on Israeli society. Aside from causing economic harm and eroding personal security, the occupation lost its legitimacy in the eyes of some segments of the Israeli population and the Jewish population in diaspora (May 2010). Such individuals recognized the injustices perpetrated on Palestinians and formed themselves into social organizations to demonstrate solidarity with Palestinians and to work to alter Israeli public perceptions (e.g., Women in Black, Jewish Voice for Peace, and the Israeli Committee against House Demolitions).

A Second Intifada followed taking place from September 2000 to 2005 and had similar causal factors – Israeli repression including extrajudicial killings, mass detentions, house demolitions, forced migrations, relocations and deportations. This was coupled with economic co-optation through using Palestinians in the Israeli labor market as a source of cheap and dependent labor and the rapid evolution of Israeli settlements and the Jewish settler population. The literal fear of *de facto* annexation of Palestine contributed to an ascending militancy in Palestinian society. People were also grievously upset that the promise that an Oslo agreement would yield a Palestinian state in five years was violated. Still worse, the Palestinian Authority which was designed to uphold and carry forward Palestinian interests badly thwarted the people's aspirations (see Carter 2006).

The Intifadas, as it happened, did not radically alter politics. The occupation actually became more entrenched and featured higher levels of suppression. The reaction by the Palestinian people on the street did trigger global attention. We have witnessed world public opinion begin to gradually veer toward the Palestinian side but this gradualism that defines the change in public attention is exasperating for the Palestinians and those who have chosen to stand with them. Importantly, the intifadas were the seed for a burgeoning Palestine Solidarity Movement.

This is because of 48 years of occupation as of June 2015, Palestinians still experience daily institutionalized persecution with little power over their daily lives, living in a constant state of trauma that results from a continuous lack of control. They face economic strangulation, collective punishment on spurious grounds, loss of basic freedoms, and diminished futures. This is especially the case for Gaza which is under a siege which leaves them in a literal open-air prison enclosed by segregation walls, electric fences, and border closings; obstructions to livelihood activities, regular curfews, roadblocks and check points; denial of basic services essential to life and wellbeing including health care, education, employment, and enough food and water; bull-dozing of their homes, crops and orchards thus threatening food security; arrest, imprisonment and torture without cause; and worst of all, repeated lethal attacks with the full force of the Israeli military with no safe haven to seek refuge (see Chapter 15 this volume; Pappe 2014).

Since we are focusing in on tourism in this chapter, these political developments have had an important impact on the development of the tourism sector in Palestine. While being home to some of the most attractive religious sites in the world one would think Palestine's tourism would be amongst the largest, but instead one finds quite the opposite. The consequences of the events, history and political conflicts recounted above are that Israel controls all access to Palestine (land and sea borders as well as access from the airport), most of the Palestinian water resources, and all movement of people and goods from, to and within Palestine. These facts have significant impacts on the development of tourism in the Palestinian territories and the dissemination of information to tourists (Kassis 2006). Jerusalem – the heart of tourism in the region – has been illegally annexed to Israel, filled with illegal settlements, besieged, surrounded by checkpoints, and encircled by the Apartheid Wall, all of which has resulted in the city's isolation from its social and geographical surroundings. This is the context for starting any understanding of tourism within Palestine and analyzing the role of the ATG.

Solidarity tourism in Palestine: an instrument of justice through peaceful resistance and mobilization

These circumstances of injustice briefly recounted in the section above are some of the conditions which see Palestine emerge as one of the prime destinations for solidarity tourism. This is not just a mere competitive claim, but rather an assertion of a sound analysis.

The Holy Land is a location that attracts a huge multiplicity of visitors. They range from religious pilgrims, to environmentalists, historians, curious travellers fascinated by the option of a striking and exotic experience, inter-religious explorers who seek dialogue as a mediatory mechanism for peace, religious scholars, researchers, volunteers, international political observers, peace makers and others. Palestine, however, is not the run-of-the-mill destination. It has all the ingredients that a destination offers – history, culture, exotic foods and religious traditions. In the main, travellers visit Palestine for a subjective experience – one which affords a time of self-fulfilment and which caters to the inquisitiveness of what the Holy Land offers as a location for religious pilgrimage as the source of the three great monotheistic faiths and more recently to a place of contestation to those who are less religious and more political (de Jesus 2013).

In Palestine the need for a new form of tourism that challenges the classical form of mass, commercially-based tourism has become essential, notwithstanding the occupation of some 47 years and counting. Tourists still visit Palestine under the supervision of guides and itineraries created and packaged by the Israeli tourist industry (Kassis n.d.). Consequently, the tourist often visits the Holy Land with little or no contact with Palestinians. The only impressions about Palestinians afforded to them are that Palestinians and Palestinian territories are 'dangerous' (see Figure 3.1). There is little exposure to the reality of Palestinian life and access to the Palestinian narrative.

Solidarity and justice tourism in the Palestinian context are forms of tourism that counter this dominant trend and allow the traveller to encounter the truth of Israeli oppression and Palestinian suffering and to offer a chance to act in solidarity with the Palestinian people. Both are based on the desire of travellers to learn and engage rather than to gain a mere glimpse and risk leaving with even greater prejudices or inadequate understanding. Solidarity and justice tourism start from a comprehensive analysis of what tourism means not just for those engaged in it, but also for the local populations in tourist destinations (Kassis 2006). In Palestine, it is essential that this sort of tourism be planned with prime regard for the needs of the local people and how tourism can help bring justice to their lives. It must challenge the monopoly imposed by Israel in the tourism industry. It must also seek to raise the awareness of travellers about the political realities who can then return to advocate for Palestine and Palestinians. Because tourism is an industry that is very susceptible to war, it is important to promote solidarity and justice as

Figure 3.1 Sign at the entrance to Palestinian controlled area of the OPT.

Source: Freya Higging-Desbiolles.

twin components in travelling to Palestine so that Palestine can become open to the world and prosper.

Growing support at civil society levels prompted increasing numbers of citizens from western countries to stand in solidarity with Palestine – despite risking being labelled as criminals and also in some cases courageously putting their lives on the line. The intifadas tended to discourage mainstream tourists from visiting the Holy Land. Cancellations of trips happened on a massive base and badly affected the Palestinian tourism sector. But it also added a whole new category of travelers who, angered by Israeli ongoing occupation and oppression, were attracted to witness and support the peaceful, legitimate mass resistance of the Palestinians. These visitors can be described as solidarity tourists as they strived to learn from Palestinians, support their resistance in projects like the olive harvests, monitor human rights violations, protect Palestinians in their everyday activities like travelling to school and to bring those stories back home to educate people with the aim to change public perception and government policy for the better.

Post-Oslo, Palestinian plans for resistance has been geared to peaceful, non-violent protest. There have been aberrations of this trend but none of the violence has had broad societal sanction. In village after village, Palestinians protest routinely making just demands to authorities or questioning illegal actions of the occupation authorities. Other forms of protest such as international camps to rebuild demolished homes, to restore olive farms, to restore agricultural fields and accompany children to school have met with success through combining local communities and international volunteers (Higgins-Desbiolles 2009b).

Alternative Tourism Group (ATG): a new paradigm of solidarity through tourism

The Alternative Tourism group (ATG) commenced formal operations in 1995 at a time when Palestine was caught up in a period of political turmoil and transition. The Palestinians were alerted to the importance of tourism in occupied Palestine during the first intifada. It was a small group of Palestinian visionaries who chose unconventional thinking to use tourism as a tool for solidarity with the Palestinian people, designing and launching the ATG from Beit Sahour in the occupied West Bank. ATG opted to create innovative tourist packages of an all-encompassing nature, including interpretative tours, homestays, food and cultural experiences and visits to mainstream sites. These would serve the basic requisites of a 'normal' tourist who visits the Holy Land too visit the historic religious sites. What made it different however was the narrative. ATG's groups did not just visit the sites; they were encouraged and facilitated to meet with the people of Palestine, what we have called the Living Stones rather than just visiting the dead stones of ancient sites and churches. It was this different and dual approach that attracted more visiting groups and individuals, as well as an uninterrupted stream of researchers and volunteers.

The ATG has cultivated a constituency of individuals and groups, from study centers in universities to church groups who come to learn and witness; these have come to serve as a base of support and solidarity. Their commitment and reliability is telling and can be counted on even when conflict such as the 2014 assault on Gaza saw tourism to Israel shrink by nearly two-thirds ('Summer tourism dries up...' 2014). However, the ATG has bucked this trend from its very inception. Participants in ATG tours are, by and large, a loyal set of people who are justice travelers and such people who seek authentic human encounters. They know that the risk factor is exaggerated in media reporting in the West and they have declared that they feel secure with their Palestinian hosts and itineraries despite the ongoing conflict, the uncertainties of checkpoints and the inconveniences that Israeli occupation imposes on travelers in solidarity. One statement which attests to this dedication is offered by a tour leader from the Eastern Mennonite University Cross-Cultural Program who claimed:

We brought our first student group to Beit Sahour in 2001 during the Second Intifada. Since then, thanks to the creative and careful planning of ATG in the midst of violence, invasions, curfews, and check-point closures, we have returned time and again. We have never canceled a single trip; we have never had a single safety problem – a testimony to both the fallacy of the media's portrayal of Palestine, and the commitment and expertise of ATG to visitors' safety. And in the process, the students learn in ways that change, not just their opinions, but their lives.

(Stutzman 2013)

ATG's tours offer some interesting permutations and combinations. One can take an ATG tour and experience a spiritual pilgrimage where pilgrimage is linked with a form of spirituality that is transformative. Such pilgrimages reject over-romanticizing the location as a religious space and engaging in pilgrimage as spiritual activity minus social and political content. Within such tours, ATG offers a transformative experience which is best summed in the words of Deenbandhu Manchala:

> If you love God, you would love the people of God, the people that God created. Many of us Christians love the church- our buildings, monuments, traditions, relics, liturgies, and symbols. In the name of God, we love what God has created but fail to love what God has created – the human being and the rest of creation.

(ATG 2010)

As part of this effort, ATG invites spiritual tourists who come to undertake pilgrimage to Palestine to get to know their fellow Palestinian Christians, to worship with them and to engage with their lived reality, rather than simply visiting the holy sites, bathing in the River Jordan and returning home with no human contact with the people of the Holy Land.

ATG has also developed some compelling and unique itineraries and projects that it offers as tourist encounters to its constituency. For instance, the Nativity Trail is not a mere travel from Nazareth to Bethlehem. It is an opportunity to meet a diverse range of people: Franciscan priests on Mount Tabor, Muslim clerics at village mosques, Greek Orthodox monks in desert monasteries, hillside farmers and their families, small-town shopkeepers and craftspeople, and Bedouin shepherds watering their flocks at ancient cisterns. It is an opportunity to understand the geopolitical situation in the Holy Land by observing it while walking through the valleys and mountains of Palestine. Indeed, it is a journey of dialogue, openness and interaction.

Another case of solidarity and awareness is a counter tactic through tourism against the occupation's atrocities. One of the worst crimes in terms of Palestinian cultural and ecological values is the concerted attacks on olive trees and olive groves. Agricultural experts in Palestine estimate that over a million olive trees have been uprooted and destroyed by Israel since it was created in 1948 (Musleh n.d.). More than half of these olive trees were uprooted and destroyed in the past decade and some of these trees are centuries old. Without regard for its religious, cultural, ecological, nutritional and economic values, the olive tree has been a constant target of the Israeli military occupation under the guise of security, the construction of the Segregation Wall on Palestinian lands and the continuous expansion of Israeli colonies (settlements). The destruction of olive trees has had intentional and destructive results on the lives of many Palestinian farmers, land owners and the Palestinian population in general. The Olive Tree Campaign has fast emerged as a tool to advocate for the Palestinians right to peace with justice.

Other encounter and exposure trips show visitors settlements in contested places like Hebron, old market places, religious sites, refugee camps, the Segregation Wall, religious locations under constant threat of attack, cultural spaces and artifacts. Some of the key experiences appreciated by solidarity visitors are homestays and meals with Palestinian families which, in addition to bringing economic benefit to these families, also serve to help such visitors get to know the lived experiences of the Palestinian people and engage with them in their full humanity.

These are not mere activities that are geared to self-fulfillment for the visitor. They are directed at deconstructing the negative myths about Palestinians, showing them as normal beings with hopes and aspirations including the hope of freedom based on equality and justice. That the messages that the ATG tries to communicate are appreciated and effective is clear from the client feedback. For instance, one client shared this evaluation on Trip Advisor:

> I had the chance to do a day tour in Hebron with ATG. For those who would like to understand more about the Palestinian struggle, Hebron explains itself what occupation is about. Samer Kokaly, our tour guide, was able to show us the political and historical parts of the city with precision, since he's a Palestinian. We were able to visit the street market, Ibrahim Mosque, the synagogue, a glass factory (worth going) and other touristic sites. What ATG promotes (and personally, this was one the best moments of the tour) is a lunch time in a Palestinian house. By meeting the family and having lunch with them, I was able to get to know more about the meaning of the quote 'to exist is to resist' and also I was able to help the family income.... All in all, my experience with ATG was worth doing and gave me another perspective about who are the Palestinian and how they resist the Israeli oppression. I strongly recommend.
>
> (comment on Trip Advisor, 6 February 2014)

The ATG works hard to ensure that interpretation is accurate and balanced. Evidence that this works and is appreciated is clear from this statement from one client who noted:

> [the tour of] the city of Hebron gave us something to think about. Our guide, Samer Kokaly, has plenty of personal stories to tell about how the occupation influences life on the West Bank. However, he keeps a somewhat optimistic and balanced view.
>
> (comment posted on Trip Advisor, 4 March 2014)

ATG takes its clients not as other travel and tour operators would on selfish, hedonistic ventures. Rather, ATG would accompany visitors on a journey with a purpose and with intent to both learn and unlearn through gaining accurate insights into Palestine and the struggle for justice as viewed through the eyes of Palestinians and based on their aspirations. It is, indeed, an attempt to foster shared aspirations for a more just and peaceful world which is vital to all of us as a common humanity.

In line with the above, ATG has set as its core intent the modification of mass tourism in 'the Holy Land' in order to establish a more human-oriented tourism and to ensure that the local community, the Palestinians, are front and center in the tourism encounter. It also endeavors to link the visitor with Palestinian families and communities so that a better understanding of Palestinian culture and history is achieved. This, in particular, has enabled the dismantling of negative stereotypes of Palestine and its people often held in western societies (Said 1993).

At the level of creating fertile grounds to enhance tourism in Palestine and make it beneficial for local entrepreneurs, ATG works to achieve a re-balancing of the revenues of the Palestinian and Israeli tourism sectors by the near-exclusive use of Palestinian infrastructure such as hotels, restaurants, transportation and guides for its tours. Recognizing the hesitancy of the tourist to stay in Palestinian territories for fear of violent assaults, ATG seeks to alter perceptions through effective education and marketing through which not only are the number of tourists augmented but equally important, their length of stay is increased.

In terms of qualitative experiences, ATG has developed approaches that facilitate visitors to develop knowledge of Palestinian culture and the socio-political situation in Palestine. This is done through instructive and authentic meetings with the Palestinian people so that the visitor is exposed to the everyday realities of the Israeli Occupation and the impact this has on the lives of Palestinians. Living with Palestinians, visitors can develop feelings of empathy which can make them feel these impacts and thereby transform their attitudes and actions as a result.

The establishment of a just and responsible tourism for Palestine has been a goal of the ATG and a point of collaboration with others. In this effort ATG led the initiative to create the Palestinian Initiative on Responsible Tourism and the efforts to develop the Code of Conduct for Tourism in the Holy Land together with many NGOs in the alternative tourism sector and industry in Palestine. This code which ATG pursues seeks to contribute to a more general effort to re-engage the tourist with Palestinian land and people in such a way that will benefit local communities, reduce over exploitation of a small number of iconic sites, and also reduce the pollution that results from coach driven mass tourism in the Palestinian towns and cities (especially Bethlehem). The code affirms that Palestine is a unique tourist destination with its long history, religious significance and natural beauty but it is also a place committed to responsible tourism and it calls on all stakeholders to consciously commit to more than hedonistic and selfish enjoyment of tours and pilgrimage and to accept an obligation to help secure justice for the Holy Land and its people (see Kassis and Solomon 2013).

We noted earlier that Israel controls all access to Palestine including land and sea borders as well as access from the international airport and that the total control of the occupation constricts all Palestinian tourism development. Despite all of this, the touristic, historic, and holy places found in Israel and the Palestine are united; they cannot be separated from each other. The code of conduct calls on tourists to visit both Israel and Palestine rather than choose to visit just one or the other. This is the route towards more fairness and justice as solidarity visitors should try to understand all aspects of this situation.

Tourism in Palestine provides visitors with a particularly rewarding and enriching experience. Not only may the tourist discover the beauty, spirituality and hospitality of the country but also come to encounter some of the political, economic, and social facts on the ground that shape the daily lives of Palestinians. This is as it should be for much can be gained – both by tourists and by their Palestinian hosts – from a proper relationship between the two. Too often the contact is very slight, consisting of rapid, coach driven visits to the Church of the Nativity in Bethlehem (perhaps with a souvenir shop stop on the way) – a style of tourism that derives from the fact that much of the itinerary is controlled by Israel and the processes of the Israeli tourism industry. ATG, thus, creates time and space for encounters with the population living in these places. The conviction is that only then will tourism realize its potential for both traveler and visited. The relationships that emerge from such encounters are the pathway to justice that can offer an authentic peace. A visitor who follows such an itinerary will naturally develop a deep and profound understanding of the Palestinian condition and what solidarity entails. It is motivational in scope because it drives people to link their experience to advocacy within their own countries. By offering a voice of comfort to the Palestinian people through their encounters, the visitor begins to stand with Palestinian demands for freedom and dignity.

ATG has also added another important instrument to its assets of tourism related products in the Holy Land. Its study centre has, in the last year alone, carried out studies on key questions that impact the tourism sector in Palestine as a result of the occupation by unfair means including how Israel's land appropriation includes Palestinian heritage sites. These are all beginning to visibly change perceptions in western audiences. It can serve as a counter to racial profiling of the Arab, for example. Or, to unmistakably establish how, under the Israeli occupation, Palestinians cannot hope to gain economically in a fair and equitable way from tourism. And even to assert that there is manipulation of the religious story to justify the occupation and distort history and logic.

Observers and friends of ATG's work characterize ATG as the promoter of peace through tourism (see Blanchard and Higgins-Desbiolles 2013). The many thousands of visitors who have travelled in Palestine under the aegis of ATG will count their visit as a pilgrimage and will preface it with descriptions such as political or solidarity, and increasingly as justice tourism. For, at the end of the day, such pilgrims 'become holders of the knowledge that will one day lead to equality, democracy, and human rights for all' (ATG 2010).

Conclusion

While it has been taken for granted in recent years that certain Western governments will continue to bankroll the Israeli government, sell weapons to its military, and provide diplomatic protection from any condemnation of its illegal actions through use of the veto at the United Nations Security Council thus serving to support and shield Israel from accountability, popular opinion in many countries is changing. As Pappe (2013a) has noted, there is some indication Israel is coming to be seen as comparable to Apartheid South Africa and censor of its illegitimate occupation and actions is growing. The recent protests around the world in reaction to repeated attacks on Gaza and advocacy of non-violent actions like the movement for boycott, divestment and sanctions indeed resemble the anti-apartheid movement of the eighties supporting the struggle to end apartheid and injustice in South Africa. This gives hope that circumstances are changing and that justice for Palestine is emerging. The ATG with its focus on developing a niche market of solidarity tourists who become the foundations of justice tourism for Palestine has a vital role to play in these efforts. Of the many solidarity tourists that the ATG has hosted, some have exclaimed before leaving: 'We came here as tourists but are returning as advocates'.

ATG's vision of the future looks forward to a free and prosperous Palestine. ATG imagines a tourism where the tourist serves the function of a justice seeker and tourism is her/his instrument to broaden her/his horizons and understanding of a common humanity. ATG believes that if one part of humanity is injured, then humanity itself is diminished; we therefore must use all tools at our disposal for justice and healing, including tourism. Tourism is therefore planned to create the space for seeing and knowing, dialogue, advocacy and active transformation in the world for equity and justice. In the current context of Israeli occupation, tourism becomes a tool for solidarity, transforming tourists into advocates for justice pressing Israel to surrender its unjust claims and occupation of Palestinian lands and resources and demanding it abide by international law and UN Resolutions. In this way a just settlement can be secured, a Palestinian state can emerge in the global community and Israel and Palestine can live side by side in peaceful co-existence where both peoples can thrive. Just as the moment when Nelson Mandela was freed and the Apartheid ideology was dismantled in South Africa, global humanity would be inspired by such a powerful outcome and we could have hope for a more peaceful and just future.

References

Alternative Tourism Group (ATG) (2010) 'Come and see: a call from Palestinian Christians. A journey for peace with justice. Guidelines for Christians contemplating a pilgrimage to the Holy Land', issued by *Alternative Tourism Group in cooperation with Palestine Israel Ecumenical Forum, Ecumenical Coalition on Tourism, and Kairos Palestine.* Online http://www.atg.ps/resources/file/pages/Guidelines.pdf [Accessed 3 June 2014].

Bennis, P. (2007) *Inside Israel–Palestine: the conflict explained,* Oxford: New Internationalist.

Blanchard, L.A. and Higgins-Desbiolles, F. (2013) *Peace through tourism: promoting human security through international citizenship,* London: Routledge.

Carter, J. (2006) 'Palestinian elections: trip report by former U.S. President Jimmy Carter'. Online http://www.cartercenter.org/news/documents/doc2287.html [Accessed 17 July 2015].

Chok, S. (2013) 'Labour justice and political responsibility: an ethics-centered approach to temporary low-paid labour migration in Singapore', unpublished PhD thesis, Murdoch University. Online http://researchrepository.murdoch.edu.au/22465 [Accessed 30 July 2014].

De Jesus, J. (2013) Visitor perception of destination image: a case study of Palestinian tourism, Master's thesis, London Metropolitan University.

Franklin, A. and Crang, M. (2001) 'The trouble with tourism and travel theory', *Tourist Studies,* 1(1): 5–22.

Halper, J. (2012) 'Roots of resistance: we all have a responsibility to turn resistance into liberation'. Online. Available http://mondoweiss.net/2012/12/roots-of-resistance-we-all-have-a-responsibility-to-turn-resistance-into-liberation#sthash.cRGpOjGv.dpuf [Accessed 3 June 2015].

Higgins-Desbiolles, F. (2006) 'More than an industry: tourism as a social force', *Tourism Management,* 27(6): 1192–1208.

Higgins-Desbiolles, F. (2008) 'Justice tourism: a pathway to alternative globalisation', *Journal of Sustainable Tourism,* 16(3): 345–364.

Higgins-Desbiolles, F. (2009a) *Capitalist globalisation, corporatised tourism and their alternatives,* New York: Nova Publishers.

Higgins-Desbiolles, F. (2009b) 'International solidarity movement: a case study in volunteer tourism for justice', *Annals of Leisure Research,* 12(3–4): 333–349.

Higgins-Desbiolles, F. (2010) The elusiveness of sustainability in tourism: the culture-ideology of consumerism and its implications, *Journal of Tourism & Hospitality Research* ,10 (2), 116–129.

Kassis, R. (n.d.) *The Palestinians and justice tourism.* Online http://www.patg.org/palestinians_and_justice_tourism.htm [Accessed 19 July 2005].

Kassis, R. (2006) 'The Palestinians and justice tourism: another tourism is possible', paper prepared for the Masters of Pilgrimage, Tourism and Cultural Heritage, Bethlehem TEMPUS Program. Online www.atg.ps/index.php?page=1177263149.1199956205 [Accessed 12 December 2013].

Kassis, R. and Solomon, R. (2013) 'The pilgrimages for transformation project: shaping tourism for peace with justice', in L. Blanchard and F. Higgins-Desbiolles (eds.) *Peace through tourism: promoting human security through international citizenship,* London: Routledge.

Khoury, E. (2012) 'Rethinking the Nakba', *Critical Inquiry,* 38(2): 250–266.

McCabe, S., Minnaert, L. and Diekmann, A. (2012) *Social tourism in Europe,* Bristol: Channel View.

McLaren, D. (2003) *Rethinking tourism and ecotravel,* 2nd edn, Hartford, CT: Kumarian.

May, T. (2010) *Contemporary political movements and the thought of Jacques Rancière,* Edinburgh: Edinburgh University Press.

Mowforth, M and Munt, I. (2003) *Tourism and sustainability: development and new tourism in the Third World,* 2nd edn, London: Routledge.

Musleh, J. (n.d.) *Help keep hope alive and join the Olive Tree Campaign.* Online http://www.worldywca.org/YWCA-News/World-YWCA-and-Member-Associations-News/Help-Keep-Hope-Alive-and-join-the-Olive-Tree-Campaign [Accessed 3 June 2014].

Pappe, I. (2007) *The ethnic cleansing of Palestine*, London: One World.

Pappe, I. (2013a) 'Q&A: Israeli historian Ilan Pappe'. Online http://www.aljazeera.com/ indepth/features/2013/06/201362583915886263.html [Accessed 3 July 2015].

Pappe, I. (2013b) 'The two state solution died over a decade ago'. Online http://www. informationclearinghouse.info/article36229.htm [Accessed 3 June 2014].

Pappe, I. (2014) 'Israel's incremental genocide in the Gaza ghetto'. Online https:// electronicintifada.net/content/israels-incremental-genocide-gaza-ghetto/13562 [Accessed 15 July 2015].

Picketty, T. (2013) *Capital in the twenty first century*, Harvard: Belknap Press.

Pitt, B., Gardner, D., Kleiner, J., Wlodkowski, S. and Noorani, T. (Producers) and Murphy,R. (Director) (2010) Eat, pray, love [Motion Picture]. United States: Columbia Pictures.

Pleumarom, A. (1994) 'The political economy of tourism', *The Ecologist*, 24(4): 142–148.

Said, E. (1979) *The Question of Palestine*, New York: Vintage.

Said, E. (1993) *Culture and imperialism*, New York: Knopf.

Scheyvens, R. (2002) *Tourism for development: empowering communities*, Harlow, England: Prentice-Hall.

Sela, A. (2012) 'The first intifada: How the Arab–Israeli conflict was transformed', Haaretz. Onlinehttp://www.haaretz.com/weekend/magazine/the-first-intifada-how-the-arab-israeli-conflict-was-transformed.premium-1.484677 [Accessed 17 July 2015].

Smith, C.D. (2010) *Palestine and the Arab-Israeli conflict*, Boston. Bedford/St Martin's.

Stutzman, L. (2013) *A cross-cultural program*. Online http://atg.ps/study-center/articles [Accessed 2 April 2015].

'Summer tourism dries up as Gaza rockets target Israel' (2014) Reuters. Online http:// english.alarabiya.net/en/business/economy/2014/07/21/Summer-tourism-dries-up-as-Gaza-rockets-target-Israel.html [Accessed 14 June 2015].

United Nations Administrative Tribunal (UNAT) (2004) *Steering committee on solidarity tourism*, Paris: unpublished document.

Wheatcroft, O. and Francis, J. (n.d.) *Should all inclusive holidays be banned?* Online http:// www.responsibletravel.com/copy/should-all-inclusive-holidays-be-banned [Accessed 3 March 2015].

4   Bike and hike in Palestine

Yiota Kutulas and Michel Awad

Introduction

The chapter has been written from the personal perspective and experiences of Yiota Kutulas, who is currently Marketing & Communications Officer for the Siraj Center, working on the World Bank funded project, 'Economic development across fragile communities' in Palestine. Contents of this chapter have been enriched by the ideas of Michel Awad, Director of the Siraj Center, who has been a pioneer of experiential tourism in Palestine for the past ten years.

What does tourism in the Holy Land bring to mind? Pilgrimage tours are quickly winding through the ancient old city of Jerusalem, and then a brief visit to the Church of the Nativity in Bethlehem. These cocooned trips prevent the inquisitive traveler from exploring, discovering and experiencing the true Holy Land with its endless opportunities. Such visits sidestep any contact or exchange with the residents of the places that are being visited, thus depriving the local communities of any financial benefits. Politically motivated? Perhaps.

Throughout history, people have been walking to Holy Land for spiritual, social or work-related purposes. During the Byzantine era, pilgrims would walk to and throughout Palestine on pilgrimages. Visitors would travel back to their respective homelands with bottles of water from the Jordan River or blessed oil from the monasteries for religious and/or healing purposes. During Islamic rule, the faithful would walk from Mecca to Jerusalem to pray and carry out their hajj.

Today, more than ever, there is a change in travelers' attitudes and their demands. The international adventure traveler pursues meaningful trips to destinations that others have yet to step out of their comfort zone to visit. According to statistics collected by the Siraj Center, visitors going to Palestine to walk/hike were numbered at 29 in 2009, and sky-rocketed to 505 by the end of 2014. This environmentally friendly traveler has the mindset of social, cultural and environmental responsibility standards. Therefore, developing and diversifying products based on their specific requests and expectations, increasing tourism capacity for those who love nature, and would like to explore ancient history, culture and religion in a unique way, either on foot or on two wheels, boosting socio-economic development of rural communities was the only way to move forward. The Holy Land's best kept secrets, in terms of archaeological and sacred sites are now being revealed to the curious visitor on another level. The heritage of walking is being kept alive with a modern twist, giving it a new meaning and purpose. So much so that the Adventure Travel 'Hot List' names Palestine as one of the top 10 most exciting Adventure Travel destinations to visit in 2015 (Curious Animal 2015) Walking, hiking and cycling in the Holy Land go beyond the physical activity, but into an appreciation of authentic Palestinian hospitality and untouched ascetic beauty.

In Biblical stories, Abraham, John the Baptist, the Disciples and Jesus walked into nature and into the Jerusalem Desert to find solitude and inspiration. Today, there are a variety of walking products which are being offered to satisfy the diverse demands of modern day travelers, whether they seek spirituality, adventure or nature related experiences. Hiking tours are becoming very popular for visitors coming to Palestine to hike through nature, and see the beautiful landscape of Palestine as they walk. Therefore, the aim of this chapter is to present this form of tourism and its social, political and financial implications for the Palestinian people. The visitor experiences warm hospitality by staying with Palestinian families – learning firsthand about the rich culture, traditions and cuisine. Experiential tourism, a combination of adventure and community oriented tourism, is paving the way for a more effective sustainable tourism in Palestine, creating jobs in marginalized rural and Bedouin communities, thus enabling them to benefit directly, enhancing their standard of living and the overall rural development

The Abraham Path is a long-distance hiking trail which connects the places where Abraham was traditionally supposed to live, and links villages throughout the heart of rural Palestine, from Jenin in the north to Hebron in the south, fostering unique exchanges between people, while at the same time creating occupational opportunities, enhancing the economy of marginalized communities along the Path. To date, the total route covers just over 1,000 kilometers of trails, which have been marked from Turkey, Syria, Jordan, Palestine and Israel. Palestine hosts 266 km of the walking trails.

The Nativity Trail is another unique trail, which has been created in order to offer the traveler a symbolic journey and the opportunity to meet a distinct range of people, such as Franciscan priests on Mount Tabor, Muslim clerics at village mosques, Greek Orthodox monks in desert monasteries, hillside farmers and their families, craftspeople and Bedouin shepherds. This is an 11-day journey of dialogue and interaction with indigenous Palestinians living along the trail. The walk is also an opportunity to understand the geopolitical situation in the Holy Land by experiencing it firsthand. Walkers will be hiking through beautiful, but sometimes challenging terrain of rocky hillsides and voyaging into the desert where silence replaces noise.

The Sufi Trails is a series of one-day hikes tailored for the nature lover who also has an interest in history, culture and religious tradition. The Sufi Trails take the walker deep into the Palestinian countryside of northern Palestine, allowing the visitor to explore a serene landscape unseen by most travelers. This backdrop is host to a scattered network of hidden ancient Islamic Sufi shrines which are situated on hilltops and in historic Palestinian villages.

The Samaritan Walks is a six-day hike which concentrates on walking to the Samaritan community at the top of Mount Gerizim, then down to Jacob's Well at the Greek Orthodox Church, and through rural villages in the Nablus region. The hikers have the opportunity to experience Palestinian hospitality by staying overnight in villagers' homes. See www.walkpalestine.com for various Walks such as the Samaritan Walks; Nativity Trail and Jerusalem Wilderness Walks.

These trails have placed the Holy Land firmly on the map, ultimately making Palestine a destination for the outdoor adventurer who is interested in broadening his/her knowledge about Palestine, its people and their cultural heritage. International tour operators offer Palestine as a destination, where visitors travel to and stay in the Holy Land for an average of eight–ten days for the sole purpose of walking or cycling in rural Palestine. Following, the role and impact of tourism in Palestine will be examined on three main levels: socially, financially and politically.

Social impact

Taking a journey to the Middle East has more than often not been put on the back-burner by the would-be traveler as political unrest in the region has become a norm. For the prospective visitor, there was lack of awareness about the diversification of the responsible tourism package that people can experience in Palestine. However, for the traveler who longs to journey to a part of the world that is steeped in history, archaeology, adventure, religion and has been one of the most visited places on Earth, it is potentially well worth the trip! Engagement with the unknown can be more than rewarding – it can go way beyond that – becoming a life-altering experience. International guests are welcomed to discover a world that is completely hidden to many Western travelers – the world of the village, family, food, customs and traditions.

Walkers and cyclists are now escaping from the large crowds and the cacophony of the busy cities, to explore the mysteries of the region, its people and their culture. The impact of such a getaway potentially brings about benefits to the travelers as they are welcomed into rural homes, experience Palestinian hospitality and day-to-day life, have intercultural exchanges, and as a result, alter and reshape the image of Palestine and Palestinians often created by mainstream western media. These same travelers may return to their homelands as 'ambassadors', advocating peace and justice for Palestine and its people.

Today, there are an abundance of opportunities to meet people and indulge in Palestinian cuisine, culture and traditions, explore and discover unspoiled nature, ancient Roman – Hellenistic archaeological sites and religious places of worship belonging to Christian, Jewish and Islamic eras hidden off the beaten track or deep within the desert. It is no wonder that in 2014 *National Geographic Traveler* (Lerwill 2014) chose Palestine's Abraham Path as its number one walking trail, which is part of the Middle East regional Abraham Path, retracing the footsteps of Abraham, the common patriarch of Christians, Jews and Muslims. Travelers from diverse cultures are welcomed in Palestine, exchanging and sharing experiences with Palestinians from rural communities along the 266 km path.

   Walkers hike through the ancient religious landscape of the Jerusalem Desert to reach the breathtaking Byzantine monastery of Mar Saba (Saint Sava) which is among the most ancient and wondrous desert monasteries in the Holy Land. Built into the rock, it clings to the cliffs of the Kidron Valley. Hikers are challenged, yet rewarded, by the trail through the isolated rocky canyon of Wadi Qelt, which hosts the Greek Orthodox Monastery of St. George. This spiritual complex appears to hang off the Jordan Valley cliffs. The walkers also hike to the desert sanctuary of Nabi Musa, which is said to be the last resting place of Moses. The walk through the wadi continues to awe the traveler with sights of unique varieties of flora and fauna. The ancient city of Sebastia, formerly Samaria, is situated on a hilltop just south of Nablus, and is home to several important archaeological and religious sites which date back to the Canaanite, Hellenistic, Herodian, Roman and Byzantine cultures.

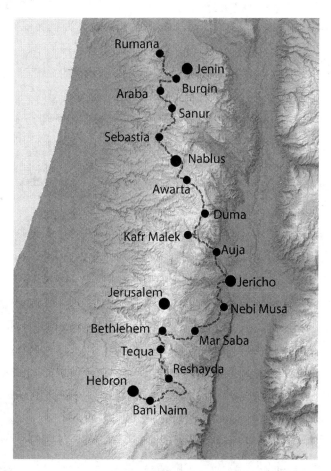

Figure 4.1 Masar Ibrahim al-Khalil route.

Source: Michel Awad.

مسار ابراهيم الخليل
masar ibrahim al khalil

Figure 4.2 Masar Ibrahim al-Khalil logo.
Source: Michel Awad.

The products offered, i.e. hiking, biking, homestays with local families, all focus on people engagement. Through these encounters, the hosts have complete ownership of the tourism product in terms of planning and decision making. There is a desire to maintain, and be the key beneficiaries of the tourism product, which is community led.

Women are becoming more confident with their new roles of catering to internationals; offering both tangible and intangible features of Palestinian life, traditions and customs. Empowerment! They are voicing their opinions within their households, helping in the management and decision making of financial issues, as well as in local community issues. It is the women of the villages who do the preparation for the overnight stays, including all of the traditional meals prepared. It is not only the women who benefit, but their immediate family members, usually the youth, are directly involved in the preparations before, during and after the homestay, and thus benefit through the intercultural exchanges. There is a positive change in the way female involvement is becoming more and more attractive to other women and their families in neighboring villages. Rural women in local associations and cooperatives are preparing themselves to host travelers who come from afar. Women are investing their time in making handicrafts, such as cross-stich embroidery, basketry and olive oil soap, which have been passed down from generation to generation, and which reflect their age old traditions and cultural heritage.

The social impact has been two-fold. The traveler's demands which are driven by an eagerness to discover and understand the Holy Land, its people, its history and religions, beyond the superficial coach-based tours, have been met through the tailor-made responsible tourism products. The residents of rural and Bedouin communities are positively impacted by preserving local traditions, taking pride in sharing customs such as religious norm, local weddings, mourning, traditional Palestinian folklore dances, food preparation, cultural heritage, architecture and the importance of their multigenerational families living within the same spaces.

Financial impact

Although for centuries the Holy Land has been an important pilgrimage destination, tourism in general has been underdeveloped in Palestine. Most of the revenues accrued from pilgrimage tourism tended to reach the more established businesses at the relevant tourist sites, rather than the people with more need of financial support in remote rural areas. Most tour operators offered packages where travelers stayed in Israeli territories and spent money there.

Nowadays, the Palestinian products aim to increase the number of visitors being accommodated in Palestinian territories, whether in rural homes, Bedouin camps, monasteries, or locally-run guesthouses or hotels. In addition, carefully developed walking and cycling products have been created to reduce the economic 'leakage' of tourism revenue, making sure that the money goes directly to the members of the rural communities who provide services to travelers. The diversified products offered are attracting more visitors who prefer to spend more quality time and money in host communities. Community tourism has generated increased revenue in local communities by creating jobs, i.e. service and food providers, trainings for women and local tour guides, via the mechanism of establishing cycling and walking trails in rural Palestine. Trainings empower local communities to offer their best services to visitors, which open new job opportunities to the residents of these economically marginalized communities.

Before 1999, rural and Bedouin communities were not involved in any form of mainstream tourism, nor were they aware of their own potential, and how their cultural heritage could be used as an incentive for a tourist destination. Thus, these communities were not prepared to receive international tourists into their homes and communities. To overcome this, a series of specific workshops were organized by centering on developing their sense of confidence through knowledge of the significance of their own cultural heritage, human rights, democracy, fostering women's social and political awareness and participation in civil society organizations and the decision making mechanisms, nutrition, First Aid, Professional Work Protocol and Ethical Guidelines for Tourism.

In the past years, there were few local trained hiking guides; therefore specific training programs were held to increase the number of qualified wilderness guides. They were trained to be ethically and environmentally responsible, and to be able to transfer knowledge about the trails, the region, its history and cultural heritage to visitors. The workshops resulted in qualification for the candidates to be certified as professional wilderness guides by the Palestinian Ministry of Tourism and Antiquities (MOTA).

Villagers, who were once reluctant to welcome foreigners into their remote communities, opened up to the world, becoming eager to embrace tourists. They are making efforts to renovate homes, restore local buildings and tents in order to host travelers. Rural communities are taking initiatives to develop their own society and economy by becoming active partners in welcoming and hosting international, as well as Palestinian walkers, hikers and cyclists. A unique element of this product is that it is sustainable in terms of having no running costs. Palestinian hosts have their own homes, and therefore, it is a product which is always readily available at no extra expense.

It is evident that a strong network of rural people, who are committed to a responsible and green tourism in Palestine, has been developed. Benefits are multilayered for the families' well-being and livelihoods, as well as for their local communities as a whole. There is social development, allowing residents of the rural communities to discover and have exchanges with people from around the world. Opportunities for job creation and income generation by providing services such as family hosting, guiding and cooking are all in place. Beneficiaries are the rural communities as a whole, and more specifically Bedouin families and women. This has resulted in positive contributions to the conservation of natural and cultural heritage, and to the promotion of cross-cultural exchange and understanding. All of the alternative products offered to visitors, involve the participation of members of rural communities in the decision making process, which ultimately affects their lives and life chances.

The range of people walking and cycling has increased in the past ten years. Visitors now know that there are historical, archaeological and religious sites along the path, with the added value of warm hospitable people waiting to welcome them into their homes to share traditional Palestinian meals to satisfy their hunger, and to quench their thirst for knowledge and intercultural exchanges about all facets of life in Palestine.

Improved communication and cooperation among local committees and other communities is taking place, thus creating a multipliers' effect to broaden the benefits from experiential and cultural tourism in Palestine. Today, the number of beneficiaries of the alternative products is increasing, therefore broadening the market of people visiting Palestine, and as a result, enhancing the direct benefits to the fragile rural communities.

Environmentally-friendly products such as walking, hiking and cycling tours in the Holy Land, which connect people and cultures along the path, have gained economic significance in rural Palestine, improving lives of people who otherwise would have never been touched by the benefits of tourism. This responsible way of travel is bringing about an increase in beneficiaries in rural communities. The local Palestinian economy is being enhanced as money being spent during the walk or cycle tour is disbursed exclusively in Palestinian areas with a wider geographical spread throughout the West Bank. In addition, local communities, guides and service providers have inevitably become partners in the development of their own economies along the path.

In these close-knit communities, Palestinian women are proudly taking the lead in developing their family financial status. Women, either individually or as part of women's unions/associations, prepare homemade traditional meals for groups of travelers, which result in financial benefits. Jobs are being created for women who otherwise would not have had opportunities to join the work force. There is an incentive to offer home cooked meals in a warm welcoming environment. As host families, they are situating themselves to accept other visitors, who are not part of an organized group; therefore, they are accessing wider markets by promoting their accommodation by word of mouth and through social media, thus increasing their household incomes. According to testimonies of beneficiaries in one of the northern rural villages of Jenin during a workshop that took place in Ramallah (Personal communication, December 23, 2014), the hosts reported that they had both financial benefits, as well as development on the personal level for themselves and their children, who have been inspired by visitors to learn other languages and to study abroad. The hosting families express that the intercultural learning experiences are a great benefit of having guests from different nationalities come into their homes.

The host families are the window to authentic traditional Palestinian customs and hospitality. Until now, the results have been amazing – intercultural exchanges, understanding, learning and friendships. These host families and their experiences can be used as models for other households and rural communities, not yet involved in the tourism product, thus allowing for a multipliers effect of economic empowerment for each community.

The beneficiaries are proudly offering their authentic Palestinian hospitality, showing that Palestinians are a peaceful people with a great history rich in cultural and religious traditions, while at the same time debunking the image of Palestine as solely a pilgrimage destination or a dangerous place to visit. An accomplishment that beneficiaries' state is that through direct contact with visitors, they are able to break down the stereotypes held by some westerners about Palestinians. Developing responsible tourism related to rural communities, culture and the environment, has been the means to change the perception of tourism in Palestine by initiating new ways to experience Palestine and its people. Traditionally, Palestine was viewed as a destination for coach-based pilgrimage tourism. Now, a thriving experiential tourism sector has evolved, where local people set the agenda and reap the benefits. Visitors appreciate the warm welcome and the opportunity to have a closer connection with Palestinians, learning about their daily lives, their challenges and their aspirations.

Political impact

Centuries old trading routes once connected the ancient markets of the Holy Land from east to west and north to south. Pilgrimage paths brought the faithful from faraway places either by sea or by land. However, since the Oslo Agreements in 1993, access to and from the Holy Land has changed. Despite the fact that all entrance points into and out of the Palestinian territories are controlled by Israel, alternative tourism in the Holy Land is gaining ground, and cannot be stifled due to the political realities. Walking, cycling and community tourism have flourished and have been resilient during on-going political and security instabilities.

Approximately 130 km long and 65 km wide, with a population of roughly 2.7 million people, the occupied West Bank was partitioned by the Oslo Accords into three zones, Areas A, B, and C. Area A consists of territory under the full civil and security control of the Palestinian Authority; Area B is land under the Palestinian Authority's civil and partial security control; and Area C remains under full Israeli control and contains the illegal Israeli settlements. Areas B and C are usually not invested in; therefore little or no development in favour of the Palestinian residents there has been taking place.

The walking, hiking and cycling trails that have been developed in Areas B and C support struggling Palestinian rural residents and the development of their economics. Lands in these areas, such as in Auja, Reshayda and in the Jordan Valley, are part of ongoing Israeli court proceedings with the aim of confiscating and clearing Palestinian land for expansion of more settlement blocs. The fact that international travelers visit and stay overnight in the Bedouin tents of Auja and Reshayda, helps the residents of these locations remain steadfast on their land, preserving their time-honored customs, traditions and Bedouin way of life. The type of tourism offered is an invaluable contribution and backing for the rural and Bedouin communities of Areas B and C in order for them to maintain their resistance, while at the same time improve their lives. To exist is to resist.

Israel once monopolized tourism throughout the decades of occupation, however, nowadays; the strength which lies within the Palestinian predicament of occupation is that a unique product has been created as a result of travelers' demands. Responsible tourism caters to their needs which take them to the heart of Palestinian rural and Bedouin communities, experiencing the mysteries of ancient archaeological ruins, mystical remote monasteries, preserved cultural heritage and the timeless serenity of the Jerusalem desert. As a result, the experiential product offered in Palestine has no competitor, and is the sole key to sustainable tourism and successful development in Palestine. A final note on the political impact of responsible tourism in Palestine is that it has greatly contributed to changing perceptions of how foreigners view Palestinians. Only when someone takes the first step to travel and discover this part of the world will he uncover and understand the realities of Palestine. These guests come and see the real Palestine, 'see for yourself experience', the one hidden behind the propaganda of western media. They leave Palestine as strong advocates for the Palestinian cause. Campaigns are held in their respective homelands, social media and word of mouth are used to call for human rights, peace and justice for Palestine. This type of advocacy, which has only been made possible through the abovementioned products, has gained tremendous ground in Europe and North America.

Conclusion

The aim of this chapter was to present hiking form of tourism and its social, political and financial implications for the Palestinian people. Despite Palestine being under occupation, international travelers choose to continue visiting the Holy Land, not for religious purposes, but instead for cycling and walking the rewarding path of cultural history. The visitor experiences warm hospitality by staying with Palestinian families – learning firsthand about their rich culture and traditions.

A sense of pride of being Palestinian has been brought to the surface of every Palestinian directly or indirectly involved in this form of tourism. The morale of marginalized villages has been enhanced. Hiking, biking and visiting archaeological sites, have had an impact on Palestinian students and residents from other regions of the West Bank, inspiring them to get outdoors, to hike, cycle and visit their very own Palestinian cultural heritage sites, fulfilling them with a sense of pride that this beauty and these treasures, which are sought out and appreciated by foreigners, belong to them as part of the diverse mosaic of World Heritage sites.

Through the responsible tourism programs, locals and Bedouins in rural communities have been locally empowered and have gained a great sense of honor about their heritage, the beauty of their natural environment and the richness of Palestine's most precious resource: the human resource. A win–win situation which has been set in motion for both visitors and hosts. The promising product is making holidays in Palestine more accessible than ever to a greater range of responsible travelers from around the world. A sustainable, environmentally friendly, self-reliant product. There are no longer silenced voices in rural communities of Palestine. There are proud voices, welcoming and hosting travelers from around the world, humbly sharing their cultural heritage and history with them. This is the Holy Land, waiting to be explored!

References

Curious Animal (2015) The adventure travel hot list: the 10 most exciting adventure travel destinations for 2015. Online http://www.curiousanimal.com/adventure-travel-hot-list/ [Accessed 5 January 2015].

Lerwill, B. (2014) Cover story: 10 of the best new walking trails, London: National Geographic Traveller. Online http://www.natgeotraveller.co.uk/smart-travel/features/cover-story-10-of-the-best-new-walking-trails/ [Accessed 25 February 2015].

5 Ongoing dispossession and a heritage of resistance

The village of Battir vs. Israeli settler-colonialism

Ryvka Barnard and Hassan Muamer

Introduction

In the summer of 2014, the small West Bank village of Battir made international news headlines when it was declared a World Heritage Site (Hetter 2014; Lewis 2014). For many tourism host communities, a UNESCO designation is key to putting them on the tourism map, and a likely boost to the tourism economy. For the village of Battir, the expectations were more modest, and simultaneously extremely high stakes. The UNESCO designation process for Battir was less about potential for tourism, but rather about the village's larger struggle for survival, a struggle that has reached and is waged far beyond the scope of UNESCO and tourism. Battir's story represents the many challenges facing Palestinian villages suffering under Israeli colonial rule. It is also the story of a long legacy of anti-colonial resistance, demonstrating the ever-evolving creativity and resourcefulness of the Palestinian liberation movement. In this chapter, we use the story of Battir as a case study to describe the wider context in which tourism development, colonialism and resistance are all at play.

Theoretical framing

International development

The dominant frame used to plan and analyze West Bank tourism is international development. In general, an international development frame focuses on different locations and societies in reference to their contemporary social and economic positions in relation to other countries, most often according to categories such as governance, economy, poverty rates, education, health care and human rights. While there are different theories and schools of thought within international development, they generally converge on the idea that there is differential development (less or more developed countries, or developing vs. developed), and they diverge on best approaches to address the problems of inequality.

In relation to Palestine, the development frame was used in British and later Israeli colonial planning, who initiated limited development plans as a form of social engineering, pacification, and image management for the colonial powers (i.e. promoting limited development to project an image of an 'enlightened colonialism') (Weizman 2007). The Oslo Accords, signed in 1993 between the Palestine Liberation Organization (PLO) and the Israeli State, were structured in such a way to continue this form of control (Hanieh 2013), with international donors committing support for the peace process from the premise that improved living conditions for Palestinians would prevent political discontent and thus improve the prospects of peace (Hanieh 2013). Large amounts of international aid money for development flooded into the West Bank and Gaza Strip, now coded as 'post-conflict' zones in need of uplifting and development (Taghdisi-Rad 2011).

Nevertheless, a post-conflict framework is problematic because it creates an illusion of two equally independent parties ('Israel' and 'Palestine'), when in reality, one is still the colonizer/occupier and the other is colonized/occupied. The historic dimension of Zionist colonialism is rendered invisible, and the structural power that Israel wields over all Palestinians is painted as a part of a new era disconnected from the past (hence the post-). Israeli attacks and repression against Palestinians are depicted as 'responses to terror' or 'security concerns' instead of a part of a colonial system designed to dominate and exploit or destroy the indigenous population. It also relies on and promotes a false model of two bounded separate geographic entities to suit two different nations. This picture invisibilizes Palestinian refugees living outside of historic Palestine, who continue to be affected by Zionism's denial of their right of return; Palestinians in Gaza under complete Israeli siege; and Palestinian citizens of Israel who suffer from a host of social and political restrictions and attacks.

Settler-colonialism

An analysis of settler-colonialism is a more appropriate frame for understanding the conditions in Palestine. Settler-colonialism is used to describe a specific type of colonial structure in which the colonizing force focuses on acquiring land, including but not limited to the natural resources and exploitation of indigenous labour (Veracini 2010). Primary examples of settler-colonial societies are Australia, the United States, Canada, South Africa and Israel. In all of these cases, white/European settlers established colonies with the intention to stay on that land, and they all involved massive ethnic cleansing and/or systematic exploitation of the indigenous population. According to Wolfe (2006), settler-colonialism is a zero-sum form of colonialism, with specific territorial aims, in which the end goal is not to exploit the indigenous population, but to replace it.

The Zionist movement was explicitly a colonizing scheme, focusing its pre-state efforts on acquiring land, building and populating settlements, and preparing a proto-state infrastructure which would be prepared to take control once the British left (Pappé 2006). Once the State of Israel was declared in 1948, the large majority of Palestinians were expelled or forced to flee from their lands and are prevented from returning to this day. The expansion of colonial settlements accelerated rapidly after 1948, and the agencies and organizations of the Zionist movement were shifted and adjusted to become state agencies (the pre-state militias were institutionalized to become the Israeli military). In 1967, Zionist ambitions for possessing a 'complete Land of Israel' were accomplished in the June war, when the Israeli military occupied the West Bank and Gaza Strip. Military occupation gave way to settlement expansion, which continues today.

Colonialism is always met with resistance, and Palestinians have always engaged in anti-colonial resistance against incredible odds. An analysis of settler-colonialism was the basis of the formation of the Palestinian national movement starting in the 1960s, which framed itself specifically as an anti-colonial national liberation movement. The third-world nationalist 'liberation through decolonization' doctrine was a prevailing understanding and political framework at the time (Salamanca *et al*. 2012). This framework animated political activism, from theoretical studies to street-level protest and communal organization, detailed and developed in the massive cultural and intellectual production generated from the PLO, in books, articles, and studies, as well as popular songs, poetry, art works, protest slogans etc. However, under the Oslo Accords, the Palestinian decolonization agenda was pushed to the background and stigmatized by Western donors as too ideological (for specific examples see Bhungalia, 2012). The context of colonialism was thus obscured, its contemporary manifestations presented as residual rather than a part of an ongoing structure.

Tourism and colonial development in Palestine

Tourism has long been a major industry in the West Bank due to the high concentration of historic sites of significant value, particularly to the three main monotheistic faiths. As such, tourism is seen as a 'natural resource' (players in the tourism industry often refer to it as 'Palestine's oil', see for example: Palestine Fitur 2014) linked with potentially large profits that could benefit individuals or individual companies, boost the besieged national economy, and even be the ticket to the economic independence so often touted by the Palestinian Authority (PA) and international donors as the key to ending the Israeli occupation (for more on the economic independence discourse see: Khalidi and Samour 2011). However, given the settler-colonial context, tourism has been used most effectively by the colonizer, both a resource to be exploited (an industry and market), as well as a tool for land confiscation.

Before the State of Israel was established, the Zionist establishment in Palestine organized a tourism committee with the explicit aim of counter-acting and pushing Palestinian tourism workers out of the market (Cohen-Hattab 2004). After the State of Israel was established, the Zionist tourism efforts were absorbed into the operations of the new state and expanded. Palestinian tourism enterprises were only able to continue insofar as they did not pose a threat to the tourism development led by the Israeli state (Cohen-Hattab 2004). In 1967, the Israeli tourism market received a major boost as it gained new territories with significant tourism sites to be counted as a part of the Israeli spoils of war. In a telling figure, in the year following the occupation, Israel reported an over 56 per cent growth in tourist arrivals, as they were now in control of significant sites in the West Bank as well

(Collins-Kreiner 2006). During that period, the numbers of tourists increased massively, but Palestinian tourism industry remained stagnant for the most part, as the military administration was intent on preventing any local alternatives that could compete with Israeli-run hotels and other facilities (Isaac 2010).

Under the development framework of Oslo, Palestinian tourism became a major target for economic development money, partly because tourism is seen as a fast-cash form of development, but also because it is generally seen as a non-political sphere insofar as it remains contained. Millions of dollars have been poured into the small enclaves of PA-administered cities like Bethlehem and Ramallah, supporting the financing and maintenance of up-scale hotels (which largely serve the foreign development contractors) and large Christmas events in Bethlehem, perpetuating a myth of normalcy despite the deepening of the military occupation (for a more general discussion of this phenomenon, see: Hanieh 2013; author's field research). In the economic development frame, tourism is seen as an indicator of stability, so the presence of large touristic events and posh hotels are used as examples of progress and success.

In the meantime, a far from stable reality is at play in the parts of the West Bank outside of PA control, which make up over 60 per cent of the West Bank and the majority of the villages. Villages are losing land at an alarming rate to Israeli state confiscations for the construction of the Apartheid Wall and other 'security' measures, and to Israeli settlements, expanding every day. The few villages that receive scraps of PA or international support for tourism development, or other forms of economic development, are struggling to simply stay on their lands. For most West Bank villages, economic development and any illusion of normalcy is not a realistic or viable option when they are under such intense political attack.

Case study: Battir

Introducing Battir

Grounding studies of tourism in an analysis of settler-colonialism lends two specific strengths. One is that it makes clear the connections between the multiple challenges facing Palestinian tourism initiatives (and Palestinian lives in general), namely, Israeli state and settler land grabs/expansion on both sides of the green line and throughout history, Israeli tourism development, and the Israeli security apparatus (including the Apartheid Wall, checkpoints, and other surveillance mechanisms). Through the lens of settler-colonialism, these multiple forms of violence and dispossession make sense as part of a structuring system, rather than random and ahistorical problems.

Equally as important, an analysis based in settler-colonialism allows us to see the powerful continuity of Palestinian resistance to colonization, and brings to the fore a narrative in which Palestinians are the main actors, whose struggle is defined as much by their creativity and dignified resistance as it is by what they are up against. A side effect of the development paradigm is that it projects a macro-political picture in which events are shaped primarily by governments, militaries, international aid agencies and NGOs, rather than looking at peoples' inspiring actions that often do not fit neatly into the frame of development. The case of Battir illustrates the depth of the challenges facing Palestinians, but also the richness of the Palestinian legacy of resistance.

Battir is a relatively small village in the West Bank, with a population just over 5,000, located between Bethlehem and Jerusalem in the Makhrour Valley, neighboured by the villages of Al Walaja, Husan, Al Khader, and Beit Jala. Battir lands used to also touch Al Qabu, a village depopulated and destroyed by Zionist militias in 1948. Despite its small size, Battir hosts some modest tourism infrastructure, including hiking trails, an eco-museum and a guest house. Parts of the village were designated as a UNESCO World Heritage Site in 2014. The designation celebrates Battir as an outstanding cultural landscape with particular focus on its unique ancient agricultural system.

According to its UNESCO nomination file (Department of Antiquities and Cultural Heritage, Ministry of Tourism and Antiquities, 2013), historically, Battir was known as the vegetable basket of Jerusalem since its main economy was based around agriculture, and Jerusalem provided a market for Battiri farmers to sell their produce. The Battir–Jerusalem connection was further strengthened in the early twentieth century when Battir became a stop on the newly constructed Jaffa–Jerusalem railroad, greatly facilitating the movement of goods and people. Battir's agricultural output was high partly because of its constructed stone terraces, connected to the main village spring by a complex network of irrigation channels dating back to the Roman era and an aqueduct that helped regulate the availability of water. The village's eight major families devised a unique 'eight day week' system, whereby each family would have access to the village water in turn, guaranteeing the equitable sharing and distribution of communal resources. The system of communal sharing co-developed over time with the ancient man-made structures, making the village strong enough to withstand various different difficulties for centuries.

Social solidarity and the legacy of Hasan Mustafa

Battir's history also reflects its role in the broader political and national landscape, well-documented (and summarized in this section) in a thesis authored by a son of Battir, Jawad Botmeh (2006). Like other Palestinian villages, Battir came under threat by the increasing power of the Zionist movement in the twentieth century, peaking in 1947 with the beginning of the systematic attacks by Zionist militias on Palestinians in advance of the declaration of the Jewish State (Pappé 2006). Like other villages, Battir residents established a village defense committee, organized by Hasan Mustafa, a prominent Battiri Palestinian nationalist. Mustafa had already been a vocal opponent of British and Zionist colonial rule, and when the dangers of Zionist military attacks became pressing, he and his comrades gathered weapons and were able to fend off attacks on Battir. Most of the villagers felt compelled to flee in summer–fall of 1948, when refugees from nearby villages arrived with tales of the horrors they witnessed, particularly the massacre in Deir Yassin, only four kilometers away. Mustafa and the other village defenders stayed behind, and they successfully prevented the village from being occupied, however the most difficult times were yet to come.

Battir was one of the frontier villages whose status was to be negotiated in the Israeli-Jordanian cease-fire of 1949 in Rhodes. During the negotiations, Hasan Mustafa traveled frequently to Amman to pressure Jordanian officials not to forfeit Battir to the newly declared State of Israel. In the meantime, the village still came under occasional fire. Committed to keeping the village in their hands, remaining and returning Battiris devised ways to continue working their fields while minimizing exposure to danger, for example, through switching to crops requiring less frequent maintenance.

When the cease-fire delegation came to the area of Battir to implement the boundaries of the armistice line (which became known as the Green Line), Mustafa and his comrades prepared ahead of time by hanging laundry and lighting lanterns in the village so that from a distance, the village appeared to be completely inhabited, hoping that this would prevent an Israeli takeover. The strategy worked, though the lands beyond the railway tracks were included on the Israeli side. Mustafa was able to pressure for a special clause in the Rhodes Agreement entitling Battir residents to continue farming their lands beyond the tracks so long as the train was not disturbed, and Battir's residents returned to the village.

Maintaining rights to cultivate their fields was helpful to preserving Battir on one level, but no place was immune to the massive disruption to the social, political and economic fabric of Palestinian life. The railway, which had so widened access to other markets for Battir, was taken out of operation, and Battiris were prevented from reaching Jerusalem using their standards routes. Overall systems of life and community were severely disjointed by the destruction of so many of the nearby villages. To counteract the despair, Hasan Mustafa worked tirelessly to implement a wide-range of programmes in the village to increase social solidarity within the Battir community. These programmes included major improvements to the educational system, most notably the opening of one of the first rural girls' schools in the area, an initiative that accounted for Battir's impressively low levels of illiteracy. Various communal clubs and organizations were also founded to help keep morale high in the short term while rebuilding the village's social infrastructure, strengthening the community's abilities in the long-run to sustain hardship that was sure to come.

Battir under occupation

In 1967, Battir was occupied by Israel along with the rest of the West Bank. Battir suffered from the same difficult conditions as other villages under occupation, including the stagnation of local development due to Israeli restrictions, forcing a majority of Battir residents to seek employment in the Israeli labour market, mostly in construction and the service industry. This contributed to a shift away from agriculture, particularly in the 1980s (Farsakh 2005; Gordon 2008), and also led great number of Palestinians to leave in search of better work elsewhere. Despite this, many Battiris continued to farm their lands, even if their main work was elsewhere, refusing to be severed from their beloved land and the land of their ancestors.

On top of the economic challenges, political repression was and still is a hallmark of the occupation. Battir residents, like all other Palestinians, were subject to arrest, incarceration, and/or physical violence if suspected of political activity. Over the years several homes and other buildings in the village were destroyed by the Israeli military, a form used commonly as collective punishment and as a deterrence mechanism to keep Palestinians from engaging in resistance (Gordon 2008). However, even during high periods of resistance to Zionist colonization, and even though Battiris were certainly involved in struggle, there were almost no incidents involving the trains that ran through the village.

Nearly three decades later under the Oslo Accords, all of Battir ended up outside of the Palestinian Authority's main jurisdiction, and about 76 per cent of the village lands were classified as Area C, under total Israeli control . This means that Battir was excluded from major development projects undertaken by the PA, and simultaneously at higher risk for land loss due to Israeli settlement expansion. In 2004 the situation became even more dire when Israel confiscated village land adjacent to the railroad tracks in order to begin building the Segregation Wall. The planned route of the wall completely encloses Battir's eastern neighbouring village of Al Walaja, and if constructed, would surround Battir from three sides, with the fourth side (west of Husan) blocked by the Israeli settlement Beitar Illit. Like many of the villages along the 1967 cease-fire line, the Wall would not only cut Battir off from its neighbours and access to Palestinian urban centres, but it would also cut people off from their lands and for many, the source of their subsistence. Reliance on agriculture is not only Battir's historic legacy, but it is also increasingly central to the local economy as fewer Battiris are allowed to legally enter Israel to work.

While certainly all Battiris opposed the construction of the wall, many were surprised that a few years into the plan, another network of opponents to the Wall surfaced, including some of the most right wing Israeli voices through the settlement movement, as well as a range of actors in the international and Israeli environmental scene (Hasson 2015). Suspicious of this dubious support, Battir oriented its anti-Wall movement in rebuilding the social solidarity in the village, and towards gaining the support and attention of international groups like UNESCO (which is detailed below). The surprising Israeli opposition to the wall in Battir opens the second topic of this chapter: the connection between Israeli eco-tourism initiatives and the ongoing displacement of Palestinians.

Open spaces and colonial expansion

Open spaces

Israeli opposition to building the Wall in Battir came primarily from two constituencies: settlers and environmentalists, though as we will demonstrate, these two seemingly separate sets of interests and positions are deeply intertwined.

Settler opposition to the Wall was not unprecedented since its construction interferes with potential settlement expansion. The settlement movement generally favours other forms of containment of Palestinians that do not interfere with the logistical and geographic elements of expansion, including the next logical step from containment, which is expulsion/eradication.

The other set of opposition came primarily from environmental groups, most notably, the influential Society for the Protection of Nature in Israel (SPNI), and ultimately, the Israel Nature and Parks Authority (INPA), the Israeli government agency responsible for national parks and nature reserves. These groups both submitted opinions in a 2012 petition to the Israeli Supreme Court, filed by the Friends of the Earth Middle East, requesting that the decision to construct the wall on Battir's lands be completely reversed (Friends of the Earth Middle East 2012). The opposition surprised many, particularly since the Israeli Ministry of Defense originally consulted and gained the approval of the INPA about the route of the Wall. However, their change of position made sense after news emerged that the INPA along with several other organizations and government agencies were planning for an Israeli national park on what would be the Israeli side of the wall (i.e., Battir's lands beyond the railroad tracks). In the opinion submitted to the Supreme Court, the INPA urges for a way to 'conserve' the agricultural lands (called in the petition 'open spaces') of Battir, including the agricultural traditions, and save it from the destruction of the wall (Hacohen 2012).

In the context of settler-colonialism, 'conservation' of 'open spaces' is a standard form of land appropriation (Poirier and Ostergren 2002; Brockington and Igoe 2006). In fact, the INPA has been at the centre of similar cases since the occupation began, resulting in scores of Palestinians losing land to Israeli national parks, nature reserves, and other 'green' projects (Rinat 2013). The concept of 'open spaces' in and of itself reveals a colonial mentality: why are Battir's lands, private properties belonging to the village, considered 'open space' by Israeli agencies? This practice is only understood properly if seen in the context of Zionist history of colonization, through which Palestinians have been consistently depicted alternately as existential threats or as virtually invisible, or more accurately, as simple flat images in the background, as part of a natural landscape, a timeless picture, which would be updated by colonial modernity, with the relics leftover as a charming touch of decontextualized local colour (for a detailed analysis of this phenomenon, see Stein 2008).

Colonial eco-tourism

Many influential players in the Israeli environmental movement are closely linked or directly involved with the settlement movement and other instigators of Palestinian displacement. The Jewish National Fund (JNF-KKL) was largely responsible for the massive planting over of Palestinian village remains in the 1950s, and it was also instrumental in the infrastructure for Israeli expansion in the West Bank. The Israel Nature and Parks Authority (INPA), the government body dealing with national parks and nature reserves, was contracted by the Israeli military to oversee the bulldozing of a Palestinian neighbourhood in the Jerusalem Old City in 1967 to make way for the visitor's plaza at the Western Wall (Masalha 2007), and is currently involved in administering (along with the local settlement authorities) dozens of nature reserves and Israeli national parks in the West Bank and occupied East Jerusalem. The Society for the Protection of Nature in Israel (SPNI) maintains various field schools in West Bank settlements, where groups of (non-Palestinian) hikers are hosted to go on West Bank nature expeditions. These three agencies also are the main organs of one of the biggest niche tourism markets in Israel: eco-tourism.

Eco-tourism is generally associated with responsible tourism initiatives worldwide, but in the context of colonialism, eco-tourism often takes on the same exploitative tendencies as the larger regime (Fairhead, Leach and Scoones, 2012; Garland 2008; Hall 1994). It becomes a tool in the land appropriation strategy of an expansionist colonial regime because the discourse of 'open spaces' and 'nature preservation' lend themselves so well to land confiscation, under the premise that it is being misused by the indigenous population or that it needs to be confiscated in order to be preserved for the common good. Variations of these premises have been put forward in making way for a new eco-tourism project being planned and built directly on the other side of the green line from Battir, Husan and Al Walaja, on the lands historically belonging to those villages, in the form of the Jerusalem Park (Park Yerushalayim (Jerusalem Park) 2015).

The Jerusalem Park (in Hebrew *Park Yerushalayim*) is a project of the JNF-KKL, INPA, Jerusalem Municipality, and the Jerusalem Development Authority, planned to form a green ring' around the city which, on the southwestern end, includes sections of the historic lands of Al Walaja, and the Battir lands beyond the railroad tracks. The section of the Green Park most relevant to the case of Battir is the Emek Refaim Valley Park, which snakes along the green line across Al Walaja (actually, Al Walaja is the most directly impacted as a large number of its lands are slotted for the new park), and into the area in question in Battir, along the railway, on the lands which were promised to continual access to Battir through the Rhodes Agreement in 1949.

Jerusalem Park in focus

While the complete plans and the trajectory of events is still murky, the intentions of the Jerusalem Park developers can be understood most clearly from a combination of the document submitted to the Israeli High Court by the INPA (Hacohen 2012), and the promotional materials about the Jerusalem Park on the JNF-KKL website under the 'tourism and recreation' category (KKL-JNF n.d.), along with the park's Hebrew website. The language in the petition is strikingly similar to the promotions of the eco-tourism project being developed. This is to say that the content of the objection to the Wall cleverly skirts around any advocacy on behalf of the rights of people in Battir, and instead talks about the significance of the natural features on the land, which are then detailed as a part of the 'landscape of the Land of Israel' in the park promotions.

For example, in the INPA petition submitted to the court, the landscape is considered important to the State of Israel and to the Jewish people because:

> [it] tells our story, the story of the land from which we were exiled and to which we returned. The landscape is indicative of spiritual cultural heritage of our ancestors…who dreamed of returning to work and live on the same land from which we were expelled.
>
> (Hacohen 2012: 2)

Its sources include biblical references to the area, as well as the ancient roots of the terraces and aqueduct system, from the 'second temple period'. According to one of their quoted sources, the construction of the landscape could be attributed to the Israeli settler-pioneers: it 'is the fruit and the grandeur of the work material and the pioneering of Israel throughout the ages' (Hacohen 2012: 5). The summary at the end of the document calls for '[Israel] to know to preserve what is ours' (Hacohen 2012: 12). The promotion for the park on the websites use much of the same language, presenting the parks as a way for visitors to enjoy the ancient agricultural heritage and the scenic terraces of the 'ancient Land of Israel' (JNF-KKL n.d.).

The Palestinian presence and ownership of the land is barely mentioned in the petition document, and even then, Palestinians are presented as the people who incidentally live in the village and farm the land, and in no place is there a mention of their legal ownership of the land, their rights to stay there, their roots in the land, or their political rights in general. In fact, they are not even called Palestinians, but rather 'our Arab neighbours' and 'the Arabs of Judea and Samaria' (Hacohen 2012: 12). The picture painted in the petition is of an ancient Jewish site that is being taken care of by these quaint people. In the same document, there are oblique references to Palestinians who dare to resist the occupation, who are best controlled through the high-tech surveillance of the Israeli military, and its effective 'improved intelligence gathering capabilities and the prevention of violent attacks' (Hacohen 2012: 3). In essence, the opinion calls for the land to be recognized as a part of Israeli heritage, and for well-behaved Palestinians to be allowed to stay, and the rest to be dealt with by the advanced Israeli military intelligence and repression apparatus!

The touristic promotion of the park puts emphasis on accessibility and inclusiveness (KKL-JNF n.d.), quite ironic since the very owners of the land are the single group excluded from its boundaries. There is no mention at all of Palestinian people in the promotion for the park, and on maps included, the Green Line is implied, but not labeled. The names Battir and Al Walaja are written on to the map in the periphery, along with the Jewish settlements in the area, but in other parts of the promotion there is mention of the 'abandoned spring of al Walaja' and 'abandoned fields', suggesting that the people associated with those places and who once tended them are long gone, and/or that they left voluntarily. A 'living museum' is slotted to open on the part of the park closest to the West Bank settlement Gilo, where there will be live demonstrations of ancient agriculture techniques, including actors dressed in clothing to make them look like ancient Hebrews, creating an educational infrastructure and a visual image branding the terraced agriculture as a Jewish concept.

When the park is completed, the area will be considered a nature reserve according to Israeli law, and it will be administered by the INPA. While this is not a Wall, its results are perhaps as odious for Battiris. Israeli nature reserves have very tight regulations and even their own police force. There are already several cases in which nature reserves and national parks were declared on Palestinian West Bank land, and consequently the Palestinian land owners were prevented from cultivating their land, and in fact fined, arrested, or beat up for trying to do so, under the excuse of trespassing and causing damage to a nature reserve (B'tselem, 2015). The process is currently underway in Wadi Qana, where the residents of the Palestinian village of Deir Istiya have been essentially banned from their own lands, as the INPA and neighbouring settlers develop it into an Israeli tourism site. There is unfortunately very little legal recourse for the residents of Battir to challenge such a process, particularly since the land in question is on the other side of the Green Line, and their historic agreement in 1949 is unlikely to hold much traction against combined claims of 'conservation' and 'security'.

The heritage of resistance

Battir's response to the Apartheid Wall

When the route of the Apartheid Wall was first made clear in the early 2000s, different Palestinian towns and villages were forced to assess ways to resist the Wall and its destructive results, a difficult task given the already strained conditions of life under occupation in the West Bank, and particularly in the midst of the Israeli repression of the second intifada. In areas where the construction of the Wall began immediately, there was little time to strategize and carefully plan, and the only feasible option was for people in those locations to wage noisy and consistent demonstrations, as became well-known in Bil'in, Budrus, and Jayyous. Given the height of the repression at the time, which included frequent closures and curfews, villages were fairly isolated in their struggles. However, Popular Struggle Committees were formed in each location and were able to begin coordination.

In Battir, popular demonstrations were not such a clearly viable choice. First of all, any demonstration would surely put the Rhodes Agreement into danger, and would immediately jeopardize a large portion of the lands that might be saved otherwise. Secondly, Battir was lucky in the sense that there would be some time before construction in that area would begin, giving some time to plan ahead, carefully assessing what particular tools of resistance were available to the Battir community that may not be accessible to others. Battir had an advantage in its historic relative visibility because of the railroad tracks, seen as a potential leverage point by strategists in the village. It is important to emphasize that refraining from popular demonstrations was a tactical choice, rather than a philosophical or political one, as Battiris saw themselves very much as a part of the larger movement against the Wall.

In 2007, a group composed of engineers and other technical experts (including Hassan Muamer, one of this article's co-authors) were commissioned to produce on an assessment of the village on behalf of the Palestine office of UNESCO as a part of an initial list of heritage sites in danger in Palestine. The assessment was conducted partly oriented around UNESCO's criteria of cultural heritage landscapes, with special attention to the unique historic co-evolution of the village and its natural landscape, and with an eye towards producing scientific and historically grounded and precise information which could detail the negative effects the construction of the Wall would have on the village. The result of the study was the production of the *Battir Landscape Conservation and Management Plan* which won the UNESCO Melina Mercouri International Prize for the Safeguarding and Management of Cultural Landscapes in 2011, awarding the village council and various other collaborators funds to commit to the plan. Part of the outcome of the assessment was the possibilities for modest tourism development in the village, both to celebrate Battir's unique features and to bring attention to its precarious position.

In the same year that the study was launched (2007), the Battir village council submitted a petition to the Israeli Supreme Court to protest the Wall. The data from the study would be used in the court case against the Wall, but serve the dual function of providing a blueprint for how the community could work to preserve its resources no matter what happened with the Wall. The Battir community decided to use the time it was afforded to build itself up internally, rather than using up all of its resources and energy in fighting the external effects of the Wall. While Battir was able to do this partly because of time, it also attests to the legacy of community solidarity in resistance to the occupation, inspired by Hasan Mustafa's ethos.

Old forms, new applications

The connection between the community-focused aspects of the heritage management project and the legacy of Hasan Mustafa is not simply a retrospective observation; it was a specific facet of research conducted by the project team. While the project was externally supported by UNESCO and various other organizations, its course was driven by the local knowledge of how difficult political conditions and repression can wear down a community, and produce melancholy and deep depression that prevent creative solutions. The project researchers began collecting photographic, documentary, and oral history archives on the village, including a specific focus on Mustafa-era strategies for keeping the village active in the most difficult times. In turn, some of these strategies were adjusted and replicated to apply to the current situation.

For example, in learning how Hasan Mustafa worked with farmers to make sure that they kept maintaining their fields even when there were Zionist militia attacks in the area, the new project worked with farmers to help them continue cultivating their fields in the area due to be cut off by the Wall. Farmers worked together with the researchers to work the lands beyond the railway tracks every day of the year. This increased local investment in opposition to the Wall by helping to sustain traditions of the village's agricultural bounty, to keep energy and morale high by protesting in advance through a productive and positive action. Farming, an increasingly difficult tradition because of Israeli policies, was revived not only as sustaining in the technical sense, but also as a refusal to be compliant and give up on the land before it is lost. In the meantime, the project was able to support the traditional forms of agriculture that are valued by UNESCO.

Studies of the ecological features of Battir also included studies of local folklore and local history around the many natural and archaeological sites on village lands, including various religious shrines, Byzantine-era burial caves and a large monumental rock on the village lands. Researchers looked into various understandings and explanations of different features on the village, and instead of focusing only on the purely scientific explanations, they collected local lore as well, demonstrating how local culture develops understandings and stories about its own surroundings. This facet of heritage interpretation is also important in resistance because it helps develop the specifically Palestinian, specifically Battiri, historic relationship to the land. In UNESCO terms, this forms a sort of intangible heritage that is undeniably connected to the indigenous inhabitants of the land, and not a top-down state-driven colonial narrative as devised by the State of Israel.

The tourism development in the village was envisioned as a way to complement the process, and the planners were careful not to let the tourism development drive for profit-making overshadow the community focus of the project. For example, hiking trails that were cleared in the village were done primarily to facilitate easier access of farmers (especially elderly farmers) to their fields, and secondarily served the function of tourist hiking trails. An eco-museum and guest house were developed by rehabilitating old buildings in the town, so as to revitalize the old spaces rather than building something new. Local guides were trained with the information gathered from the research project, again as a way to ensure that the voices at the forefront of talking about Battir would be those most directly invested, a particularly significant point as its fate was literally being quarreled over in the colonial court with no real room for the local voices to be recognized as the experts that they are.

UNESCO strategy

When they started, the Battir activists working on the UNESCO assessment did not know ahead of time how relevant UNESCO would become, when the Palestinian Authority used its upgraded status in the UN to apply for full membership in UNESCO. After some initial stalling, the PA finally put forward Battir as a World Heritage Site in Danger, and it was designated as such in 2014. While this designation was widely celebrated as a symbolic victory for Palestinians, including by Battiris, those close to the process regard it as one of many tools, rather than a completely winning strategy for heritage protection, particularly since the UN (including UNESCO) has no power to implement or enforce its recommendation.

In the meantime, the UNESCO designation can be a powerful tool for Battir. Firstly, it gives formal international recognition to Battir as a Palestinian site. Secondly, it internationalizes and increases the stakeholders invested in Battir's struggle, making it at least a bit more difficult for the Israeli government to proceed with its plans. For example, it is likely to have played significant role in the January 2015 Israeli Supreme Court ruling which indefinitely closed the Ministry of Defense's case for building the Apartheid Wall. With so many organizations and people around the world watching the case of Battir, it was strategic of the State of Israel not to pursue the construction so as to take the spotlight away from the issue. For the people of Battir, this was a major relief, if possibly only temporarily. The case also presents a useful trial to see if UNESCO may prove to be a potentially useful tool in other Palestinian settings. While not every place can claim the same unique cultural landscape as Battir, the victory opens up the potential of new ways of trying to challenge Israeli Apartheid through international bodies and the courts.

Unfortunately, the threat of the Jerusalem Park remains imminent, and it presents a much more complicated challenge that Battir activists, as well as other Palestinians, will have to keep working on. If the pressure is kept up, Battir may be able to devise a strategy to expose and challenge the use of parks and nature reserves as a colonial tool of land confiscation, and having UNESCO recognition may help in that process. However, it will require a new phase of intensive energy, careful planning, strategic coordination with other villages and international organizations and maintaining a critical stance towards Israeli eco-tourism which continues to eat away at Palestinian land.

Conclusion

Reflecting on the case of Battir, there is much to learn from the complex challenges and inspiring victories won by the village. While there is much left unclear in the future, the legacy of Hasan Mustafa provides a useful guide. Mustafa well understood the importance of internal social building for the long-term struggle of decolonization and the conservation and protection of heritage. While the village defenders were able to protect the village during the fighting in 1948, Mustafa knew that this was only a temporary victory, and that the real work would only begin afterwards. He and others in the village worked tirelessly at that point to maintain the lands until the Rhodes Agreement was implemented. Even this was seen as merely another temporary victory, and Mustafa and others used the time to build up internal systems in the village to plan for more difficult times ahead. Similarly, the 2015 victory of Battir in the court case is only a temporary one, and Battir residents now have the task of building the longer term social and technical infrastructure in the village to fight for the next challenge, one which is already unfortunately on the doorstep.

References

B'tselem, The Israeli Information Center for Human Rights in the Occupied Territories (2015). 'Wadi Qana – from Palestinian agricultural valley to settlements' tourism park'. 23 April 2015. Online http://www.btselem.org/area_c/wadi_qana [Accessed 7 July 2015].

Bhungalia, L. (2012) '"From the American people": sketches of the US national security state in Palestine'. *Jadaliyya*. 18 September 2012. Online http://www.jadaliyya.com/pages/index/7412/%E2%80%9Cfrom-the-american-people%E2%80%9D_sketches-of-the-us-nati [Accessed 18 September 2014].

Botmeh, J. (2006) 'Civil resistance in Palestine: the village of Battir in 1948', Master of Arts, Coventry University.

Brockington, D. and Igoe, J. (2006). 'Eviction for conservation: a global overview'. *Conservation and Society*, 4(3): 424-470.

Cohen-Hattab, K. (2004) 'Zionism, tourism, and the battle for Palestine: tourism as a political-propaganda tool', *Israel Studies*, 9: 61–85.

Collins-Kreiner, N. (2006) *Christian tourism to the Holy Land: pilgrimage during security crisis*, Cheltenham: Ashgate Publishing Ltd.

Department of Antiquities and Cultural Heritage, Ministry of Tourism and Antiquities (2013) 'Palestine: land of olives and vines – cultural landscape of Southern Jerusalem, Battir'. World Heritage Site Nomination Document, UNESCO World Heritage Centre, Palestine.

Fairhead, J., Leach, M., and Scoones, I. (2012) 'Green grabbing: a new appropriation of nature?', *Journal of Peasant Studies*, 39(2): 237–261.

Farsakh, L. (2005) *Palestinian labour migration to Israel: labour, land and occupation*, Abingdon: Routledge.

Friends of the Earth Middle East. (2012) *Route of separation barrier threatens to destroy shared Palestinian/Israeli cultural landscape site*. Press Release http://foeme.org/www/?module=media_releases&record_id=107 [Accessed 5 June 2015].

Garland, E. (2008) 'The elephant in the room: confronting the colonial character of wildlife conservation in Africa'. *African Studies Review*, 51(3): 51–74.

Gordon, N. (2008) *Israel's occupation*, California: University of California Press.

Hacohen, Z. (2012) *Machshol kav ha-tefer: keta Batir-Mahsom HL"H. Amdat reshut hateva vehaganim (Seam-line barrier: section Battir-Checkpoint HL"H. Position of Nature and Parks Authority)* (In Hebrew).

Hall, C.M. (1994). 'Ecotourism in Australia, New Zealand and the South Pacific: appropriate tourism or a new form of ecological imperialism?', in E. Cater and G. Lowman (ed.) *Ecotourism: a sustainable option?* Chichester: John Wiley.

Hanieh, A. (2013) *Lineages of revolt : issues of contemporary capitalism in the Middle East.* Chicago: Haymarket Books.

Hasson, N. (2015) 'Palestinians, settlers, greens declare victory in court ruling on separation barrier', *Ha'aretz*. 4 January 2015 Online http://www.haaretz.com/news/diplomacy-defense/.premium-1.635293 [Accessed 5 July 2015].

Hetter, K. (2014) 'Palestinian landscape is newest World Heritage Site'. CNN. 21 June 2014. Online http://edition.cnn.com/2014/06/20/travel/unesco-battir-new-world-heritage-site/ [Accessed 5 July 2015].

Isaac, R.K. (2010) 'Palestinian tourism in transition: hope, aspiration, or reality', *Journal of Tourism Peace Research*, 1: 23–42.

Khalidi, R. and Samour, S. (2011) 'Neoliberalism as liberation: the statehood program and the remaking of the Palestinian National Movement', *Journal of Palestine Studies,* 40: 6–25.

KKL JNF – Keren Kayemeth LeIsrael – Jew. Natl. Fund. (n.d.) *Jerusalem Metropolitan Park: a green lung for Israel's capital.* Online http://www.kkl.org.il/eng/tourism-and-recreation/forests-and-parks/jeruslem-park.aspx [Accessed 18 January 2015].

Lewis, R. (2014) 'UNESCO names West Bank's Battir a protected World Heritage Site'. *Al Jazeera America.* 23 June 2014. Online http://america.aljazeera.com/articles/2014/6/23/unesco-palestinebattir.html [Accessed 5 July 2015].

Masalha, N. (2007) *The Bible and Zionism: invented traditions, archaeology and post-colonialism in Palestine–Israel,* London: Zed Books.

Palestine Fitur 2014, video, Destination Experts, 31 January 2014, viewed 5 June 2015, https://www.youtube.com/watch?v=qfPBZXqAqTk.

Pappé, I. (2006) *The ethnic cleansing of Palestine.* Oxford: Oneworld.

Park Yerushalayim (Jerusalem Park) (2015). Online http://www.jerusalempark.org.il/ [Accessed 18 January 2015].

Poirier, R., and Ostergren, D. (2002) 'Evicting people from nature: indigenous land rights and national parks in Australia, Russia, and the United States'. *Natural Resources Journal,* 42, 331–351.

Rinat, Z. (2013) 'Why Palestinians Despise Nature Reserves'. *Ha'aretz.* 18 December 2013. Online http://www.haaretz.com/news/national/.premium-1.564264 [Accessed 20 December 2014].

Salamanca, O.J., Qato, M., Rabie, K. and Samour, S. (2012) 'Past is present: settler colonialism in Palestine', *Settler Colonial Studies,* 2: 1–8.

Stein, R.L. (2008) *Itineraries in conflict: Israelis, Palestinians, and the political lives of tourism,* Durham: Duke University Press Books.

Taghdisi-Rad, S. (2011) *The political economy of aid in Palestine: relief from conflict or development delayed?* New York: Routledge.

The Applied Research Institute (2010) 'Battir village profile, Palestinian localities study', *The Applied Research Institute Jerusalem.* http://www.ochaopt.org/documents/opt_arij_villageprofile_battir.pdf

Veracini, L. (2010) *Settler colonialism: a theoretical overview,* Basingstoke: Palgrave Macmillan.

Weizman, E. (2007) *Hollow land: Israel's architecture of occupation.* London: Verso.

Wolfe, P. (2006) 'Settler colonialism and the elimination of the native', *Journal of Genocide Research,* 8: 387–409.

6 World Heritage Site in Bethlehem and its potential reflections on tourism

Nada Atrash

Introduction

The inscription of Bethlehem, 'Birthplace of Jesus: Church of the Nativity and the Pilgrimage Route' on UNESCO's World Heritage List in 2012 formed an important milestone on different levels – while this achievement was considered as a victory on the national level for Palestine, it was considered a tool to enhance community-based tourism throughout the inscribed area. This chapter briefly highlights the history and process of inscribing Bethlehem on UNESCO's World Heritage Site (WHS), a brief history on the development of the Pilgrimage Route, and shall mainly aim to present a thorough analysis of the potentials of the Route as a site that could boost the cultural tourism in the town of Bethlehem, depending mainly on the research and work conducted during the work on the 'Heritage for Development Project' – an EU funded project aimed at building the local authorities in Bethlehem Ramallah and As-Salt in Jordan in the conservation and management of historic city centres through involving them in the preparation of conservation and management plans that serve the goal. In addition, this chapter shall mainly aim to present a view of the potential impacts that the WHS should offer to tourism in the town, taking into consideration the current situation and the future expectations based on the outputs of the plan.

Bethlehem: a World Heritage Site

On 29 June 2012, the World Heritage Committee voted during it thirty-sixth session, which was held in St. Petersburg, Russian Federation, in favour of the inscription of Bethlehem, Birthplace of Jesus: Church of the Nativity and the Pilgrimage Route on the World Heritage List in Danger [World Heritage Committee (WHC), Decision 36 COM 8B.5]. The inscription was a significant event and the result of a long journey that started with the call of the World Heritage Convention in its twenty-sixth session held in Budapest, Hungary, to consider the exceptional universal value of the Palestinian cultural heritage and the request to take the appropriate measures to protect it [WHC, Decision 26 COM 6.1].

The decision to inscribe Bethlehem gained important dimensions since it was the first result of admitting Palestine as a full State member to UNESCO, and it represented an international recognition of the cultural rights of the Palestinians. It also contributed to removing part of the historical injustice that was caused to the Palestinians. Bethlehem is the second Palestinian site inscribed on the List, following the Old City of Jerusalem and its Walls, which was inscribed in 1981 and on the Danger List in 1982 [WHC, Decision 06COM X.28-35].

Initially, the decision of the World Heritage Committee in its twenty-sixth session came as a result of the Israeli occupation of the Palestinian land in 2002, and the intended destruction of sites of cultural significance in Nablus, Hebron and Aboud, and the long siege of the Church of the Nativity in Bethlehem. The decision of the World Heritage Committee emphasized the exceptional universal value of cultural heritage in Palestine, and called to take appropriate measures to protect it. The Committee also decided to provide technical and financial assistance to Palestine to ensure establishing an inventory of cultural and natural heritage, assessing state of conservation and measure for its preservation and protection, and training and capacity building of Palestinian specialists in the World Heritage.

Following the admission of Palestine as a full state member to UNESCO, Palestine adopted four agreements the most important of which was the Convention Concerning the Protection of the World Cultural and Natural Heritage (1972). On 8 March 2012 the membership of Palestine and its adoption of the Convention text were approved. This has enabled Palestine to submit nomination files to inscribe sites of cultural and natural heritage value. The first step was to list Bethlehem, Birthplace of Jesus: Church of the Nativity and the Pilgrimage Route on the tentative list, and to submit immediately the nomination document to inscribe the site on the World Heritage List in danger. The inscription was considered at the time as an important accomplishment in the Palestinian struggle to achieve freedom and independence; and that it represented a momentous step towards right of self-determination (Fayyad 2012).

The inscription of Bethlehem was immediately followed by submitting to the World Heritage Centre a tentative list of sites that are of 'outstanding universal value'. The list aims at listing sites that shall be nominated to be inscribed on the World Heritage List in the future (Taha 2012). The Palestinian tentative list at the time included: 13 cultural and two natural: Ancient Jericho: Tel es-Sultan, Anthedon Harbour, El-Bariyah: wilderness with monasteries, Mount Gerzim and the Samaritans, Old Town of Hebron al-Khalil and its environs, Old Town of Nablus and its environs, Qumran: Caves and Monastery of the Dead Sea Scrolls, Sebastia, Tell Umm Amer, Throne Villages, Um al-Rihan Village, Wadi Gaza Coastal Wetlands and Wadi Natuf and Shuqba Cave (Taha 2009).

The Bethlehem site was inscribed as an emergency case based on various reasons among which the most important are the state of the roof of the Church, the general condition of the Church prior to and during the siege of the church of the Nativity, and the vibrations that were caused by the Israeli military tanks that was moving in the periphery of the Church in 2002, and then comes the water leakage inside the Church that was mentioned by local and international experts who were working for the National Committee for the Restoration of the Roof of the Church of the Nativity in Bethlehem (Taha 2012).

Birthplace of Jesus: Church of the Nativity and the pilgrimage route, Bethlehem

The following description of the property is compiled according to the nomination document to inscribe the site on the World Heritage List (Ministry of Tourism and Antiquities (MoTA 2010). Bethlehem lies 10 kilometres south of the city of Jerusalem, in the fertile limestone hill country of the Holy Land. Since at least the second century people have believed that the place where the Church of the Nativity now stands is where Jesus was born (Pringle 1993). One particular cave, over which the first Church was built, is traditionally believed to be the birthplace itself. In locating the Nativity, the place both marks the beginnings of Christianity and is one of the holiest spots in Christendom. The original basilica church of 339 AD (St. Helena), parts of which survive below ground, was arranged so that its octagonal eastern end surrounded, and provided a view of, the cave; this church is overlaid by the present Church of the Nativity, essentially of the mid-sixth century (Justinian), though with later alterations. It is the oldest Christian church in daily use. (MoTA 2010)

Since early medieval times the Church has been increasingly incorporated into a complex of other ecclesiastical buildings, mainly monastic. As a result, today it is embedded in an extraordinary architectural ensemble, overseen by members of the Greek Orthodox Church, the Custody of the Holy Land and the Armenian Church, under the provisions of (the Status Quo of the Holy Places) established by the *Treaty of Berlin* (1878) (Cust 1980).

For most of the last 1700 years, Bethlehem and the Church of the Nativity have been, as is still very much the case, a pilgrim destination. The eastern end of the traditional route from Jerusalem to the Church; known as the Pilgrimage route, marks the road that connects the traditional entrance of Bethlehem, near King David's Wells with the Church of the Nativity, and extends along the Star Street through the Damascus Gate or *Qos Al-Zarara*; the historical gate of the town, towards the Manger Square. The route continues to be celebrated as the path followed by Joseph and Mary during their trip to Bethlehem during Christmas ceremonies each year, and is followed ceremonially by Patriarchs of the three churches at their several Christmases, and during their official visits to Bethlehem.

The pilgrimage route, identified as a WHS in Bethlehem, refers to the route approaching the Church of the Nativity via Star Street and Paul VI Street. It retains the street width and line fossilized by urban development since c. 1800 AD. This 'width and line' formalizes a commemorative route for religious ceremonies. The significant historical and religious features in this line are in the urban fabric rather than the architectural and historical features of the individual buildings, which collectively delimit that line. Nevertheless, a few buildings from earlier periods still stand and the street is now mainly defined by facades of the nineteenth and twentieth centuries. The general aspect, almost completely in pale yellow limestone, is attractive. Most of the buildings incorporate traditional design and appearance, for example with living accommodation above and workshops at street level opening out on to the street. Most importantly, the relatively few unsympathetic modern intrusions are along the south side of Paul VI Street and around Manger Square.

The buffer zone of the WHS is identified as the historic town of Bethlehem. Its urban fabric is composed of traditional buildings and the majority of these buildings dates back to the Ottoman period. The fabric also contains some churches, monasteries, schools and the Mosque of Omar, which were built between the mid-nineteenth and mid-twentieth centuries. This buffer zone is able, through the recently adopted 'Bylaws for Regulating the Conservation of the Architectural Heritage in Bethlehem, and the Categorization of the Traditional Areas and Traditional Individual Buildings' (CCHP 2014), to ensure proper protection for the WHS. This area is also able to ensure proper physical and visual transition between the WHS and the surrounding territories.

Birthplace of Jesus: Church of the Nativity and the Pilgrimage Route was inscribed under World Heritage criteria (iv): be an outstanding example of a type of building, architectural or technological ensemble or landscape which illustrates (a) significant stage(s) in human history and (vi): be directly or tangibly associated with events or living traditions, with ideas, or with beliefs, with artistic and literary works of outstanding universal significance (UNESCO 2013). Criterion (iv) was indicated because the Church of the Nativity represents an outstanding example of an early church in a remarkable architectural ensemble. It illustrates two significant stages in human history including the conversion of the Roman Empire to Christianity, which led to the development of the Church of the Nativity on the site believed to be associated with the birth of Jesus (fourth century AD), and to the power and influence of Christianity in the period of the Crusades that led to the development of three major convents in its environs (eleventh and twelfth century AD). Criterion (vi) was indicated because the site is directly associated with the birth of Jesus, an event of outstanding universal significance, through the buildings of which were constructed in the fourth century AD and re-constructed in the sixth century AD – the site is considered holy to more than two billion Christian believers in the world, both Christians and to Muslims.

Urban development of the site

Until the early twentieth century, Bethlehem remained a satellite town of Jerusalem and was historically connected to it. The only approach to the Church of the Nativity was through the Star Street, which is traditionally the road followed by Mary and Joseph on their way to the town some 2000 years ago. Bethlehem has been always described by the various travellers and pilgrims who visited it as being a small village surrounded by agricultural terraces located on the hill facing the Church of the Nativity, and separated from the Church by an esplanade that also serves as the market place for the town.

On the eastern brow of the ridge, separated from the crowded village by an open esplanade, is the convent, like a large feudal castle. It is a huge pile, consisting of the Church of the Nativity and the three convents-Latin, Greek, and Armenian abutting on its north, east, and south sides.

(Porter 1887: 116)

The town of Bethlehem was composed of seven quarters, each inhabited by one of the town's seven clans. The houses were built close to each other as a method of ensuring security for the people living in these quarters. The urban development was normally within these quarters or immediately adjacent to them. Five major changes between the mid-nineteenth and mid-twentieth century has left a noticeable print on the urban development of the town.

The adoption of the *Ottoman Reform Edict* of 1856 allowed foreigners to own property throughout the Ottoman Empire (Nasser 2005). As a result, various Christian missionaries were able to purchase their own property in Bethlehem and immediately commenced with the construction of various buildings around the historic city centre. Buildings included churches, schools, monasteries and hospitals that were massive in scale compared to the residential complexes in the town. These buildings have affected the townscape, and have defined the shape and direction of the urban development of the town, which tended to connect these structures with the city centre.

The *Ottoman Reform Edict* of Sultan Abdülmecid I promised equality in education, government appointments, and administration of justice to all regardless of creed. The decree is often seen as a result of the influence of France and Britain, which assisted the Ottoman Empire against the Russians during the Crimean War (1853–1856) and the *Treaty of Paris* (1856), which ended the Crimean War (Shokeh 2012).

In 1860, the Mosque of Omar was constructed on a plot of land that was donated by the Greek Orthodox Church, and located to the north-western side of the Manger Square. The Mosque, in its existing form, was demolished and rebuilt in 1958. Moreover, the fire inside the Grotto of the Church of the Nativity in 1873 due to dispute between the Greek Orthodox and the Franciscans led to a decision by the Ottoman government to build a police station 'As-Saraya' in the empty plot of land facing the church from the west. During the British mandate period, As-Saraya was used as a police station, municipality and a courthouse. As-Saraya was burnt during the Palestinian revolt in 1936, and replaced by a British Tegart Building, which continued to be in use as a police station by the Israelis, and was replaced in 1998 by the Bethlehem Peace Centre.

In 1905, a decision by the Ottoman government to move all cemeteries from the city centre to its margin resulted in moving the cemeteries that were located to the north of the manger Square to their current location to the south western part of Al-Anatreh Quarter. Moreover, in 1927, Bethlehem Municipality decided to move the marketplace from the Manger Square to its current location at Al-Farahiyeh Quarter. These two decisions contributed to a major change in the activities that used to take place in the Manger Square (Centre for Cultural Heritage Preservation (CCHP) 2014).

Figure 6.1 (above) and 6.2 Two general views of Bethlehem from the entrance of the Star Street towards the Church of the Nativity. The photos display the contrast in the urban fabric of Bethlehem between mid-nineteenth and early twentieth century; Top 1857 – Bottom c. 1930.

Source: Nada Atrash

Figure 6.3 (above) and 6.4 Two general views of Bethlehem from the Church of the Nativity towards the west. The photos display the contrast in the urban fabric of Bethlehem between mid-nineteenth and early twentieth century; Top c. 1880 – Bottom c. 1940.

Source: Nada Atrash

Between 1956 and 1966, during the Jordanian Jurisdiction over the West Bank, Bethlehem Municipality evacuated and demolished the buildings located between the Church of the Nativity and the Mosque of Omar, and a row of the buildings which were located to the southern side of the Star Street extending from the Mosque of Omar to Al-Manara Square (Shokeh 2012). The demolition was followed by the construction of the municipality Building on the southern end of the Square (1965) and the municipality building on its western end (1973), and thus defining the Manger Square as it is today. The demolition of the traditional quarters and the creation of the Square was foreseen by the municipality as an important step to meet the increasing tourism incoming to the town, but it did not take into consideration the loss of the traditional fabric of the town.

In 1926, and in order to meet the new transportation developments, Manger Street, which is the main street that connects Bethlehem with the city of Jerusalem, was planned and implemented. The project was one of the most vital projects that enabled tourists' buses to arrive directly to the Manger Square. As a direct result of the project, souvenir shops along the Star Street, which used to be the only road that connected Bethlehem with Jerusalem, were replaced with other handicrafts shops that served the local community. Moreover, the locating of the marketplace along Paul VI Street, and the expansion of the town towards the west has contributed to the majority of the shops and trades being concentrated along Paul VI Street.

The rehabilitation of Star Street was one of the important projects that were implemented during the works on Bethlehem 2000 Project. The project, which was funded by the Spanish Government, has remarkably contributed to enhancing the infrastructure and the physical situation of the area (Kassis 2001). Nevertheless, and due to commencement of the second intifada and the events that followed, including the siege of the Church of the Nativity, Star Street was not revitalised.

After the inscription

On the national level, the inscription of Bethlehem gained an important momentum since it represented the international recognition of the cultural rights of the Palestinians and contributed to removing part of the historic injustice that was caused to the Palestinian over the years. On the local level, the inscription of the site was foreseen as an important tool that should be employed to ensure the sustainable tourism of the town; while the local community was pleased for the event which was considered to directly contribute to the economy of the town, the various stakeholders, mainly the Ministry of Tourism and Antiquities (MOTA), Bethlehem Municipality and the Presidential Committee for the Restoration of the Church of the Nativity, were requested to provide a management plan for the WHS [WHC, Decision 36 COM 8B.5] (UNESCO, 2015b).

Upon the inscription of the site on the World Heritage List, the Centre for Cultural Heritage Preservation (CCHP) employed the *Heritage for Development Project (Her4Dev)* to set guidelines for a management plan for the site. The project, which was funded by the European Commission and implemented in Bethlehem by CCHP in association with Bethlehem Municipality with the technical guidance of RehabiMed Association in Spain, aimed directly to build the capacities of the local authorities (Bethlehem Municipality in Bethlehem) in the protection and management of the cultural heritage resources in the town.

The preparation of the guidelines came as a direct response to the request of Bethlehem Municipality for the assistance of the CCHP to assist its technical team in the task, and the project was foreseen by both partners as an opportunity to achieve the task. It is worth noting that the CCHP is a semi-governmental organization established in 2001 in order to preserve cultural heritage resources in Bethlehem. The Centre works under the administration of a steering committee headed by the Minister of Tourism and Antiquities.

The work on the *Guidelines for the Management of the World Heritage Site in Bethlehem* (CCHP, 2014) took into consideration two major issues that shall contribute to a comprehensive management plan. The first was the aspirations of the local community and their willingness to contribute in the various issues that shall be addressed in the plan, and the second was the roles and capacities of the various stakeholders and the legal frameworks that shall form their roles and responsibilities within the plan.

The local community

In order to form a comprehensive understanding about the aspirations and of the local community and their willingness to contribute in the various issues that shall be addressed in the plan, CCHP held a community mapping activity within the historic centre of Bethlehem. *Diwan Al-Ballad*, which literary translates to the hall of the town; *diwan* in Palestinian traditions is a large hall located at the house of the elder man or the sheikh of the clan where people meet to discuss matters related to the clan or the town, is a mapping activity during which CCHP team placed living rooms within the open spaces of the historic centre and asked the people passing by to stop for coffee and fill a form that shall contribute to drawing a map of the town according to the information provided by the local community. The activity was held on 30 September and 3 October 2013 at the Manger Square and Al-Manara Square.

A survey was developed based on various interviews with the local community conducted between June 2012 and July 2013 during the work on the survey of the traditional buildings in Bethlehem. The survey gathered more than 600 questionnaires. Final figures varied from a maximum of 602 responses to a minimum of 248 responses. The data computer-based collection process, including the removal of partial or generally illegible data, led to these variable outcomes. Elements on the basic socioeconomic profile of surveyed citizens were asked in order to estimate the general outcomes accuracy.

The survey acknowledged a more than positive overview of the public awareness. The local community demonstrated to be aware of the importance to preserve tangible and intangible heritage within the historic centre of Bethlehem. Ninety-seven per cent of answering users acknowledged an existing heritage to be preserved, providing an impressive popular statement regarding the value of such local heritage. Furthermore, the local community mostly stated that the value of Bethlehem is to be fully recognized. In that extend, the town users considered essential that UNESCO acknowledged the universal value of Bethlehem heritage. Ninety-four per cent of participants were confident in such recognition, considering that the inscription of Bethlehem was profitable for the city.

It is important to point out that the local community involved in the survey not only considered the importance of official recognition, but also the necessity of public awareness. They ranked public awareness as a powerful tool for heritage preservation. Public awareness was considered as the second best way to encourage built heritage preservation within the historic centre. Besides, the local community ranked incentive preservation policies in first position in what concerns the best ways to encourage cultural heritage preservation. Thus, the local community underlined themselves that any implemented preservation measure is to come with public awareness in order to be successful.

A positive public acknowledgment of development potentialities within the historic centre was acknowledged through the survey, the participants highlighted the Manger Square as the area with the highest development potential. Damascus Gate 'Qoss Al-Zarara' and the Star Street in addition to Al-Anatreh Quarter were also considered as urban areas with high development potential. The indicated areas represent the most preserved examples of Bethlehem traditional urban fabric. Exactly the same districts were described as the most attractive areas in the professional survey outcomes. In terms of intangible heritage, it is worth mentioning that the users also highlighted the value of commercial areas within the Old City, such as *Al-Madbaseh* Street and the Old Market (Suq).

Through the survey, the users as well as the inhabitants of the historic centre shared the importance of preserving the traditional urban fabric of the town. As they underlined the necessary weight of public awareness in the preservation process, they provided a positive overview of the several practices regarding the built heritage within the city, thus providing highly encouraging data over the inner situation of traditional building. Along with the common willingness to preserve the traditional heritage, adaptation of such heritage to the contemporary ways of life came in a logical perspective. Rehabilitation of the architectural heritage within the centre is therefore to enable contemporary living standards. In this way, adaptation of the heritage to contemporary needs constitutes an intrinsic part of the whole preservation process.

The survey outcomes stressed the general wish for the historic centre to remain a lively urban area. The participants acknowledged the historic town as the core of urban life within the city of Bethlehem. Several religious ceremonies were indicated to play a key role in the overall local urban activities. The participants underlined, the need for a revitalization of the cultural platform within the area. Thus, the implementation of major touristic and recreational projects came in third position in what concerned the emergency measures to be taken in the historic town.

In the meantime, since many responses came from already renovated urban areas, their requirements may have focused on measures to revitalize the historic town. Such revitalization is in this case to come as a coherent long-term approach for the overall preservation of the built-up heritage. The lack of public services constituted a crucial issue in the historic centre of Bethlehem. The local community also highlighted the need for welcoming public spaces. Moreover, they insisted on the inadequacy of the local public infrastructure in a coherent approach, based on the whole importance of public spaces. Structural weaknesses of the built-up fabric were indicated the most crucial threats affecting the local living environment. In fact, the inhabitants of the historic centre widely highlighted poor living conditions. Various issues including humidity and air circulation problems inside the housing unit were underlined as important matters that need to be addressed in the future. The problem of the lack of fresh water was also pointed out by the inhabitants, as the Bethlehem region suffers from the lack of water during the summer.

The survey outcomes stressed on the necessity of a comprehensive regulation of traffic within the historic town. The urban environment of the historic centre remains unsuitable for the growing traffic pressure. Major streets of the centre are overcrowded by cars, and corresponding facilities do not meet the local requirements, congestion was indicated as a main threat to the local working and housing environment. Furthermore, providing parking facilities in the outskirts of the historic town came out as the second most urgent measure to be taken within the by the local authorities.

The collected data also pointed out to the local customs of parking vehicles in closeness to the destination of the driver, which is to be taken account. Although the surveyed users insisted on the inadequacy of the local urban framework for a smooth car flow, the perspective of such car traffic as representing a threat to the traditional urban fabric was not extensively acknowledged. The Old City users involved in the survey ranked car pollution among the minor threats to the local built heritage. Indeed, the weight of car displacement represents a characteristic feature in the local ways of living. In this way, public awareness regarding this issue should be considered as crucial for future projects.

Another crucial issue that legitimated the work on bylaws for the conservation of the historic centre was the identification of unauthorized building works as a major threat to the traditional urban fabric. Private construction works often include practices threatening the overall value of the built-up heritage, from the building scale to the general urban environment. Additions of further floors on the top of traditional buildings are not only destroying the historic value of such buildings but also affecting the whole urbanscape of the historic centre. The fact that local community recognized the necessity of building control within the Old City, also underlined the corresponding necessity of enforcement and reinforced the role of the local public authorities in preserving the built-up heritage of the town.

The local authorities

The WHS in Bethlehem includes within its borders: the Church of the Nativity and its three adjacent convents; the Greek Orthodox Convent, the Franciscan Convent and the Church of St. Catherine and the Armenian Convent, public, private and religious buildings and public spaces. Accordingly, various local authorities and religious institutions, either separately or together, are responsible for the various issues related to these places including the daily care and maintenance, follow up and management.

However, the responsibility of the local authorities in regards to the WHS, is divided between Bethlehem Municipality and the Ministry of Tourism and Antiquities regarding the Pilgrimage Route and the buffer zone (the historic centre of Bethlehem) and the Presidential Committee for the Restoration of the Church of the Nativity regarding the works relate to the restoration of Church of the Nativity; it is worth noting that the three Convents are directly managed by the concerned churches without any interference of the local authorities.

Bethlehem Municipality, the acting local authority in the town, plays the major role in the management of the Pilgrimage Route and the buffer zone. The municipality is responsible for various issues related to the site including the day-to-day maintenance of property, issuing building permits and following up construction throughout the property, and other issues related to the physical structure of the Holy Land. The MOTA also approves the building permits. The ministry also plays a major role in case of any archaeological discovery; the decision is the sole responsibility of the ministry.

The management of the Pilgrimage Route and the buffer zone (the historic town of Bethlehem) is ensured through the Building and Planning Law no. 79/yr 1966 enforced in Palestine, and the Buildings Bylaw no. 5/yr 2011, and the 'Regulatory Bylaws for Conservation of the Historic Centre and Traditional Individual Buildings in Bethlehem – 2014' (Bethlehem Municipality 2014).

The implementation of the 'Regulatory Bylaws for Conservation of the Historic Centre and Traditional Individual Buildings in Bethlehem – 2014' fall under the responsibility of the Bethlehem Municipality. However, according to Article 5 of the 'Regulatory Bylaws', a committee was formed to review the building permits and present their recommendations to the Building and Planning Committee at the Municipality. The Committee is composed of the Head of the Engineering Department at Bethlehem Municipality, a member of the Municipal Council, a representative of the Centre for Cultural Heritage Preservation, a representative of the Ministry of Tourism and Antiquities and a representative of the Local Government Office (Bethlehem Municipality 2014: Article 5).

The Church of the Nativity is overseen by the Greek Orthodox Patriarchate, the Custody of the Holy Land and the Armenian Patriarchate of Jerusalem according to the Status Quo of the Holy Places (MOTA 2010). While the ongoing restoration works are directly implemented and managed by the Presidential Committee for the Restoration of the Roof of the Church of the Nativity in direct cooperation with the custodians of the church. The three adjacent convents are managed by the three churches separately; the Armenian Convent is managed by the Armenian Patriarchate in Jerusalem, the Greek Orthodox Convent is managed by the Greek Orthodox Convent in Jerusalem and the Franciscan Convent is managed by the Custody of the Holy Land.

The Church of the Nativity and its surrounding convents are protected according to the effective laws in Palestine; namely the *Antiquities Law* no. 51/yr 1966 applied in the West Bank, Article no 2/c, which indicates that an Ancient Archaeological Remain is defined as 'any mobile or fixed object constructed, engraved, built, discovered, made or modified by the human race before the year 1700'; 'and/or 'any object, mobile or fixed, that dates back to after the year 1700, declared by the minister as an archaeological ancient object' (Kingdom of Jordan 1966). It is worth noting here that in 1995 the Palestinian Authority ratified the Jordanian Laws that were applicable in the West Bank during the Jordanian Jurisdiction until the ratification of new laws, and that the Temporary Jordanian Law of Antiquities (no. 55/1966) is applicable in Palestine until the preparation of this report (Kingdom of Jordan 1966).

In addition, the protection of the Church of the Nativity is coordinated and monitored by the Palestinian Presidential Committee for the Restoration of the Church of the Nativity in direct cooperation and follow up with the three dominations (the Greek Orthodox Church, the Franciscans through the Custody of the Holy Land and the Armenian Church; the rights, privileges and possessions of these communities are protected by the *Status Quo of the Holy Places* (1852) as guaranteed in Article LXII of the *Treaty of Berlin* (1878)) (Cust 1980).

Christmas celebrations, and all other activities that co-occur in during the Christmas season, are organized by the Bethlehem Municipality in close cooperation with the Ministry of Tourism and Antiquities. It is worth noting that the Christmas Season in Bethlehem starts on the First Advent Sunday (last Sunday of November or first Sunday of December) and lasts until 19 January; the date the Armenians celebrate Christmas and the Orthodox celebrate Epiphany; various active stakeholders that represent both the public and private sectors participate in the organization of this event including the three churches.

Guidelines for the management of the WHS

In order to ensure a proper management of the Bethlehem WHS, the *Guidelines for the Management of the World Heritage Site in Bethlehem* introduced a management frame that engages the stakeholders at two stages (CCHP 2014). The management frame aimed to ensure the commitment of the stakeholders and to meet the aspirations of the local community. Moreover, it took into consideration the effective laws applicable in Palestine, which shall directly affect any proposed Management Plan in the future.

The Guidelines includes the establishment of a 'Management Unit for the World Heritage Site'. The Management Unit shall include at the first stage of its formation the stakeholders directly involved in the management of the site (CCHP 2014). These include Bethlehem Municipality and the Ministry of Tourism and

Antiquities as the active state actors in the site, in addition to the Presidential Committee for the Restoration of the Church of the Nativity and the Centre for Cultural Heritage Preservation as active non-state holders involved in the management of the site. During the second stage, and upon setting proper internal bylaws for the 'Management Unit' additional stakeholders that represent local community organizations shall be invited to join the unit; the selection shall be based on the various actions that shall be proposed by the unit and the role that the local community organizations shall play in the implementation of these actions. Moreover, during the first stage of the establishment of the 'Operational Unit', the Presidential Committee for the Restoration of the Church of the Nativity shall act as a focal point for all issues concerning the Church of the Nativity.

The 'Operational Unit' shall be responsible of the various issues related to the Site, including the follow up on the daily tasks; the follow up on the different requirements of the World Heritage Centre; setting programmes that ensure the conservation of the site; and the follow up with the various stakeholders on the different issues that shall be set by the unit. According the Guidelines, the operational unit shall have a technical unit that ensures that implementation of its activities, and a steering committee to oversee its work. The steering committee shall be composed by the four stakeholders.

In addition to the institutional frame for the management of the WHS in Bethlehem, the guidelines also included a brief proposal of financing the various issues related to the actions that shall enhance the Site. The financing section indicated various resources of financing depending on the public system, taxation regime, public-private partnerships and private sector. Moreover, the Guidelines proposed a set of actions that aim at enhancing the built up heritage within the Site; the actions included the urban management of the open spaces, tourism development and control, signage, housing improvement and traffic control (CCHP 2014).

Conclusion

The WHS in Bethlehem 'Birthplace of Jesus: Church of the Nativity and the Pilgrimage Route' is considered one of the Palestinian achievements in the international arena. Immediate reactions took place in Bethlehem; these included the celebrations on the inscription day and one week later (Tuma 2012). Locally, the inscription was foreseen by the local community as a tool to enhance tourism in the site; more precisely, the local community took it for granted that tourism to the town would no longer be limited to a quick visit to the Church of the Nativity and some other places in the town. They soon discovered that achieving this goal would require more than an inscription on the World Heritage List. Moreover, the realization that the inscription is not the end of the journey, represents a new set of responsibilities in ensuring effective conservation and management of the site have pushed the various stakeholders to start working on a management plan for the site.

The realization of a comprehensive management plan might not be an easy task, and might take some time to become applicable. However, the stakeholders have been working hard since the inscription to realize this goal, and were able to implement various actions indicated in the 'Guidelines for the Management of the World Heritage Site in Bethlehem' [State of Conservation Report by the State Party 2015], (UNESCO 2015a). These actions are foreseen by the different parties as first steps towards a comprehensive conservation and management of the site.

It is worth noting that Bethlehem, Birthplace of Jesus: Church of the Nativity and the Pilgrimage Route remained on the World Heritage List in Danger. This is valid until meeting the corrective measures indicated by the World Heritage Committee, i.e. until the completion of the restoration of the roof of the Church of the Nativity.

References

Bethlehem Municipality (2014) *Regulatory bylaws for conservation of the historic centre and traditional individual buildings in Bethlehem – 2014*, Bethlehem: Bethlehem Municipality.

Centre for Cultural Heritage Preservation (CCHP) (2014) *Manual for the rehabilitation of the historic town of Bethlehem*, Bethlehem: CCHP.

Centre for Cultural Heritage Preservation (CCHP) (2014) *Guidelines for the management of the World Heritage Site in Bethlehem*, Bethlehem: CCHP.

Cust, L.G.A. (1980) *The status quo in the Holy Places with an annexe on the status quo in the Church of the Nativity – Bethlehem by Abdullah Effendi Kardus*, Jerusalem: M.B.E.

Dabdoub-Nasser, C. (2005) *Anatreh Quarter: evolution and architecture*, Bethlehem: CCHP.

Fayyad, S. (2012) 'The story of inscribing Bethlehem on the World Heritage List', *This Week in Palestine*. Online http://archive.thisweekinpalestine.com/details.php?id=3766&ed=209&edid=209 [Accessed 28 June 2015].

Kassis, N. (2001) *Bethlehem 2000 Diaries, Bethlehem 2000 Project*, Bethlehem: Palestinian National Authority.

Kingdom of Jordan (1966) Temporary law of antiquities *(51)*, Amman Online http://www.dft.gov.ps [Accessed 28 June 2015].

Ministry of Tourism and Antiquities (MOTA) (2010) *Birthplace of Jesus: Church of the Nativity and the Pilgrimage*, Bethlehem: MoTA.

Porter, J.L. (1887) *Jerusalem, Bethany, and Bethlehem*, Jerusalem: Ariel Publishing House.

Pringle, D. (1993) *The Churches of the Crusader Kingdom of Jerusalem: a corpus, Volume 1 A–K (excluding Acre and Jerusalem)*, Cambridge: Cambridge University Press.

Shokeh, K. (2012) *Bethlehem municipality: its establishment and development 1880–1967*, Bethlehem: Bethlehem Municipality.

Taha, H. (2009) *Inventory of cultural and natural sites of potential outstanding universal value in Palestine*, Bethlehem: Ministry of Tourism and Antiquities.

Taha, H. (2012) 'The story of inscribing Bethlehem on the World Heritage List', *This Week in Palestine*. Online http://archive.thisweekinpalestine.com/details.php?id=3767&ed=209&edid=209 [Accessed 1 March 2015].

Tuma, N (2012) 'PA marks placing Nativity Church on UNESCO list', *JPost*. Online http://www.jpost.com/Middle-East/PA-marks-placing-Nativity-Church-on-UNESCO-list [Accessed 28 June 2012].

UNESCO (2013) *Operational guidelines for the implementation of the World Heritage Convention*, Paris: UNESCO World Heritage Centre.

UNESCO (2015a) Document on birthplace of Jesus Church of the Nativity and the Pilgrimage Route. Online http://whc.unesco.org/en/list/1433/documents/ [Accessed 28 June 2015]. State of Conservation Reports (2015) State of conservation report by the State Party SOC Reports, SOC Report 2015.

UNESCO (2015b) 'Committee decisions 36 COM 8B.5. Nominations to be processed on an emergency basis – Birthplace of Jesus: Church of the Nativity and the pilgrimage route, Bethlehem, Palestine. Online http://whc.unesco.org/en/decisions/4776 [Accessed June 27].

7 Experiential community-based rural tourism potential in Palestine
Challenges and potentials

Raed Saadeh

Introduction

Tourism in Palestine often finds itself like a little bush trying to break its way through the trees in an attempt to see the sun. This chapter provides a description of the key sustainability elements that are necessary to develop not only the tourism industry but also the environment needed to create the local readiness and the differentiation to improve the competitive advantage of the National Palestinian product. A specific treatment will be given to community-based tourism (CBT) both as a potential approach for sustainability and a source for new products. In the second part of the chapter, interpretation methods for community based tourism programs and guiding will be introduced and the process of working with the local community will be illustrated. Current and ongoing community based initiatives will be discussed and a correlated gap analysis will be explored.

Analytical background

Tourism in Palestine is no doubt sensitive to the prevailing political situation. Prior to 1967 tourism in Palestine was the leading industry compared to the neighboring Jordanian or Israeli tourism offers. Today, Palestinian tourism and services are dragging behind their regional counterparts. Although the Oslo Accord agreements have attracted a number of tourism investments and hotel projects to a number of Palestinian cities, the development was not equal or proportional in every city. On the contrary, the number of hotels and the percentage of room capacity in Jerusalem have declined by half. In fact, the instability of the political situation has dictated extreme fluctuations in the hotel business and has contributed to the deformation of the tourism industry. This deformation has been controlled by price competition and by service limitations threatening investments and frightening potential interest. The Palestinian tourism has often been hard hit by a number of incidents such as the Gulf wars, Sharon's visit to the Holy sanctuary and several attacks on Gaza. It has also suffered due to a number of cumulative losses that have affected each city diversely.

The Israeli Wall and the Israeli matrix of control (Halper 2008) have limited and deprived several Palestinian cities from their hinterlands. In Jerusalem, for instance, the Wall's impact on the city has not only deterred people from entering and spending in the city, it has contributed to shifting the center of Palestinian life in it to other neighboring cities particularly Ramallah. This has negatively affected both the Palestinian local tourism and the foreign expat business/investment potential in the city. Similarly every city or community faces a different set of obstacles and hindrances and serves different market segments and types of business.

By the same token, all sectors whether directly or indirectly linked to tourism have faced a set of challenges and opportunities respectively as indicated by the fluctuations in the hotel industry. Hence the question is how can a sustainable difference in the Palestinian touristic, cultural and socio-economic future be made taking into consideration the imposing situation and the local ability to exploit the available and potential resources and capacities?

The answer to this question resides in understanding and appreciating the need for investment and innovativeness in two developmental tracks, namely the industry and the community. These are two parallel tracks; the former includes investments in tourism establishments such as hotels, restaurants and tourism transport. The latter, focuses on enabling the tourism environment and is closely linked to issues such as cultural integration, identity and community empowerment and awareness. This chapter will provide an overview of community-based tourism development in Palestine.

Threats and challenges

The Palestinian tourism industry faces a considerable number of threats and challenges. However, it is worthwhile discussing those that have the most impact on the tourism industry.

Threats

Fragmentation

The current Israeli policy is to fragment the Palestinian society by a number of check points, barriers, dirt mounds, ditches, gates in addition to the Segregation Wall has contributed and intensified the fragility of the existing Palestinian economy. The loss of contiguity has its toll not only on the economic situation and access to markets but also on the social cohesion, the cultural reference and the role of the community in the development process. Tourism being a freedom of movement dependent sector has been hardly impacted by this policy.

Isolation

The deprivation of certain cities and their communities from their hinterlands is another Israeli policy that has limited tourism growth and sustainable capacity in these areas. This is particularly evident in Jerusalem where the city is cut off the rest of the Palestinian body and has completely lost its domestic market rendering it dependent on the seasonality of the international tourism. This policy has contributed to the marginalization and de-urbanization of the city draining its central socio-economic and cultural role and capacity.

Instability

The Palestinian tourism industry, despite all the odds has adapted to a certain mode of survival based on a minimum threshold of stability particularly in the absence of a concrete political solution. Instability is damaging to the tourism industry. It is commanded by a fluctuating political situation that keeps many travellers away from the country. The lack of political will to give the needed priority for tourism hampers the sustainable development of tourism and threatens the continuity of its establishments.

Challenges

Similarly, there are also a number of explicit challenges that faces the Palestinian tourism industry. Tourism stakeholders have the specific task to overcome them if the tourism industry is to advance forward.

Differentiation

The Palestinian tourism for the most part depends on Christian pilgrimage to the Holy Land. Although there is a very small margin for Islamic tourists to reach the country, the current tourism in Palestine remains a pilgrimage undertaking. However, Palestine has a lot to offer within and beyond the Holy Land package. The Palestinian's ability to exploit these resources and capacities is inevitable to achieve the necessary differentiation to improve the competitive advantage of their tourism offer. The Palestinians need a new way of thinking and a new vision in order to identify their competencies and consequently their competitive advantage. Once the Palestinian offer is able to generate the necessary added value, Palestine is positioned to differentiate itself as a destination.

Perception

The general perception of Palestine is generally negative as a tourism destination regardless of all the statistics that reflect the safety of the traveller. Foreign countries and their travel advisories are often too hasty to issue travel warning to Palestine as a result of political upheaval even though the situation does not impose a necessity. Palestinians are hospitable people and their attitude towards travelers is naturally welcoming. The challenge remains as to how to create a positive and sustainable perception to visit Palestine. The Palestinian Ministry of Tourism and Antiquities (MOTA) has invested a lot to attend international fairs and has exerted a lot of efforts to portray a positive image of the country. After all, tourism is an industry of perceptions. However, direct advertising and marketing are not enough to achieve this goal. Local, regional and international partnerships, networks and media management should be advocated in this endeavor.

Seasonality

Pilgrimage, being the prevailing source of tourism influx into Palestine, has a major setback that is inherent with the way it is run and managed. The seasonal nature of pilgrimage has a detrimental impact on tourism as an industry and as a developmental process because it leaves most of the year running on fumes. New products that can be integrated into the tourism package as well as new stand-alone products that promote other types of tourism such as cultural, environmental and experiential tourism gain importance in attracting different niche markets that are able and willing to visit Palestine during the low seasons.

Sustainability pillars for the Palestinian tourism

Depending on the discussion above and taking into consideration both the objective and subject circumstances that overwhelm the Palestinian tourism, both as an industry and as a developmental tool, this section will present a number of supporting activities and initiatives that if implemented, can form a safety valve to advance and protect the Palestinian tourism. These operate as basic pillars and principles and should be understood as such. How to implement them and translate their quintessence into practice depends on the combined effort, innovation, creativity and consistency of the Palestinian tourism operators.

The first sustainability pillar: cross-sectorial development and synergies

Tourism does not only belong to the tourism sector, it belongs to the entire community and to all the sectors that are directly or indirectly linked to it. In the past, tourism associations such as the hotel association, the tour operator association, the guides union, the tourism transport and others planned for tourism development in complete isolation with the rest of the sectors that are related and often fundamental to the tourism dynamics. The principle idea here is to invite stakeholders from other sectors to participate in the planning, the vision and the future of tourism industry in Palestine. Looking for reciprocal synergies among the sectors becomes basic when designing and creating tourism packages (Figure 7.1). This pillar does not only advance a more holistic approach to tourism management but, in the case of Palestine, it will contribute to reducing the existing alienation between the tourism establishment and the local community as a result of many years when tourism operators maintained a certain distance from the rest of the community.

The role of the community in the tourism development process is essential not only on the participatory level but also as a contributor to the cultural, social and demographical identity creation of the Palestinian tourism. These are essential elements of differentiation that are capable of enriching the national tourism product. Principles of Community-Based Tourism (CBT) are important in areas that are accustomed to tourism but they gain further importance when working in marginalized areas. Through CBT encounters with the local communities are augmented with local culture, hospitality and friendship. CBT indulges both the visitor as well as the local residents in memorable experiences and creates a lot of opportunities for employment generation, entrepreneurship, social cohesion and cultural exchange. Figure 7.2 illustrates the basic principles of CBT.

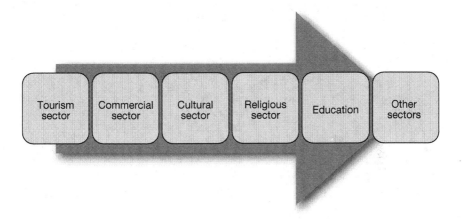

Figure 7.1 Cross sectorial synergies in Palestinian tourism.

Source: Raed Saadeh.

Figure 7.2 Basic principles of community-based tourism.

Source: Raed Saadeh.

Local guides

Community-based principles advocate the development, training and employment of local capacities and skills. Young men and women in villages and other marginalized communities leave their homes to find work in other places in the country or abroad. CBT opens opportunities to encourage local production and services to cater to visitors and guests. Home-stays, food caterers, transportation, handcrafts and local guides are examples of such opportunities. Local leadership is encouraged and young guides and community escorts play an important and natural role in promoting their village's services.

Planning as community

CBT is a bottom up approach. The role of the community in planning their programs and packages is essential not only for inclusion purposes but more importantly to establish their ownership of these programs and packages. This is an essential element of sustainability at a time when Palestine faces a number of uncertainties and challenges. The Palestinian public sector might not have all the resources to backup local development and the private sector might shy away from investing in certain areas. The civil society actors, on the other hand, will continue to work, research and produce particularly if the local community endorses their initiatives as part of their own.

Benefiting stakeholders

One of the principles to develop in working with the community is how to maximize the socio-economic and cultural benefits of its members and stakeholders. It is not enough just to encourage visitors to buy from the shops and bakeries or to eat at women centers or nearby restaurants. The involved community members and organizations need to be organized in umbrella associations and/or tourism cooperatives in order to best manage and maximize their benefits. Interested tour operators, agents and suppliers should be encouraged and persuaded to buy their entire package directly from the local communities at net rates to allow for future development and maintenance of the local programs and packages. Local packages' rates will calculate for such allowances to secure the sustainability of these programs and to maintain their standards. The local references should take into consideration the proper management of other social, cultural and environmental benefits when designing their packages.

Community balances

Human beings need to manage their lives while preserving their resources and capacities, identifying their needs and respecting their social structures and sense of community. This is essential and must be made clear to visitors and guests in order to encourage a collective effort to maintain the human presence in equilibrium with the surrounding environment and the need for education, research and knowledge. If a village offers an important habitat for a certain type of animal or bird life, this habitat needs to be protected and the locals need to learn how to survive while protecting what could be an important resource for their tourism packages. Similarly, if a certain community chooses to adopt tourism as one of its economic drivers, the need to integrate tourism awareness in educational programs becomes important. This type of holistic and horizontal development takes into consideration such balances and contributes to the protection and preservation of potential resources and capacities.

The third sustainability pillar: diversifying product

The main type of tourism that reaches Palestine is Christian pilgrimage. This type of tourism is currently seasonal and quite competitive with similar Israeli and Jordanian packages. Palestine, however, is not only the Holy Land. There is a lot of diversity inherent in such a small country that renders it very exciting and capable of providing a unique variety of experiences, literally within a walking distance from each other. Palestine is like a sparrow hawk, a small and capable destination. Among the Palestinian list of product diversity is spirituarlty. Palestine needs to learn how to re-offer the same experience that conceived the prophets of the monotheistic religions. It is the Palestinian culture that is fully capable of interpreting the metaphors and proverbs of the different scriptures as such examples were realized through its daily life and production. Palestine offers a unique cultural presentation, many years of history that portray traditions and heritage from different periods beyond Christianity and a matchless encounter with a wide spectrum of ethnic backgrounds and people. Only in Palestine a traveler can cross the country passing by three different landscapes from the Jordan valley through the mountains and into the cost in a couple of hours. This diversity also suggests a large variety of flora and fauna found in close vicinity to each other. The Palestinian cuisine is another area of stimulating exploration and sensational taste. These examples and others need to be incorporated in any visit to Palestine. Only through this diversity, the capabilities of such a small country can be comprehended.

The fourth sustainability pillar: enhancing supporting sectors

Cultural production, traditional handcrafts and artisanship, youth programs and local producer groups represent activities that can foster and enrich the tourism experience. Yet, these sectors are not well supported and their production has not found its way into the tourism package. Tourism operators are by large negligent of the value that such contributions can bring to the development of their programs, activities and packages. In order to realize the value of such contributions, these sectors must be enhanced and supported. Their programs must be integrated into the tourism package and their activities must be promoted to tourists, visitors and guests. Cultural production, for example, is a stand-alone activity at the time being and is very seldom referred to in the tourism establishment and vice versa.

Figure 7.3 Supporting sectors.

Source: Raed Saadeh.

Working close and interacting with the local community opens the door for visitors to experience the daily life and its many thousands of years of evolvement through simple activities such as cooking with a local family, visiting a farm, telling and listening to stories and myths, exploring the landscape, the architectural heritage, discovering community challenges, investigating their opportunities and their plight to create social, cultural, environmental and economical possibilities. CBT and experiential travel opportunities in Palestine are not only about visiting, they are also about protection. This is the essence of interpretation (Figure 7.4). Learning alone does not lead to loving and interpretation is about establishing this link. Interpretation methods consider building both an emotional as well as an intellectual link with the visitor. However, interpretation avoids too many facts that are often forgotten when visitors leave and attempts to leave an impression by telling stories and indulging both the visitor and the host in a unique cultural and humanistic exchange. Interpretation is reciprocal and depends to a great deal on understanding the guests and relating to them. People are much more readily receptive to remembering stories and experiences that resonate with their interests. Community objectives are pivotal to this method and they need to be incorporated into the design of the program and the guiding approach. Through interpretation, there is understanding; through understanding, there is appreciation; through appreciation, there is protection. Hence, the visitor is encouraged to delve into the specifics of the experience, to understand its limitations and opportunities, to appreciate its value and need and to participate in the ongoing or proposed protective efforts.

Figure 7.4 illustrates the particulars of the interpretation method and defines its approach.

Conveys a message or theme

The interpretation method depends on conveying a certain message or introducing a certain topic that is both linked to the host and related to the visitor as much as possible. The topic can be environmental, educational, anthropological or

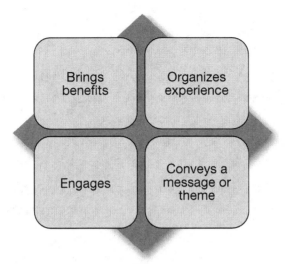

Figure 7.4 The specifics of the interpretation method.

Source: Raed Saadeh.

educational. Local guides are trained to identify pertinent themes and are encouraged to custom design their tours in order to best convey the desired message. For example, if a bird habitat needs to be conserved and is threatened by new urban planning, it might be a worthwhile theme to present during such a tour.

Organizes experience

In order for a tour to identify an issue, understand it, link to it and perhaps indulge in supporting or protecting it, the design of the tour and its different stages should be carefully thought of. It requires sensitivity and skill to organize a tour that deliberately starts from a certain point and ends with the appreciation required to link emotionally to it. In the case of the bird habitat above, the tour needs to lead the visitor to learn and appreciate that birds might disappear if the habitat is destroyed.

Engages

Interpretation is a tool of indulgence. It is an experiential venture and it is a window to meet people, make friends and work jointly for the benefit of mankind. This type of tourism is new in Palestine but its potential is promising and diverse. Perhaps it is what Palestine really needs to order to utilize tourism as a tool of heritage, identity and existence.

Brings benefit

The interpretation method brings benefits to the local stakeholders and to the community at large. Benefits are defined as socio-economic, cultural, environmental, educational, technological, and political. Benefits can be expanded through local, regional and international partnerships that deal with the various concerns and specializations undertaken by the local community.

Creating a quality visitor experience

Tourism remains an industry of perceptions; hence it is of utmost importance to create an impressionable experience for the guests and visitors, an experience that combines the goals of cultural exchange, environment protection and economic enhancement with guest needs. The basic guest needs are actually quite simple and are founded upon the provision of a safe and clean environment, mutual respect and clarity. The latter describes the clarity and accuracy needed to respond to visitors' expectations and tour descriptions. When a guest decides to visit any country or establishment, the concern is to achieve the required commitment for the business to prosper. Tourism operators, tour operators and guides need to understand this process as well from the point when a person decides to travel until they leave. This process is described in Figure 7.5 and its success contributes to the differentiation of the tourism package and the services provided. This process is particularly important for Palestine to improve its competitive advantage and service quality. It is also important to help organize the experience as discussed in the interpretation method above.

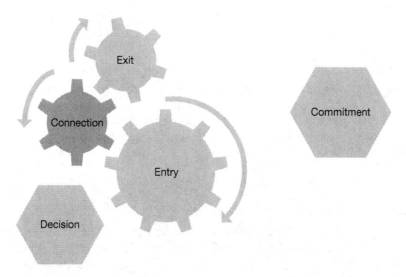

Figure 7.5 Creating quality experience.

Source: Raed Saadeh.

Decision

The point of decision when a guest decides to travel to a certain destination is the first step in creating a quality experience. It starts when this guest makes a phone call, sends a message or meets an agent abroad. The impression established at this point is of utmost importance as it could dictate and probably alter the guest's mind about the entire trip. At the time Palestine faces a number of obstacles and hindrances that render its communication with the outside world limited and controlled, an exciting, intimate and welcoming first impression can break many barriers.

Entry

The point of entry is when the guest or guests arrive at the destination. The way they are greeted and welcomed impacts their first impressions of the upcoming experience. The feelings of mutual respect they receive from their ground agents and the clarity of the program presentation prepares the guests' expectations of a unique and worthwhile experience. Again, as Palestine lacks control of its own borders and as the Israeli authorities are reluctant to set clear border crossing policies and regulations, this first encounter with the Palestinian ground agent must be well thought through to bring people back from any imposed negativity. There is a Palestinian proverb that suits such a situation and says 'meet me, don't feed me' with a specific reference to the importance of this stage of the tour.

Connection

This is when the guests start their itinerary and program. The description of each of the program activities should not only be clear, they should be exciting and should include language and elements and foster the emotional linkage with the specific itinerary. The entire program should be well organized in order nourish the visitors experience and link it to the place. If Palestine is able to convert its visitors into guests; if it is able to achieve this level of connection, satisfaction and appreciation, then this stage of the experience becomes mature to provide the projected program added value. Elements of culture, cuisine, handcrafts, local production, landscape and community should find their way into the ongoing itinerary to establish this level of connection.

Exit

When the visit is over, a proper overview of the trip should remind people of its main highlights and this should not include further information but rather stress themes and experiences. It should show the gratitude of the agent and emphasize the appreciation of the local hosts where the visitors stayed. Leaving is as important as arriving and should be well thought of.

Commitment

The objective of the entire effort is to establish an impressionable experience and hence a commitment to return, to pursue friendships and to indulge in genuine promotion of the visit and the stories exchanged. This kind of commitment is a reflection of the sustainable capacity of the visit.

What does Palestine has to offer to foster a differentiated experience?

The land of Palestine is a land of friendship and hospitality. Since the beginnings and since the early stories of the first patriarchs, the people of Palestine disseminated this culture from one generation to the other through stories, food and traditions.

Palestine's culture offers much more than an authentic experience with its heterogeneous mosaic of people, backgrounds, religions, landscapes and environs, it offers an interpretation of all the metaphors and proverbs that compact the scriptures and an inspiration for all the poems, the paintings, the sculptures and the music that molds its identity.

Like many other countries that belong to the ancient world, Palestine's culture has been shaped throughout the years by all the civilizations, people, empires and religions that came across its land from the times of early human settlement starting with the Natufian civilization through the present times. These civilizations have not only left behind a wealth of antiquities, sites and histories, they left their trace on the culture, heritage and traditions that exist today.

Palestine's nature on the other hand is as unique as its cultural identity or identities. It embraces the lowest point on earth, the Dead Sea, and retains the micro bird habitats of Jericho, the oldest continuously inhabited city in the world. The Jordan Valley, offers a unique climate and a diverse flora and fauna system influenced by a unique climate ruled by 300 meters of added atmospheric pressure and a particular intimacy induced by its below sea level location. Palestine's mountain range is part of the ridge that links the Syrian and Lebanese mountains with Egypt. They provide a different ecological and geological experience from the Jordan valley. Hiking off the beaten track in the mountain ranges is typically commanded by the olive trees, fresh water springs, Ottoman water mills, Roman water canals and harvest watchtowers commonly known in Palestine as 'palaces'. Rural Palestine with its historically immersed serene Palestinian villages spread throughout the mountain ranges and hilltops graciously provide some of the first few places that might come to mind when starting a nature tour.

The Palestinian desert, or better described as wilderness, conceals in its topography many desert palaces, Byzantine monasteries and Sufi shrines. Desert hilltops are likely locations of ancient Canaanite kingdoms or Roman garrisons. Still, somewhere in the desert skies, a Sparrow hawk would be quietly circling the landscape with effortless stature and keen overview.

The relationship between the local community and its environment may be one of the most enticing pursuits that could attract the attention of the nature goer. The many centuries of continuous existence in rural Palestine has created a natural knowledge of the indigenous plants and shrubs that grow nearby and the many uses and benefits they offer. It is not unlikely to meet people from nearby villages picking plants and shrubs along rural trails to make food or to prepare and use for medical treatments to relieve pains and cure illnesses.

This cultural and natural wealth offers many elements of differentiation and competitiveness for the national Palestinian tourism product. If it integrates the community based approach and methodology described in this chapter, it will open a new world of interest and a global network of people and initiatives that are pursuing similar endeavors. Their connection to Palestine will grow because of the similarity of effort and specialization. They will learn about Palestine through its individual and specialized endeavors.

Figure 7.6 describes some of the most important community-based initiatives that are currently taking place in Palestine. These programs are specifically chosen because of their intensive and holistic community-based effort. There are many other programs that follow suit and can be found on the website of the 'Network of Experiential Palestinian Tourism Organizations' (www.nepto.ps). The description below is not intended to describe each initiative in full and does not attempt to lay out the competencies and the business structures proposed to manage them as these elements are still in the making. However, these initiatives have acquired a distinctive position on the National Palestinian Tourism map as competitive examples of CBT and are presented here based on this significance.

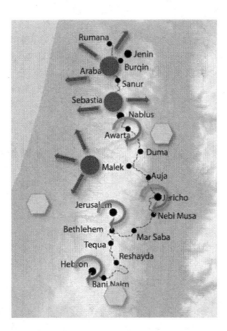

Figure 7.6 CBT initiatives in Palestine.

Source: Raed Saadeh.

- Masar Ibrahim (Abraham Path) – This is a long path that crosses Palestine from the north to the south as depicted in the dotted line in Figure 7.6. It offers 17 days of walking in the country's most exquisite natural landscapes. Visitors of the path travel from one town to the next listening to stories, telling stories and enjoying a rare diversity of landscapes in a single hike. Masar Ibrahim is based on the friendship and hospitality associated with the story of Abraham, which in turn provides the foundation of its interactive experience. Masar Ibrahim has been rated number 1 new trail in the world by National Geographic traveler section and one of the ten most attractive trails in the world by the *Curious Animal* magazine.
- Sufi Trails – Palestine had a long history of Sufism lead by religious dedicates and Islamic leaders starting from the Ayyubi period through the decline of the Ottoman Empire. The trails shed light on this history through the many shrines and tombs that are spread around the Palestinian countryside and within several cities like Jerusalem, Hebron and Nablus. Many of the shrines are built on top of Crusader or Byzantine churches which in turn are built on top of Roman Tombs or sites and the story goes on to tell the legacies of all the civilizations that settled in Palestine at one point or another and how it forged the contemporary Palestinian identity. The added value of these shrines is their locations on hilltops, their dense tree covers and their commanding views of the landscapes nearby. The dark circles representing hub villages from which a number of Sufi Trails start their excursions show the Sufi trails model.
- Centers of Local Culture – A center of local culture is a village, a cluster of villages, a historic site or a neighborhood in a city. They offer a variety of unique identities and competencies packaged and developed to offer visitors with a number of natural and cultural itineraries. One such example is Battir, west of Bethlehem. Its local leadership succeeded in attracting people to visit their eco museum of historic terraces and their unique agricultural irrigation ducts that go back in history to the pre-Roman period. Battir is now a world heritage site. The hexagons in Figure 7.6 represent the distribution of the centers of local culture in Palestine.
- Inner City Trails – The arrows in Figure 7.6 show the potential of inner city thematic trails, walks and other community linked ideas. These could be a bird's trail in Jericho to introduce its diverse habitats and historic centers, or a community excursion in Jerusalem to learn about the diverse demographic and cultural mosaic of the city or a handcrafts tour in Hebron to learn of its heritage in this regard.

Working with the local communities

To advance the tourism potential to different parts of Palestine regardless of their previous significance as whether or not they were part of the local or international packages, it is important to organize and prepare the local communities' capacity and readiness to receive guests (Figure 7.7). This is particularly true the more marginalized these communities are.

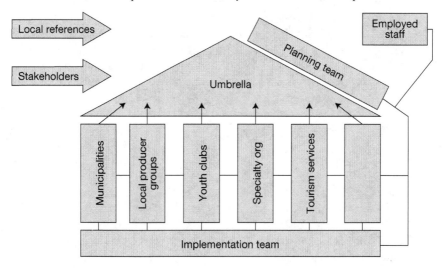

Figure 7.7 Working with the local communities.

Source: Raed Saadeh.

The role of CBT in this respect is pivotal both because it is a necessary prerequisite for the developmental process and because it provides the platform to transfer ownership of the local packages and itineraries to the local community. Tour operators might argue that this is not a mandatory approach and that tour packages can be developed in agencies' offices and sold regardless of the role of the community. This is obviously a viable track, but it will lose its sustainability and differentiation elements if diverted from the local interest and benefits. In Palestine the local community involvement is also a factor of safety, hospitality and cultural exchange, which further contributes to its importance due to the imposing political situation, Hence, if the community formulates such a principal pillar in the hospitality development process a great deal of investment is required to advance its role, participation and impact. However, working with the community is not a straight forward thing, but Palestine has envisioned an approach that is both respectful and indulging, an approach that is keen not to bypass the local population but rather creates awareness and opportunities for it.

Figure 7.7 describes this approach. The structure is a socio-economic organization of the targeted communities and has a tendency to respond better in marginalized areas where need is more evident. The structure also resonates well with the sustainability elements that were discussed earlier in this chapter and applies similar synergy fostering principles among the different stakeholders. The structure also assumes a foundation for a business model that is capable of selling community products at net rates to tour operators. This means that the local itinerary is priced and sold as a package including all food, accommodation and guiding services taking into account the budgets needed to sustain the required standards and maintenance of the underlying infrastructure and hospitality.

- The structure resembles a house whose pillars are the local stakeholder organizations and people providing tourism services to visitors.
- Each organization or reference should have some sort of a representation in the organizational structure. The institution building could take the form of tourism cooperative or an association. The type of this structure depends on the dynamics, readiness and maturity of the local community.
- The planning team resembles the solar panel that provides the house with energy. The planning team should include both local and professional organizations with emphasis on involving community leadership in the process.
- All of the above are part of the stakeholders' pool. The local references, however, are tribal leaders, political or religious references or even governmental agencies or ministries that possess the power to impede the entire initiative if they are incorrectly positioned. The local culture and traditions must be taken into consideration here. Some sort of a zigzag approach must be observed in order to guarantee periodic consultations with these references and ensuring that they are still on board. Their approval and blessings can save a lot of effort and can protect the proper, uninterrupted implementation of the action.

The measure of success of tourism initiatives among the different communities during the developmental process is not only the number of visitors attracted to a certain destination, but more importantly the level of acceptance and adoption the local community conveys in this respect. The more local ownership of initiatives, the more success.

Gap analysis

Working in new areas and even with current sites and destinations will shed light on needs, deficiencies and future developmental investments. Indeed, this is an ongoing process; the more visited, the more apparent the gaps and the need for intervention. Some of the immediate issues that surfaced during the delineation and development of the currently ongoing initiatives particularly in the more marginalized areas are presented in Box 7.1.

Conclusion

The development aspect in the Palestinian tourism industry needs to create all the necessary prerequisites for success. Encouraging private investment only is not enough to ensure a holistic development. The community needs to grow, mature and respond to its future needs. The community needs to be aware of the benefits and threats of private investment and how much it should be allowed. The community needs to find ways to employ its capacities, resources and tools in order to figure out the most appropriate engine to push its economy and opulence forward.

Box 7.1 On-going initiatives in the more marginalized areas

- Rehabilitation: Tourism infrastructure in Palestine generally requires a certain amount of facelift. However, there are many resources, shrines, archeological sites and architectural heritage that are spread all over the country that are completely overlooked. Such resources possess inherent values of identity and culture. They are elements of differentiation and deliver a considerable competitive advantage for the current national tourism product. Villages and remote areas have a lot to offer:

- Village Historic Centers: Many villages in Palestine have reasonably intact historic centers although often neglected, overlooked and deserted. Depending on the architectural fabric in these centers, which is decreed by their history and hierarchal position, a set of urban rehabilitation plans can ensue to revive them and convert them into attractive and bustling hubs of activity, vulture and business.

- Shrines and Historic Sites: Palestine has many such sites. They are spread all over the country and often situated on top of hills with commanding views of the attractive Palestinian hills. There are many stories associated with these sites, which can only add value and appeal to their significance and connection to the local heritage.

- Public Parks: One great way to establish public parks is to design them around certain shrines and historic sites. If properly done, they can provide a breathing space for the local families and their children while reintroducing their affluence and value in a cultural and touristic form.

- Centers: Many if not most communities lack an address that operates as a visitor information center or an interpretation Center that sheds light on the important competencies of a village or a cluster of villages. Such a center can have an exhibition space, interaction displays, videos and other tools that tell the main historic stations of the community, stories of its leaders and their achievements, the lineage of its inhabitants and elements of its environment.

- Capacity Building: Currently, a number of actions are taking place to improve the tourism and hospitality services offered in the different towns, villages and neighborhoods where CBT initiatives are taking place. Home Stays and Hospitality training as well as local tour guide preparation are among some of these efforts.

- Products: Another area that requires intervention both on the developmental and the promotional levels is handcrafts and Local productions. Most guests are happy to take back a relevant souvenir particularly if it is linked to their visit and triggers a memory of their experience.

- Infrastructural investments in signage, public toilets, roads, stairs, curbs and lights, to name a serve their purposes and provide a feeling of safety and confidence that the visited community is willing and ready to take care of its guests.
- Environmental, social, educational, economic, architectural and cultural equilibrium is another area to consider during the development process. These are pivotal elements of the planning processes. They need to be integrated in the urban planning of the involved towns and villages if the local leadership is interested in pursuing a tourism development.

This is why Palestine needs to invest in its people and in their resources. Palestine needs to advance its civil society, as it is a safety valve for a sustainable prosperity. Planning and preparing the platforms for a diverse and a holistic tourism product requires vision, sincerity and commitment to the principles and pillars of sustainability particularly that the Israeli occupation hovers above all Palestinian initiatives. Involving local people in the tourism development process is a target by itself as it generates the awareness, wisdom and knowledge of their competencies and how to employ them.

CBT is not only about generating visitors to a certain destination or attraction, it is about the formulation of a process that takes into consideration all elements of a horizontal development where the community plays a central role and where protection of diversity, culture, identity and resources takes a precedence.

Reference

Halper, J. (2008) *An Israeli in Palestine: resisting dispossession, redeeming Israel*, London: Pluto.

8 Diaspora and VFR

An exploratory study

Suhail Khalilieh

Introduction

Emigration has been a longstanding feature of human activity for a number of reasons, including environmental, social, economic, and particular in the case of Palestine, political and security causes. The establishment of diasporas has been one result of such movement of people. Increasingly, in recent years, emigrants have been returning to their homelands for holidays and visiting friends and relatives (VFR), and this form of tourism grown significantly. Palestinians are one of the great diasporic communities in the global community. They live as far afield as the Americas, the Asia-Pacific, Africa, Europe and of course, throughout the Middle East. Palestinian diasporic communities have formed from at least the 1800s, but grew significantly since the aftermath of the *Al-Nakbah*. This has resulted in these diasporic communities periodically returning to the homeland to re-connect with family and friends and to reconnect children with language, culture and history.

While Israel is well known for its fostering of connections between the Jewish diaspora and the state of Israel through officially organized tours like the Taglit Birthright tours, it is only recently that Palestinians have started to organize tours among the diverse diaspora communities. These tours serve multiple functions that will be explored in this chapter. They also serve as a potentially vital foundation for future tourism opportunities for Palestinians and the Palestinian economy. The chapter will start by analyzing literature on diasporas and the relationship with VFR. The discussion then followed by the history and different periods of forced displacement of the Palestinian people during the last 60 years and finally will present an example of the Palestinian birthrights that are starting to gain ground in Palestine.

Diaspora

In the view of Mitchell (1997: 534), the term diaspora has been used by most scholars in a working sense to describe 'the situation of a people living outside of their traditional homeland'. Helmreich (1992: 243) states, the etymology of word 'diaspora' may be traced back to the Greek words 'dispersion' and 'through', and originated in the Greek translation of the Book of Deuteronomy in the Bible. For Cohen (1997: ix), 'when applied to humans, the ancient Greeks thought of diaspora as migration and colonization' but for several groups – Jews, Palestinians and Armenians notable among them – diaspora has had much more sinister historical connotations, signifying as it does a sense of group identity resulting from collective trauma, collective punishment and exile.

In addition, the concept diaspora was originally used in the context of dispersion of the Jews from Palestine, but in recent years has become to mean 'dispersion, as of people originally belonging to one nation' (Collins 1998: 310 cited in Butler 2003: 318). It is usually used in the context of recognizable groupings of people of common ethnic or racial origin living in close proximity to one another in a country to which they have emigrated. Thus Scots and Irish in North America, Italians in the USA, Palestinians in Latin America, specifically in Chile and Honduras all represent such diasporas. The catastrophic aspect of the creation of such communities is that most of them have been created because of problems in the original homeland, many are the result of war and conflict and enforced exile, such as the case of Palestine, while some are the effect of economic migration, reminiscent of the emigration resulting from the Potato Famines of Ireland in the nineteenth century (Butler 2003).

Diaspora and VFR

It is argued by many authors, (see Hall and Williams 2013) that there are a strong relationship and links between those who have emigrated to other countries and VFR segment of international tourism, and these relationships received lots of attention in recent years. VFR travel has been discussed to some extend with regards to its social significance, particularly in the context of the close link between migration and tourism (Coles and Timothy 2004; Hall and Williams 2000). For example, Hay (2008) elucidate that the term VFR emerged around after World War II, a period characterized by much displacement of people and the liberalization policy between many countries. Accordingly, migration generates a two-way flow of tourists: immigrants who pay a return visit to their country of origin and their friends and relatives who visit them in their new home (Bywater 2005; Jackson 1990). While King (1994: 174) preferred the term 'ethnic tourism' to illustrate the phenomenon, rather than VFR, as the current 'categorization may in fact result in a failure to gain full understanding of a significant market'. In a similar vein, Duval (2003) selects for 'return visit' and Scheyvens (2007) for 'diaspora tourism' when discussing migrants visiting their traditional country of origin. Shani (2013: 4), for example states 'the social-economic significance of VFR as a crucial connection between ancestral homeland and Diaspora – for both hosts and guests, has received some attention in literature'. Regarding VFR travelers, the return visit permits them to express their sense of belonging and identification with the homeland and its way of life (King 1994), in addition to re-establishing old ties and re-affirming blood ties (Asiedu 2005, 2008). Duval (2003), for example, investigating the Commonwealth Eastern

Caribbean Diaspora in Toronto, Canada, explored various meanings that expatriates within the community associated with their return visits to their root island States. VFR tourism also offers significant social, cultural and political benefits for the migrant-sending regions themselves, while Scheyvens (2007: 313) drew some parallels between domestic travel and Diaspora tourism and argued that 'travel by… country nationals now leaving abroad can expand their knowledge and understanding of their home country, with a subsequent increase in national pride'. Many destinations also often not only benefit from an important source of financial remittances, material and equipment donations, but also of knowledge, technology and transfer of skills (Asiedu 2005; King and Gamage 1994).

The following section will examines the different periods of the Palestinian forced displacements and forced migration that could grow significantly and to be one of the most important forms of tourism, once a fair and just final status agreement reached between Israel and Palestine.

Palestine: up until 1947

Historic Palestine became a province of the Ottoman Empire in 1516, and continued to be for the next 400 years. The Anglo–French agreement of May 1916 (AKA: the Sykes–Picot Agreement) came to be under the pretense of agreeing to the demands of the 1915 Arab Revolt, which ultimately seek Arab independence. The Sykes–Picot Agreement also incorporated the division of the Arab region to zones of permanent British-French influences. Later on; in November 1917; an infamous British document 'Balfour Declaration' ceded the establishment of a Jewish national home in Palestine, provided it did not prejudice the civil and religious rights of the other inhabitants (the Arab Palestinians) of the country. At that point of time, there was 642,850 individuals living in that land; the Palestinians (Muslims and Christians) formed 89.8 per cent (577,550) of the population, while the Jews made 10.1 per cent (65,300).

Later in 1922, the mandate was formalized based on the Balfour declaration designating the area west of the Jordan River as Palestine, while the area east of the Jordan River was made a separate British mandate and would be called Transjordan (now the Hashemite Kingdom of Jordan). Form this point on, mass immigrations of Jews to Palestine became an alarming phenomenon, encouraged and facilitated by the Jewish Agency. At the time, the population of mandate Palestine was 752,048, of which Palestinians formed 660,941 (87.9 per cent) opposite to 83,790 Jews; some 11.1 per cent.

The consequential administrations in Palestine played an essential role in the Palestinians' immigration, whether in a mandatory or optional fashion. In this regard, this chapter will examine this matter over certain periods of time in relation to the fluctuating numbers of population on the various accounts of changes on the status of the ruling power over the land.

The consecutive waves of Jewish immigrants to Palestine continued leading to systematic increase of the Jewish population from 15,000 (3.2 per cent of the total population) in the year 1879 to some 65,000 (10.2 per cent of the total population) in 1917; an annual increase of 14 per cent.

By 1947, the total population of Palestine was 1,955,260. At that time, the British mandate rule over Palestine came to an end and the United Nations introduced a partition plan. The UN proposal set to designate some 56 per cent of mandate Palestine for the Jews to establish their State and 43 per cent for the Arab-Palestinians to establish a Palestinian State, while the remaining 1 per cent was designated for Jerusalem area, which was to go under a *Corpus Separatum* status; meaning to be administered by an international body.

The UN calculation and division of the land was far off from fair for the Arab-Palestinians; for the least part; the Jewish population counted for some 650,000 (33.2 per cent) of the total population in mandate Palestine; in opposite to 1,288,890 Arab-Palestinian forming 66 per cent of the population. Hence, it is easily concluded that the increase in the number of Palestinians (123 per cent) have gone through a natural and normal increase in the population life cycle during the British Mandate between 1917 and 1947. In contrast, the mutated 895 per cent increase in the number of Jewish population, is categorically due to the systemized mass migration organized by the World Zionist Organization (WZO) formally known as the Zionist Organization.

Palestine: 1948 Al-Nakbah – 1966

When the 1948 war broke out, it forced more than 770,000 Arab-Palestinians to flee outside of mandate Palestine, to what later on came to known as the West Bank, the Gaza Strip and also inside to what became known as Israel. The latter was declared as a state on 15 May, 1948 on 78 per cent of mandate Palestine. At that time, the forced migration of the Palestinians was carried out in three waves and was the biggest ever to hit the Palestinians. The main causes may be attributed to the following:

The first wave was associated with the revelation and the declaration of the partition plan extending between January 1947 and March 1948, which was associated with hostile acts by the Jewish militias against the Palestinians creating a sense of vulnerability that led to the displacement of more than 100,000 Palestinians.

The second wave, extended between April 1948 and May 1948 and was instigated by attacks led by the Stern, Haganah and Irgun, militia groups. The climax of this wave was the massacre in the village of Deir Yassin, in which some 254 Palestinians were killed, upon which the Jewish militias occupied the western part of Jerusalem (the present day 'West Jerusalem'). The massacre had an immense impact on many of the Palestinian communities, Tiberias, Haifa, the Hula Valley, Jaffa and, Safad among others; spreading fear and terror in the hearts of many, which ultimately led to the displacement of more than 330,000 Palestinians.

The third wave, covered the time between July and November 1948 as the attacks of the Israeli militias continued. Massacres in Safad (29 October, 1948

– 70 killed) and Eilbun–Tiberias (30 October, 1948 – 13 killed) spread fear and terror but were not the only factor leading to the mass expulsion of Palestinians. In addition, the newly established Israeli army was involved in the expulsion and transfer of more than 300,000 Palestinians from hundreds of communities including Al-Lud (Lydda) and Al-Ramleh.

Following the war

When the 1948 war broke out the Jewish militias went to and seized 78 per cent of mandate Palestine; exceeding the 56 per cent designated to the Israeli state in the UN partition Plan. In the aftermath of the war; between February and July 1949, Egypt, Lebanon, Jordan and Syria signed armistices with Israel; and according to the findings stated in the First Interim Report of the United Nations Economic Survey Mission for the Middle East of November 16, 1949 the number of the Palestinian refugees does not exceed 774,000; including 97,000 in Lebanon, 70,000 in Jordan, 75,000 in Syria, 200,000 in Gaza, 280,000 in West Bank (The United Nations Information System on the Question of Palestine (UNISPAL) 1949).

Consequently, Jordan and Egypt administered the West Bank (5661 km²) and Gaza (362 km²) respectively spreading over 22 per cent of Mandate Palestine including East Jerusalem. From this point on tension continued to mount especially when Jordan and Syria undertook military agreements with Egypt and this eventually led to the 1967 war.

Palestine: West Bank–the Gaza Strip and the 1967 war

On June 5 1967, Israel launched what it claimed to be a preemptive strike against Syria, Egypt and Jordan, which came to known later on as the 'Six Day War'. According to Israeli claims, the war it won and lasted six days was set off in the face of imminent planned invasion from Jordan, Egypt and Syria. The war ended with the Israel capture of the West Bank including East Jerusalem from Jordan; the Gaza Strip and the Sinai Peninsula from Egypt; and the Golan Heights from Syria.

The 1967 war had a tremendous impact of what remained of mandate Palestine; geographically and demographically; for it instigated yet another wave of forced migration of about 325,000 Palestinians from the West Bank and the Gaza Strip to border countries; and especially to Jordan with at least 95 per cent of the displaced Palestinians settled in Jordan (Abuljebain 2015).

On November 22, 1967, the United Nations Security Council (UNSC 1967: 4) unanimously approved resolution 242, which stressed 'the inadmissibility of the acquisition of territory by war' and called for Israel to withdraw from 'territories occupied in the recent conflict' as well as an end to 'all claims or states of belligerency and respect for... the sovereignty... of every state in the area and their right to live in peace... free from threats or acts of force'. After the war, Israel was made to allow the return of approximately 21,000 Palestinian to the areas occupied in mandate Palestine during the 1967 war under the pretext of family reunification.

Palestine: 1987–the first intifada

On December 9, 1987, twenty years after Israel's military occupation of the West Bank and Gaza, an accident in Jabaliya Refugee Camp instigated a spark of outrage at the crowded checkpoint at the northern entrance of Gaza, which later on swept through the Gaza Strip and spread to the West Bank. The spark soon turned out to be oppressed feelings of nationalism making its way into the Palestinian society. Soon enough this popular movement was named, the uprising better known as 'the *Intifada*', a demonstration of desire for freedom and independence led by the younger Palestinian generation in order to seek liberation. The Intifada was in fact a dawn to a new era as it brought global attention to the Palestinian struggle for freedom after years of political and international apathy.

The Intifada was not just a passing element in the Palestinian conflict but more like a game changer that led Jordan in 1988 to sever its legal and administrative ties to the West Bank. At this point; the Palestinian Liberation Organization (PLO) embraces the Palestinian Declaration of Independence in Algeria, and subsequently accepts the UN Resolution 181 that calls to establish two states in Palestine. After which the PLO and the late President of Palestine Yasser Arafat issued the Stockholm Declaration, which acknowledges Israel's right to exist and renounced terrorism issues and the acceptance of Resolutions 242 and 338.

Palestine: a new Palestinian exile 1990–1991

In August 1990, Iraq decides to invade Kuwait, which rallied in February 1991 an international U.S.-led coalition of 33 countries that included Saudi Arabia, Egypt, Syria, and Gulf States set to force out and liberate Kuwait. The PLO President Yasser Arafat visited Iraq in what was expounded as Palestinian support of Iraq's invasion of Kuwait, which led to the expulsion of 300,000 (Galbraith 2003) to 400,000 (Aljazeera 2009) Palestinians from Kuwait.

Palestine: 1993, the Oslo Accord–1999

In October 1991, the United States and Russia co-sponsored a peace talk initiative in Madrid, which went through rounds of meetings with no result. However, in the second half of 1993, news of parallel secret negotiations surfaced with an imminent signing of an understanding. In the fourth quarter; in September 1993 a ceremonial event took place in the front yard of the White House before the world that witnessed the signatories.

Israeli Prime Minister Yitzhak Rabin and PLO Chairman Yasser Arafat, shake hands and signed what came to known as the 'Declaration of Principles' (Oslo I Accord) that basically conclude Israel's withdrawal from the Gaza Strip and certain areas of the West Bank, and handover local government administration to what came to known as the 'Palestinians Authority'. In May 1994, the Israeli Army forces withdrew from the certain parts of the Gaza Strip and the West Bank (Jericho), hence it was commonly known as the Gaza–Jericho Accord.

On 28 September 1995, in Taba, Egypt, the Interim Agreement on the West Bank and the Gaza Strip commonly known as Oslo II or the Taba Agreement was signed. It fell short of a Palestinian independent state but instead established a Palestinian interim self-government in areas where Israel ceased to have jurisdiction. The Israeli Army would go through a phased withdrawal based on areas A, B and C definitions indicating various levels of control in the prospect of initiating the final status negotiations over issues of: settlements, borders, water, refugees and Jerusalem. Following, the political events in the Middle East as a result of the Gulf War and the aftermath of the 1993 Oslo Accord, more than 267,000 Palestinians from the Gulf countries, Jordan and other countries returned to the West Bank and Gaza (Lubbad 2007).

Palestine: 2000–the Second Intifada

The Second Intifada was instigated when Ariel Sharon visited Al-Aqsa Mosque in September 2000 provoking mass Palestinian protests in Jerusalem and throughout the West Bank and Gaza. More than 3000 Palestinians died and thousands other injured.

Between the years 2007 and 2009, some 22,000 Palestinians emigrated (PCBS 2013a: 25). All and all, 6.7 per cent of Palestinian households have at least one member as emigrant (3.4 per cent of households have only one member as emigrant, 1.1 per cent have two members as emigrants. As to reasons or motives behind emigration, about 34.4 per cent of total emigrants left for education and studying purposes, 14.6 per cent for improving living conditions, and 13.7 per cent left because of the lack of job opportunities in the Palestinian Territory. There were approximately 5,000–7,000 returned emigrants during this period (PCBS 2011). The decline in the percentage of returnees to the Palestinian territory between 2000 and 2009 was mostly due to the instigation of the second Palestinian *Intifada* and the associated economic and political instability .

Palestine: population in Palestine and the Diaspora

The events that led to the 1948 war and the aftermath had significant implications on more than 770,000 Arab-Palestinians as it encapsulates the misery, the loss of their homeland and life in the Diaspora. That is why the Palestinians remember that time as 'the Catastrophe' – better known as and referred to as 'Al-Nakbah'. At the time, the Palestinians were actually convinced that they would return to their homes as soon as the war ended. This conviction of return is based on the fact that the 400+ depopulated and destroyed villages were filled with their personal belongings. The unfortunate reality for the 80 per cent of the Palestinian population expelled is that they were banned to return from the newly established 'State of Israel'. This is what created the term 'Al-Nakbah'.

On the 5th June 1967, the Palestinians were faced with the similar misfortune upon the break of the 'six days war' that ended with Israel capturing the rest of Mandate Palestine, the Gaza Strip from Egypt and the West Bank including East Jerusalem from Jordan. The war was referred to and continues to be called to today as the Setback or 'Al-Nakseh' for during the six days of the war, some 325,000 Palestinian felt forced to run for their lives and for some of them it was the second time that they had to do it after they were refugees of the 1948 war.

According to the PCBS (2013b: 1):

> The Palestinian population has increased eight-fold since the Al-Nakbah, so by the end of 2012 the estimated world population of Palestinians totaled 11.6 million, which means it multiplied eight fold in 65 years. The PCBS and the UNRWA records show that there were 5.3/4 million Palestinian refugees registered in mid-2012–2013, they constitute some 45.7 per cent of the total Palestinian population worldwide, of which 59 per cent live in Jordan, Syria and Lebanon, 17 per cent in the West Bank, and 24 per cent in the Gaza Strip. About 29 per cent of registered Palestinian refugees live in 58 refugee camps, of which 10 are in Jordan, nine in Syria, 12 in Lebanon, 19 in the West Bank and eight in the Gaza Strip.

A Palestinian birth right trip

Every young Jewish member of the Diaspora around the world knows 'Birthright', an all-expenses-paid trip for anyone of full or partial Jewish descent of a certain age who has not visited Israel to see the Jewish Homeland. However, what is less known is that there is also an opportunity for young Palestinians of the Diaspora to visit the Palestinian homeland in a new program called 'Know Thy Heritage'.

This is not a vacation, Know Thy Heritage founder Rateb Rabie (The Daily Beast, 2013) stressed in several interviews 'we made the point that [delegates] have to be ready for this, to commit to the program, and to commit to Palestine'.

In 2011, Rabie, a Palestinian businessman and President of the Holy Land Ecumenical Foundation, raised enough money between Palestinian businesses in the West Bank and the United States to sponsor 33 young Palestinian-Americans to take a two-week trip to Palestine. To be accepted, the applicant had to be between the ages of 18 and 25, have at least one Palestinian parent and speak some Arabic. The final group of selected delegates was purposefully selected to be half Christian and half Muslim.

Although there is certainly overlap between Birthright Israel and Know Thy Heritage, Rabie hesitates to make the comparison. The Palestinian delegates of Know Thy Heritage experience their homeland quite differently. For one thing, Know Thy Heritage delegates land at Queen Alia Airport in Amman, Jordan rather than the more conveniently located Ben Gurion Airport in Tel Aviv, Israel. The reason for this is that Palestinians with dual citizenship, foreign nationals of Palestinian or other Arab heritage, and sometimes even potential activists who might be affiliated with the Palestinian cause are frequently held for hours and interrogated, in some cases leading to denied entry into Israel, for 'security reasons'.

Once the delegation arrives in Palestine, they begin their tour. Understandably, their itinerary differs radically from that of Birthright Israel. The young Jewish participants of Birthright Israel are guided through the Israeli history of the Golan Heights and Negev Desert, the beaches and nightlife of Tel Aviv and the Jewish religious sites of Jerusalem. Meanwhile, it seems that the Palestinian delegation is in another country altogether, beginning their trip with the Church of the Nativity and Aida Refugee Camp in Bethlehem, the Ibrahimi Mosque in Hebron, the Samaritan Museum in Nablus and both the Christian and Muslim sites of Jerusalem. Both groups visit Haifa, which the Birthright Israel website calls the 'city of coexistence', though many Palestinian citizens of Israel think otherwise (Miller 2013).

Birthright Israel is advertised as a trip for young Jews to spend time in the homeland and connect to Israel. But Know Thy Heritage has a different motive for bringing young Palestinians from the Diaspora to Palestine. They want to encourage young Palestinians to do business in Palestine – to invest there.

Palestine's economic boom first began after the Oslo Accords, which allowed monetary sovereignty and economic freedoms that yielded business opportunities. Many Palestinians in Diasporas who lived – and made money – abroad, saw this as an opportunity to come back and help build a Palestinian state. When the Second Intifada's restrictions on movement between the West Bank and Israel became institutionalized, most of this development was relocated to Ramallah as a way to cater to Palestinians who could not travel to Jerusalem.

However, this economic development is often criticized as being limited to Ramallah and leaving out the rest of the West Bank – coining terms like the 'Ramallah Bubble' and the 'Five Star Occupation' – and normalizing Israel's occupation with the illusion of prosperity. However, while state-building and economic development is on Rabie's mind, most of the participants seem to come away from the trip more focused on peace and reconciliation in the Israeli-Palestinian conflict. When asked about his generation of Palestinians in the conflict, Wissam Rifidi, a delegate from Houston, Texas expressed, 'You never forget, but we need to start learning how to forgive' (Miller 2013).

Green Olive Tours was established in 2007, originally offering a single on-day tour of Jerusalem. The original name was Tours in English, and changed to Green Olive Tours in early 2010. In 2012 a Company was registered and a charter was drafted that radically changed the nature of the business. The new company, Green Olive Collective is managed democratically by the people working in the organization, and has a broad mandate. Green Olive Collective Inc. is registered in the USA, has Palestinian and Israeli working partners, and almost 100 Investors and Members from 19 countries around the globe (Green Olive Tours 2015).

> Our Unplugged trip primarily seeks to expose North American people to the realities of Palestinian life though travel and conversations with a variety of Palestinian people. In six days, we visit Palestinian cities, villages and refugee camps in the West Bank and spend time with internally displaced Palestinian

people living inside Israel. Throughout the journey, we help participants develop an understanding of daily life under occupation and the history of the region from people profoundly affected by and under-represented in Western discourses about the occupation. We encourage participants to be deeply reflective and after the program we support their involvement in human rights and justice oriented efforts.

(Green Olive Tours 2015)

Conclusion

One of the enduring features of human development has been the movement of people from one location to another. In this context, the catastrophic aspect of the creation of such Palestinian diasporic communities is that most of them have been created because of problems in the original homeland, namely is the conflict between Israel and Palestine, many are the result of war and conflict and enforced exile. This chapter aimed at exposing the underlying reasons for such as exile and diasporas as well as exposing some of the tours are starting to gain ground in Palestine. Palestinian VFR travelers, the return visit allow them to express their sense of belonging and identification with the homeland and its way of life. In addition the return visits permits to re-establishing old ties and re-affirming blood ties. VFR tourism also offers significant social, cultural and political benefits for the migrant-sending regions themselves. These tours may serve multiple functions as well as potentially vital foundation for future tourism opportunities for Palestinians and the Palestinian economy. Nevertheless, this all can be achieved once a final status agreement reached between both parties, as currently the situation does not allow for full access for this particular market segment due to the restrictions of movements by the Israeli military and control of borders of all Palestinian cities and towns.

References

Abuljebain, N. (2015) Palestine refugees more than 50 years of injustice. Online http://www.arabworldbooks.com/arab/injustice.htm [Accessed 1 June 2015].

Aljazeera. (2009) Arafat's costly Gulf war choice. Online http://www.aljazeera.com/programmes/plohistoryofrevolution/2009/2009/08/200981294137853350.html [Accessed 15 March 2015].

Asiedu, A.B. (2005) 'The host should get lots: paradigms in the tourism theory', *Annals of Tourism Research*, 28(3): 736–761.

Asiedu, A.B. (2008) 'Participants characteristics and economic benefits of visiting friends and relatives (VFR) tourism – an international survey of literature with implications for Ghana', *International Journal of Tourism Research*, 10(6): 609–621.

Butler, R. (2003) 'Relationships between tourism and diasporas: influences and patterns', *Espaces Populations, Societies*, 2: 317–326.

Bywater, M. (2005) 'New Zealand outbound', *Travel and Tourism Analyst*, 1: 19.

Cohen, E.H. (1997) *Global Diasporas,* London: Routledge.

Coles, T.E. and Timothy, D.J. (eds) (2004) *Tourism, diasporas and space*, London: Routledge.

Duval, D.T. (2003) 'When hosts become guests: return visits and diasporic identities in a Commonwealth Eastern Caribbean community', *Current Issues in Tourism*, 6(4): 267–308.

Galbraith, P. (2003) 'Refugees from war in Iraq', *Migration Policy Institute, February, 2003* No.2, Policy Brief.

Green Olive Tours (2015a) Tours in English, about. Online http://www.toursinenglish.com/2007/11/about-alternative-tours.html [Accessed 1 June, 2015].

Green Olive Tours (2015b) Birthright unplugged. Online http://www.toursinenglish.com/2007/07/birthright-unplugged.html [Accessed 1 June, 2015].

Hall, C.M. and Williams, A.M. (eds) (2013) *Tourism and migration: new relationships between production and consumption*, Dordrecht: Springer Science and Business.

Hay, B. (2008,) 'An exploration of differences in the volume and value of visiting friends and relatives tourism in the UK', paper presented at the CAUTHE conference, Surfers Paradise, Queensland, Australia, February 2008.

Helmreich, S. (1992) 'Kinship, nation and Paul Gilroy's concept of diaspora', *Diaspora*, 2(2): 243–249.

Jackson, R.T. (1990) 'VFR tourism: is it underestimated?', *The Journal of Tourism Studies*, 1(2): 10–17.

King, B. (1994) 'What is ethnic tourism? An international perspective', *Tourism Management*, 15(3): 173–176.

King, B., and Gamage, M.A. (1994) 'Measuring the value of the ethnic connection: expatriates travellers from Australia to Sri Lanka', *Journal of Travel Research*, 33(2): 46–50.

Lubbad, I. (2007) *Demographic profile of Palestinian migration: migration and refugee movement in the Middle East and North Africa*, Cairo: The American University of Cairo.

Miller, A. (2013) A Palestinian birthright trip. Online http://www.thedailybeast.com/articles/2013/04/03/a-palestinian-birthright-trip.html [Accessed 10 April 2015].

Mitchell, K. (1997) 'Different diasporas and the type of hybridity', *Environment and Planning D: Society and Space*, 15: 533–553.

PCBS (2013a) Palestinian National Authority Palestinian Central Bureau of Statistics Migration Survey in the Palestinian Territory, 2010 Main Results March, 2011, Ramallah: PCBS.

PCBS (2013b) Special Statistical Bulletin 65th Anniversary of the Palestinian Nakba. Online http://www.pcbs.gov.ps/site/512/default.aspx?tabID=512&lang=en&ItemID=788&mid=3171&wversion=Staging [Accessed 2 June, 2015].

Scheyvens, R. (2007) Poor cousins no more: valuing the developmental potential of domestic and Diaspora tourism. *Progress in Development Studies*, 7(4), 307–325.

Shani, A. (2013) 'The VFR experience: "home" away from home?', *Current Issues in Tourism*, 16(1): 1–15.

The Daily Beast, (2013) Know Thy heritage. Online http://www.thedailybeast.com/articles/2013/04/03/a-palestinian-birthright-trip.html [Accessed 1 June, 2015].

The United Nations Information System on the Question of Palestine (UNISPAL). (1949) *First Interim Report of the United Nations Economic Survey Mission for the Middle East*. Online http://unispal.un.org/UNISPAL.NSF/0/648C3D9CF58AF0888525753C00746F31#sthash.o8ACn8oe.dpuf [Accessed 16 March 2015].

United National Security Council (1967). Online http://unispal.un.org/unispal.nsf/0/7D35E1F729DF491C85256EE700686136 [Accessed 2 June, 2015].

9 Pilgrimage tourism to Palestine

Rami K. Isaac

Introduction

Pilgrimage tourism is a significant and rapidly growing segment within the tourism industry. It is sometimes referred to as faith tourism, faith-based travel, Christian travel, Muslim travel, or any other religious denomination linked with the words 'travel' or 'tourism'. However, regardless of the name, the inference is that this is a form of tourism that is driven by a given faith. Pilgrimage tourism is a well-known phenomenon in religion and culture and it exists in all the main religious of the world: Buddhism, Hinduism, Islam, Judaism, and Christianity. Barber (1993: 1) states that pilgrimage is defined as 'a journey resulting from religious causes, externally to a Holy site, and internally for spiritual purposes and internal understanding'. Pilgrimage, whether traditional and religious or modern and secular, is experiencing revival around the world and long-established shrines still act as magnets for those in search of spiritual goals (Digance 2003). Debate of the pilgrimage metaphor has produced many intriguing discussions in tourism but too few discussions on the pilgrimage itself (Attix 2002; Cohen 1979; Graburn 1989; Vukonić 1996). Pilgrims and pilgrimage are also recognised by local and national authorities in charge of pilgrimage routes and sites by issuing certificates or passes. In Japan, for example, pilgrims have special books in which they collect stamps and inscriptions from the shrine visited during pilgrimage. Alike is also issued on the pilgrimage to Santiago de Compostela (Stausberg 2011).

There is significant evidence, despite the lack of reliable statistics, that religious tourism has experienced considerable growth over the past 30 years, although it appears that the greatest increase has taken place over the last decade. The number of foreign pilgrims travelling to perform the Hajj in Saudi Arabia has increased from 1.4 million in 2001 to 1.8 million in 2011, according to the Saudi Supreme Commission for Tourism and Antiquities. The Religious Conference Management Association reports that delegates at religious conferences increased from 4.4 million to 14.7 million between 1994 and 2006 (Mintel Group 2012).

The number of pilgrims visiting the Vatican has more than doubled in the last decade, recording over five million for the first time (Mintel Group 2012), although not all visitors will be pilgrims. A common mistake is assuming that a visitor must be of a particular religion in order to visit a particular religious site.

For example, although the Vatican holds special meaning for followers of the Catholic faith, millions of non-Catholics also visit the Vatican both for its spirituality and for its architectural beauty. The vast majority of other famous shrines and sites have also experienced similar substantial growth, including Lourdes, Fatima, San Giovanni Rotondo, Assisi, Canterbury Cathedral, German Reformation sites, and biblical sites along the route of Apostle Paul in Greece and Turkey. Holy Land destinations such as Jordan, Palestine and Israel have also enjoyed record numbers in recent years.

New segments within religious tourism have also appeared in recent years, such as faith-based cruises. Almost non-existent 20 years ago, today more than 12 cruise operators carry around 3,000 people each year on cruises that are themed for Christians and other religious beliefs. Around 44 million Americans embarked on volunteer holidays with churches and religious groups in 2011, and although most of these were domestic trips, it does demonstrate the potential for international travel in the future (Tarlow 2014). According to the now defunct World Religious Travel Association (WRTA), in 2009 (cited in United States Agency for International Development (USAID 2014) the worldwide faith travel market was valued 1$ 18 billion and composed over 300 million travellers.

A typical pilgrim-tourist spends 9 to 10 days in Palestine and Israel and an average itinerary includes 4 to 5 days in Jerusalem (including visits to Bethlehem, Jericho, and the Dead sea) and 3 or 4 days in northern Israel, where the focus is on Nazareth, the Sea of Galilee, and other sites (Isaac and Ashworth 2012). Specific sites are visited depending on the religious denomination of the pilgrims as different churches have their own sacred sites. Christian pilgrimage is not a unified phenomenon (Fleischer 2000). There are differences between the Protestants and the Catholics in their needs and therefore in their behaviour (Bowman 1991). These dissimilarities are manifested in different tourist activities, motivations and expectations.

This chapter will deal with the most important market segment, which is the pilgrimage that is still the back bone of the Palestinian tourism economy, particularly in Bethlehem and in Palestine in general. This chapter will also touch the difficulties and challenges dealing with this form of tourism, in which Israel has a stranglehold of the flow of this market segment in terms of visa issuing, using Israeli touring buses, using Israeli tour guides, and control of the whole market.

Global and regional perspectives

International tourist arrivals keep growing and prospects are bright for the current decade. United Nations World Tourism Organization (UNWTO) has announced that international tourist arrivals (overnight visitors) grew by 4 per cent in 2012, surpassing a record of 1 billion tourists globally for the first time in history (UNWTO 2013) The Middle East represents only 5 per cent of the total (53 million). The most dynamic markets were Asia and the Pacific with 7 per cent more international tourists. In spite of the on-going economic challenges, UNWTO's long-term outlook is optimistic.

According to the World Travel and Tourism Council (WTTC) (2014) the tourism industry globally generated some US $2,056 billon directly in 2012 and is expected to grow by an annual rate of 4.4 per cent until 2023. The forecast growth of the tourism sector globally confirms the importance for the State of Palestine of further developing and diversifying its tourism offer. Tourism should keep growing worldwide by 3.8 per cent per year on average between 2010 and 2020. For the Mediterranean region, the direct contribution of tourism to regional GDP in 2012 was estimated at US $377.5 billion, or the equivalent of 4.5 per cent of the region's total GDP. In addition, it is estimated that tourism directly supported 7.9 million jobs at the regional level or the equivalent of 4.8 per cent of total employment. It is forecast that tourism will directly contribute to 5.1 per cent of total regional employment in 2013 (WTTC 2014).

There are many scholars who have tried to define and tackle the concepts of tourist and pilgrim, from the well-known continuum established by Smith (1992) to classic authors such as Cohen (1979), Nolan and Nolan (1989) or Turner and Turner (1978), among many others. What seems to be evident in the discussion between tourist and pilgrim is that the latter was characterized by religious motivation. However, Collins-Kreiner (2010a: 446) goes a step further when clearly recognizing that the differences between these two groups are fading as a lot of similarities start to emerge, and concludes that 'pilgrims cannot be differentiated from tourists, both kinds may be motivated to undergo an experience which will add more meaning to their lives'.

The word pilgrim in the Roman Empire referred to foreigners, vagrants or exiles who visited cities or regions and were hardly any different from a tourist. The word 'pilgrim' essentially comes from the Latin word 'tornus', referring to one who takes a journey of one or more days before returning to one's place of origin (Collins-Kreiner 2010b; Lopez and Lois 2011; Smith 1992). During medieval times the word pilgrimage was used to express movement for sacred reasons while the word tourism emerged from the Grand Tour of the seventeenth and eighteenth centuries and was connected with a secular character (Cohen 1992; Rinschede 1992). In spite of this historical difference, the various authors who have studied this matter agree that the pilgrim and tourist often become one and the same (Eade and Sallnow 1991).

Faith travel market

The U.S. has always and remains an important source of overnight tourist visitors to the Holy Land, but the number of U.S. visitors and their share of total visitors has fallen in the past five years. Studies conducted by the U.S. Office of Travel and Tourism and by Globus, a U.S. tour operator provide information on the size and growth of the overall U.S. outbound travel market. The Globus (2011, cited in USAID, 2014) study found that 46 per cent of U.S. potential faith travellers feel compelled to take a religious vacation – 26 per cent agreed somewhat and 23 per cent strongly or mostly agreed. Past faith travellers were even more likely to view a faith vacation as a necessity – over one-half (54 per cent) agreed somewhat and almost one-third (32 per cent) strongly or mostly agreed. The majority of both potential and past faith travellers are motivated to travel in order to deepen their faith, visit spiritual destinations, and explore historic roots of their faith. In addition, the 2011 Globus study sheds light on the type of overseas potential faith travellers are somewhat, very strongly to take biblical tours. All potential travellers indicated they are likely to take a biblical trip, combining sites of Biblical significance with experiencing the culture and history of the areas. Christian tours – almost three quarters of potential travellers indicated they were likely to take a Christian trip, where one grows their faith while visiting major sites of Protestant Christianity and the Reformation. Catholic tours – almost one-half of potential travellers stated they were likely to take a Catholic trip, where one visits treasured Catholic shrines, historic sites and cultures as well as learning about the lives of the Saints.

The Globus survey found that most faith travellers are looking for a variety on their overseas faith trips. About four in ten potential faith travellers preferred a mix of religious and nonreligious activities. In the 2007 and 2011 Globus studies, the same countries made the top three rankings for destinations that potential faith travellers are most interested in visiting, but there were several significant differences in the percentages. Israel topped the list with 58 per cent and 54 per cent in 2007 and 2011, respectively. Italy was selected by 41 per cent of survey respondents in 2007 but by only 30 per cent in 2011. England was selected by 28 per cent in 2007 and fell to 21 per cent in 2011.

Christian pilgrimage in Palestine

Palestine plays vital an important and role in attracting and motivating the tourists whom find interest in religions, history, cultures, traditions and environment. Palestine is sacred for the three monotheistic world religions: Islam, Christianity and Judaism. In regards to the Christian religious sites of Jerusalem, these places are regarded as the most important in the world containing various churches and monasteries of the Christian religion such as The Church of Holy Sepulcher (Palestinian Association for Cultural Exchange (PACE) 1999; Shahin 2007). As Jerusalem is a unique place and major consideration in religious tourism, there are a lot of villages, districts and towns considered sacred which attract tourists and pilgrims to visit and stopover in them such as Hebron, Bethlehem, Jericho, Nazareth and Nablus. Alternative Tourism Group (ATG) (2005) presented the religious and historical significance of Bethlehem town dating back to the fourteenth century BC this city is mentioned in the Amarna letters, and also mentioned in the bible. The city called it Lehmo in the Canaanite period which meant the god of fertility for them, for many centuries pilgrims were visiting it and some of them were of nobility and Patriarchs such as, the mother of the Emperor, Constantine 'Queen Hilana', She requested from her son to build the Church of the Nativity, which was built on the Holy cave of Jesus. In the period of Caliph's 'Omar Bin Al Khattab' he visited this town and then there is his mosque near the nativity church which is a sign of the freedom of religious property of the Christians. The town of Jericho at the crossing between Jordan and Palestine, has the (Allenby crossing), which is the only access for residents of the West Bank to visit neighbouring countries and the nations of the world via Jordan. Jericho is an important city for tourism through a variety of tourist attractions in it, and its considered the town for winter vacation for the Palestinian people, because of its warmth in winter season and also for having the best dates, citrus fruits and bananas in the world, the ancient town of Jericho has been associated with ancient walls, (oldest city in the world, which dates back to 10,000 BC) as well as having a lot of historical and religious sites.

Revenues generated by tourism in Palestine are made up of 50 per cent incoming international tourism and 50 per cent domestic tourism (including Palestinians travelling from Israel). Over 85 per cent of tourism revenues generated by international visitors come from pilgrimage. As a tourist offering, pilgrimages have five special characteristics (Palestine Trade Centre 2014). See Box 9.1.

The seasonality of the pilgrimage industry affects the entire sector in Palestine. For example, the hotel occupancy rates, utilization of other services and employment are all affected. The annual average room occupancy rate in the State

---

Box 9.1 Pilgrimage special characteristics in Palestine

- In contrast with other types of tourism, the decision to undertake a pilgrimage is much less susceptible to influence by means of marketing because the main motivation is spiritual and hence deeply personal. In consequence, it appears difficult to stimulate international demand in this area.
- The pilgrim market has a fluctuating high season between March and April (due to Easter, increasing the number of pilgrims) and between September and November (as a by-product of Jewish holidays which lead to high occupation rates in Israel, pushing pilgrims into Palestinian accommodation).
- Pilgrims in most cases follow a fixed programme which generally includes meals, accommodation in and tours of almost exclusively sacred places such as the Holy Sepulchre in Jerusalem or the basilicas of the nativity in Bethlehem, together with visits to churches, monasteries, and convents.
- Pilgrims usually have a relatively low budget, not least as often one purpose of their trip is to rediscover simplicity. Many are thus looking for simple accommodation and meals and do not intend to spend a lot of money, in particular not on luxuries. This means that margins are rarely significant (with the possible exception of devotional artefacts).
- Pilgrimage cannot be easily bundled with other types of tourism. Additional services that can be bundled with the traditional ones need to be 'religion-friendly'.

of Palestine was only around 30 per cent in 2012. Hotels enjoy full occupancy for only a few months and are empty for the rest of the year. This unsteady demand generates management issues that are difficult to handle. The State of Palestine experiences two high seasons: Easter holidays and the period between September and October. There are different reasons for the high seasons. The Easter seasonality is caused by the Christian holidays (Palm Sunday, Good Friday and Easter) attracting heightened numbers of pilgrimage tourists. The September/ October high season results from Jewish holidays that fill up Israeli hotels, causing an overflow of other tourists (who would have otherwise stayed in Israeli hotels) into Palestinian accommodation, primarily in East Jerusalem. During the low season tour operators and most service providers offer discounts but this does not seem to increase demand significantly (Palestine Trade Centre 2014).

The tourism sector's direct contribution to GDP is approximately 4 per cent, which is less than the immediate region economies (6 per cent in Israel, 20 per cent in Jordan, 13 per cent in Egypt and 37 per cent in Lebanon). This weakness also applies to the contribution of the tourism sector to total employment (WTTC 2013). The tourism sector contributes approximately 2 per cent to total Palestinian employment. This is the lowest rate compared to the immediate region economies (8 per cent in Israel, 19 per cent in Jordan, 11 per cent in Egypt, and about 4 per cent in Lebanon) (Al-Falah 2012). However, the limited availability of reliable statistics makes it difficult to describe with accuracy the size and dynamics of the State of Palestine's tourism sector both in terms of volumes and value. According to Palestinian Central Bureau of Statistics (PCBS) (2013), tourism revenues for the State of Palestine may have decreased by between 1 per cent and 2 per cent between 2010 and 2011, and the number of foreign tourist arrivals fell by almost the same percentage (1 per cent to 2 per cent), while domestic tourism remained virtually unchanged.

A second data set suggests a 5 per cent increase in visitor arrivals and a 12 per cent increase in overnight stays (1.5 million) in 2011 (Travel Palestine 2012). Similarly, of two million visitors to the State of Palestine in 2012, approximately 1.7 million were recreational tourists (the rest were business travellers), 3 per cent more than in 2011 and 7 per cent more than the previous year (Fox 2012). According to PCBS (2013) of the 2.6 million visits to tourist sites between January and August 2012, 1.4 million were by non-residents (visitors not residing in the West Bank and Gaza). This second data set is aligned with regional performance over the same period. The total number of overnight inbound tourism to Palestine reached 1,066,281 million tourists, whereas the number of inbound and domestic visitors reached 5,079,399 million (Ministry of Tourism and Antiquities, 2015).

Table 9.3 shows the distribution of number of inbound overnights during 2008–2014 by region in the State of Palestine.

According to MOTA (2015) the three top markets of overnight stays in Palestine are the Russians, the Polish and Palestinians residing in Israel.

The State of Palestine's pilgrimage tourism potential is closely entangled with that of Israel. Most tourists visit the State of Palestine while visiting Israel. Except for the diaspora or Palestinians in Israel, very few tourists come to visit the State

Table 9.1 Number of overnights for inbound tourism

Year	Number of overnights for inbound tourism	Years percentage change
2008	500,511	
2009	484,332	−3.2
2010	717,117	48.1
2011	766,423	6.9
2012	915,126	19.4
2013	977,951	6.9
2014	1,066,281	9.0

Source: MOTA, Palestine (2015).

Table 9.2 Number of inbound and domestic visitors

Year	Number of inbound and domestic visitors	Years percentage change
2008	2,115,799	
2009	2,593,606	22.6
2010	4,945,464	90.7
2011	4,832,053	−2.3
2012	4,790,236	−0.9
2013	5,047,714	5.4
2014	5,079,399	0.6

Source: MOTA, Palestine (2015).

Table 9.3 The distribution of inbound overnights during 2008–2014 by region in the State of Palestine

District /	2008	2009	2010	2011	2012	2013	2014
Jericho /	62510	49798	75054	68531	80108	65673	61457
Hebron /	1564	2505	2284	3825	3196	2913	2379
Bethlehem /	392523	364053	547502	589360	698274	776169	848124
Jenin /	230	2308	4180	9278	25342	18550	19349
Ramallah /	35399	60164	73483	86179	100330	103932	122161
Nablus /	8285	5504	8446	9250	7876	10670	12734
Tulkarm /			6150			20	77
Tubas /			18				
Qalqeliah /						24	

Source: MOTA, Palestine (2015).

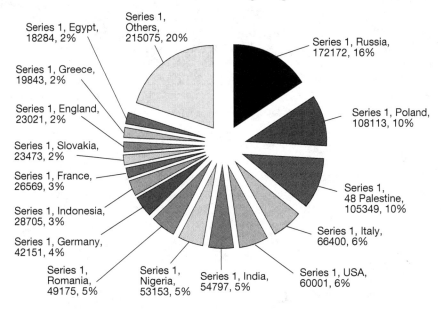

Series 1, Egypt, 18284, 2%

Series 1, Others, 215075, 20%

Series 1, Russia, 172172, 16%

Series 1, Greece, 19843, 2%

Series 1, England, 23021, 2%

Series 1, Poland, 108113, 10%

Series 1, Slovakia, 23473, 2%

Series 1, France, 26569, 3%

Series 1, 48 Palestine, 105349, 10%

Series 1, Indonesia, 28705, 3%

Series 1, Italy, 66400, 6%

Series 1, Germany, 42151, 4%

Series 1, Romania, 49175, 5%

Series 1, Nigeria, 53153, 5%

Series 1, India, 54797, 5%

Series 1, USA, 60001, 6%

Figure 9.1 Distribution of overnight numbers by top nationalities.

Source: MOTA, Palestine (2015).

of Palestine mainly or exclusively. However, tourism in Israel should not be seen as a rival destination but, on the contrary, as the main attracting force for tourists to visit the State of Palestine.

The State of Palestine's status as a de facto submarket of the Israeli market also carries advantages, as the 2013 Diagnostic Study (Palestine Trade Centre 2014) finds that the State of Palestine and Israel to some extent are perceived by potential tourists as distant and separate from the region. Visitors often identify Israel as part of another region more connected to Europe, and the State of Palestine (or at least its classical Holy Land features) are largely included in this perception. When surrounding countries complain about a sharp drop in tourism due to unrest in these countries and their neighbours, the State of Palestine and Israel are still getting a moderate number of arrivals.

Bethlehem has always been one of Palestine's leading destinations, attracting millions of visitors and pilgrims from around the world. Being home to the Church of Nativity, Bethlehem's religious appeal has made it a 'must see experience' for any pilgrim or visitor to the Holy Land.

Over the past few years, Bethlehem continued to see record numbers of both one day and overnight visitors. Traditional as well as new source markets continue to show signs of growth. The tourism industry is booming once again and new tourism investments are being established every year. New hotels, resorts, restaurants, museums and attractions are opening and complimenting the destination's appeal by catering to a more diverse range of visitors, both local and international. Despite these record numbers in the economic sphere and despite being a host community, Bethlehem has not been able to fully capitalize on its tourism potential. There remain substantial revenue leakages that are outsourced from the local economy, mainly to Israel. One of the reasons behind that is that the majority of visitors to Bethlehem are day visitors (their visits are sometimes merely half a day long) (Isaac 2010a) and their pre-packaged programs tend to only include short stops at the Church of Nativity, followed by a visit to the Shepherd's Field in nearby Beit Sahour and then shopping at one of the large souvenir shops. Most of the other sites and attractions around Manger Square and across the governorate are not visited by the majority of these tourists. There is no doubt that as a tourism destination, Bethlehem (and Palestine as a whole) faces significant obstacles and challenges. At the centre of these obstacles are the Israeli occupation and the on-going conflict. That said, and putting the political environment and other external threats aside, Bethlehem is still left facing many internal weaknesses and challenges that it must overcome in order to live up to its true destination potential (see Chapter 6, this volume).

To achieve growth of exports a key imperative is to broaden the tourism offer beyond classical pilgrimage. Apart from Christian pilgrimage, other types of tourism that exist and might have potential in the future is Islamic heritage. The disputed city of Jerusalem is the third holy city of Islam. Muslims from all over the world might be interested in visiting this holy site, particularly the Al-Aqsa Mosque and the Dome of the Rock, Nabi Musa, or Ibrahimi Mosque. The main potential market to be targeted would be Palestinian residing in Israel, the Palestinian diaspora (see Chapter 8, this volume), Muslim countries or Muslim communities in non-Muslim countries, for example in Europe and North America. In addition, the diaspora as well as the Palestinians living in neighbouring countries such as Lebanon, the Syria Arab Republic, Egypt, and Jordan, offers the Palestinian tourism sector an opportunity to develop and diversify their products focusing on Islamic heritage.

Difficulties and challenges facing the pilgrimage market in Palestine

Currently, the primary obstacle facing the Palestinian tourism industry is lack of accessibility. Isaac (2010a: 581) noted that 'currently freedom of movement and access to Palestinians and visitors within the West Bank is the exception rather than the norm, contrary to the commitments undertaken in a number of agreements between Israel and Palestine'. Palestinian authorities should be aware of constraints which lie on their tourism industry: first the Israeli military checkpoints at the entrance of Bethlehem and throughout the West Bank and Gaza Strip. These check-points and border control obstruct the free movement of local people and tourists, and second, the Palestinian National Authority does not have either the power of issuing visas or controlling the borders (Isaac 2009). Also, Palestinian agencies lack communications with the rest of the world. Furthermore, the Palestinian tourism industry should have its mission accompanied with goals and objectives in relations to these new forms of tourism. A strategy should be developed to reach such goals. Israeli behaviour and policies are severe and hinder Palestinian tourism aspiration. Such policies will remain until true peace is achieved between the Palestinians and Israelis. The first step to overcome this structural violence would be to start by constituting a tourism policy in the Holy Land based on equality (of resources, income, guides, policy inputs) between actors. Palestinian objectives can only be achieved by negotiating on an equal basis. Palestinian independence will allow authorities to establish their control over borders which are considered the cornerstone of tourism success.

The lack of control over borders (air, land and sea), the vulnerability to regular invasion and consequent physical damage to tourism infrastructure, the lack of freedom of movement for Palestinians and tourists, the regular closures of Palestinian areas, and the Segregation Wall, which cuts deep into Palestinian areas, are only some of the problems resulting directly from the Israeli occupation. Furthermore, or as a consequence of, this occupation, Palestinians have been unable to fully develop their pilgrimage tourism potential and, more importantly, have been unable to plan for future development without a clear indication of when the conflicts will end and how Palestine will look once a final status agreement is reached (Isaac 2014).

Israeli measures in Holy places and throughout occupied Palestine explicitly target religious and cultural heritage, including damaging and demolition of mosques and ancient sites. Constant military incursions and unilateral measures taken in occupied Palestine, severely damage pilgrimage tourism through creating threats to any developments or investments in the sector (see Isaac 2010b).

The development of the pilgrimage tourism sector is the responsibility of the Palestinian private and public sectors, however, the Israeli restrictions highly limit the sovereignty of the Palestinian government in many areas and consequently affecting the governmental performance regarding improving and supervising the sector and mainly by closing roads, placing random checkpoints and through military power prevent any Palestinians from accessing certain areas that have potential for development and tourism growth. Consequently, the Palestinian (private and public sector) is unable to access many touristic places and sites for infrastructure development or sites development, due to the fact that significant number of the locations and sites in Palestine are in areas which are controlled by the Israeli military (Area C), according to Oslo II – (Article XI), Area C is supposed to be transferred to be under Palestinian National Authority control but in the redeployment phase, but since the peace agreement was freeze due to the Israeli policies, the transformation never happened and hence a permit should be granted from the Israeli military administration to the Palestinian government to implement any development activities, which as a result limits the development progress and weaken the management ability of Palestinian government (International Chamber of Commerce 2013).

In the context of organized group travel/pilgrimage tours, however, there are in many cases long delays for permits or travellers are eventually not authorized to enter Israel, which causes losses to tour operators. For instance, the Muslim world, and especially the Arab world, would obviously represent a very significant potential for tourism and FDI inflows into the State of Palestine if it was in full control of its borders. This would permit a significant improvement in the development and marketing of the different tourism subsectors. The State of Palestine's lack of control in this regard is a serious obstacle to the development of services exports.

A summary of the difficulties and challenges facing the pilgrimage market are the followings: However, a comprehensive description of the difficulties facing the tourism industry in Palestine in general and the pilgrimage market in particular to be found in Chapter 2 in this volume.

- Tour operators manage most of the tourism entry because of lack of structured marketing efforts from other players in the value chain.
- The State of Palestine does not control its borders, access, points of entry/exist or visa delivery.
- Circulation between Palestinian territories is restricted.
- Information on the viability of complementary products/markets are lacking, resulting in a lack of tour operators' initiative to widen tourism offers.

Conclusion

The aim of this chapter is to present the most important market segment, which is the pilgrimage that is still the back bone of the Palestinian tourism economy, particularly in Bethlehem and in Palestine in general. This chapter also revealed the difficulties and challenges dealing with this form of tourism, in which Israel has a stranglehold of the flow of this market segment in terms of visa issuing, using Israeli touring buses, using Israeli tour guides, and control of the whole market. Unless a fair and just final status peace agreement is reached between Israel and Palestine, tourism planners, public and private stakeholders and others cannot plan any long term pilgrimage tourism strategies. There are too many uncertainties and worries to plan long term, at least from the Palestinian public sector perspective. Questions, which include: Will East Jerusalem, which is still under occupation, be part of the Palestinian's tourism offer? Will there be a Palestinian airport? Will Palestine control its borders? Where will these borders be drawn?

References

Al-Falah, B. (2012) *Tourism in the Palestinian territory: analysis of significance and impact*, Ramallah: Palestine Economic Policy Research Institute.

Alternative Tourism Group (ATG) (2005) *Palestine and Palestinians*, Beitsahour: ATG.

Attix, A.A. (2002) 'New age-oriented special interest travel: an exploratory study', *Tourism Recreation Research*, 27(2): 51–58.

Barber, R. (1993) *Pilgrimages*, London: The Boydell.

Bowman, G. (1991) 'Christian ideology and the image of a Holy Land: The place of Jerusalem in the various Christianities', in M.J. Sallnow and J. Ead (eds.) *Contesting the sacred: the anthropology of Christian pilgrimage*, London: Routeledge.

Cohen, E. (1979) 'A phenomenology of tourism experience', *Sociology*, 13(2): 179–201.

Cohen, E. (1992) 'Pilgrimage and tourism: convergence and divergence', in A. Morinis (ed.) *Sacred journeys. The anthropology of pilgrimage*, Wesport, CT: Greenwood Press.

Collins-Kreiner, N. (2010a) 'Geographers and pilgrimages: changing concepts in pilgrimage tourism research', *TESG Journal of Economic and Social Geography*, 101(4): 437–448.

Collins-Kreiner, N. (2010b) 'The geography of pilgrimage and tourism: Transformations and implications for applied geography', *Applied Geography*, 20(1): 153–164.

Digance, J. (2003) 'Pilgrimage at contested sites', *Annals of Tourism Research*, 30(1): 143–159.

Eade, J. and Sallnow, M.J. (1991) 'Introduction', in J. Eade and M.J. Sallnow (eds.) *Contesting the sacred. The anthropology of Christian pilgrimage*, London: Routledge.

Fleischer, A. (2000) 'The tourist behind the pilgrim in the Holy Land', *Hospitality Management*, 19(3): 311–326.

Fox, J.T. (2012) 'Israel's hotels to bring back star rating system', *Travel Agent Central*. Online http://www.travelagentcentral.com/israel/israels-hotels-bring-back-star-rating-system-36673 [Accessed 3 September, 2015].

Graburn, N.H. (1989) 'Tourism: The sacred journey', in V. L. Smith (ed.) *Hosts and guests: The anthropology of tourism*, Philadelphia: University of Pennsylvania Press.

International Chamber of Commerce (2013) 'Palestine tourism sector', Palestine: The World Business Organisation.

Isaac, R.K. (2009) 'Can the segregation wall be a tourist attraction?' *Tourism, Hospitality, Planning & Development*, 6(3): 247–254.

Isaac, R.K. (2010a) 'Moving from pilgrimage to responsible tourism: the case of Palestine', *Current Issues in Tourism*, 13(6): 579–590.

Isaac, R.K. (2010b) 'Alternative tourism: new forms of tourism in Bethlehem for the Palestinian tourism industry', *Current Issues in Tourism*, 13(1): 21–36.

Isaac, R.K. (2014) 'Palestine: Tourism under occupation', in R. Butler and W. Suntikul (eds.) *Tourism and War*, London: Routledge.

Isaac, R.K. and Ashworth, G. (2012) 'Moving from pilgrimage to 'dark' tourism: leveraging tourism in Palestine', *Tourism, Culture and Communication*, 11(3): 149–164.

Lopez, L. and Lois, R.C. (2011) 'The pilgrims and their wills: historical sources for geography', paper presented at IGU/UGI, Regional geographic conference, Santiago de Chile (Chile).

Ministry of Tourism and Antiquities (MOTA) Palestine. (2012) *Tourists Statistics*, Bethlehem: MOTA.

Ministry of Tourism and Antiquities (MOTA) Palestine. (2015) Tourists Statistics, Bethlehem: MOTA.

Mintel Group. (2012) 'Religious and pilgrimage tourism', *Mintel Report – International - February*, USA: Mintel.

Nolan, M. and Nolan, S. (1989) *Christian pilgrimage in Modern Western Europe*, Chapel Hill: The University of North Caroline Press.

Palestine Trade Centre. (2014) *Tourism Sector Export Strategy 2014–2018*, Ramallah: Palestine Trade Centre.

The Palestinian Association for Cultural Exchange (PACE). (1999) *PACE tour guide of the West Bank & Gaza Strip Palestine: Historical & Archaeological Guide*, Ramallah: PACE.

Palestinian Central Bureau of Statistics (2013) *Around 2.6 Million Visits to Tourist Sites in the West Bank During the First Half of 2013*. Online http://www.pcbs.gov.ps/portals/pcbs/PressRelease/Press_En_Tourism-2013-e.pdf [Accessed 23 January, 2014].

Rinschede, G. (1992) 'Forms of religious tourism', *Annals of Tourism Research*, 19(1): 51–67.

Shahin, M. (2007) *Palestine: a guide*, 1st edn, Ramallah: Arab Scientific Publisher.

Smith, V.L. (1992) 'Introduction. The quest in guest', *Annals of Tourism Research*, 19(1): 1–17.

Stausberg, M. (2011) *Religion and tourism: crossroads, destinations and encounters*, London: Routledge.

Tarlow, P. (2014) The importance of religious tourism market. Online http://www.eturbonews.com/50998/importance-religious-tourism-market [Accessed 2 March 2015].

Travel Palestine. (2012) *Destination Palestine 2011 Overview*. Online http://www.travelpalestine.files.wordpress.com/2012/01/2011-tourism-industry-overview-final.pdf [Accessed 3 September, 2015].

Turner, V. and Turner, E. (1978) 'Image and pilgrimage in Christian culture', *Anthropological Perspectives*, Oxford: Blackwell.

United Nations World Tourism Organization (UNWTO) (2013) *World tourism barometer*, Volume 11 (January), Madrid: UNWTO.

United States Agency for International Development (USAID). (2014) *Faith and adventure tourism market profiles*: Prepared by Holy Land Incoming Tour Operators Association (HLITOA). Bethlehem: HLITOA.

Vukonić, B. (1996) *Tourism and religion*, London: Elsevier Science Ltd.

World Travel and Tourism Council (WTTC) (2014) *Travel & tourism economic impact 2014: Mediterranean*, London: WTTC.

10 Gaza

The missing tourism assets

Rania Filfil Almbaid

Introduction

The Gaza Strip is one of the most ancient civilizations in mankind's history; it actually spans over 5000 years of history. Communities first developed in Gaza during the Stone and Iron Ages. The enduring quality of these two elements continues to characterize its people. Throughout the ages Gazans have been fated to live on the frontiers of the competing kingdoms of the world. Kings, emperors and sultans have fought bloody battles on Gaza's soil, laid waste to its cities and rebuilt them. Beneath Gaza lies layer upon layer of tales so terrible, fantastic, and heroic that they rival the legends of the gods. But Gaza's story is no fairytale. The Gazans who lived through these epic events at the crossroads of the world were real men and women who suffered under humanity's lust for power but always rose again from tragedy to live on in the next generation. Their blood, culture and spirit live still in the people of Gaza today. Woven with the threads of many kingdoms, Gazans continue to adapt while preserving their distinctive identity (Filfil and Louton 2008: 25)

This chapter will start with a brief history of Gaza, investigates the potential of tourism through identification of the archaeological and cultural sites that are of interests for tourism, as well as the social and cultural assets of Gaza.

History

The Gaza Strip is a land of area located along the Mediterranean Sea in the southwestern side of Palestine and northeast of Egypt. The size of the area is about 365km².

Gaza was founded during the Canaanite age (3000 BC). As a Canaanite city, Gaza is considered as one of the oldest cities in the world at large as described by many historians (Almughany, El-Wazir and Al-Qeeq 2009). Gaza was said to mean strong, treasures, or stores. Persians called it *Hazato*, while the Arabs called it Gaza of Hashem after Hashem bin abd Manaf, grandfather of the prophet who died in his return from Syria. His tomb is in the mosque named after him Said Hashem Mosque in Al-Daraj old neighborhood. The oldest known inhabitants of Gaza were Canaanites, thereafter the Palestinians (Al-Mubaid 1995). Old Gaza was built on a hill 45 meters above sea level. When the city grew, buildings extended north, east and south (Al-Aref 1943). Old Gaza is divided into two parts: the eastern part which includes the Al-Shijaiya neighborhood named after Shujauddin Ottoman bin Alkan Al-Kurdi who met martyrdom there during the crusades. The western part includes the walled old town with its old quarters Al-Tuffah, Al-Zaitoun and Al-Darj (Al-Dabagh 1996).

Because of its strategic location between Asia and Africa, Gaza was a prosperous trade centre, located on the ancient coastal road linking Egypt to Palestine and beyond. Gaza was built and continuously developed to become a transit place where traders can rest before continuing to travel to Asia and Africa (Skaik 1980). Throughout history, Gaza has been viewed amongst the most important cities of Palestine, and underwent many changes. Gaza city is amongst the most important sites in the city and contains over four hundred historic buildings. Given the increase of populations and various activities during the Ayyubid era, the core of the old city expanded beyond the limits of the surrounding wall, in so doing forming the four known old neighborhoods of Gaza city: The Tuffah (Apple), The Zaitoun (Olives), Al-Suhja'iyya (Braves) and Al-Daraj (Steps) (Dawod 2005). Today the Gaza Strip retains several historical sites in spite of Israeli attacks in recent years and demolition of its architectural heritage and history.

Entering into Gaza

In order to be able to enter into the Gaza Strip, you need a permit from the Israeli administration in order to travel by road via the Eretz Checkpoint to the north of the Strip. Obtaining such a permit needs a 'valid' cause in the eyes of the Israeli government. But, it is always worth trying. The other entrance to Gaza is traveling via Egypt through the Rafah Crossing Point, which is also subject to a decision from the Egyptian government. You should be prepared for a long trip and days of waiting for the Crossing Point to be open. It should be noted that with the advent of the Palestinian National Authority in 1993, an international airport was constructed and operated starting in 1998. The airport was able to handle 700,000 passengers per year. It operated 24 hours and 364 days a year. The airport was closed in 2001 after being severely damaged in the massive Israeli incursion of the Palestinian Territory following the outbreak of the second Palestinian *Intifada* in September 2000 (International Civil Aviation Organization (ICAO) 2002).

People of Gaza

Today, Gaza's population is divided into three categories: the indigenous Gazans, the settled refugees (Palestinians from the 1948 who had fled the Zionists' attacks against their cities) and refugees of the camps. The refugee population constitutes almost two-thirds of the population of Gaza. The Gaza Strip population, in 2005 according to the Palestinian Information Centre (2005, cited in Almughany et al. 2009) are: North Gaza 265980 people; Gaza 493621; Deir Al-Balah 202707; Khan Younis 271787; and Rafah with a population of 166701.

Figure 10.1 Remaining part of airport in Gaza.

Source: Rania Filfil.

Figure 10.2 Old seaport in Gaza.

Source: Rania Filfil.

Accommodation

Gaza offers a range of unique hotels to its visitors. It is also known for the hospitability of its people. Many tourists end up in a Gazan home sharing the culture, food and shelter. Before the PNA takeover in 1993, Gaza had few hotels, the most prominent being Abu Heuwidi by the beach, which offered a unique fish restaurant under the name of 'The Love Boat'. However, starting 1994, the hotel industry boomed mainly in the city of Gaza featuring tens of hotels and restaurants, mainly specializing in seafood. The hotels of Gaza include Aldiereh, Gaza Comodor Hotel, Roots, Adam and Palestine Hotel. On the beach lies also the Budapest Chalets, with cabins overlooking the Mediterranean.

Al-Mathaf

Al-Mathaf stands on a quite location next to the beach of the northern Gaza Strip. It is built as a private investment to help preserve the historical and cultural identity of Gaza and offers a new standard hospitability and cultural services. As its name suggests *Al-Mathaf* (Arabic for 'The Museum') is the home of Gaza's finest archaeological museum, which is filled with beautiful artifacts that celebrate Gaza's rich cultural heritage. The Museum shows rare Gazan antiquities and artifacts. The collection includes ancient tools, columns, motifs, coins, glass and pottery. In addition to its hospitable hotels, Gaza offers a variety of restaurants and cafés offering different fish dishes and seafood.

Figure 10.3 Al-Mathaf hotel in Gaza.

Source: Rania Filfil.

Gaza city has a long-standing ice cream shop – Kazem. It is located on the main street, Omar Almokhtar, right in the city center. Although it may not be as famous as other branded ice creams, Buza Kazem remains a brand name in Gaza

Marna House is a motel in the city of Gaza, historically hosting scholars and visitors from all around the world; its former owner, Ms. Alia Shawwa, transformed it into a cultural hub. And after her passing away, the new owner preserved its legacy.

Entertainment and nightlife

The beach hotels in Gaza hold special nights with music and dance for visitors and local people to enjoy. In addition, visitors can take part in Gaza's active cultural life in centers like Rashad Alshawa Cultural Center and the YMCA Gaza. Before the tightened Israeli siege, Gaza used to have a highly active cultural scene with art exhibitions, film festivals, sports events and carnivals. Unfortunately, much of this activity has stopped due to the protracted siege and repetitive Israeli onslaughts against Gaza. However, this vibrant culture can still be felt as you tour the streets, talk to the people and share their day-to-day life.

Attractions

Mosques, churches, public buildings and private residential houses constitutes the main historic buildings in the Gaza Strip. However, the majority of historical sites in Gaza are residential areas composed of houses built during the Ottoman period with an age ranging from 100 to 400 years pld (Almughany *et al.* 2009).

Gaza beach

Gaza beach is considered the only coastline recreational site for a population of more than one million in the Gaza Strip (Afifi 1998). It is usually very crowded during the summer, mostly with local inhabitants.

The Great Omari Mosque

The story of this Mosque is similar to the history of its city; and reflects different layers of religious structures and ruling powers. It is believed to have begun as a temple of Marnas (Aramaic for Marnas, 'the Lord'), god of fertility and rain. It was then transformed into a church by the Byzantines in the fifth century AD. The latter ordered 42 Greek marble columns to be shipped to Gaza to construct the church, which was named in honor of Saint Helena. It then became a mosque during the Islamic era in Palestine and was named the Omari Mosque, after the second Khalif, Omar bin Alkhattab, who conquered Palestine and Alsham. The Crusaders then made it into a Norman church, the Cathedral of John the Baptist, until it became a mosque again under the Mamlouki rule.

When you enter the mosque, you find a huge area of 1190 m² of courtyard that contains the old tribune and model of Jerusalem. If you pass this yard before entering the mosque, you find against the door of the mosque, a place for ablution. In addition to its distinguished minaret and outstanding architecture, the mosque hosts a library that includes many of manuscripts in various fields of science and the arts. The library contains thousands of books and was named after Zahir Baybars, who loved Gaza, and was very kind. The library used to contain 132 manuscripts but unfortunately, the manuscripts are now in poor condition due to humidity, and some of them have ruptured and eroded due to weather, old age, neglect and lack of maintenance. According to Gaza Municipality (Interview, 25 June, 2015), these manuscripts included Korans (8), Koran and its interpretations (9), Faith discussions (5), sophism and ethics (14), Prophet sayings (text and interpretation): 14, Islamic Jurisprudence (53), Arabic language and literature (15), Life of the Prophet (8), Arabic and Islamic History (4), Education and learning methodologies (1); Arabian Medicine (1), mathematics (1).

The oldest manuscript dates back to 920 Hegira, titled 'explaining the ambiguities of religious rituals – *sahrh alghawmedh fi ilm alfara'edh*', but Badreddien Mahoammad Bin Ahmad Almardiny (died 867 Hegira), transcribed by Ahmad Bin Moahmmad Alassali Almalik, an Azhar graduate. The manuscript by donated to the Mosque from the library of Shiekh Ali Abu Almawaheb Aldajani, former Mufti of Jafa before 1948 through is grandson Yousef Aldajani. Most of the manuscripts of the Mosque library were either gifts or donations.

The Gold/ Zawya Market (Caesaria)

The market is named after Julius Caesar who built it as stables for the horses of the different armies passing through Gaza. Linked to the Mosque is what serves now as the gold market. With the transformation of the St. Helena Church into a mosque, the vaulted alley was used as a market, specializing in selling gold. Families of Gaza known to be the jewelers of the city include Hakura, Tarazi, Sayegh, and Ashi among others.

Hammam alsumara

Gaza had several public baths established to serve its people in different historical eras. Islam is a religion that requires ablution and cleanliness as a pillar of the faith. Therefore the baths were constructed for the needs to passengers traveling to Gaza on trade and to citizens who lacked private baths in their homes. One of the oldest baths, which is the only remaining, is Alsumarah Bath in Alzaytoun headquarter. It used to be part of the structure comprising the Greater Omari Mosque, the Caesarea market and khan Alzeit, all of which are located in the old city of Gaza, currently known as *Albalad* (downtown).

The bath was built in the Mamluk era in 685 by King Sinfar bin Abdallah, a Mamluk from Egypt. You enter the bath via a narrow corridor that leads to three rooms: *Mashlah* (vestry) to leave your clothes before coming into a large hot room that is close to the heating system. It is a high temperature steam room with hot water bath tub. The third part comprises a main (*Iwan*) whole with sofas to sit and relax. The *Iwan* has pillows with Palestinian embroidery and serves beverage to customers. It also has a skylight ceiling that lets in natural lighting reflecting on the sumptuous marble tiles with diversified ornaments (Saffad Press 2015).

Church of St. Prophyrius

Dumper and Abu-Lughod (2007) state that this fourth century church is where St. Porphyrius, Bishop of Gaza died and was buried (420 AD). It is located in the Zaytoun Quarter of Gaza's old city and is still in use by the Greek Orthodox Community.

The Church of Saint Porphyrius has a rectangular shape, ending with a half-domed roofed temple. Its pavement is 1.8 meters below ground level in its southern part, and three meters below ground level in the northern end. The church consists of a single aisle made up of two groin-vaulted bays, with a projecting semi-circular apse preceded by a barrel-vaulted presbytery. The church has architectural and constructional similarities to the former Cathedral of Saint John the Baptist (Currently the Great Mosque of Gaza).

In the Israeli onslaught on Gaza in summer 2014, the church hosted families whose houses were demolished. As the war coincided with the holy month of Ramadan, prayers of *Laylat Alqadr*, the night of revelation of Prophet Mohammed, were held in the church.

Napoleon's Fort – Qasr Al-Basha

Qasr Al-Basha, on Al-Wahda Street in AlDaraj Qaurter in the old City of Gaza, is an imposing stone building that dates back to the Mamluk period. It was the headquarters of the *Wali* (Deputy) of Gaza during the Mamluk and the Ottoman periods. Under the British mandate of Palestine it was as a police station. Napoleon spent three nights there during his campaign against Egypt and Syria in 1799. This is why it is sometimes called 'Napoleon's Citadel'. The Fort is characterized by the beauty of its façades which are decorated with different patterns such as the emblem of Al-Thaher Babers (a sculpture of two facing lions) in addition to geometrical patterns and unique archaeological elements such as domes, fan and cross vaults. The building has now been converted into the Alzahra' Secondary Girl's school but can still be visited.

Anthedon Harbour

Anthedon is the first known seaport of Gaza, mentioned in Islamic literature with the names of Tida, apparently an abbreviation of Anthedon, or Blakhiyeh. The city was inhabited from 800 BC to 1100 AD, and witnessed a series of different cultures: Neo-Assyrian, Babylonian, Persian, Greek, Roman, Byzantine and early Islamic rulers (Umayyad, Abbasid, Tulunid and Fatimid).

Anthedon was a significant seaport along the ancient trade route that linked Europe with the Levant during the Phoenician, Roman, and Hellenistic periods. Abundant archaeological evidence provides a complete and comprehensive picture of the historical and archaeological evolution in the region, which reflects the rich socio-cultural and socio-economic interchange between Europe and the Levant.

One kilometer south of the seaport of Anthedon lies the ancient harbour of Maiumas, then identified with the harbour of Gaza. The city flourished in the Roman period with Maiumas mentioned only in late classical sources. The name Maiumas drives from an Egyptian word, which means 'maritime place'.

The Gaza ports were a hub of trades on the so-called the Route of the Philistines; the route they are believed to have taken from Crete to land in Palestine. It became then known as the *Via Maris* (from Latin: route of the sea). The name is based on a passage from the Vulgate (the New Testament in Latin translation, Matthew 4:15) (Wafa Info 2015).

Wadi Gaza Coastal Wetlands

Wadi Gaza springs from the Negev hills and the southern heights of *Khalil* (Hebron). The length of the Wadi is about 105 km from its source to the sea, and extends from the Truce line in East Gaza to the coast where it discharges into the sea. It is considered as one of the most important wetlands on the Eastern Mediterranean Basin because of its biodiversity and it is a significant layover site for migrating birds.

Tell Umm Amer

The site of Tell Umm Amer is located in Al Nusairat village, near Dier Albalah, on the Mediterranean Coast, 8.5 km south of Gaza City. The first settlement in the site was established during the Roman era. It appears on the Madaba map with the name Tabatha. The site contains the ruins of Saint Hilarion (born 291 AD), which consist of two churches a burial site and a baptism hall, a public cemetery, an audience hall, and dining rooms. The first fourth-century building of the Monastery is attributed to St. Hilarion, a native of the Gaza region and the father of Palestinian monasticism. It was abandoned after a seventh-century earthquake and uncovered by local archaeologists in 1999.

Tel Umm Amer was occupied over four centuries from the late Roman Empire to the Umayyad period. It is the site of five successive churches, bathing and sanctuary complexes. It is distinguished by its geometric mosaics and an expensive crypt. It constitutes part of the Byzantine monastic desert centers in Palestine. It is believed to have been a center of missionary work in Gaza region, seemingly isolated in the desert but in reality at the crossroads and center of communication between Egypt, Palestine, Syria and Mesopotamia. As the only archaeological site accessible to the public in Gaza, Tell Umm el-'Amr is important and treasured heritage in an area torn by conflict.

Other sites of Dier Al-Balah

Dier Al-Balah's name is derived from the Aramaic *Darum*, which means south. It is known for its cemetery that contained coffins in the form of human body that date back to the late Bronze Age. The sarcophagi are believed to be of the kings of the Philistines. The cemetery dates back to 400–1200 BC. The unique coffins are characterized by their mobile head covers. They were discovered in groups of three or more, placed at a 3–4 meter distance of each other in tombs curved of karkar stone or red clay facing the sea. Other numerous sarcophagi are made of Alpaster and Canaanite, Cypriot and Egyptian clay were also found. It seems they were used as immolations upon burial. In 1971, General Moshe Dayan, then Israeli defense minister, looted the site and add the uncovered coffins to his personal collections, which he kept until his death. Afterwards, the pieces were moved to a museum in Jerusalem (Wafa Info 2015).

Tel Alraqeesh

Excavations at this coastal archaeological site revealed a prosperous Phoenician colony on an area of 150,650 m², surrounded with walls extending over length of 1600 meter. The site has a Phoenician cemetery for the incineration of corpses that dates back to the late Iron Age and the Persian era (538–332 BC). The site and its wall give the impression that it used to be an important seaport on the ancient trade route. Archaeologists unearthed pots of local clay, Alraqeesh, in addition to other Phoenician and Cypriot pottery.

Khan Younis

Khan Younis is 25 kilometers south of Gaza, 20 kilometers north of the Egyptian borders and 4 kilometers from the Mediterranean Sea. Its name means *Khan* (Hostel) *Younis* (of Younis). It was Prince Younis Dawadar who built a garrison in 1387 to serve soldiers grading travelers and pilgrims on their way to Jerusalem and Mecca and also functioned as a station for commercial caravans. The town square is dominated by a square fortress. The Mamlouk sultan, Barqouq had commissioned his secretary Prince Younis Dawdyar to build the castle. The name of the Sultan was curved on its door.

Khan Younis is a market town for agricultural produce from the surrounding villages and holds a weekly, colorful Bedouin Market, where merchants sell everything from embroidery to fish. There are also several cafés around the town center.

Rafah

The ancient city of Rafah is and has been for many years the southern port to Palestine. This strategic location left it vulnerable to competing powers. The city formed a natural border between Egypt and the Fertile Crescent. Marble colonnades and obelisks were erected to mark the boundary between Palestine and Egypt. It was mentioned in the Pharoahs' scripts dating back to sixteenth century BC and constituted a strategic guard point along the Hawaras coastal road.

Rafah was known in the Islamic era as a rest station for travelling merchants. Historians in the eleventh century described the city as an industrious hub, featuring a market, a mosque, and several hotels and shops. Archaeologists believe that the sands of the western part of Rafah cover ruins belonging to the Roman era.

Arts and crafts village

Gaza, as other old towns in the area, is famous for its traditional handicrafts that played a role in both physical and socio-economic life of its citizens. The famous handicrafts are pottery, glass, bamboo, embroidery and textile. Despite its image of a conflict zone, Gaza has a long tradition of arts and crafts. Those skills passed from a generation to another in Gaza's seven millennia. For this purpose, the Arts and Crafts Village was created in 2010 to host a centre that contains an art gallery and handicraft workshops which offer high quality articles for sale.

The village was designed by a Palestinian architect using local building material. It offers workshops for ceramics, cupper items, rugs, weaving and embroidery as well as burning woods. In addition, it hosts cultural activities and the Café Abu Nawwas in the complex.

The pottery workshop

Situated near the el-Faras market, the pottery workshop is unique. Pottery-making in Gazah has a long tradition. From the Greek to the Byzantine period, amphorae called "Gaza jars" filled with olive oil, wine or brine could be found all over the eastern Mediterranean. Today, the jars are principally decorative in purpose. They are usually of generous proportions, but one may also find smaller versions, in particular, water coolers whose unglazed clay is perfect for keeping water fresh and cool.

Woven rugs

Throughout Gaza, weavers can be seen creating brightly colored rugs on wooden looms. The patterns are simple geometric shapes or stripes. They tend to come in bright colors such as red, orange, yellow and green.

Bamboo in Gaza

The industry was introduced in Palestine under the British Mandate when wicker furniture was highly fashionable. The British established workshops in Jafa and Jerusalem. The industry came to Gaza in 1950s with the refugees fleeing the Zionist attacks in historical Palestine.

Different forms of tourism

In Gaza time may appear frozen. The days are so similar and the faces do not change. It is the place where you can say, "People of Gaza used to have electricity before they shifted to using candles." The Via Maris, or the Horus Road, hub of ancient trading centers is subject to a tight siege imposed by the Israeli occupation forces. The restriction on the mobility of its people undermines their indigenous identity as travelers and international traders. Tourism is regarded as a means to listen to the day-to-day stories of the Palestinian people, to help them survive and prosper again. In their veins runs the blood of warriors, traders, rulers and kings; most importantly, in their veins runs the blood of humanity. In Gaza, tourism is seen as way of telling their story and reporting on their narrative of history and is regarded as integral means of economic, social and political support.

Help the orphans

The protracted conflict and repetitive attacks on the Gaza Strip left many children without parents. Some of them no longer have a home to go to since the last war in 2014 resulted in the demolition of entire neighborhoods. Part of them lost a limbo or an eye; their hopes for life are increasingly shrinking. They do not only need bread and water, but dignity and freedom, tourism is a means of achieving this.

Our last word

Historians reported that Cleopatra and Antonio travelled through ancient tunnels from Egypt to the Palestinian city of Rafah where they wed. They challenged Rome and the powers of their time and smuggled themselves into this land to unite in marriage. Instead of sending aid boats to bring daily bread and no more, tourism provides a means to bring the world to live an experience of time and life still waiting to be born. A place portrayed by the media as one of the most violent places in the world with wars and conflicts and poverty is yet a place of many stories and lives yet to come. In this narrow strip where children aging 10 years old have already experienced three major wars and devastation and where their parents and grandparents have been forcibly displaced several times, tourists can discover a new meaning and perspective of life.

Conclusion

This chapter has exposed the missing assets of Gaza as a tourism destination. Despite the recent Israeli military invasions and bombardments and the devastations of Gaza, the region still has many historical, cultural and archeological sites that are of interest for tourism. Just as significantly, tourism could play an important role in the socio-economic life of its citizens as well as to be used as an economic instrument in job generation and income. One of the major benefits of tourism is the revival of traditional craftworks and the promotion of social life and building use in the city. For example, it may include the establishment of a land plot, a work space for artisans to produce products and to train interested trainees to follow up the production and development of handicrafts.

References

Afifi, S. (1998) *Identification and evaluation of seawater and beach quality state in Gaza Governorate: final report*, Gaza: Environmental and Rural Research Centre, Islamic University.

Al-Aref, A. (1943) *History of Gaza*, Jerusalem: Orphan House for Publishing.

Al-Dabagh, M. (1996) *Palestine, our country*, Beirut: Al-Talia Printery.

Al-Mubaid, S. (1995) *Islamic and historic buildings in Gaza city and the Gaza Strip*, Cairo: General Egyptian Assembly for Books.

Almughany, N., El-Wazir, M., Al-Qeeq, F. and Dawood, H. (2009) 'A sustainable approach for urban integration of Hammam Samarah in the historic city of Gaza', *Archnet-IJAR. International Journal of Architectural Research*, 3(1): 171–185.

Dawood, H. (2005) 'Preservation of cultural heritage for historic buildings in Gaza Strip', Unpublished Master dissertation, Cairo: Al-Azhar University.

Dumper, M. and Abu-Lughod, J.L. (2007) Cities of the Middle East and North Africa: a historical encyclopedia, California: ABC-CLIO.

Filfil, R. and Louton, B. (2008) 'The other face of Gaza: the Gaza Continuum', *This Week in Palestine*, 125: 20–25.

International Civil Aviation Organization (ICAO). (2002) *Council adopts resolution strongly condemning the destruction of Gaza International Airport*. http://unispal.un.org/UNISPAL.NSF/0/4C7354F26BB24F1685256B8000612610 [Accessed 3 March 2015].

Saffad Press. (2015) *Hammam alsumara*. Online http://www.saffad.com [Accessed 21 March, 2015].

Skaik, K. (1980) *Gaza through history*, Cairo: General Egyptian Assembly for Books.

Wafa Info. (2015) *Dir A-Balah*. http://www.wafainfo.ps/atemplate.aspx?id=3292 [Accessed 20 March 2015].

Part III
The ways in which Palestine matters to tourism

11 Tourism, travel and academic (and cultural) boycotting

Bisan Mitri

Introduction

Israel's treatment of Palestinians in Israel and the occupied territories of Palestine constitutes an overall discriminatory regime with the primary purpose of controlling the maximum amount of land with the minimum amount of indigenous Palestinians residing on it (Masalha 1992). The main components of this structure serve to violate Palestinian rights in areas such as nationality, citizenship, residency and land ownership (Alqasis 2012).

Israeli policies of land grab; forcible displacement; creation and expansion of settlements; and restriction of movement control almost every aspect of the daily life of the Palestinian people. Numerous UN resolutions have not stopped Israel from the continuous violation of international law and basic human rights of the Palestinian people. In addition to this, the support Israel enjoys from some superpowers on an official level is leaving it extremely difficult for Palestinians to see a glimpse of hope for the future. Decades of peace-talks and negotiations' cycles full of compromises on the Palestinian side are proving to be void and have, in effect, added even further to the dispossession of the Palestinians (Russell Tribunal on Palestine 2011; Dugard 2007; Falk 2011).

Like the right of return of Palestinian refugees, the right to self-determination and the right to housing, the right to resistance – interpreted through the right to freedom of opinion and expression – is also guaranteed as a human right. The United Nations (UN) General Assembly Resolution 3246 (XXIX) of 29 November 1974, 'reaffirms the legitimacy of the peoples' struggle for liberation from colonial and foreign domination and alien subjugation' (UN 1982). However, the Palestinian aspiration of independence and freedom will not be achieved without struggle. This chapter will start briefly by explaining how tourism's relationship to academic and cultural boycott fits into the struggle for liberation and self-determination of the Palestinian people. Secondly, it will provide a historical overview of the history of the Palestinian Campaign for the Academic and Cultural Boycott of Israel (PACBI) as part of the global Boycott, Divestment and Sanctions Movement (BDS), its objectives and goals and how they coincide with the general objectives (and pillars) of the BDS Movement. Third, it will highlight the importance of PACBI within the struggle, this section will concentrate on defining

PACBI through the concepts outlined in the first two sections. It will offer an explanation that legitimizes this sort of struggle, as well as examples of the success within it. It will also briefly seek to deconstruct the rising attack that is attempting to delegitimize it. Finally, the last section (the way forward) will discuss PACBI as a resistance means for the future, and what can be done to strengthen it. The Boycott, Divestment and Sanctions Movement (BDS), a rapidly growing one, on local, regional and international levels, with its various campaigns and initiatives offers available, non-violent means to end Israeli occupation by mobilizing the international community to hold Israel accountable to international law.

Boycotting and tourism

Boycotts have an honorable history, both as a weapon of the weak and as non-violent alternative to more powerful action. It was Captain Charles Boycott's tyrannous regime as a grasping English land agent in County Mayo, Ireland in the 1880s that provoked his employees to deny him and his family of all assistance. In this process they gave this form of collective action a human name. Nevertheless, the history of boycotts long antecedes Boycott (British Committee for Universities of Palestine (BRICUP) 2007).

Not all boycotts achieve their objectives, but the roll-call of success is considerable. An example of celebrated boycott was the refusal of Britain's colonial settlers in North America to buy products on which the Townshend Act of 1767 had imposed taxes. Within three years the reduction in sales led to its repeal. Gandhi's 'March to the Sea' in the 1930s was a boycott of commercial salt in protest against the imposition of tax. The UK boycott of South Africa, and particularly the sporting boycott, were instrumental in fostering a climate in which the confidence of that country's anti-apartheid regime began to weaken (BRICUP 2007).

The essence of a boycott is the shared decision, by those who if acting individually would have no power, to provide a compelling moral and practical argument against the continuation of unacceptable practices. They mutually commit to withhold from engaging in certain activities that provide support to the perpetrator of the targeted practices. It is of the essence that the boycotter also loses, which gives this form of pressure an unusual moral force. The issues here have been presented in abstract terms, however, the translation of the specifics' s grip on the occupied territories of Palestine, as has been presented in this book, and subsequent sections, are straight-forward.

Political consumerism has emerged as a relevant form of political expression, and a form of active civil disobedience used to put pressure on governments or corporations to pursue a cause. Boycotting lies at the heart of political consumerism. Seccartini (2006: 3) states that political consumerism has emerged as a form of political expression apparent in the rejection of formal or traditional political institutions and traditional modes of politics. He suggests that, 'Contemporary democracies, in fact, are living an intense change in the relationship between society and politics. Traditional political actors such as parties, unions and structured and formal organizations, are progressively more detached from society. The membership decline is a manifest indicator of this process', a process where citizens take political, social and even environmental actions in their hand (Stolle *et al.* 2005; Micheletti *et al.* 2006). Further examples of social, political and environmental events for political consumerism, see for example (Holden 2003; Micheletti *et al.* 2006). Political consumerism is a non-traditional avenue where people, organizations or governments voice their concerns for or against a policy, action of a body, such as the state of Israel that is believed to not conform to the ethical values of political consumer. Political consumerism comes in different forms. Citizens boycott to express political sentiment to support a corporation, government or policy that represents a social, political or environmental value that is supported by the actor (Micheletti *et al.* 2006). Political tourism can also be considered to be a type of political consumerism. Political consumers support a cause by choosing to buy or not to buy a product or service that related to the principles they are fighting against, or for tourists choose to visit or not to visit a destination or boycott it align with the case they are supporting, such as the case of Myanmar (Hall and Ringer, 2000).

Furthermore, ethical travel as a concept is now common discourse, with tourists increasingly asking now they can minimize the impact they have on local communities, as well as expressing growing interest in volunteerism and working with communities to endorse change. Travelers hold a unique position of economic power over the whole tourism supply chain – transport, accommodation, hospitality and other vital aspects of many burgeoning economies. Tourism boycotts are a common and somewhat popular way to cash in on this power (Reeves 2003). Tourists contemplating a visit to any country with a history of human rights abuses are faced with a similar ethical dilemma; keep yourself and your money away, or go and bear witness, facilitate the exchange of ideas, and support local businesses (Hudson 2007). For example, in the case of Myanmar, tourism was used as a weapon with which the opposition party can attack the authorities and exert pressure for political reform (Henderson 2003). The number of boycotts related to tourism has increased significantly in the past years (Glaesser 2003). Coles (2008), for example, offered more recent accounts of political tourism where tourism boycotts were used, as in the case of the 1999 East Timor struggle for independence from Indonesia. 'For the first time, the travel writing community in Britain put out a press release suggesting tourists and tour operators should boycott Indonesia' (Coles 2008: 35). Glaesser (2003) offered other examples of boycotts in the tourism industry serving the purpose of political, social and environmental causes, such as the call for boycott against travel to Zimbabwe because of general political situation, and call for boycott against travel to Thailand because of an alleged failure to deal with child sex prostitution.

In the case of Israel, not only does Israel control all the borders, entry visas, tourists' stay permits, tour guides licenses to operate, as well as freedom of movement of both Palestinians and tourists alike, it also controls touristic sites (both historic and religious) that are supposed to fall under the mandate of the Palestinian Authority as per the subsequent accords. The Alternative Tourism Group (ATG) has published a research in 2014 discussing the various touristic sites that fall within this category. Israel's control on these sites effects the Palestinian tourism sector and those involved in it immensely (Alternative Tourism Group 2014). In this sense, Israel deals with the Palestinian tourism sector in the same colonial framework as it applies its racist policies of land-grab and exclusiveness on sites belonging per agreement to the PA. This is why ethical tourism measures in Palestine is not enough, it should be furthermore mirrored by a boycott of tourism in Israel. In its dealing with the Palestinian tourism sector, Israel is in clear violation of international law and human rights, and therefore it should be dealt with the same way the international community has dealt with other examples in this regard.

What is BDS?

The Palestinian Boycott, Divestment and Sanction (BDS) National Committee describes BDS as:

> the global movement for a campaign of Boycotts, Divestment and Sanctions against Israel until it complies with international law and Palestinian rights... and was initiated by Palestinian civil society in 2005... BDS is a strategy that allows people of conscience to play an effective role in the Palestinian struggle for justice.

(PBDSNC 2011)

In July 2004, the International Court of Justice (ICJ) in The Hague issued its advisory opinion that the Wall Israel is building on confiscated lands throughout the West Bank, including East Jerusalem, is in violation of international law and should be dismantled (ICJ 2004). With a total planned route of 440 miles, (Al-haq 2012) the construction of the illegal Israeli Wall began in 2002 and continues to this day. Its path is not restricted to the 1967 Green Line (internationally recognized as the border between Israel and the future Palestinian state as part of a two-state solution), but instead strays deep into the West Bank.

Although the ICJ decision did not make the hoped for change in politics translated in the actual dismantling of the Wall, it generated dynamics within the Palestinian as well as the international civil society which lead to the founding of the BDS movement in 2005 on the first anniversary of the Court's advisory opinion. An important dimension within the tactics of the movement is that next to state and official actors, there is also an important role for civil society to play in lobbying for and advocating enforcement mechanisms and in raising awareness regarding the lack of trials and accountability for Israeli perpetrators of international law. This has been recently exemplified by the establishment of the Russell Tribunal which took place early November 2011 in South Africa to determine whether the state of Israel is committing the crime of apartheid (Russell Tribunal on Palestine 2011). But in particular through the BDS campaigns which aim at imposing broad boycotts and implementing divestment initiatives against the state of Israel similar to those applied to South Africa during the apartheid era and to maintain these non-violent punitive measures until Israel meets all its international legal obligations.

The Call was signed by more than 170 Palestinian civil society organizations, political parties, unions, and councils. Therefore, it represents the largest coalition of civil society organizations in Palestine. The movement is based on a holistic approach, targeting the whole Palestinian populace in the West Bank, the Gaza Strip as well as Palestinians in Israel and the millions of Palestinian refugees in the Diaspora. In this way the BDS Call is the initiative that includes all Palestinians under one umbrella – that is its strength: one movement comprising of all the Palestinian people as a whole and demanding the realization of their full rights.

The overall demands of the BDS Call are enshrined in three pillars that target the rights of the Palestinian people. Based in accordance with international law, the BDS Call demands that Israel:

- Ends its occupation and colonization of all Arab lands occupied in June 1967 and dismantling the Wall.
- Recognizes the fundamental rights of the Arab-Palestinian citizens of Israel to full equality.
- Respects, protects and promotes the rights of Palestinian refugees to return to their homes and properties as stipulated in UN Resolution 194 (PBDSNC 2005).

The BDS Call entails three sections: B for boycott; D for divestment and S for sanctions

Boycott

In the B-section of the BDS Call, the academic and cultural boycott is an instrumental element (Palestinian Campaign for the Academic and Cultural Boycott of Israel (PACBI) 2004). As such the movement asks people of conscious in the world to boycott Israeli cultural and academic institutions that contribute to maintaining, defending or whitewashing the oppression of Palestinians. Therefore, various campaigns and initiatives are launched regularly to encourage academic institutions to severe their ties with Israeli academic institutions that are supporting the occupation, either by being directly involved in creating doctrines for launching attacks and by developing technology for the military or by being indirectly supportive of and/or complicit with the occupation. The academic boycott campaign is gaining momentum and internationally renowned academic figures, such as the physicist Stephen Hawking (discussed below), have joined the Boycott Call. A significant and landmark success in this regard was when the South African University of Johannesburg heavily debated the issue of severing its ties with the Israeli Ben-Gurion University (PBDSNC, 2011). The decision to end ties between the two universities is considered a moral victory since the Palestinian BDS Movement was created following the footprints of the South African one. Furthermore, many student associations and unions worldwide replied to the BDS Call by boycotting Israeli academic institutions. The first academic union in Europe to call for an academic boycott of Israel was the Teachers Union of Ireland, voting unanimously for an academic boycott at its annual congress in 2013. The Teachers Union's Call referred to Israel as an apartheid state and encouraged all members to 'cease all cultural and academic collaboration with Israel including the exchange of scientists, students and academic personalities, as well as all cooperation in research programmes' (Irish Palestine Solidarity Campaign (IPSC) 2013). Another striking example is the American Studies Association (ASA) which voted to endorse the academic boycott of Israeli academic institutions and the motion passed by a majority of 66 per cent (ASA 2013). The ASA has received over 700 new members since its endorsement of the academic boycott of Israeli academic institutions (Horowitz 2014).

Another example is scientist Steven Hawking, who in 2013 cancelled his participation in a conference which was taking place at the Hebrew University in Jerusalem and published an article explaining his careful consideration of the matter of participation in the scientific conference he decided not to take part in it because Israel is in clear violation of international law (Rose 2013). In addition, an important and influential dimension of the boycott is the cultural boycott which targets celebrities such as authors, singers or movie actors and makers; artists in general. Approaching these famous figures generate attention in the media which in turn advances the BDS Call and its overall message. The cultural boycott has received a lot of support worldwide, for example from Alice Walker, Jacques Rancière, Roger Waters, Cassandra Wilson and Ken Loach. Usually artists who are planning to perform in Israel receive letters from the BDS supporters encouraging them to cancel their event/tour/participation. Those letters address the essential reasons of why to join the BDS movement and why to abstain from Israel. If successful, it is important for the movement that the artist in question states the reason for abstaining. Only this way his or her decision might generate support for the overall goal. Some artists however, choose to link their cancelling to technical reasons rather than clearly and openly supporting the Boycott Call.

Divestment

Divestment stands for withdrawing stakes, funds or shares from corporations or institutions complicit in the violation of Palestinian rights. Many multi-million corporations, both Israeli and international either directly support the occupation and colonization of Palestine and/or profit from it. Activists target these corporations and those who have funds or stakes in them and address them to disinvest. These targets are usually approached by a letter-writing campaign with heavy (social-) media exposure. There are also other tactics used in divestment campaigns such as lobbying and shareholder activism (meaning a group of people buy shares in a company to guarantee they have a say in the decision making process in order to address the issue of divestment). The strength of the divestment strategies is to have the targets withdraw their funds and stakes, or severe contracts, or terminate agreements with these corporations that are contributing to the systematic denial and continuous abuse of Palestinian rights. Regardless of the outcome of each divestment campaign and its target, the media coverage and heated debates that follow contribute to the awareness raising regarding the oppression imposed upon the Palestinians and the importance of the BDS campaigns in helping to end this oppression.

The divestment campaign with its many sub-categories is a rapidly growing one and it is becoming mainstream as multi-million worth of stakes and shares are being disinvested from major, internationally renowned, companies due to their complicity with the Israeli occupation. This argument is solidified by many examples similar to the move of a Dutch pension giant (known as PGGM) which divested tens of millions worth of investment from five Israeli banks (Winstanley 2014). The fact that PGGM manages the pensions of 2.5 million people and has assets equivalent to €153 billion, and that this is not a singular example or an isolated incident, is proof that the divestment campaign is having a concrete impact.

Important key actors in the divestment section are the churches and church related organizations. A key momentum for such engagement all around the world was the launch of the *Kairos Palestine* document in 2009 (Kairos Palestine 2009). It was written and launched by Palestinian Christians and is modeled after the Kairos document which was launched in South Africa in 1985. The Kairos Palestine document addresses the 'peace-loving people of the world' and especially the Christian community to actively oppose the occupation and oppression imposed upon the Palestinians. The call discusses the theological justification of the Israeli occupation of Palestine and demands the realization of justice in the conflict as it is the only way to a real peace in the region. Since its launch in 2009, Kairos Palestine has received tremendous support from international groups worldwide and faith-based groups are launching their own reflection and response to the Palestinian call by writing a Kairos document of their own (Kairos Palestine 2009). The Kairos Palestine document, similar to its South African counterpart, is playing an instrumental role amongst the churches and church related organizations in concerting the efforts in the struggle against oppression on a global level. The document also triggers debates within the Christian community in regard to divestment strategies of church funds and stakes in companies supporting and/or profiting from the occupation. The Kairos document addresses the BDS Call and states:

> ...we see boycott and disinvestment as tools of non-violence for justice, peace and security for all...[1]we understand this to integrate the logic of peaceful resistance. These advocacy campaigns must be carried out with courage, openly sincerely proclaiming that their object is not revenge but rather to put an end to the existing evil, liberating both the perpetrators and the victims of injustice. The aim is to free both peoples from extremist positions of the different Israeli governments, bringing both to justice and reconciliation. In this spirit and with this dedication we will eventually reach the longed-for resolution to our problems, as indeed happened in South Africa and with many other liberation movements in the world.
>
> (Kairos Palestine 2009: section 4.2.6.)

The result is that church councils are voting on divestment, with an increasingly growing group of churches passing the vote.

Sanctions

Sanctions are a powerful tool to force a member of the international community to adhere to international laws and principles. The European Union defines sanctions as, 'instruments of a diplomatic or economic nature which seek to bring about a change in activities or policies such as violations of international law or human rights, or policies that do not respect the rule of law or democratic principles... Such measures imposed by the EU may target governments of third countries, or non-state entities and individuals' (European Union External Action n.d.). Sanctions are official state policies and could include diplomatic sanctions – withdrawal of diplomatic missions or staff; economic sanctions – full or partial ban on trade goods including arms embargos; and sport sanctions – denying national athletes to compete in international events (Chesterman and Pouligny 2003). Next to these more traditional forms options include the imposition of travel bans or the freezing of assets.

International wrongful acts or crimes might trigger specific state obligations, most importantly not to render aid or assistance in maintaining the situation created by the act in question. For example, in relation to South Africa's illegal presence in Namibia, the ICJ ruled that states had a duty 'to abstain from entering into economic and other forms of relationship or dealings with South Africa on behalf of or concerning Namibia which may entrench its authority over the territory' (ICJ 1970). Regarding Israel, the United Nations General Assembly called in 1982 for financial and diplomatic sanctions against Israel in a resolution relating to the Golan Heights (UN 1982). Even though the resolution has not been adopted and/or enforced; calls for sanctions against Israel are increasingly accepted in international forums. The ICJ has emphasized in its 2004 decision on the legal consequences of the construction of a Wall in the occupied territories of Palestine the need to refer the situation in Palestine to the relevant bodies, 'the United Nations, and especially the General Assembly and the Security Council, should consider what further action is required to bring to an end the illegal situation' (ICJ 2004). More and more states, state officials and private companies are aware of the possible legal consequences their corporations with Israel may entail; thus the Call for sanctions against Israel will become louder.

The Palestinian Campaign for the Academic and Cultural Boycott of Israel (PACBI)

There has undoubtedly a degree of confusion resulting from the variety of different boycott proposals that have been aired at different times. The crucial point is that the boycott advocated by PACBI, and supported by BRICUP, is an *institutional* boycott.

PACBI was the accumulated build-up of various calls for boycott of Israeli academic and cultural institutions worldwide. Since 2000, groups and individuals have been calling for a boycott of Israel until it complies with international law in its dealings and policies toward the Palestinian people. Academics and academic institutions in Europe and the United States have started to realize that Israeli academic institutions, which are mostly controlled by the state, are contributing either directly or indirectly to the policies of oppression and thus have started calling for a boycott of those Israeli academic (and cultural) institutions as a means of pressuring Israel to adhere to international law. In July 2004, a group of Palestinian intellectuals and academics issued a call of boycott of Israel. The call, which was signed by major academic and cultural groups, individuals, networks and organizations, is comprised of the following (PACBI 2004).

'Call for academic and cultural boycott of Israel'

Whereas Israel's colonial oppression of the Palestinian people, which is based on Zionist ideology, comprises the following:

- Denial of its responsibility for the Al-Nakbah – in particular the waves of ethnic cleansing and dispossession that created the Palestinian refugee problem – and therefore refusal to accept the inalienable rights of the refugees and displaced stipulated in and protected by international law.
- Military occupation and colonization of the West Bank (including East Jerusalem) and Gaza since 1967, in violation of international law and UN resolutions.
- The entrenched system of racial discrimination and segregation against the Palestinian citizens of Israel, which resembles the defunct apartheid system in South Africa.

Since Israeli academic institutions (mostly state controlled) and the vast majority of Israeli intellectuals and academics have either contributed directly to maintaining, defending or otherwise justifying the above forms of oppression, or have been complicit in them through their silence. Given that all forms of international intervention have until now failed to force Israel to comply with international law or to end its repression of the Palestinians, which has manifested itself in many forms, including siege, indiscriminate killing, wanton destruction and the racist colonial Wall.

In view of the fact that people of conscience in the international community of scholars and intellectuals have historically shouldered the moral responsibility to fight injustice, as exemplified in their struggle to abolish apartheid in South Africa through diverse forms of boycott. Recognizing that the growing international boycott movement against Israel has expressed the need for a Palestinian frame of reference outlining guiding principles. In the spirit of international solidarity, moral consistency and resistance to injustice and oppression, we, Palestinian academics and intellectuals, call upon our colleagues in the international community to comprehensively and consistently boycott all Israeli academic and cultural institutions as a contribution to the struggle to end Israel's occupation, colonization and system of apartheid, by applying the following:

1   Refrain from participation in any form of academic and cultural cooperation, collaboration or joint projects with Israeli institutions.
2   Advocate a comprehensive boycott of Israeli institutions at the national and international levels, including suspension of all forms of funding and subsidies to these institutions.
3   Promote divestment and disinvestment from Israel by international academic institutions.
4   Work toward the condemnation of Israeli policies by pressing for resolutions to be adopted by academic, professional and cultural associations and organizations.
5   Support Palestinian academic and cultural institutions directly without requiring them to partner with Israeli counterparts as an explicit or implicit 'condition for such support' (PACBI 2004).

Israeli universities (mostly state controlled) are complicit with the occupation and the policies of atrocities committed against the Palestinian people. For instance, Technion is a most prestigious scientific institute in Israel that prides itself in the development of Israeli weapon systems, especially drone technology, which are deployed by the Israeli military targeting Palestinians in Gaza and the West Bank. Moreover, Tel Aviv University designs weapons for the Israeli army and also houses the Institute for National Security Studies (INSS) which develops doctrines of attacks and military strategies for the Israeli army like the 'doctrine of disproportionate force' used by the Israeli army in several attacks on Gaza. Furthermore, The Hebrew University has an army base on its campus, which is partly built on confiscated Palestinians land. These universities are also promoting gratitude and appreciation towards students who serve in the Israeli army, and are applying a system of economic merits and scholarship to those who serve in the army.

The academic complicity goes beyond the collaboration between academic institutions and the occupation, but also includes academics themselves. Tel Aviv University professor Avraham Katzir argues that:

One of the things which helps the State of Israel [...] is the fact that each one of us is both an Israeli citizen and working in these fields [...] I'm an academic at university and I've also done my [military service], and I was also at [state arms manufacturer] RAFAEL for some years. All of those things come together; we're helping one another – something which doesn't happen elsewhere]; I've been in the US and Europe, and there is a disconnect between the workshops and the army; they hate the army! [With us], I think that we succeed by virtue of the fact that we help one another so much.

(Katzir 2009 cited in SOAS Palestine Society 2009)

Tel Aviv University academic and Israel Prize laureate in Philosophy AsaKasher has also co-authored a code of conduct for the Israeli army promoting a 'moral justification' behind the killing of innocent civilians while targeting 'terrorists'.

There are numerous registered accounts of repressing freedom of expression or political activism of students, both of Palestinian descend or anti-Zionist Jews who express a different opinion than that of the allowed for spectrum of activism. A study by the Alternative Information Center about Israeli universities and their complicity with the occupation indicated several accounts of apprehension, official letters, monitoring of political activists, harassment and detention of students on various occasions regarding opinions or activism against the policies of occupation and violations committed by the Israeli state (Keller 2009).

The way forward

The urgency imperative is an important aspect of the struggle against Israeli atrocities. If we compare, as an example only, the attacks on Gaza during 2010–2015, we see a pattern of a rising use of force, a rising disregard for human life and the destruction of public infrastructure, as well as an increasing targeting of civilians including children. The Israeli public opinion polls are showing support for such policies; the Israelis are shifting more and more to the right and far-right, the rise of extremist voices inside Israel who are calling for the rape, murder, expulsion and/or transfer of the Palestinian people is a worrying indicator of the graveness of the situation (Cook 2014). The striking fact in this regard is that Israeli politicians (MP's as well as ministers) are calling for such atrocities to be committed, as noted in their social media outcries (Cook 2014). Every delay in changing this situation is costing the Palestinian people more of their lives and is pushing the situation in a violent abyss which will have severe percussions on the entire region.

This is why the Palestinians are calling on the international community and mainly on people of conscious worldwide to support, endorse, join and promote the BDS call in order to isolate Israel on all levels in the international arena until it complies with international law and ends its brutal oppression of the Palestinian people. BDS is a strategic tool of resistance which offers a non-violent mean to combating one of the gravest injustices in our world.

In this sense, academic boycott is an important tool in this struggle. Israel uses its academic institutions for developing weapons and forming of policies and doctrines for maintaining the occupation on the one hand, and to whitewash its image worldwide by engaging in cooperation and mutual projects with the academia on an international level, on the other. Academia for Israel is thus an important field wherein it seeks to strengthen its position, rallies for sympathetic crowds, as well as lobby to maintain a positive image already being tarnished due to its policies of aggression towards the Palestinian people.

In this light, the African National Congress (ANC) Secretary General announced in September 2014, '[we are] joining the call for [a] cultural, academic and education boycott of Israel, including travel bans for members and leaders of the ANC, the alliance, members of Cabinet, Members of Parliament and government officials' (PBDSNC 2014).

In a statement concerning the situation in Palestine, the ANC joined the boycott movement. The South African Call for boycott was a moral victory to the Palestinian BDS movement considering the resemblance between the two experiences. While the South African struggle to end apartheid ended with the collapse of the regime, the South Africans' struggle to end international impunity, complicity and aggression continues to this time with the Palestinian people and their supporters. The struggle for Palestinian rights must be seen as a global struggle for rights. In the words of Nelson Mandela, 'we know too well that our struggle is not complete without the freedom of the Palestinians. Justice is nowhere if there is no justice in Palestine' (African National Congress 1997).

The overall situation in Palestine reflects elements of oppression everywhere in the world. Palestinians face colonialism, racism, apartheid, exploitation of their natural resources and ethnic cleansing. All people have the right to resist such oppression and to strive for their inalienable right to self-determination. The preamble to the Universal Declaration of Human Rights recognizes that: 'whereas it is essential, if man is not to be compelled to have recourse, as a last resort, to rebellion against tyranny and oppression, that human rights should be protected by the rule of law' (UN 1948). Furthermore, General Assembly Resolution 2625 'affirms the legitimacy of the struggles of peoples under colonial and alien domination recognized as being entitled to the right of self-determination to restore to themselves that right by any means at their disposal' (UN 1978).

The BDS Movement with its campaigns, notably PACBI is a non-violent form of resistance aiming, as seen above, to hold Israel accountable for its international law violations and to ensure durable solution in accordance with international law and standard. Israel will only adhere to international law if it gets isolated on all levels instead of the support it enjoys. The international civil society has a duty to step in, especially in this case where on official state level inability or unwillingness is noticeable, to end the injustice in Palestine. The practice of endorsing, promoting and joining the BDS Call is a conscience choice for non-violent resistance and for supporting justice and equality. Simply speaking, the concept of the 'rule of law' should surpass the 'survival of the fittest' concept. Justice is not a selective principle; it is absolute. Therefore it should be applied everywhere and to everyone. Injustice in Palestine is injustice everywhere and the conscious citizens of the world have a duty to end this injustice.

References

African National Congress (1997) *Address by President Nelson Mandela at the International Day of Solidarity with the Palestinian people* http://anc.org.za/show. php?id=3384 [Accessed 31 December 2014].

Al-Haq (2012) *The Annexation Wall and its associated regime* http://www.alhaq.org/publications/publications-index/item/the-annexation-wall-and-its-associated-regime [Accessed 31 December 2014].

Alqasis, A. (2012) 'The ongoing Nakba – the continuous forcible displacement of the Palestinian people', *Al-Majdal*, 50: 7–15.

Alternative Tourism Group Study Center ATG (2014) *Raising awareness: tourist locations occupied post 1967 by Israel* http://www.atg.ps/resources/file/pages/Raising%20awarness%20on%20tourists%20sites%20final%20version.pdf [Accessed on 08 June 2015].

American Studies Association (ASA) (2013) 'ASA National Council calls for boycott of Israeli academic institutions', *Academic and Community Activism Caucus* http://www.theasa.net/caucus_activism/item/american_studies_association_calls_for_academic_boycott_of_israel/ [Accessed 31 December 2014].

British Committee for Universities of Palestine (BRICUP) (2007) *Why boycott Israeli universities*, London: BRICUP, http://www.bricup.org.uk/documents/WhyBoycott IsraeliUniversities.pdf

Chesterman, S. and Pouligny, B. (2003) 'Are sanctions meant to work? The politics of creating and implementing sanctions through the United Nations', *Global Governance*, 9(4): 503–518.

Coles, S. (2008) *Tourism, culture and development: hopes, dreams and realities in East Indonesia*, Clevedon: Channel View Publications.

Cook, J. (2014) *Call for genocide enter Israeli mainstream*, Palestine, Intifada Voice of Palestine http://www.intifada-palestine.com/2014/07/calls-genocide-enter-israeli-mainstream/ [Accessed 08 June 2015].

Dugard, J. (2007) *Report of the special rapporteur on the situation of human rights in the Palestinian territories occupied since 1967*, United Nations, General Assembly (A/HRC/4/17) http://unispal.un.org/UNISPAL.NSF/0/B59FE224D4A4587D8525728B00 697DAA [Accessed 31 December 2014].

European Union External Action (n.d.) *Sanctions policy*, Brussels: European External Action Service http://eeas.europa.eu/cfsp/sanctions/index_en.htm [Accessed 31 December 2014].

Falk, R. (2011) *Report of the special rapporteur on the situation of human rights in the Palestinian territories occupied since 1967*, United Nations, General Assembly (A/HRC/16/72). http://unispal.un.org/UNISPAL.NSF/0/A72012A31C1116EC8525782C0 0547DD4 [Accessed 31 December 2014].

Glaesser, D. (2003) *Crisis management in the tourism industry*, Burlington, MA: Butterworth-Heinemann.

Hall, C.M. and Ringer, G. (2000) 'Tourism in Cambodia, Laos and Myanmar: from terrorism to tourism', in *Tourism in South and South-East Asia: critical perspectives*, (eds) C.M. Hall and S.J. Page, pp.178–194, Oxford: Butterworth-Heinemann.

Henderson, J.C. (2003) 'The politics of tourism in Myanmar', *Current Issues in Tourism* 6(2): 97–118.

Holden, A. (2003) *Tourism studies and the social science*, London: Routledge.

Horowitz, A. (2014) *American Studies Association adds over 700 new members since Israel boycott call*, Chicago, IL: Mondoweiss http://mondoweiss.net/2014/04/american-association-boycott [Accessed 31 December 2014].

Hudson, S. (2007) 'To go or not to go? Ethical perspectives on tourism in an outpost of tyranny', *Journal of Business Ethics*, 76: 385–396.

International Court of Justice (ICJ) (1970) *Legal consequences for states of the continued presence of South Africa in Namibia (South-West Africa) notwithstanding security council resolution 276*, The Hague, The Netherlands: ICJ http://www.icj-cij.org/docket/files/53/5597.pdf [Accessed 31 December 2014].

International Court of Justice (ICJ) (2004) *Legal consequences of the construction of a wall in the Occupied Palestinian Territory*, The Hague, The Netherlands: ICJ http://www.icj-cij.org/docket/files/131/1671.pdf [Accessed 31 December 2014].

Irish Palestine Solidarity Campaign (IPSC) (2013) *Teachers Union of Ireland calls for academic boycott of Israel in unanimous vote*, Dublin, Ireland: IPSC http://www.ipsc.ie/press-releases/teachers-union-of-ireland-calls-for-academic-boycott-of-israel-in-unanimous-vote-first-academic-union-in-europe-to-do-so [Accessed 31 December 2014].

Kairos Palestine (2009) *A moment of truth: a word of faith, hope, and love from the heart of Palestinian suffering*, Bethlehem, Palestine http://www.kairospalestine.ps/sites/default/Documents/English.pdf [Accessed 31 December 2014].

Keller, U. (2009) *Academic boycott of Israel: the Economy of the Occupation*. Socioeconmic Bulletin: 23, Jerusalem: The Alternative Information Centre. http://www.bdsmovement.net/files/2011/02/EOO23-24-Web.pdf [Accessed 31 December 2014].

Masalha, N. (1992) *Expulsion of the Palestinians: the concept of 'transfer' in Zionist political thought, 1882–1948,* USA: Institute for Palestine Studies.

Micheletti, M., Follesdal, A. and Stolle, D. (2006) 'Introduction: the market as a site of politics', in M. Micheletti, A. Follesdal and D. Stolle (eds) *Politics, products and markets: exploring political consumerism past and present*, New Brunswick: Transaction Publishing.

Palestinian BDS National Committee (PBDSNC) (2005) *Palestinian Civil Society Call for BDS* http://www.bdsmovement.net/call [Accessed 31 December 2014].

Palestinian BDS National Committee (PBDSNC) (2011) *University of Johannesburg ends Israeli links* http://www.bdsmovement.net/2011/uj-bgu-5379 [Accessed 31 December 2014].

Palestinian BDS National Committee (PBDSNC) (2014) *ANC joins call for complete boycott of Israel including travel bans in solidarity with Palestine* http://www.bdsmovement.net/2014/anc-joins-call-for-complete-boycott-of-israel-including-travel-bans-in-solidarity-with-palestine-12709 [Accessed 31 December 2014].

Palestinian Campaign for the Academic and Cultural Boycott of Israel (PACBI) (2004) *Call for academic and cultural boycott of Israel*, Ramallah, Palestine http://pacbi.org/etemplate.php?id=869 [Accessed 31 December 2014].

Reeves, L. (2003) *To boycott or not to boycott: the ethics behind your travel dollars*, Berkeley, CA: Ethical Traveler http://www.ethicaltraveler.org/2013/04/to-boycott-or-not-to-boycott-the-ethics-behind-your-travel-dollars/ [Accessed 16 January 2015].

Rose, H. (2013) *Stephen Hawking's boycott hits Israel where it hurts: science*, London: The Guardian. http://www.theguardian.com/science/political-science/2013/may/13/stephen-hawking-boycott-israel-science [Accessed on 31 December 2014].

Russell Tribunal on Palestine (2011) *Third international session – Cape Town. South Africa Session – full findings* http://www.russelltribunalonpalestine.com/en/sessions/south-africa/south-africa-session-%e2%80%94-full-findings [Accessed 31 December 2014].

Seccartini, L. (2006) *Why boycotting: the reasons behind fair-trade consumption acts in Italy*, University of Urbino: Laboratory of Social and Political Studies.

SOAS Palestine Society (2009) 'Urgent briefing paper. Tel Aviv University – a leading Israeli military research centre', *Tel Aviv University Review*, Winter http://electronicintifada.net/files/090708-soas-palestine-society.pdf [Accessed 31 December 2014].

Stolle, D., Hooghe, M. and Micheletti, M. (2005) 'Politics in the supermarket: political consumerism as a form of political participation', *International Political Science Review*, 26: 245–269.

United Nations (1948) *Universal declaration of human rights*, New York: United Nations http://www.un.org/en/documents/udhr/ [Accessed 31 December 2014].

United Nations General Assembly (1978) *Importance of the universal realization of the right of peoples to self-determination and of the speedy granting of independence to colonial countries and peoples for the effective guarantee and observance of human rights*, New York: United Nations General Assembly Resolution A/RES/33/24 http://unispal.un.org/unispal.nsf/a06f2943c226015c85256c40005d359c/d7340f04b82a2cb085256a9d006ba47a?OpenDocument [Accessed 31 December 2014].

United Nations General Assembly (1982) *The situation in the occupied Arab territories*, New York: United Nations General Assembly Resolution GA A/ES-9/PV.4 Online http://unispal.un.org/unispal.nsf/a06f2943c226015c85256c40005d359c/6085dc3bb28cb9b205256561005be5e3?OpenDocument [Accessed on 31 December 2014].

Winstanley, A. (2014) *Dutch pension giant divests from Israeli banks*, Chicago, IL: The Electronic Intifada http://electronicintifada.net/blogs/asa-winstanley/dutch-pension-giant-divests-israeli-banks [Accessed on 31 December 2014].

12 The folds of place

Re-visiting questions of travel in Israel/Palestine

Waleed Hazbun

Introduction

Travel writing functions as a form of mapping with words. These words usually combine direct observations with personal reflections. Both can be highly subjective. Most colonial-era travel writing, and much of it today, presents partial, fragmented observations that are too often extended to serve as maps of complex landscapes (Lisle 2006). In a similar way, the experience of tourists, especially when directed by an ideologically-framed guide or tour group, can similarly promote the experience of travel as a colonial form of mapping. Raja Shehadeh (2008: 47) observes that travel writing about the 'Holy Land' reflects 'travelers and colonizers who see the land through the prism of the biblical past, overlooking present realities'. More recently, an Israeli–North American organization Birthright Israel, has funded ten-day educational visits to Israel for young Jews 'with the hope that engagement with Israel would strengthen participants' Jewish identities and counter the threat to Jewish continuity posed by assimilation and intermarriage' (Saxe *et al.* 2002: ix, but see also Joffe-Walt 2007). In these cases, the experience of travel seeks to foster personal attachment to a distant place. The experience of those places, however, operates in a shallow register of an exclusive attachment, blind to complex rival attachments and indigenous communities inhabiting those places.

In this chapter, I explore how travel can, in contrast, offer a more complex experience of place. While a journey may take place in one moment in time, the 'place' visited can be viewed and experienced as reflecting multiple moments in time. When one visits a Greco–Roman ruin in the Mediterranean region, the viewer might imagine a civilization at the height of its power, wealth, and artistic creativity, but at the same time, the sight of decay might also remind one of its era of decline. Moreover, the reuse of some blocks of stone in a nearby structure might reflect reappropriation by later civilizations or even the dwellings of a recent community. Thus travelers can visit places like archeologists who see the layers of history built one on top of (the ruins) of the previous. Archeologists, however, usually select a layer at a time to focus on, with each layer representing a piece of a broader picture set in a temporal frame composed of fragments gathered from other places. In the writing of traditional narrative history, these horizontal pictures can be assembled like a moving picture to tell a story through time.

In contrast to the archeologists' or historians' approaches, travel writing can narrate a palimpsest, composed of views and memories from multiple eras, as if reading down through layers across time. Iain Chambers (2008) offers such an approach in his cultural history of the Mediterranean. He presents the region as the hybrid product of cultural and material flows that resist the Cartesian mapping of borders and linear notions of progress. To do this, Chambers (2008: 18) follows the baroque logic of 'the fold' as developed by French theorist Gilles Deleuze, according to which a portrayal 'acquires depth when it is bent and deviated by excluded rhythms and dislocating narratives'. Thus unlike the typical archeological excavation, such an approach attempts to map 'co-presences', where layers of history seem to fold on top each other and where there is no clear beginnings and ends. In a wonderful example of the productive merging of history, cultural critique, and travel writing, Chambers's text is closely interwoven with his travels and experiences of place.

The history of the Israeli–Palestinian conflict and the Palestinian experience is rarely told through a similar lens, though this region is part and parcel of the heterogeneous Mediterranean landscape depicted by Chambers. Most discussions of the Israeli–Palestinian conflict and the post-1948 Palestinian experience center around stories shaped by the rival territorial bases of Zionist and Palestinian nationalist identities that hold mutually-exclusive understandings of attachments to the same territory. At the same time, efforts to resolve the Israeli–Palestinian conflict – from the 1947 United Nations partition plan to the Oslo peace process of the 1990s – have tried to undo the folds of history and experience. To address the mutually-exclusive understandings of attachments to the same territory, peace-making efforts have promoted territorial partition that is giving each party a separate space to define their own exclusive territorial attachments.

Such partitions, however, require each side to suppress their attachments extending outside that space and across the partition line. To do so requires a seemingly permanent unfolding of multiple strata of history to create a single layer of the present on which to draw a line, either ignoring or cutting through the layers at lower levels. This chapter attempts to show how writing about contemporary experiences of travel in Israel/Palestine can depict a folded history of places that attempts to recognize and accommodate co-presences and their political implications. In the process, the chapter tells a spatially-inflected history of the rise and fall of the Israeli–Palestinian peace process.

I begin with a recap of the rise of the Oslo peace process and describe the new forms and experiences of tourism and travel it enabled. I note how as Israeli tourism to Palestinian Arab villages increased, these experiences, framed as 'ethnic tourism', were constructed to offer a seemingly un-folded landscape for Jewish Israeli travelers. The chapter then moves on to survey Palestinian experiences of travel within Israel/Palestine. Drawing from the account of his daughter, I note how Palestinian-American academic Ibrahim Abu-Lughod, a native of Jaffa (Yafa), late in life 'returned' to Palestine to teach at a Palestinian university in the West Bank at the beginning of the Oslo peace process. Abu-Lughod sought to live in the present, with Jaffa now transformed into an Israeli city, while seeing the half-ruins of the past. In parallel, the chapter also explores the writings of fellow Palestinian-American academic Edward Said, who at first seeing the West Jerusalem house he was born in was unable to enter. He had trouble processing the folds of experience. Years later he came to consider the meaning and implications of such co-presences in Israeli and Palestinian experiences. Rejecting the notion of unfolding through partition or another round of displacement and forgetting, he came to suggest that the interwoven histories and overlapping spaces inhabited by Palestinians and Israelis Jews could only be accommodated in some form of bi-national state.

The last text considered is *Palestinian Walks* by the lawyer and activist Raja Shehadeh (2008). It recounts a series of journeys he has made through the natural landscape of the Palestine. These narratives recount stories of places with their multilayer complexity. Like the other Palestinian authors, rather than mirror exclusivist Zionist claims to territory with a set of Palestinian counter claims and displacement strategies, he highlights how the Oslo peace process never, in fact, unfolded space and partitioned the land, but enabled the extension of the settlement project and actions by settlers which have increasingly encroached on Palestinian spaces and livelihoods. This approach leads him to a complex, nuance position that rejects exclusivist territorial attachments while at the same time refuses to deny an Israeli settler's appreciation of the natural landscape. Like Said, Shehadeh was an early Palestinian advocate for the two state solution, but through his experiencing of the impact of the Oslo process has had on the experience of Palestinians and landscape of Palestine, Shehadeh finds his agency stripped bare and his domestic dwelling no longer a place for quite retreat. Rather than suggesting a means or structure for resolution, his text maps the increasingly complex and problematic folds that define then Palestinian experience.

Reimagining the geography of Israel/Palestine

In the early 1990s, the US-sponsored Madrid peace conference launched a series of multilateral meetings on issues such as regional economic cooperation that helped foster a new wave of thinking about the future political and economic geography of the Middle East. The 1993 Israeli–PLO Declaration of Principles and the ensuing 'Oslo peace process' led to the establishment of the Palestinian Authority with control over most of Gaza and most Palestinian population centers on the West Bank. This breakthrough helped give rise to the so-called 'New Middle East' vision. Proponents of this vision, most notably the Israeli Foreign Minister Shimon Peres, argued that Arab-Israeli peace could generate mutual economic benefits that would solidify closer interstate relations by forging shared material and strategic interests between the governments and their respective private sectors and societies (Peres 1993). A critical feature of this vision was to be open borders with a regional transportation infrastructure. Tourism was widely viewed as the sector that would most rapidly see the realization of this vision (Peres 1993; Twite and Baskin 1994; Clawson 1994). In October 1994, Jordan and Israel signed a peace treaty that established a path-breaking framework for regional economic cooperation and tourism development (see Hazbun 2008). Meanwhile, Israeli and Palestinian negotiators worked out an interterm agreement giving expanded territorial powers to the Palestinian Authority.

While the Oslo Process negotiators' maps specified a complex series of spaces and borders demarking gradations of control and zones of mobility, tourism promoters and travelers began envisioning a contiguous territory in which the green line between Israel and the West Bank disappeared (Stein 2008: 24-28). The dominant lines on such maps were not the longstanding militarized borders. Rather these maps projected a new era of cross-border travel routes and tourists itineraries. Within the idiom of tourist brochures and maps drawn up by the Israel tourism ministry seeking to advance the cause of normalization between Israel and its Arab neighbors, the legends of theses maps – be it the footsteps of Christ or colonial era guided tours – present them as resuscitating memories of a past era of regional travel before the bordering of states.

Territory and memory

These new maps of a projected future, however, did more to suppress memories than invoke pre-Mandate era cultures of travel. In their effort to undo the folds of memory that define the experiences of Palestinians and Israelis, the map makers of the 'New Middle East' seemed to ignore how territory and memory are closely interwoven. As Gil Hochberg (2006: 49) observes, 'Like most national conflicts' the Israeli–Palestinian conflict 'is articulated primarily in terms of a "territorial battle": a war carried out in the name of rights of possession over land. Such "rights", however, are themselves a matter of memory'. Memories and practices of remembering have played a critical function in the dynamics of the Israeli–Palestinian conflict. While particular events are key signposts in that landscape of memory, including the Holocaust and the Palestinian Al-Nakbah of 1948, just as critical are memories and representations of territory and places. For Palestinians, many of these memories are of places in pre-1948 Palestine, many of which were destroyed and erased from future maps.

What is often not fully recognized is that the Oslo process was based on the notion of partition but also on forgetting. In the midst of international enthusiasm for the Arab–Israeli peace process in late 1993, Anton Shammas, a Palestinian novelist who grew up in Israel and writes in Hebrew, noted that as part of embracing the Oslo process, Palestinians were being asked to 'master the art of forgetting'. In a short essay for the *New York Times,* Shammas (1993: 33) writes that Palestinians 'now have to forget the names of those 400 villages razed in 1948; they now have to forget the way Yafa is spelled and forget the other Arab names of the land; they now have to forget their cartography and start memorizing the Israeli nomenclator's map'. Shammas correctly read the geopolitics of the Oslo process. While requiring Israeli accommodation of Palestinian autonomy in Gaza and the West Bank, viewed by some Zionists as part of 'Greater Israel', Palestinians were required to sever their attachments to territory within Israel proper (referred to as '48 Palestine'). Not only was this 'forgetting' a means to overwrite the memory of displacement required to declare a resolution of the 'Palestinian question', it was also essential for granting Israelis a sense of security over their own exclusive attachment to their territory and the legitimacy of the maintenance of Israel as Jewish state.

Following Nietzsche, several political theorists have noted the role that forgetting can play in helping to 'overcome the scars of intense violence and conflict' (Linda Bishai cited in Hochberg 2006: 51). With the view that political conflict and violence is often driven by efforts to sustain fixed identities, William E. Connolly emphasizes 'the political efficacy of forgetting for opening new social spaces from which new configurations for the future and new social identities may emerge so as to transgress the perpetual attachment to suffering, allow change, and promote the process of social "becoming"' (cited in Hochberg 2006: 51).

The Oslo process, however, abandoned the goal of seeking new, shared aspects of identity and, worse, it constrained the ability of Palestinians to fully express and realize their own identity. In particular, the Oslo peace process failed to recognize differences between (nevertheless interwoven) Zionist and Palestinians modes of territorial attachment. The Zionist identity that has sustained Israeli nation-building called for Jews in the diaspora, including those from Arab countries, to abandon their old ties and livelihoods. Not only did Zionism call on Jews to make Israel their exclusive territorial attachment, it defined places outside the newly secured Zionist homeland as spaces of insecurity. The Oslo process, however, failed to remove Israeli settlements in the West Bank and secure Palestinians a homeland, a sovereign state, or a space of security. Meanwhile, territorial attachments to '48 Palestine' remain an essential component of Palestinian identity defined by displacement from those spaces after 1948 during events regarded by Arabs as 'Al-Nakbah' or the catastrophe (Sa'di and Lila Abu-Lughod 2007). Abandoning those attachments would not help settle claims between Israelis and Palestinians. A central feature missing in most efforts to promote a 'two state solution' is that Palestinian identity requires the realization and public recognition of Palestinian attachment to '48 Palestine' which is at the heart of the Palestinian demand for the 'right of return'.

Within the structure of the Oslo Process, Jewish Israelis came to recognize, consume, and 'desire' places, cultural tourist experiences, and foods associated with Israel's own (Palestinian) Arab community (see Stein 2008). These practices, however, took place with in highly de-contextualized and seemingly apolitical experiences that functioned to shore-up rather than challenge aspects of Zionist nationalist mythology. In the 1990s, Jewish Israelis became increasingly interested in what was referred to as 'ethnic tourism' within the Palestinian towns and villages of the Galilee. Stein (2008: 46) views these practices as representing 'a recalibration of the terms of [Palestinian] symbolic inclusion within the [Israeli] nation-state'. Noting that state officials who promoted ethnic tourism and most Israelis drawn to it viewed themselves as enacting peace and coexistence, Stein (2008: 48) highlights its limits as 'Most Jewish Israeli clients sought Arab culture stripped of recognizable Palestinian histories and sentiments.' The experience of ethnic tourism, in fact, naturalized the rural, isolated, and underdeveloped characteristics of these communities which can be understood as, in part, legacies of previous Israeli state policies of neglect, repression, and dispossession that the new era of peaceful coexistence sought to bury. Stein (2008: 73) notes how efforts to present more 'authentic' tourist experiences – consisting of home cooked meals, private musical performances, and picturesque village landscapes – helped associate Palestinian spaces with 'interiority' and worked to 'fix Palestinians in space' where they seem naturally rooted thus mollifying Jewish Israeli fears about the accommodation required for coexistence.

Ibrahim Abu-Lughod: seeing half-ruins

To offer a view from inside the folds, I consider the experience of the Palestinian-American academic Ibrahim Abu-Lughod, a native of Jaffa, who late in life 'returned' to Palestine to teach at a Palestinian university in the West Bank at the beginning of the Oslo peace process. Abu-Lughod's daughter, the anthropologist Lila Abu-Lughod (2007), writes about his ability to live in the present, with Jaffa now transformed into an Israeli city, while seeing the 'half-ruins' of the past. Ibrahim Abu-Lughod became a refugee in 1948 and eventually made his life in the United States as a professor of political science and political activist for Palestinian causes. Like many diaspora Palestinians, for most of his life he refused to visit Israel not wanting to see how Israel had transformed his homeland. He did not wish to experience the folded space of post-1948 Palestine. But in the early 1990s, as he grew older, he had a change of heart and 'returned' (in a sense) to the West Bank and taught at the leading Palestinian university Bir Zeit. From there, still carrying a US passport, he could visit his childhood neighborhood in Jaffa, now in Israel, and become acquainted with the Palestinians who still lived there. He visited at least once every few weeks (Segev 2001). As Lila Abu-Lughod (2007: 79) explains, her father's move:

> changed his experience of...the Al-Nakbah, 'the catastrophe'. He inserted his memories of Palestine directly into the present, into a living history. My father's insertion of memory into the historical present made possible a different knowledge and identification for his children as well.

Ibrahim Abu-Lughod's return to Palestine was made possible – and meaningful – by his ability to reconnect with the places he and his family held attachment to. He developed an eye for seeing 'half ruins' from inside the fold. He was able to look out at contemporary Jaffa and see the traces of pre-1948 Palestine and the existing Palestinian community in Israel, along with the present reality of modern Tel Aviv and Israeli society.

Abu-Lughod died in 2001 and his family, undeterred by threats from Israeli Shin Bet security service, was able to follow his wishes and have him buried in Jaffa next to his father. Abu-Lughod left instructions that if this was not possible, his body should be burned and ashes scattered in the Jaffa cemetery. A small story in the Israeli daily *Ha'aretz* reported that at the funeral 'everyone noted that

Abu-Lughod was realizing his right of return – even if after his death' (Segev 2001: 1). The fact that Abu-Lughod could only become rooted in his hometown after death reflects something about the Palestinian displacement. Abu-Lughod's friend Edward Said (2001/2) wrote that 'so much in [Abu-Lughod's life] bears out the Palestinian situation in all its irresolution'. While noting that unlike himself, Abu-Lughod seemed to feel at home in Ramallah, at his death 'He was still unfulfilled and unsettled'. Like their mutual friend the late Pakistani-American Eqbal Ahmad, Said (2001/2: 1) noted the men 'didn't actually go back home. In trying to capture their memory, one confines and solidifies it, and in this sense betrays it: What these men stood for was energy, mobility, discovery and risk'. Returning to Ramallah in life, and Jaffa in death, only generated new folds. Once folded, such memories of place can only be re-folded in new ways.

Edward Said: nomadic attachments and the experience/right of return

Forty-five years after his extended family was forced to leave Jerusalem, Edward Said returned with his own family (and his friend Abu-Lughod) for a visit to see the house in the Talbieh neighborhood of West Jerusalem were he was born (Said 1992). During this visit Said could not initially insert his memories into the present and see the half-ruins as Abu-Lughod did. Said literally sought to visit the house he was born in using a map his cousin had drawn from memory. Palestinian refugees tend to cling to such mental maps that represent a nearly buried layer of history. Many Palestinian families construct memory books that collect such maps, artifacts, and oral histories to preserve the memory of their 'lost', often destroyed, homes as well as the landscapes and geographies of pre-1948 Palestine (see Davis 2007). In his recounting of this visit, Said (1992: 50) noted 'only by sticking very carefully to this map did we finally locate [the house]'. When he got to the house, he could point to the room he was born in but he could not get himself to enter the house. He would write that this house 'symbolized the eerie finality of a history…Palestine as I had know it was over' (Said 1992: 50).

Said's first visit was conducted just before the 1993 agreement between Israel and the PLO that launched the Oslo peace process. Said would condemn that process as a form of Palestinian capitulation that would fail to achieve Palestinian rights of self-determination. Many would later recognize his warning was valid. It was a decade later, however, while writing his memories of his early life, that Said would come to rethink his relationship to his past. In an interview with an Israeli newspaper, he noted:

> It was then, while looking back, that I realized that the world I grew up in, the world of my parents, of Cairo and Beirut and pre-1948 Talbieh, was a made-up world. It wasn't a real world. It didn't have the kind of objective solidity that I wanted it to have. For many years, I mourned the loss of this world. I truly mourned it. But now I discovered the possibility of reinterpreting it. And I realized that it's true not only for me, but for most of us: we move

through life shedding the past – the forgotten, the lost. I understood that my role was to tell and retell a story of loss where the notion of repatriation, of a return to a home, is basically impossible.

(Said 2001: 50-51)

Thus, in one way, Said recognizes the loss, and pushes the past into a memory of the 'Palestine' where/when he was born. But while Shammas notes Palestinians have been asked to learn to live in a new transformed geography with Israeli names and spelling, Said suggests an alternative, by evoking the metaphor of 'traveler.' He remarks: 'I see myself as a wanderer. My position is that of a traveler, who is not interested in holding territory, who has no realm to protect' (Said 2001: 51).

As Kaplan (1996) argues, the move of claiming the position of a traveler or nomad who can wander across various positions within a de-territorialized landscape of memory and identity without becoming territorially attached to places masks the privileged conditions that enable such mobility. Said, however, also holds that recognizing the experience of displacement at the heart of the Palestinian condition is critical to the pursuit of justice regardless of his own personal attachments (or lack thereof) to his family's house. In other words, Said recognizes the folded nature of Palestinian experience. More critically, he argues that the folds must be recognized while they cannot be undone. In other words, memories must be sustained as they define the nature of injustice, but they do not in themselves offer a map for attainting justice. Any such map will have to trace over existing lines while not erasing those that exist in Palestinian memory or contemporary Israeli reality. I would suggest these moves of Said's are tied to his more recent judgment that the two-state solution, which he had previously long advocated, is no longer viable, leading him to embrace the idea of a bi-national state for achieving Palestinian rights and equality (see Said 1999). Said (2001: 51) explains to his Israeli interviewer:

> [Theodor] Adorno says that in the twentieth century the idea of home has been superseded. I suppose part of my critique of Zionism is that it attaches too much importance to home. Saying, we need a home. And we'll do anything to get a home, even if it means making others homeless.

Instead, Said (2001: 51) explains that he supports the idea of bi-nationalism because, 'I want a rich fabric of some sort, which no one can fully comprehend, and no one can fully own'.

Said's urban cosmopolitan position is clearly a privileged one that does not represent the experience and identity of most Palestinians, but it offers a critical reading of the folded nature of Palestinian experience in general and the complexities of the Palestinian–Israeli conflict. And his rethinking of his relationship to his Palestinian 'home' was likely in part shaped by his 'return' travel. In a sense, his experience, of seeing his old house, led him to consider the problem at the heart of the Israeli–Palestinian conflict. With his embrace of bi-nationalism Said stakes out a position that adopts a pluralist attachment to territory that he suggests could be a basis for shared, mutual attachments. He does not offer an easy solution. He tells his interview he is not interested in evicting anyone. Rejecting the notion of unfolding through partition or another round of displacement and forgetting, Said suggests that the interwoven histories and overlapping spaces inhabited by Palestinians and Israelis Jews could only be accommodated in some form of bi-national state.

Raja Shehadeh: writing against a vanishing landscape

The last text considered is *Palestinian Walks* by the Palestinian lawyer and activist Raja Shehadeh (2008). It recounts a series of journeys he made through the natural landscape of Palestine. These narratives recount stories of places with their multilayer complexity. Shehadeh resides in the West Bank town of Ramallah. While his family is from the town, once a predominantly Christian village, Shehadeh narrates the experience of his father and uncles who had made their lives in the coastal city of Jaffa before their displacement in 1948. Shehadeh's focus, however, is not on the Palestinian displacements of 1948 or even the impact of the occupation beginning in 1967, but on the more recent phase of the Palestinian experience since the beginning of the Oslo peace process and how it has reshaped the experience of Palestinian space.

Shehadeh was a pioneering human rights activist who as a lawyer focused on issues of land and property. He sought to challenge in Israeli courts Israeli efforts to expropriate Palestinians lands in the West Bank. One stunning revelation of the book is that the Oslo process ended his career as a lawyer as in the wake of the initial peace agreement that established the Palestinian Authority (PA) and zones of relative Israelis and PA control in the West Bank, Israeli courts no longer would consider such challenges. Shehadeh had dedicated his career to a strategy of opposing the Israeli occupation but found mid-career it was no longer viable, so he turned to writing. In *Palestinian Walks* Shehadeh, writing in English, frames his narrative as a counter-text to tracks of travel writing to the Holy Land that too often ignore the indigenous population. In much of this literature the native (Christian and Muslim) Palestinians were viewed as if remnants from a biblical era, or worse, intruders into a land 'promised' to the Jewish people. But like the other authors discussed in this chapter, rather than mirror exclusivist Zionist claims to territory and strategies for displacement with a set of Palestinian counter claims and displacement strategies, he highlights how the Oslo peace process never, in fact, unfolded space and partitioned the land, but enabled the extension of the settlement project and actions by settlers which have increasingly encroached on Palestinian spaces and livelihoods.

The text's subtitle, noting a 'vanishing landscape', refers to two interconnected landscapes. One is the natural landscape that is being destroyed by massive settlement and road building in a fragile environment. The other is the vanishing space of Palestinian livelihoods. Rather than offering an end to the Israeli occupation, or even a partitioning between Israeli and Palestinian spaces,

Shehadeh describes how the Oslo peace process resulted in an insidious process of folding up of the ever-constricting Palestinian space as it become wrapped in a network of Israeli settlements, by-pass road, walls, and surveillance. Shehadeh's ecocriticism also highlights the issue of environmental degradation, which the Palestinian authority has also contributed to. As Shehadeh's explains, Israeli policies of protecting green spaces, limiting development, and appreciating nature have too often been advanced in ways that constrain Palestinian communities and livelihoods while advancing Israeli efforts to control more territory and limit Palestinian mobility. Shehadeh (2008: 108) notes the consequences of an Israeli highway building project across hills that were once crossed by small winding roads from which travelers could notice the multiple layers of colored rock forged in geological time: 'To make the road run straight…the new Israeli-built highway now cuts through the hills…With the hills massacred you could no longer see the layers of rock. The colours seemed to have run, staining with swabs of pigment the exposed sides of the rocks through which the road ran'.

Recounting his journeys through the landscape, Shehadeh is always aware of the folds of place and the shifting configuration of space, be they a product of human experience or the workings of nature. While many historical travel narratives and even Israeli Ministry of Tourism advertising campaigns celebrate the landscape without recognition of the indigenous inhabits who formed the landscape, Shehadeh is always aware that people and land are co-dependent, co-presences. This approach leads him to a complex, nuance position that rejects exclusivist territorial attachments while at the same time refuses to deny the appreciation any Israeli, including settlers, might have of the same natural landscape. Like Said, Shehadeh was an early Palestinian advocate for the two state solution, but through his experiencing of the impact of the Oslo process on Palestinian lives, the behavior of Israeli settlers, and the ecology and landscape of Palestine, Shehadeh finds his agency stripped bare and his domestic dwelling no longer even a place for quiet retreat. He wishes he could simply imagine the present as a passing phase in geopolitical history, in the way it might look temporary within a passing of geological time, but he realizes the need to recognize the co-presences of the present.

Conclusion

The political, social and environmental trends discusses in this chapter make the need for rethinking the spatial relations within Palestine all the more pressing because the folded nature of Palestinian and Israeli experiences is being manifest in increasingly unsustainable architectures and spatial practices. Rather than suggesting a means or structure for resolution, the texts discussed map the increasingly complex and problematic folds that define the Palestinian experience. In the end, when Shehadeh recognizes he is unable to map a viable future for the Palestinians, he acknowledges that his only means for being able to cope with present day reality is through writing about his experiences. Shehadeh, like Said, comes to embody an Adorno-like figure. In a remembrance of Edward Said after his passing, Anton Shammas (2003) noted a passage from Adorno that Said was fond of quoting, that 'the writer sets up house…For a man who no longer has a homeland, writing becomes a place to live'. But as other chapters in this volume attest to, Palestinians continue to resist these conditions using tourism as a tool in this struggle challenging the barriers to Palestinian mobility and Israeli control over the tourism economy. Solidarity tourism programs now bring visitors to, for example, the Israeli-built Segregation Wall to better understand the material aspects of the Palestinian experience and at times to actively protest it. Just as writers like Said and Shehadeh offer radical alternatives to the bulk of travel writing about the 'Holy Land' that reproduces colonial narrative and tropes, these new forms of tourism to Palestine seek to takes visitors into the folds of Palestinian history and lived experience.

References

Abu-Lughod, L. (2007) 'Return to half-ruins: memory, postmemory, and living history in Palestine', in A.H. Sa'di and L. Abu-Lughod (eds) *Nakba: Palestine, 1948, and claims of memory*, New York: Columbia University Press.

Chambers, I. (2008) *Mediterranean crossings: the politics of an interrupted modernity*, Durham, NC: Duke University Press.

Clawson, P. (1994) 'Tourism cooperation in the Levant', *The Washington Institute Policy Focus* Research Memorandum No. 26.

Davis, R. (2007) 'Mapping the past, re-creating the Homeland: memories of village places in pre-1948 Palestine', in A.H. Sa'di and L. Abu-Lughod (eds) *Nakba: Palestine, 1948, and claims of memory*, New York: Columbia University Press.

Hazbun, W. (2008) *Beaches, ruins, resorts: the politics of tourism in the Arab World*, Minneapolis: University of Minnesota Press.

Hochberg, G.Z. (2006) 'Edward Said: 'The last Jewish intellectual',' *Social Text* 24(2): 48–65.

Joffe-Walt, B. (2007) 'Counter tourism', *Boston Globe*, 22 July.

Kaplan, C. (1996) *Questions of travel: postmodern discourses of displacement*, Durham, NC: Duke University Press.

Lisle, D. (2006) *The global politics of contemporary travel writing*, Cambridge: Cambridge University Press.

Peres, S. (1993) *The New Middle East*, New York: Henry Holt.

Sa'di, A.H. and Abu-Lughod L. (eds) (2007) *Nakba: Palestine, 1948, and claims of memory*, New York: Columbia University Press.

Said, E. (1992) 'Palestine, then and now', *Harper's Magazine,* December.

Said, E. (1999) 'The one-state solution', *New York Times Magazine,* 10 January.

Said, E. (2001) 'The Palestinian right of return: an interview with Ari Shavit', *Raritan* 20(4): 34–52.

Said, E. (2001/2) 'A living idea', *Al-Ahram Weekly*, 27 December–2 January http://weekly.ahram.org.eg/2001/566/20015.htm [Accessed: 3 June 2015].

Saxe, L, Kadushin C. , Kelner S., Rosen M. and Yereslove E. (2002) *A mega-experiment in Jewish education: the impact of Birthright Israel*, Waltham, MA: Center for Modern Jewish Studies, Brandeis University.

Segev, T. (2001) 'The return of Ibrahim Abu-Lughod', *Ha'aretz,* 1 June.

Shammas, A. (1993) 'Palestinians now must master the art of forgetting', *New York Times*, 26 December.

Shammas, A. (2003) 'Looking for someplace to call home', *New York Times*, 23 December.

Shehadeh, R. (2008) *Palestinian walks: notes on a vanishing landscape*. London: Profile Books.

Stein, R.L. (2008) *Itineraries in conflict: Israelis, Palestinians, and the political lives of tourism*. Durham, NC: Duke University Press.

Twite, R. and G. Baskin, eds. (1994) *The conversion of dreams: the development of tourism in the Middle East*. Jerusalem: Israel/Palestine Center for Research and Information.

13 Walled off from the world

Palestine, tourism and resisting occupation

Freya Higgins-Desbiolles

> The 21st Century is witnessing the most blatant ghettoization of a people since the Second World War.
>
> (Australians for Justice in Palestine – pamphlet, n.d.)

Introduction

Our world has globalized and as some would have it, the world is the tourists' oyster (Bauman 1993). The ability to travel and e mobile is becoming the essence of being a modern human. This is well articulated in Urry (2007) when he talks about cultures of mobility and the 'importance of travel to the constitution of culture' (2001: 239). Elsewhere Urry claimed the whole world 'is on the move' (2007: 207). This new direction of analysis has opened up our eyes to the ways in which hyper-mobility has reshaped the human condition, human civilisation and the ways we envision our world. While studies such as Urry's acknowledge there are those who are immobile due to poverty, particularly in developing countries, rising middle classes in Brazil, India, China and Russia for instance make optimists assure us that mobility is within the grasp of all today. But even those remaining cut off from our mobile world can be consoled that even they get a chance to reap the rewards of our mobile world as they can always host tourists and thereby get advantages from others' mobility (Urry 2001). Urry only briefly treats those engaged in mobility as a forced or traumatic condition (what he calls 'transports of despair' (2001: 244) which pertains to refugees and forced migrations. A brief review of the literature reveals there has been insufficient thinking about what it means when attempts are made to cut off whole populations from the positive influences that mobility offers (e.g. education, employment, cultivation of cosmopolitan consciousness, expanded networks, enhanced 'social capital'). The case of Palestine since the establishment of Israel in 1948 and its occupation of the Palestinian Occupied Territories from 1967 have resulted in a regime of restrictions on mobility that are worthy of study not only for the extreme negative impacts on Palestinian people but also for what they show us about the privilege of mobility in our world.

Context of the right to travel and tourism in the twentieth century

The twentieth century can be characterized in multiple ways, but one clear feature of the era is the opening up of tourism and travel to greater numbers and classes of people. In the unique era in the aftermath of the world wars, countries built economies where leisure and consumerism could thrive, middle classes developed, countries gained independence and global interconnectedness grew through globalization. In the idealism of this era, the psychological, social, economic, and environmental benefits of travel and tourism were deemed so powerful that the right to travel was incorporated in key international documents including the Universal Declaration of Human Rights of 1948, the International Covenant on Economic, Social and Cultural Rights of 1966, the World Tourism Organization's Tourism Bill of Rights and Tourist Code of 1985 and the Global Code of Ethics for Tourism of 1999. It is specifically the Universal Declaration of Human Rights that is often perceived as underpinning the right to travel with its two passages in articles 13 and 24. Article 13 (1) states 'everyone has the right to freedom of movement and residence within the borders of each state' and Article 13(2) states 'everyone has the right to leave any country, including his own, and to return to his country' (United Nations (UN) 1948), which O'Byrne (2001) describes as underpinning the human right to travel. Combined with article 24, which states 'everyone has the right to rest and leisure, including reasonable limitation of working hours and periodic holidays with pay' (UN 1948), this fundamental document of international law is credited with situating travel and tourism as part of human rights. The vision behind this assertion that travel and tourism are worthy of inclusion beside such rights as the right to life, liberty and security can be found in the words of the UN World Tourism Organization (UNWTO), who declared tourism's potential value in 'contributing to economic development, international understanding, peace, prosperity and universal respect for, and observance of, human rights and fundamental freedoms for all' (UNWTO 1999). It is for these lofty reasons that the idea that travel and tourism should be made as widely available as possible through an articulation of human rights (and in fact a movement for social tourism to practically enable this access to occur) advanced in this era (Higgins-Desbiolles 2006).

In a globalized world, the mobility afforded by travel and tourism is the key to being an educated, prosperous and thriving individual in an era when more people are hyper mobile. There are of course people disempowered from activating their rights because of poverty, illness, caring responsibilities or other barriers, but with cheaper travel and increasing leisure time, many individuals in both the developed and developing worlds are able to travel like never before at least in domestic spheres if not in international ones. It is in such a context that we witness unprecedented suppression (in duration and extent) of the Palestinian right to movement, travel and open access to tourism in the modern era.

Palestine

There is arguably no tourist destination that has a similar experience to Palestine. Because of the decades of conflict and occupation, the Palestinian people have been under a complex and ever-changing regime of restricted movement. While in the past, Israel's economy depended on cheap labour from Palestine and so movement was easier, it was the two intifadas that saw free movement severely curtailed. Israel's military used the issuance of permits to travel into Israel allegedly as a means to prevent terrorism. As Bronner noted, in 2011 about 60,000 permits were issued; a token amount for a population of 2.5 million people (Bronner 2011). It is particularly the threat of suicide bombers that saw the current era of restrictions imposed, but as Hage has pointed out, lying behind that was a struggle by Israel 'to consolidate a "normal peaceful life" inside a colonial settler state...' (2003: 68) predicated on the permanent dispossession of Palestinian people (for greater detail on the background to Israeli restrictions see B'Tselem – The Israeli Information Center for Human Rights in the Occupied Territories (B'Tselem 2012); UN Office for the Coordination of Humanitarian Affairs Occupied Palestinian Territory (OCHAOPT) 2011). Arguably, it was the failure of the Oslo Process and the continuous failure to see the foundations for a viable Palestinian state which generated the hopelessness, humiliation and desperation that suicide bombing embodies (Hage 2003). The full blockade of Gaza began with the democratic election of Hamas in 2006 (Europe and the USA suspended aid designating Hamas a terrorist organization). This rejection of a democratically elected party was because it was likely to prove less compliant or corruptible than the Fatah Party which held rule in the West Bank. Despite requirements that Gaza not be separated from the West Bank, this blockade in fact has reinforced the cantonization of Palestine undermining hopes for a unified state in the future.

This restriction of movement is carried out through physical structures of hindrance, including permanent structures such as the well-known 'Separation Fence' (in Israeli parlance) or 'Apartheid Wall' (in Palestinian parlance), but also including numerous gates, trenches, checkpoints, guard towers, earthworks and by-pass roads, but also temporary and unpredictable barriers through things like 'flying checkpoints'. This is also supported by a complex system of permits administered by the Israeli military which issues far too few passes for the number of Palestinians who need to travel to other places for work, education, medical care, to visit family or conduct religious pilgrimage, for instance. Some sites of Palestine are becoming almost completely cut off, including Jerusalem and Gaza.

The impediments to travel to and within Palestine imposed on Palestinians

The issue of the mobility of Palestinians has multiple angles, including the ability of Palestinians to travel within Palestine (under occupation or into the territories of 1948), travel on return journeys outwardly from Palestine and non-Palestinians travelling to Palestine. This gets more complicated with the necessity to then adapt considerations of Palestinians living under occupation in the West Bank, East Jerusalem and Gaza Strip, Palestinians living as citizens of Israel, Palestinians living stateless in refugee camps in the region and Palestinians living in diaspora throughout the world.

The restrictions on movements of Palestinians is part of Israel's closure policy and sees such things as inability to travel within the West Bank, between the West Bank and Gaza, to East Jerusalem, into Israel, exit from any point of Palestine or travel efficiently on public roads or transport systems (B'Tselem 2015). Arbitrary impositions include the need for a permit which can be very difficult to obtain, particularly for men of a certain age and with any record of imprisonment (when a majority of men have served time as political prisoners at some point during the occupation). There are the inconveniences of these obstacles to travel which impose considerable time and economic costs that have worked to damage the emerging Palestinian economy. For instance, this occurs for all Palestinians forced to use the Allenby Bridge to exit through Jordan for international travel as a taxi is taken to the border, considerable time is needed to pass through the Israeli checkpoint and a significant fee is payable, another taxi is needed to Amman and usually a hotel room must be booked in order to ensure meeting an international flight schedule.

Some testimonials of impacted individuals gathered by B'Tselem as well as a few additional case examples will be offered here to provide some insight into the significance of the problems experienced by Palestinians. One key damage wrought by the regime of restrictions is the blocking of Palestinians from accessing higher education overseas. The testimony of a young woman from Gaza gathered by B'Tselem (2008) indicates the way that border closures block such students from taking up fellowships at prestigious universities. Additionally, checkpoints, border restrictions and policies work to undermine an emerging Palestinian tourism sector. It is highly recommended to read the testimonial offered by the Manager of the Jericho Resort, which provides vital insights into how Palestinian domestic travel, diaspora travel and international travel has been curbed by the inclusion of Jericho in Area A and the imposition of checkpoints and barriers on this important tourism city in 2000 (B'Tselem 2011). Aishalaat Amusement Park located in a small town near Nablus experienced a similar impact when the Israeli Defence Forces shut the main access road; but this business folded when even the people of Nablus were blocked from reaching the park (B'Tselem 2006). At a more personal level, Raja Shehadeh (2008) evokes the ways in which Palestinians who love the whole of Palestine and want to pay homage to it by lovingly walking its hills, valleys and pathways are blocked from doing so as these barriers and checkpoints prevent them from doing so; but even more than that, the Palestinian places of Palestine are vanishing under Israeli occupation and settlements. Another example concerns the ability of Palestinians of all categories to undertake 'visiting friends and relatives' forms of travel which are seriously impeded by these policies. B'Tselem captured the story of Nihayah Seif who explains how she is separated from her family in Jordan as a result of marrying a resident of Tulkarm and how she may never see her elderly mother again (B'Tselem 2007). Finally, there are the more famous cases of the Palestinian soccer team who are 'the only team in the world who competes under occupation', find it difficult to get sufficient training as a team because of the myriad of restrictions players face in getting together due to movement restrictions and also have suffered the loss of players in the bombing of Gaza in 2009 (see Booth 2015).

The 'Apartheid Wall'

The worst development in recent times is the building of the 'security fence' or 'Apartheid Wall', which describes a separation barrier built by Israel allegedly to protect itself from attacks originating in the West Bank. It is particularly controversial because it, in places, goes inside the 1949 Armistice Line (or 'Green Line') and therefore expropriates Palestinian land. It also separates Palestinians from their schools, their fields, their kin, and from each other and together with limited crossings with limited opening hours, arguably localizes people affected in a way that is more suited to the dark ages. On completion, it will be approximately 700 kilometres in length. As Chapter 5 in this volume provides a very detailed case study of the village of Battir, this chapter will not explore the significance of the Wall in any greater detail. However, to underscore the ways in which these impediments to movement undermine possibilities to harness tourism for Palestinian benefit a brief reference to the ways in which the Wall have separated the holy site of Rachel's Tomb is worth noting here (see Selwyn 2011).

More significantly such actions work to negate feelings of autonomy and well-being for Palestinians. Writing inscribed on the wall entitled 'The Wall is on my heart' expressed this:

> After the Wall around Rachel's Tomb was built, I felt terrible. Nobody was walking here, only the cats and dogs. The wall creates a feeling… the feeling that it surrounds you; that you are not permitted to move. Every time, every day you see the Wall. When I look outside through the window to see the sunrise or the sunset the Wall is in front of me. When I go to the Wall I feel that something closes in my heart, as if the Wall is on my heart… When I see the Wall I also feel ashamed of myself, because it is created by human beings
> – Melvina, Bethlehem.
>
> (Arab Educational Institute 2012: 22)

The International Court of Justice (ICJ) made a ruling in 2004 that the 'construction by Israel of a wall in the Occupied Palestinian Territory and its associated régime are contrary to international law' (ICJ 2004).

Jerusalem

> The city we love most and visit least.
>
> (Rifat Odeh Kassis (Kassis 2014))

One of the most contested sites in the right to travel is the religious and political centre of Jerusalem. With the creation of Israel Jerusalem was divided and both sides in the conflict have considered it vital for their peoples' future. With the Occupation from 1967, Israel took control of East Jerusalem but went further in illegally annexing it and saying an undivided Jerusalem is its capital (Zahriyeh 2014).

In East Jerusalem Israel has committed gross violations of international law. Kassis describes this:

> The violations themselves are copious and ongoing: historical expropriation (since 1967 and through the present day) of private Palestinian-owned land, paving the way for illegal Israeli settlements (referred to as 'neighborhoods' in internal Israeli discourse) and demolition of Palestinian houses, leaving many people homeless along with discriminatory housing permit policies; Israel's 'quiet transfer' policy, revoking the residency of East Jerusalemites who moved away from municipal borders and countless others.
>
> Israel is not simply trying to find its place in Jerusalem. Rather, it is trying to monopolize Jerusalem (again, on both quotidian levels and on universal, sacred ones) and exclude Palestinian Christians and Muslims from the city.
>
> (Kassis 2014)

Connected to this inability for Palestinians outside of Jerusalem to travel into Jerusalem, is the attempt to expel Palestinians from residing in East Jerusalem. As Cole stated:

> The Palestinians of East Jerusalem are in a special legal category under modern Israeli law. Most of them are not Israeli citizens, nor are they classified the same way as people in Gaza or the West Bank; they are permanent residents.
>
> There are old Palestinian families here, but in a neighbourhood like Sheikh Jarrah many of the people are refugees who were settled here after the Al-Nakbah ('catastrophe') of 1948. They left their original homes behind, fleeing places such as Haifa and Sarafand al-Amar, and they came to Sheikh Jarrah, which then became their home. Many of them were given houses constructed on a previously uninhabited parcel of land by the Jordanian government and by the UN Relief and Works Agency. East Jerusalem came under Israeli control in 1967, and since then, but at an increasing tempo in recent years, these families are being rendered homeless a second or third time.
>
> (Cole 2015)

The impacts of these restrictions have been in fact well considered by a World Bank technical team in 2007 who issued a report entitled *Movement and access restrictions in the West Bank*. This document is well worth reading for understanding the impediments and their impacts. While limited to largely a focus on the economic implications of these restrictions, it does briefly address some of the politics of usurpation and colonization:

While Israeli security concerns are undeniable and must be addressed, it is often difficult to reconcile the use of closure for security purposes from its use to expand and protect settlement activity and the relatively unhindered movement of settlers in and out of the West Bank. Limiting Palestinian access to the important agricultural and tourist potential of the Jordan Valley is one such example.

(World Bank 2007: 12)

This section has only briefly addressed the impediments to free movement of Palestinians and offered brief comments on the Wall and Jerusalem specifically. When one asks why such a regime of impediments is necessary, one arrives at partial and rival answers of ensuring Israeli security or alternatively a blatant land grab and secret agenda for ethnic cleansing. However, here another testimony gathered by B'Tselem is informative; an IDF soldier testifying under anonymity suggested the purpose was to make Palestinians not want to travel:

The spirit of things was to make life unbearable for the Palestinians. Stop them, inspect them a thousand and one times so that they won't want to drive that route. It seemed stupid to me. You harm people's livelihood, harm people's life, detain children on the way to school, what good can come from this to the army, or to the country?

(B'Tselem 2002)

The impediments to travel to and within Palestine imposed on international visitors

Another key aspect of the immobility that adheres to Palestine is the Israeli domination which allows Israel to determine who can visit Palestine and under what degree of difficulty. It is significant that tourists cannot get to Palestine without passing through an Israeli control point; since 1967 Israel has controlled all borders of Palestine. One key entrance is Ben Gurion International Airport (called AlLedd by Palestinians). There are also land crossings from Jordan, with access by the Allenby Bridge or Wadi Araba, and from Egypt, with the Taba Crossing; however, Israeli authorities control all of these entry ways into Palestine. If one is travelling with the clear intent to visit Palestine, it in fact can be quite difficult to pass through such border points.

As one guidebook inviting visitors to see Al Quds or Jerusalem from a 'grassroots' perspective noted:

Landing in Palestine can be stressful. Expect to face rigorous questioning about your political and religious affiliations, your recent travels and your plans while in the country. If you have stamps from other Arab countries in your passport you can expect prolonged questioning upon arrival and departure. Keep in mind that social media profiles may be accessed by guards as a condition of entry. Israeli authorities are interested in limiting the number of international activists and visitors to the 'Palestinian territories'.

(Grassroots Jerusalem 2014: 1)

However, it is often even worse for Palestinian visitors with dual nationality, visitors of Palestinian descent as well as visitors of Arabic heritage. There is also no guarantee that people attempting to enter Israel as a gateway to Palestine through any crossing will not be turned back altogether, particularly if they are identified as supporters of Palestine (see Ahmad 2005).

Tourists are confronted with a series of impediments to movement into and around Palestine. One can simply be the lengthy and arduous extra border crossings that Israeli occupation entails. For instance in 2005, Daher reported there was widespread disaffection as Israel implemented new arrangements forcing visitors travelling from Jerusalem to Bethlehem to exit their buses and be processed through a hall for passport and border control taking up to two hours of their brief touring time; and compounded by another international border if they use this pathway to exit the country from the international airport (Daher 2005). If one hopes for the development of conflict resolution and reconciliation between Israelis and Palestinians, the fact that since 2001 it has been discouraged if not illegal for Israeli citizens to travel into Area A (areas under full Palestinian control) in the West Bank makes any hope that understanding can develop through cross-cultural contact is certainly curtailed (see Figure 13.1).

Figure 13.1 Sign at the entrance to Palestinian controlled area of the OPT.

This matters in a multitude of ways. Firstly, economically many of the world's developing nations look to tourism as an engine for economic opportunity and development. Palestine should have a natural competitive advantage and tourism represents one of its best economic hopes. But more fundamentally in a world predicated on globalization and the interaction of peoples, a country is left in a state of profound social isolation if cut off so starkly from the global community. This may in fact be a key reason why the Palestinian narrative of the Al-Nakbah and oppression has so little traction against the Israeli narrative of the plucky little Western democracy in a sea of danger in the Middle East (e.g. Bernis n.d.). Finally, there is a special category of visitor that is denied free movement into and around Palestine: human rights monitors and similar actors. Former Special Rapporteur on Occupied Palestine Falk recently stated 'the Special Rapporteur on Occupied Palestine continues to be denied entry to Palestine, a situation that has existed ever since … 2008' (Falk 2015).

Tourism as a tool for resisting enforced isolation

While Israel has worked very hard to isolate and control Palestine and Palestinians through the measures recounted here, there has been considerable creative resistance. Tourism in this context has become a means for connecting Palestinians to the external world and fomenting solidarity (see also Chapter 4).

> In the Palestinian Occupied Territories, tourism has been deployed by a number of civil society groups and grass-roots operators as a means for overcoming the economic isolation that is reinforced by the Israeli occupation, and simultaneously advancing the wider struggle for Palestinian freedom and political self-determination.
>
> (Bianchi & Stephenson 2014: 206)

Palestine is noted to be the staging ground for new forms of tourism and travel but sometimes not labelled consistently or even as tourism (with its connotations of hedonism); appellations include solidarity tourism, transnational solidarity activism, justice tourism, political tourism, peace through tourism (Higgins-Desbiolles 2008, 2009). (For in-depth insights into solidarity tourism please see Chapter 3).

It is important to note that there is resistance to these impositions and it has become an important catalyst to solidarity as numerous civil society bodies, groups and individuals act to harness tourism. For instance, in reaction to the travel restrictions imposed on Palestinians which sees them landlocked and blocked from the 'simple joys at the beach' a group of Israeli women formed a movement they called 'We will not obey' with an aim to smuggle Palestinian women into Israel to visit the beach and other places they are prohibited from visiting (Bronner 2011). In a newspaper announcement they explained their motivation:

> We cannot assent to the legality of the Law of Entry into Israel, which allows every Israeli and every Jew to move freely in all regions between the

Mediterranean and the Jordan River while depriving Palestinians of this same right. They are not permitted free movement within the occupied territories nor are they allowed into the towns and cities across the green line, where their families, their nation, and their traditions are deeply rooted.

They and we, all ordinary citizens, took this step with a clear and resolute mind. In this way we were privileged to experience one of the most beautiful and exciting days of our lives, to meet and befriend our brave Palestinian neighbours, and together with them, to be free women, if only for one day.

(Bronner 2011)

Specifically focused on the Palestinian diaspora, the 'Know thy heritage' programme founded by Palestinian businessman Rateb Rabie created to re-connect youth in the Palestinian diaspora with their homeland demonstrates another approach (Miller 2013). With funds raised from Palestinian businesses in the West Bank and the USA, these tours have had less of a political focus than the Israeli Birthright tours they are compared to and instead focus on economic ties for future investment and state development (Miller 2013).

Other initiatives such as the olive harvest tours model a practical approach to harness tourism for meaningful activities which help improve Palestinian lives; it is a form of volunteer tourism. Organizations offering such tours include Zaytoun, the International Women's Peace Service and the Alternative Tourism Group (see Chapter 3) and they concern one of the most important economic, cultural and symbolic resources of Palestine, the olive. In a context where impediments like the Wall block Palestinian access to their olive groves and harassment from Israeli soldiers and settlers can threaten Palestinian farmers, visitors are brought to help in the harvest of the olive crop on solidarity tours (see www.zaytoun.org/harvest/olive-picking-trip/).

Travel and mobility has also been used by transnational solidarity activists as a tool for advocacy, consciousness-raising and tangible action. Prominent examples include the Gaza flotilla and the 2011–2012 'aerial flotillas' which were/are aimed at drawing attention to Israel's border restrictions and the impacts of occupation as well as tangibly breaking the imposed isolation of the Palestinian people. The Gaza flotillas started in 2008 by a group of Palestinian, Israeli and international activists with an aim to break the blockade imposed on Gaza by the Israeli military by bringing in humanitarian assistance and to express solidarity with the oppressed population (de Jong 2012). The aerial flotillas followed with a campaign called 'welcome to Palestine' and involved internationals attempting to fly into Israel to reach Palestine. Event organizer Fahdi Tantas was quoted saying: 'The idea was for them to come in and say, "we are going to Palestine," to change the discourse and what is required usually from a foreigner coming to Palestine. It is a basic right for them and for us Palestinians to receive our guests' (Flower 2011). However, the dangers of transnational solidarity activism were starkly revealed with the killing of nine activists in May, 2010 when Israeli naval commandos boarded the Gaza flotilla ship the Mavi Marmara sparking international outrage but little change to Israeli practices (de Jong 2012).

One final initiative which should be briefly addressed here is the 'Open Bethlehem' campaign and the Bethlehem passport initiative of 2005 which had a declared aim of making the city open to anyone in the world. In reaction to the isolation imposed by the building of the Wall around Bethlehem and other impediments to access to and from the city, 'the initiative is designed to transcend imprisonment' (Open Bethlehem 2005). As the website stated:

> Open Bethlehem's vision is to support a lasting peace settlement between Palestine and Israel using Bethlehem as a doorway for global engagement. As an iconic city, and a Palestinian city, Bethlehem has both power and responsibility to act and use its global outreach to promote positive change.
>
> Since its launch in 2005, Open Bethlehem has succeeded in building a large base of supporters through a campaign focused on the Bethlehem passport – a symbolic citizenship of an iconic town that stands for Joy and Goodwill to all. The passport was created by Open Bethlehem in partnership with the Bethlehem Governorate to invite engagement with the city and the wider cause of the region.
>
> (Open Bethlehem n.d.)

Chief Executive of the campaign and filmmaker Leila Sansour has made a film to support the campaign and spread the message of the need to act to ensure Bethlehem remains open (see www.openbethlehem.org/).

However, it is necessary to note that these efforts represent small niches reaching only small numbers of tourists to the area. It is clear that Israel controls the vast majority of tourists that travel to Israel/Palestine and this has ramifications on the ability of Palestinians to connect with the outside world. As Rifat Kassis of Kairos Palestine stated:

> During the past few decades, Israel has actively prevented Palestinians from taking the initiative in their own tourism industry. Since Israel controls all of Palestine's borders and regulates all movement inside those borders, impeding Palestinian-led tourism is just another tactic employed by a comprehensive occupation.
>
> Most tourists (including pilgrims) are received in Israel by Israeli tour guides, accommodated in Israeli hotels, and fed Israeli stories and Zionist interpretations of the Old Testament. While visiting the Church of the Nativity in Bethlehem, an Israeli tour guide may offer a quip about Arab backwardness, or a warning about Arabs' exploitative nature. The tourists may be discouraged from wandering beyond the immediate vicinity of the tourist site and from patronizing Palestinian businesses. They are then ushered back onto their buses and sped through the checkpoint back to Jerusalem.
>
> (Kassis 2015: 23)

The Palestinians nonetheless are forced to use tourism to the best of its capacities to foster solidarity through the social contact it might offer. In fact Kassis has been one of the leaders of the Kairos Initiative which was launched in 2009 and challenged visitors, particularly pilgrims, to 'come and see'. As Kassis argued, these initiatives are based on truthfulness and 'was born of our belief in the significance of tourism as an economic, political, and spiritual force that can effectively and truthfully advocate for the Palestinian struggle and for peace with justice through Palestinian-organized tours' (Kassis 2015: 25). Remembering the inclusion of travel and arguably tourism in the *Universal Declaration of Human Rights* in articles 13 and 24 (UN 1948), we clearly can see that the free and unrestricted movement these clauses should secure are the guarantors to a people securing their full humanity and being able to connect with the rest of the world to build better understanding, prosperity and peace. The Palestinian people deserve this access as much as any other people do and in fact any resolution to the almost 70 year-long conflict depends upon it. Of course, Gaza is almost completely blocked from any of these solidarity visits and the capacity of tourism to foster support and comfort for the people of Gaza. This is indeed the very raison d'etre of the Gaza Flotilla, which tried to break this imposed isolation. As Chapter 15 demonstrates, the only solidarity allowed the people of Gaza at this point are virtual tours and encounters.

Discussion

The question underlying almost all discussion of Palestine and Israel is how can you resolve what seems to be incompatible claims on the right to inhabit the historical geography of Palestine. While the concern of this analysis has been with the tourism implications of these movement restrictions, it must be made clear that there are far more important issues at stake than tourism movements, of course. For instance, human rights groups have documented the appalling number of people who have suffered grave medical consequences due to the barriers of checkpoints blocking access to medical care, particularly pregnant women who in some cases have suffered horrible tragedies (Hashayka 2012). It is also important to point out that analysts such as Hanafi (2009) have described the colonial project that underpins these actions by the Israeli government as 'spacio-cidal'; and turning to the theories of 'states of exception' and 'bio-power', Hanafi describes how such acts are meant to render Palestinians powerless and with only 'bare life' and lacking any recourse to rights. However, mobility and tourism is one of the sites of this contest and an important site of rendering Palestinians subject to living only 'bare life' (Higgins-Desbiolles 2013).

Turning to Hage's (2003) analysis of the phenomenon of suicide bombers, which were and are one of the key justifications of Israeli security practices including the travel restrictions of interest here but also the attacks on Gaza, house demolitions and massive incarceration, indicates the exploration of the catalysts to the phenomenon of the suicide bomber in Palestine is worthwhile. Hage offers an analysis demonstrating Israel's goal of imposition of a colonial order has sparked an obsessive and 'relentless search for anything that might cause "vulnerability"' (2003: 81). But the methods it employs to secure invulnerability of its occupation of the land causes a loss of hope, meaning social opportunity for the Palestinians as the occupation seems without end. Hage stated:

> More important for us, however, this 'politicidal' drive, as it is implemented on a daily basis by the Israeli colonizers, generates the affective condition many Palestinians consider as one of the main factors behind the rise of suicide bombings: colonial humiliation. Humiliation is the experience of being psychologically demeaned – treated like less than a human being, by someone more powerful than you, without a capacity to redress the situation. This is experienced not only at a national level – though the experience of having another nation enter your territory at will, arrest your leaders, and talk about them as if they were disposable entities is clearly and significantly humiliating. It is also experienced at a personal level: being shouted at, abused, searched, stopped, ordered around, checked, asked to wait, 'allowed to pass', and so forth.
>
> (2003: 82)

This is why the solidarity activism/tourism is so important as it helps to counter this isolation and humiliation. Hage's essay offers a social explanation for the Palestinian suicide bomber phenomenon to counter the trend in global societies of fear, exclusion, rejection of the Other and the building of borders. In this work he notes a trend to exighophobia or fear of explanations and the shutting down of analysis that attempts to understand what makes violence occur. Here though we can use his analysis to think through the larger meaning of the restrictions of the right to travel and tourism and Palestine. At one level it is an imposition of an Occupier on an occupied people in an attempt to stabilize and normalize a colonial project – in an era where colonial projects are rejected. But at another level we have a contest for the future of our world.

For in fact, while nowhere else arguably sees a whole people restricted the way the Palestinian people are, as Bianchi and Stephenson noted: 'the proliferation of borders at the gates of Europe and North America, has entrapped the majority of the world's inhabitants even more forcefully in a vicious circle of poverty and immobility' (2013: 19). In her discussion of the meaning of Qalandia checkpoint on the West Bank, Tawil-Souri noted:

> The Palestinian landscape is used as a playground and laboratory by the Israeli state/military to exert power, create new modes of organization, parcel out and govern territories and people in ways heretofore undreamed of. Israeli policies of territorial segmentation of the West Bank into Areas A, B, and C, combined with the erection of settlements, by-pass roads, walls/fences, checkpoints, and closures demonstrate how directly and explicitly domination and control are inscribed into the way space is organized...
>
> Additionally, while Qalandia is unique and checkpoints have sprouted across the Palestinian Territories in astounding numbers and formations, they inform our understanding of other spatial mechanisms of stratifying,

separating, fragmenting, and/or immobilizing (sub-altern) populations across the world: not only at checkpoints and border zones such as in Iraq, Cyprus, or along the US/Mexico border, but spaces such as ghettoes, reservations, Bantustans, gated communities, and all kinds of no-go zones and no-man's lands.

(2010: 32–33)

What this analysis hints at is the nature of the struggle for political order and especially a 'new world order' that we are undergoing at this time. Any thoughts of international cooperation under visions of equity and sharing are dwindling as neoliberal globalization defines who gains access to opportunities, resources and meaningful lives, and while doing so dictating those confined to the margins, blocked by barriers and confined to only living 'bare lives'. While tourism may seem trivial in these struggles for the nature of world order being secured for the future, as this chapter has tried to demonstrate this is clearly not so; tourism has significant economic, political, social and cultural value and it marks an important site in the struggle. For example, the Open Bethlehem campaign represents a model of an open, inclusive and cosmopolitan world that invites us to imagine an alternative to the fearful era characterised by the War on Terror with its gated communities of privilege and the bare life of the excluded.

Conclusion

As this chapter has argued, mobility is a significant factor to living a fulfilled and prosperous life in our globalized world. While the more idealistic days of the 1960s and 1970s, when counterculture movements and visions of a New Economic Order, could countenance ideas of travel and tourism as a human right and see initiatives to realize this, the current era in contrast is characterized by borders, gated domains of privilege and stark dichotomies of the 'haves' and the 'have nots'. The details recounted here of the myriad ways in which Palestinians are systematically cut off from the benefits of mobility should alert us to a gross injustice which cannot stand under the authority of international law nor the moral authority of a civilized, globalizing world. However, it must also be considered in the context of wider struggles marked by imposed dichotomies of privilege/ underprivilege, mobility/immobility, oppressor/oppressed that feature in our world. This is a world increasingly characterized by: fear of any vulnerability to the demands of an alien Other; barriers and borders to block such individuals out; and to an authoritarian, militaristic and nihilistic future which results from such paradigms. In such a world, we all risk becoming Palestinians unless we dedicate ourselves to building a more just, open, inclusive and cosmopolitan world.

References

Ahmad, S. (2005) 'Holidays in the Holy Land', *Contours*, 15(3): 10–12.

Arab Educational Institute. (2012) *The 'Wall Museum': Palestinian stories on the wall in Bethlehem*, Bethlehem: Arab Education Institute Culture and Palestine Series.

Australians for Justice in Palestine. (n.d.). 'The Apartheid Wall – Israel's ghetto wall of shame'. Online http://www.ajpp.canberra.net .au [Accessed 3 May 2012].

B'Tselem. (2002) *H.L., Staff Sgt testimony*. Online http://www.btselem.org/testimonies/20020201_soldiers_testimonies_witness_h_1 [Accessed 16 July 2013].

B'Tselem. (2006) *Baslan Al-Fares testimony*. Online http://www.btselem.org/testimonies/20061129_amusement_park_closed_because_of_blocked_road [Accessed 16 July 2013].

B'Tselem. (2007) *Nihayah Seif testimony*. Online http://www.btselem.org/testimonies/20070819_family_separation_nihaya_seif [Accessed 17 July 2013].

B'Tselem. (2008) *Rasha Abu Sha'ban testimony*. Online http://www.btselem.org/testimonies/20080708_rasha_abu_shaaban_student_stuck_in_gaza [Accessed 16 July 2013].

B'Tselem. (2011) *Riad Mahmud Muhammad Hamad testimony*. Online http://www.btselem.org/testimonies/testimony-effects-israeli-restrictions-jericho-resort-village-may-2011 [Accessed 16 July 2013].

B'Tselem. (2012) *Background on the restriction of movement*. Online http://www.btselem.org/freedom_of_movement [Accessed 16 July 2013].

B'Tselem. (2015) Closure. Online http://www.btselem.org/closure [Accessed 16 July 2013].

Bauman, Z. (1993) *Postmodern Ethics*, London: Routledge.

Bernis, J. (n.d.) 'Identifying Israel's enemies'. Online http://www.jewishvoice.org/media/publications/articles/identifying-israels-enemies.html [Accessed 20 June 2015].

Bianchi, R.V. and Stephenson, M.L. (2013) 'Deciphering tourism and citizenship in a globalized world', *Tourism Management*, 39: 10–20.

Bianchi, R.V. and Stephenson, M.L. (2014) *Tourism and citizenship: rights, freedoms and responsibilities in the global order*, London: Routledge.

Booth, W. (2015) 'Fans love underdogs, but few face greater odds than the Palestinian soccer team', *Washington Post*, 1 January. Online http://www.washingtonpost.com/world/middle_east/fans-love-an-underdog-few-are-more-under-doggy-than-the-palestine-soccer-team/2015/01/01/af7b912a-7fd6-11e4-9f38-95a187e4c1f7_story.html [Accessed 15 March 2015].

Bronner. E. (2011) 'Where politics are complex, simple joys at the beach', *New York Times*, 26 July. Online http://www.nytimes.com/2011/07/27/world/middleeast/27swim.html?_r=0 [Accessed 3 March 2013].

Cole, T. (2015) 'Slow violence, cold violence', *The Guardian*, Australia edition, 17 April. Online http://www.theguardian.com/books/2015/apr/17/bad-law-east-jerusalem-ethnic-cleansing-palestines-teju-cole [Accessed 20 April 2015].

Daher, Y. (2005) 'Bethlehem recent border arrangements slammed by tourists and tourism stakeholders', *ETurbo News*, 17 November. Online http:///www.travelwirenews.com [Accessed 30 March 2006].

de Jong, A. (2012) 'The Gaza Freedom Flotilla: human rights, activism and academic neutrality', *Social Movement Studies: Journal of Social, Cultural and Political Protest*, 11(2): 193–209.

Falk, R. (2015) *Weakening and discrediting the UN: the mission of Israeli QGOs*. Online https://www.transcend.org/tms/2015/04/weakening-and-discrediting-the-un-the-mission-of-israeli-qgos-quasi-government-organizations/ [Accessed 21 April 2015].

Flower, K. (2011) 'Israeli officials detain pro-Palestinian protesters at airport', *CNN*, 8 July. Online http://edition.cnn.com/2011/WORLD/meast/07/08/israel.aerial.flotilla/index.html [Accessed 12 July 2013].

Grassroots Jerusalem. (2014) *The grassroots guide to Jerusalem*, Jerusalem: Grassroots Jerusalem.

Hage, G. (2003) 'Comes a time we are all enthusiasm: Understanding Palestinian suicide bombers in times of exighophobia', *Public Culture*, 15(1): 56–89.

Hanafi, S. (2009) 'Spacio-cide: colonial politics, invisibility and rezoning in Palestinian territory', *Contemporary Arab Affairs*, 2(1): 106–121.

Hashayka, A. (2012) 'Human rights, pregnancy and Israeli checkpoints', *Jurist*. Online http://jurist.org/dateline/2012/07/abeer-hashayka-israeli-checkpoints.php [Accessed 13 April 2015].

Higgins-Desbiolles, F. (2006) 'More than an industry: tourism as a social force', *Tourism Management*, 27(6): 1192–1208.

Higgins-Desbiolles, F. (2008) 'Justice tourism: a pathway to alternative globalisation', *Journal of Sustainable Tourism*, 16(3): 345–364.

Higgins-Desbiolles, F. (2009) 'International Solidarity Movement: A case study in volunteer tourism for justice', *Annals of Leisure Research*, 12 (3–4): 333–349.

Higgins-Desbiolles, F. (2013) 'Tourism as politics: the case of Palestine', in L. Blanchard and F. Higgins-Desbiolles (eds.) *Peace through tourism: promoting human security through international citizenship*, London: Routledge.

International Court of Justice (ICJ) (2004) *Legal consequences of the construction of a wall in the Occupied Palestinian Territory*. Online http://www.icj-cij.org/docket/index.php?pr=71&code=mwp&p1=3&p2=4&p3=6 [Accessed 3 July 2014].

Kassis, R.O. (2014) *Jerusalem: The city we love most and visit least*. Online http://www.maannews.com/eng/ViewDetails.aspx?id=689634 [Accessed 15 April 2014].

Kassis, R.O. (2015). 'A Kairos perspective of tourism and pilgrimage: come and see', *This Week in Palestine*, 204: 22–28.

Miller, A.L. (2013) 'A Palestinian birthright trip?', *The Daily Beast,* 3 April. Online http://www.thedailybeast.com/articles/2013/04/03/a-palestinian-birthright-trip.html [Accessed 17 May 2013].

O'Byrne, D. (2001) 'On passports and border controls', *Annals of Tourism Research*, 28(2): 399–416.

Open Bethlehem. (n.d.) *The campaign*. Online http://www.openbethlehem.org/the-campaign/ [Accessed 22 April 2015].

Open Bethlehem. (2005) 'The Bethlehem passport', *Contours*, 15(3): 9.

Selwyn, T. (2011) 'Tears on the border: the case of Rachel's Tomb, Bethlehem, Palestine', in M. Kousis, T. Selwyn and D. Clark (eds.) *Contested Mediterranean spaces: ethnographic essays in honour of Charles Tilly*, Oxford: Berghan.

Shehadeh, R. (2008) *Palestinian walks: Notes on a vanishing landscape*, London: Profile.

Tawil-Souri, H. (2010) 'Qalandia Checkpoint: the historical geography of a non-place', *Jerusalem Quarterly*, 42: 26–48.

United Nations (UN). (1948) *Universal Declaration of Human Rights*. Online http://www.un.org/en/documents/udhr/ [Accessed 15 March 2015].

United Nations Office for the Coordination of Humanitarian Affairs Occupied Palestinian Territory (UN-OCHAOPT) (2011) *Movement and access in the West Bank*, Online https://www.ochaopt.org/documents/ocha_opt_movementandaccess_factsheet_september_2011.pdf [Accessed 13 January 2015].

United Nations World Tourism Organization (UNWTO) (1999) *Global code of ethics for tourism*. Online http://www.world-tourism.org/pressrel/CODEOFE.htm_[Accessed 8 March 2000].

Urry, J. (2001) 'Transports of delight', *Leisure Studies*, 20(4): 237–245.

Urry, J. (2007) *Mobilities*, Cambridge: Polity Press.

World Bank. (2007) *Movement and access restrictions in the West Bank: Uncertainty and inefficiency in the Palestinian economy*. Online http://siteresources.worldbank.org/INTWESTBANKGAZA/Resources/WestBankrestrictions9Mayfinal.pdf [Accessed 13 July 2013].

Zahriyeh, E. (2014) 'Who owns Jerusaelm?'. Online http://america.aljazeera.com/articles/2014/10/30/jerusalem-statusinternationalregime.html [Accessed 3 June 2015].

Part IV

Conclusion

Future visioning

14 Towards the future of tourism and pilgrimage in Bethlehem, Jerusalem and Palestine

Tom Selwyn and Rami K. Isaac

Introduction

The tourism sector has always been a primary sector in the Palestinian economy and an essential income generating industry accounting for 15.2 per cent of GDP in 2014, and approximately 14 per cent in 2013 (International Trade Centre 2013), and an employment generator either through direct employment in the tourism field or indirect employment in other related fields accounting for 19.9 per cent in 2004 (Isaac and Ashworth 2012). This reflects the fact that its cultural and natural heritage has historically formed Palestine's most significant capital resource and will continue to do so in the future.

The present chapter looks critically at the past, present, and future of tourism and pilgrimage in Bethlehem, Jerusalem, and Palestine. There are three parts. The first presents a case study of a single street, now known as Star Street, in Bethlehem. It examines the failure of a three-year pre-millennial project to open up this street to tourists: a project that would have also effectively opened up the city of Bethlehem itself to visitors. The second part discusses how this study helps us identify the malaise in the organization and administration of Palestinian tourism and pilgrimage. The third section offers a comprehensive, if also compressed (given the space constraints of a book chapter), outline of a Palestinian tourism strategy capable of addressing both the particular case raised here and also the wider challenges that this case raises. The chapter is intended to be as relevant to other Palestinian cities, including (and pre-eminently) Jerusalem, as to Bethlehem, its overall aim being to contribute to discussions about the future of tourism and pilgrimage in Palestine as a whole (also see Dabdoub and Zoughbi-Janineh 2011, a chapter in a book, which ideally should be read in conjunction with the present chapter).

The underlying reason why we consider the issues raised here of significance is that although tourism and pilgrimage are, and will continue to be, the backbone of the present and future Palestinian economies and although there are several strategic reports (for example, International Trade Centre 2013) there seems little 'official' strategic work being actually carried out on the ground. According to the International Trade Centre (2013), the strategic 'organization of the sector is inefficient' (International Trade Centre 2013: 32). Incredibly, for example, although an official decision to establish a Palestine Tourism Board was made by the authorities in 2010, this vital institution is still not established in 2015 (International Trade Centre 2013: 28). Arguably, such lack of strategic efficiency lies at the heart of the failure of the Star Street project as described below.

Geographical and political context: Bethlehem and Bethlehem Governorate

Bethlehem, the eponymous town of Bethlehem Governorate is located south of the city of Jerusalem (in fact for much of its history, Jerusalem and Bethlehem have been a single urban space that is now divided by the Segregation Wall) in the southern part of the West Bank. The governorate borders Hebron Governorate to the south/southwest, the Dead Sea to the east, and the 1949 Armistice Line (the 'Green Line') to the west. Within the governorate there are Palestinian built up areas, Israeli settlements, closed military areas, military bases, nature reserves, forests and cultivated areas (Applied Research Institute 2010).

The population of the city consists of a mixture of old established residents (mostly Christian), more recent immigrants from surrounding villages (especially since 1948 and 1967), Bedouin from the vicinity, and the residents of three refugee camps. Today, slightly more than two-thirds of the population are Muslim whilst slightly less than a third are Christian. Bethlehem, together with Jerusalem and Nazareth, comprises one of the most sacred urban areas for Christianity in the region. The Basilica and Grotto of the Nativity are sacred to Catholics, Protestants, Orthodox and Armenians, most of which have ownership rights in the church. Other sacred sites in the town include the churches of St Catherine and St Jerome, the Milk Grotto and the pilgrimage site of Shepherds' Field. Bethlehem is one of the cities under the control of the Palestinian Authority (known as 'Area A') (see Chapter 2 as well as Chapter 6 in this volume) and, together with the towns of Beit Sahour (to the east), Beit Jala (to the west), and the three refugee camps of Aida, Beit Jibrin, and Deheisheh constitutes an agglomeration of over 76,000 people. Bethlehem District, encompassing the surrounding villages, contains approximately 180,000 people (Isaac 2013).

The city has a young population (nearly half being less than 15 years old). Many people in Bethlehem live in overcrowded conditions with most living in rooms housing more than one person. Bethlehem, Beit Jala and Beit Sahour are all marked by substantial (and increasing) emigration – many local Christian families presently living in diaspora communities in the USA, South America and Europe (See Chapter 8 as well as Chapter 16 in this volume).

The urban and rural economies of city and district are heavily dependent on tourism. The city has upwards of 2.5 million visitors per year and the industry employs up to twenty per cent of the working population. But the tourism industry is seasonal and this leads to many of those working in some capacity in the tourism in the summer being laid off in the winter months. A large proportion of the employees in the hotels are casual. Historically the principal enterprises linked to tourism have been the production of olive wood and mother of pearl souvenirs (previously handmade, now increasingly machine produced) as well as clothing.

At the time of writing, however, there is a noticeable increase in Chinese made items filling the souvenir shops.

From 1967 until 1995, Bethlehem, as much of Palestine, was occupied and administered by the Israeli army. Following the Oslo agreement in 1993, the Israeli army withdrew from Bethlehem's urban centre and the Palestinian Authority (PA) took control. With the outbreak of the second intifada in September 2000, the Israeli army re-occupied the city and blocked the roads leading in and out of the district. In 2002, Bethlehem was placed under 24-hour curfew for 156 days (United Nation Office for the Coordination of Humanitarian Affairs occupied Palestine Territory (UNOCHA) 2004). For the duration of the second intifada, Israeli actions severely affected the tourism industry in Bethlehem through its bombardment of two hotels (the Paradise Hotel and the Inn), its widespread shooting and infliction of damage to the city infrastructure, and the imposition of roadblocks, military closures and checkpoints. This made entry to Bethlehem difficult and periodically impossible. The same was true of other Palestinian towns and cities (Isaac 2010). At present, the Wall and surrounding checkpoints effectively imprison Bethlehem, Beit Sahour and Beit Jala (ATG 2008).

A series of Israeli incursions between November 2001 and summer 2002 led to an eight-year collapse of tourism. In 2006, unemployment reached 60 per cent in Bethlehem, compared with 25 per cent across the rest of Palestine (The Guardian Weekend 2010: 37). However, temporary incursions still continue – often at night.

Tourism in Bethlehem and Palestine

Pilgrimage and tourism in Bethlehem have long revolved around the Nativity Church, thought to be the birthplace of Jesus. However, as Dabdoub and Zougbhi-Janineh (2011) show and this chapter reinforces, the concentration by the tourism industry on the Church has been a mixed blessing for the city as a whole. Whilst ensuring the centrality of Bethlehem to the tourism map of the 'Holy Land' generally it has generally been the case that tourists and pilgrims have not visited the rest of the city and/or the governorate, even though these contain a vast array of other attractive and interesting sites. Two important points also need to be considered here. First of all, Bethlehem, as Palestine more widely, has no direct control over the entry of visitors from the outside world. All access points (air, sea and land) to the West Bank and the Gaza Strip are controlled by Israel. Hence, international visitors and pilgrims wishing to visit Palestine must first pass through Israeli borders, using Israeli entry points: Ben Gurion Airport, the Allenby Bridge crossing near Jericho, Sheikh Hussein Bridge in Bissan, the Arava crossing in Eilat and the Rafah crossing in Gaza. Secondly, this closure is one of the main reasons why the majority of visitors to Bethlehem are day visitors, although the number of overnight stays in the city has been rising since early 2005. The countries that are presently the top three sources of visitors to Palestine and Bethlehem are Poland, Italy and Russia whilst Germany, Spain, France and United Kingdom remain amongst the top ten (See Chapter 9 in this volume). Palestine has also seen an increase in visitors from emerging and growing markets such as

Indonesia, India and Brazil. Palestinians living inside Israel also account for a substantial portion of visitors to the city.

The remainder of the chapter begins by tracing the recent history of attempts to revive the fortunes of Star Street for locals and tourists alike, and by so doing to open up Bethlehem for visitors. It then analyses the reasons for the failure to achieve this and concludes by offering the outlines of a Palestinian tourism strategy that, if operative, could have ensured that the Star Street succeeded.

Part I: the Case of Star Street

For centuries before the beginning of the British Mandate in Palestine in 1917, the main entrance to the city was through the street known as *Ras Fteis*, which was given the name of Star Street around 1960. The modern name symbolises the narrative of the star that led the Magi into Bethlehem to see the newly born Jesus Christ. During the British Mandate, Bethlehem municipality built a beacon at al-Manarah Square (demolished in 1945 on the grounds that it hindered traffic) where it is believed that the Magi-leading star stopped. Star Street is also known as the 'Patriarch's Route' since it is the last stage of the pilgrimage from Jerusalem to Bethlehem made by the patriarchs of the individual churches on their annual Christmas processions. Star Street is thus both a pilgrimage route and historical entry point to Bethlehem and also a recognized part of Bethlehem's historic religious heritage. It contains much of the outstanding architecture of the Old City.

Families and trades

According to Dabdoub and Zoughbi-Janineh (2011) it is believed that Star Street was first populated by the at-Tarajmeh clan, comprising the families of 'Abit, Abu al 'Arraj, Abu Fheileh, Abu Gheith, Abu Jaber, Abu Khalil, Batarseh, Dabdoub, Dahburah, Dawed, D'eik and many more. Revault, Stantelli and Weill-Rochant (1997: 14) state that the at-Tarajmeh Quarter (comprising Star Street and the surrounding area) was established around the seventeenth century. at-Tarajmeh are believed to be the remnants of the crusaders, originally Italians, who married locals from Bethlehem and worked as translators for the Franciscan fathers as well as for the Italian pilgrims visiting Bethlehem. Prior to seventeenth century, the population of Star Street, as the rest of Bethlehem, were farmers, peasants and stockbreeders.

During the second half of the twentieth century, Star Street – which at the beginning of the century had developed into an active commercial centre – suffered a drastic decline, many enterprises relocating to newly emerging areas outside the historic core of the city. This decline continued apace following the outbreak of the first Intifada in December 1987 and came to a total standstill at the beginning of the second Intifada in September 2000. Many of the shops and artisanal workshops located in Star Streets have closed. As noted above, the street which at one time had been the commercial centre for the whole of Bethlehem is today a shadow of its former self, the few remaining small shops (offering at best only a very limited selection of goods) attracting the residents of the street but few others.

Star Street and the colonial/contemporary tourism narrative of Bethlehem

The colonial narrative of Palestine, rooted in the European tours of the nineteenth century, persists in the tourism industry today and is most dominant in the traditional 'pilgrimage tourism' that dominates the Bethlehem economy. These days, as already noted, upwards of two and a half million tourists visit Bethlehem each year, the vast majority on organized pilgrimage tours through church-affiliated groups from all over the Christian world. The tours follow fairly similar itineraries to the mass pilgrimages of the late nineteenth century. Coaches enter Bethlehem in charter buses transporting groups of pilgrim/tourists to the Nativity Church for a fast tour and photo opportunity, following which they return to the bus before returning through the Israeli-built Wall surrounding the city, probably calling at a pre-selected souvenir shop. The selection process depends (entirely) on negotiated commissions. Recent figures (authors' field work) have included a report that a souvenir shop owner plying for trade would need to pay five thousand dollars to the bus driver (for subsequent distribution to significant others including guides) for a busload of American pilgrims and one thousand dollars for a busload of Nigerians.

Most pilgrimage tours spend little more than two hours in Bethlehem. One of the consequences of this is that the local community sees few tourists outside buses as they speed though the city on their way in or out. Visitors to the Nativity Church have a very tightly controlled view of Bethlehem including little or no reference to its modern society. Part of this is a carryover from the nineteenth century when Palestinians were seen, in the main, as part of the scenery, but also has more recent provenance. Palestinian tour guides were, and remain, tightly censored by Israel who look for any signs that they are offering their clients any sort of Palestinian narrative. This is just one of the reasons that visitors gain little or no understanding of the city and its inhabitants. Indeed the lack of interaction between the tourists and the local community is quite striking and has long been a source of concern by those engaged in an 'alternative' type of tourism in which local people are depicted as 'living stones' who enable visitors to gain a much more rounded narrative of what it means to be a citizen of the city. The concern is partly economic. As will be clear by now a large segment of the town's industry is dedicated to services related to tourism, yet many (small and medium sized) businesses see very little revenue.

The reasons for the continuation of what are essentially nineteenth century pilgrimage practices (and the resulting blindness on the part of visitors to the realities of life in the city) are complex and will be examined further below. One factor is that, given the multitude of restrictions faced by Palestinian operators without Jerusalem or other Israeli identity, it is considerably easier for tour operators in Israel (Israelis and Palestinians alike) to make comprehensive arrangements for visitors to the 'Holy Land' than their counterparts without an Israeli identity in Palestine.

Opening Star Street and Bethlehem to visitors

In 1997, three years before the Christian millennium, the Palestinian Authority (PA) set up an organization, 'Bethlehem 2000' (BL2000), with funding from a number of international agencies including the World Bank. The PA gave BL2000 the status of a ministry. Following the millennium, the cultural heritage unit of BL2000 became the Centre for the Preservation of Cultural Heritage (CCHP). Today the CCHP, staffed as it is by architects, planners and experts in the built environment, tangible, and intangible cultural heritage of the three city cores of Bethlehem, Beit Jala, and Beit Sahour, is the leading centre concerned with the theory and practice of cultural, spatial, and architectural heritage of these cities.

Two of BL2000's earliest projects consisted of planning and mapping a 'Nativity Trail' from Nazareth to Bethlehem and the preparation of Star Street as a pedestrianized route for visitors entering Bethlehem. The former was a (primarily) walking/hiking route based on the journey made by Mary and Joseph before the birth of Jesus. This project, though expertly planned, never materialized partly because of the difficulties posed by the fact that the trail crossed the border between Israel and Palestine at a time (after the start of the second Intifada in 2000) when such border crossings were becoming increasingly problematic. The latter did not work either, but for a different reason as follows.

The staff at 'BL2000' developed a plan for Star Street that would involve buses/ coaches dropping their tourist/pilgrim passengers off at the entrance to Star Street before the buses proceeded to the bus station enabling tourists to walk down Star Street to Manger Square, passing as they did so, numerous small shops, cafés, artisanal and craft workshops, and other spots of interest for visitors to the city. Visitors could, of course, branch off the street to visit the other sites of interest in the town. Carol Dabdoub, one of the leading planners of this enterprise, thought in terms of the opportunities the plan would bring both for those who could offer attractive items (from the traditional mother-of-pearl and olive wood souvenirs to more contemporary fashion items and beyond) and also to a new kind of 'cultural tourist' who could discover the streets, alleys, and steps around the street. She and her colleagues devoted three years to the project, much of the time spent in explaining, persuading, and cajoling tradesmen and craft workers to return to the street and open/re-open their premises in the expectation of doing profitable business in a revitalized part of town. This long-term vision was linked in the short-term to a radical extension of a Christmas market that had been encouraged (by USAID amongst others) to take place in the street. Dabdoub and BL2000 proposed that the market should take place throughout the year (see Dabdoub and Zougbhi-Janineh 2011). BL2000 also successfully persuaded several foreign donors to invest in the refurbishment work in the street. The overall purpose in raising the profile and availability of Star Street to visitors/pilgrims was not only to bring them into what is arguably the most beautiful street in Bethlehem but also to provide an opportunity for them to peel off into the surrounding streets and passage-ways, and in this way come to see much more of Bethlehem than they normally do.

In the weeks before 2000 the plans were just about to bear fruit when BL2000 learnt that PADICO (the largest company in Palestine and first to enter the

Palestinian stock exchange with investment interests, inter alia, in real estate, industry and agriculture, financial and communication services, and tourism) had signed an agreement with Bethlehem Municipality that all tourist buses (without exception) were required, on their entry to the city, to park first of all in the new PADICO built bus/coach station, paying $59 a time for the privilege. The agreement involved the municipality receiving a share of this fee. At a stroke the ideas and plans to open Star Street to pedestrian visitors fell apart, in the process leaving a number of potential enterprises in the lurch and thus producing feelings of considerable bitterness amongst planners and small traders alike.

Star Street as United Nations World Heritage Site

A decade and a half after PADICO destroyed the efforts of BL2000 to open up Star Street there was a new development in the saga of the street. The nomination by Palestine of several sites (including Star Street) as World Heritage Sites (See Chapter 6 in this volume; Kershner 2012) is discussed below. Whether or not this will bring new hope to the street and/or Bethlehem itself remains to be seen.

Part II: analysis of the debacle – lessons from Star Street for tourism in Bethlehem and Palestine

The debacle that resulted in the collapse of the plans for Star Street brought into clear relief the structural, political, economic, and cultural, and organizational shortcomings of tourism organization in Bethlehem and in Palestine more generally. In order to understand the failure of the attempt by a combination of parties and institutions, led in this case by BL2000, to enable more visitors to discover Bethlehem by foot the chapter follows Dabdoub's and Zougbhi-Janineh's (2011) suggestion of identifying the various actors, voices and organizations involved in tourism in the city at the same time as gaining a sense of the contours of Bethlehem's civil society. The latter is especially important given that any Palestinian tourism strategy (encompassing Bethlehem, Jerusalem, and other cities) needs to be anchored in Palestinian civil society.

Small and medium sized actors, institutions and associations

The residents of Star Street include Muslim and Christian families with relatively low incomes and with a fairly high level of unemployment. The former *hwash* (singular: *hosh* – house, or large habitable space within a house containing extended families) in the street (*Hosh Dabdoub, Hosh al Sirian*, for example) are now no longer inhabited by large and often well-to-do Christian families but by groups of families renting separate rooms. Questions of ownership of buildings in the street are complex with an interweaving set of owners. These include absentee landlords, a Catholic charitable organization that rents out properties, and mainly elderly owner-occupiers. The complex mixture of ownership and lack of neighbourhood associations is typical of other streets and neighbourhoods in the city.

Despite residents typically having very close relationships with neighbours in their streets, quarters, and across the town, there appear to be few street or neighbourhood associations with any kind of collective political influence. The same seems largely true of small businesses. There is a chamber of commerce in the city but this institution does not seem to have routine relations with the smaller souvenir shops, souvenir producers, workshops, or artisanal enterprises associated in one way or another with tourism. These small businesses operate in a largely independent way and seem lacking the capacities to exercise collective representation, this means they have little visible influence on public institutions involved in tourism policy or planning. These features are of direct relevance to the case of Star Street since it is precisely such small businesses, souvenir shops, cafés, workshops, and other enterprises, that would have been at the forefront of activity in the event of the street becoming, once again, a pedestrian hub. The commissions referred to above (payments from large souvenir shops to bus drivers and others) would and could not realistically be paid by the small businesses that BL2000, CCHP, and others envisaged would populate the street. There are also numerous individual workers (from guides to street pedlars to taxi drivers and many others) either directly or indirectly involved with tourism who do not have any discernable way of exercising influence in the formulation or direction of tourism policy or planning.

The above very preliminary and inadequate paragraphs need a great deal more detailed research to present anything like a convincing ethnographic coverage of the position of many small and medium sized businesses engaged in tourism in Bethlehemite tourism. However, for the moment we may make a tentative generalization as follows: tourism in Bethlehem depends on the city's citizens and the small and medium sized businesses with which some of these are associated. Few if any of these have any means of making effective collective representations to any regulatory body or institution associated with the administration and organization of tourism in the city. This is a generalization that is possibly also applicable to some of the traders in the Old City of Jerusalem.

Looking at these various institutions, there is very little to no cooperation among these players. There is a lack of cooperation and consultation when it comes to tourism planning, or a vision (Faulkner 2003) for the future in answering the question where we would like to be in ten years ahead as a tourism destination in Bethlehem in general and Palestine in particular.

Large-scale institutions including international donors

Our narrative of Star Street ended with its failure to become an alternative route for visitors on foot into Bethlehem following the agreement between PADICO and the municipality. In the third of our extremely brief considerations of some of the institutions involved in tourism in Bethlehem we will consider two large institutional structures: PADICO itself and foreign donors.

PADICO has a broad range of interests from telecommunications to tourism to property development. It is also the majority shareholder of the Palestinian

Box 14.1 Medium and larger institutions in both public and private sector – some associated directly or indirectly with the governance of the city and its tourism sector

Bethlehem Municipality has 15 elected members from a range of political parties and their branches. There is a statutory condition that the mayor, deputy mayor, and majority of councillors are Christian whilst there are a number of other seats open to all. In the most recent elections (in 2005) Hamas gained the majority of seats.

Mayors of Bethlehem Municipality have historically held prominent positions in Palestinian political affairs. In recent history, for example, before the setting up of the PA in 1994 and for a period immediately after that, the mayor, the nationally and internationally known Elias Freij, who owned several souvenir shops in Bethlehem and who was a member of various Palestinian negotiating teams, held, in effect, the position of Palestinian delegate/representative/minister for tourism affairs. Freij attended, as the main Palestinian delegate, the 1994 conference in Taba in the Sinai peninsula which was attended by many Ministers of Tourism from Middle-Eastern states, including Israel. There was talk, during and after this conference of making a 'Middle-Eastern Riviera' from the Mediterranean and Red Sea coasts of Lebanon, Israel, Egypt, and Jordan. The PA appointed Freij as Minister of Tourism in 1995, a post he held for two years before stepping down as mayor. During his time as mayor he managed to attract considerable financial support from foreign donors for infrastructure projects.

In 2012 Mrs Vera Baboun, a member of *Fatah*, was voted mayor and is now on the committee preparing Bethlehem to be a capital of Arabic Culture in 2019. The deputy mayor is Issam Juha who is also director of the Centre for Cultural Heritage Preservation (CCHP). That the deputy mayor of the municipality is also director of the CCHP is perhaps a sign that in some important senses the CCHP, which leads the city in its heritage initiatives, also (unsurprisingly) takes a prominent interest in tourism. After all there is no department in the municipality dealing specifically with tourism although there are a number of departments dealing with other matters such as infrastructure and education.

CCHP's reputation was recently enhanced when Star Street and the village of Battir, near Bethlehem, were granted World Heritage Site (WHS) status (See Chapter 6 in this volume). Staff of the CCHP composed the plans for both sites, having worked closely with a Palestinian team of experts established in 2002. This committee gained technical and financial support from foreign donors to develop WHS and encouraged Palestinian authorities to take measures for the protection of Palestinian heritage. From its inception the committee expressed concerns over the damage and destruction of Palestinian heritage. It submitted an inventory of 20 Palestinian holy sites, of which 17 are cultural and three are natural. The inventory includes historical cities such as Bethlehem (as a whole), Hebron and Nablus, cultural and natural landscape sites (such as El-Bariyah), major archaeological sites (e.g. Ancient Jericho, Qumran, Sebastia), natural sites (e.g. Wadi Gaza, Umm er-Rihan) and potential trans-boundary sites (The Dead Sea). The Old City of Jerusalem was inscribed on the World Heritage list in 1982. At its meeting in 2012, the UNESCO World Heritage Council discussed new WHS, including the 'pilgrimage route' and Battir (Taha 2012). Both were inscribed following an emergency application in an urgency motion. The PA delegation argued that these sites were in particular danger: from a leaking roof in the case of the former and Israel's proposal to build an extension to the Wall in the case of the latter.

A sense of the CCHP's growing influence vis-à-vis the municipality in matters of tourism and heritage, partly stimulated in the following case by the United States Agency for International Development (USAID), may be gleaned from a very recent project carried out jointly by the CCHP and the Municipality of Beit Sahour. A Memorandum of Understanding signed by the Mayor of Beit Sahour and the director of the CCHP (also, as already noted, Deputy Mayor of Bethlehem) was drawn up in 2015. This involved (in the words of the MOU) 'the rehabilitation of Shepherds Field Street' to become a tourist street under the supervision of the CCHP. The project aims to improve street lighting and asphalt the street and pavement.

This project was launched without consultation with local residents and businesses. Indeed, some businesses may suffer as a result of the project, mainly because a pedestrianised street in this location will make it impossible for coaches to park near that part of the street where several restaurants are presently located. Visitors will need to alight further away thus making it less likely that they will in the future be able to reach the restaurants that were responsible for the development of the area in the first place.

The Alternative Tourism Group (ATG) is the longest running and nationally and internationally most distinguished and successful group that has, over many years, critically challenged the dominance of the "classic" pilgrimage route in which tourists visit the Nativity Church, a souvenir shop, and little else. ATG operates imaginative and informative tours and encourages their tourists to stay in local homes and eat in local restaurants. Its director was a member of the 2008 TEMPUS group (see below).

Bethlehem University has been involved in tourism, cultural heritage, and hospitality in at least three ways. Firstly, the Institute of Hotel Management, founded in 1973 and for much of the recent period under the leadership of Nabil Mufdi has offered courses in the hospitality industry. Throughout its history it has been involved in international networks of hospitality and tourism specialist university departments. Secondly, the

Turathana Centre for Palestinian Heritage was set up with the help of Ireland Aid following the millennium in 2000 in the University library. Thirdly, the MA in Tourism, Pilgrimage, and the Cultural Industries was composed and funded from the European Commission's TEMPUS programme with the participation of Joensuu University, Finland; University College London; and London Metropolitan University (Isaac, 2008). Research conducted in the programme is extremely valuable with respect to knowledge transfer for policy-making and planning. The TEMPUS MA has given rise to a new MA in Tourism validated by the PA that commenced in 2014.

Dar Annadwe, the International Centre of Bethlehem (ICB), is a long established and also rapidly growing ecumenically minded institution rooted in the Lutheran tradition under the direction of the Rev. Mitri Raheb (International Centre of Bethlehem, 2015). It has generated a substantial number of educational and training programmes in the arts and cultural industries. It also has a guest house that is recommended by Lonely Planet. Over the past ten years, with funding from the US and several European countries, the ICB has built Dar al-Kalima School, college, and Health and Wellness Center. The college will be offering degree courses in tourism from 2016.

Bethlehem Bible College is one of three centres for the training of tour guides (the other two being Dar Annadwe and the university) within its wider remit of training Christian priests for work in Palestine.

The Ministry of Tourism and Antiquities is based in Bethlehem. The minister is the symbolic head of Palestinian tourism and routinely appears at international events and conferences as well as marketing initiatives in such market sources as London and Berlin. Over the years aid from the UNDP has been given to strengthen the work of the ministry, a fact that finds eloquent testimony in the substantial collection of specialist reports by foreign consultants in its library (including Burns and Selwyn, 1997). Despite such aid the ministry has chosen not to generate a Palestinian tourism strategy.

Securities and Equities Commission (PSEC), the Palestinian stock exchange supervised by the Palestinian Ministry of Finance. PADICO is thus a private/public partnership active in all sections of the Palestinian economy, financed by private investors and banks. In addition PADICO articulates the receipt and use of investment funds from USAID, The World Bank, and EU. Its stated intention is to promote new businesses and, as they are floated, reduce its own shareholding to around, preferably under, 50 per cent.

Dabdoub and Zougbhi-Janineh (2011), suggest that shortly after PADICO concluded its agreement with Bethlehem Municipality, it transferred the running of the bus terminal to a partially owned subsidiary, Al-Aqaria (51.8 per cent owned by PADICO). The chief reason for the failure of BL2000's attempt to revive Star Street was that the agreement was neither expected nor accepted by the public. Although BL2000 possessed the power of a ministry when it was first founded, certain weaknesses, both external and internal partially explain why it was blindsided by the PADICO deal. As Dabdoub and Zougbhi-Janineh (2011) suggest the main structural weakness of the Star Street plan was that there was a notable lack of communication and co-operation between the institutions involved (including BL2000, Bethlehem Municipality, Ministry of Tourism, shop owners, and PADICO itself) most of whom were pre-occupied with their own particular interests.

Finally, many of the institutions identified here have been, and are periodically, the recipients of foreign aid. Several observations can be made. The first is that the largest tranches of aid are given to PADICO, a fact that ensures its primacy in the management of the Palestinian economy, including the tourism industry, of liberal 'free market' development. PADICO is a private company dedicated to attracting private investment including foreign direct investment so that new companies can develop in order for them to become independent (or, rather, dependent on their shareholders rather than donors). Many observers would argue that this places the power to determine strategy, including tourism strategy, squarely in the hands of the private sector and out of the hands of Bethlehemites. The second is that lesser amounts of aid are distributed to institutions such as the CCHP. But here, as in the case of the development of the Beit Sahour tourism beautification project, the donor stipulates time constraints that make proper and professional consultation difficult if not impossible. Once again the donor holds the power over the way tourism policy is pursued. Thirdly, the seemingly benign role of UNESCO (not strictly speaking a donor but a foreign presence with very considerable influence on tourism and heritage policy) does not, in itself, lead to coherent tourism strategic policy. For example, at the time of writing Battir suffers from a *surfeit* of visitors, leading to quite a dramatic increase in rubbish, and from financial strains in the village municipality.

The above (once again very preliminary and ethnographically inadequate) account of some of the actors and institutions involved in the politico-economic structure of the city's tourism industry may be briefly summarized in the following way. It highlights the significant fact that there are several institutions have undertaken innovative work that has made long-term contributions to practices in tourism. Despite this there is no overall plan or strategy for tourism in Bethlehem and the industry is dominated by a mixture of a powerful private sector investment company (PADICO) and foreign donors simultaneously pulling in different directions, with Palestinian public sector bodies apparently powerless to steer the process. Whilst such a structure persists there is little chance that any project such as the Star Street project stands any chance of success. To emphasize yet again, the administration and direction of tourism and pilgrimage in Bethlehem is dominated by a privatized 'free market' that has resulted, *inter alia*, in the continuation of tourism practices dominated by the Nativity Church and some large souvenir shops to the economic detriment of the wider population of the city.

An opening up of the spaces of Bethlehem would effectively open up the revenues from the tourism business to a much larger constituency of residents. But this would only realistically happen if an institutional body with members representing all those (particularly small and medium sized) businesses associated directly and indirectly with tourism and pilgrimage possessed the power and authority to compose a tourism strategy, mobilize residents and traders behind it, and ensure that it is put into practice. Presently civil society in Bethlehem has little power in the planning or organization of tourism in the city.

Part III: towards a Palestinian tourism strategy encompassing Bethlehem and Jerusalem

The third part of this chapter builds on the analysis offered above of the failure of the Star Street project and the lessons it offers about the lack of tourism planning and strategy. The aim in what follows is to discuss what a professional tourism strategy could consist of. First, it refers to a significant conference held in Jerusalem in 2015. Secondly, it outlines some of the essential aspects of a tourism strategy using the experience of other largely Mediterranean destinations to do so. Thirdly, it integrates research on various key aspects of tourism strategy conducted by graduates of the 2008 EU TEMPUS project at Bethlehem University.

The 2015 Jerusalem Tourism Cluster (JTC) conference: aims and objectives

This significant conference was held in Jerusalem in May 2015 with the objective of discussing the establishment of a democratically and civil society run Palestinian tourism strategy with Jerusalem at the centre. The conference was called to determine how such a strategy could move beyond traditional pilgrimage towards development of new types of tourism built on new niches and markets in a way that would encourage a greater number of independent tourists to visit Jerusalem and which thus, partly as a result, would benefit the largest possible number of residents of the city (Jerusalem Tourism Conference, 2015).

The conference organizers emphasized that there is presently no Palestinian regulatory body overseeing the organization and administration of tourism in Jerusalem and that the city's tourism industry lacks any sort of normal tourism governance or legal framework vis-à-vis the Israeli sector. Thus all the aspects of a professional tourism sector such as the expansion of hotels/hospitality outlets, expansion of the cultural industries, issues of guiding, site development, mapping and the making of new routes for visitors to the city, and so on seem to be dependent on the political whims of the Israeli authorities. Moreover, the city's municipality is clearly not a municipality in any normal sense but an institution that serves Israeli communal interests to the detriment of Palestinian interests. In every visible sense Jerusalem in its divided and occupied condition is (obviously) a depressingly special case. Nonetheless it cannot realistically be claimed that the rest of Palestine has an effective tourism policy or strategy either. Occupation is partly to blame – but so are the politico-economic structures and processes that we have described above in relation to the case of Bethlehem and Star Street. To put the matter rather bluntly and crudely the organisation of Palestinian tourism appears, in many important respects, to be subject to the private interests of a large and powerful investment company operating in a politico-economic field of frankly pliant public institutions.

A potential tourism strategy defined

Using comparative examples from various parts of the mainly Mediterranean world, nine core aspects of what a professional tourism strategy is normally thought to be may be identified. Data presented here derives from ongoing work, much of it conducted in the context of EU supported inter-university research projects civil society institutions (including universities) concerned with tourism in the cities of Alexandria, Malta, Ancona, Bologna, Marseille, Chania (Crete), Sarajevo, Palma/Ciutat de Mallorca and its neighbouring municipality Calvia (in which one of the largest mass tourism resorts, Magaluf, is to be found) in the Mediterranean region, in addition to Borlange in Sweden and Addis Ababa in Ethiopia. At various points along the way we may also draw attention to initiatives in both Bethlehem and Jerusalem themselves. The experiences of tourism in all these cities are highly relevant to the question of a Palestinian tourism strategy. Evidence suggests that there are at least nine elements of what tourism authorities in our mainly (but not exclusively) Mediterranean cities would recognize as a reasonable and effective tourism strategy.

Furthermore, the section will describe the research and development work carried out by those who graduated in 2008 from the EU TEMPUS funded MA in Tourism and Pilgrimage at Bethlehem University and those who are currently involved in the degree, newly validated as it has been by the Palestinian Authority. The purpose here is to show that every single feature of the professional tourism strategy as we have defined it has been, or is, subject to research by the BU MA graduates and/or their followers.

(i) Tourism governance

A well-organized and democratic system of tourism governance is the bedrock of any tourism strategy (Hughes 1994). As the failure of the Star Street project demonstrated, tourism cannot successfully operate according to the erratic whims and private interests of one particular branch of the private financial sector. Governance may take a number of forms. Although, in the cities we have mentioned, there is normally a physical centre (such as the municipality itself) the key to successful governance is that it involves a large collection of democratically committed civil society actors and institutions, of all sizes, which are involved in tourism. In the cases of Jerusalem and Bethlehem there is, at present, no such centre. Nevertheless the JTC conference itself, gathering together such a wide cross section of tourism professionals – souvenir shop owners, artisans, artists, hoteliers, operators, agents, craftspeople, tourism information specialists, academics, planners and others – strongly suggests that such a centre is on the point of emerging. This issue is returned to below. Two dissertations derived from the TEMPUS project at Bethlehem University, one on tourism governance, the creation of a Palestinian tourism board (Daher, 2008) and another in tourism law (Abu Jaber, 2008).

(ii) National and international civil society networks

Unlike most other industries, tourism and pilgrimage are founded upon the nature (land, landscape, flora, fauna, and so on) and culture (social life as expressed in life in streets and markets, architecture, as well as the overtly 'cultural' practices of a city) of tourist destinations. As such, tourism is, by its nature, dependent on social groups of all kinds: community groups, faith groups, women's and youth groups, municipalities, voluntary societies, unions, schools, universities, and all the other groups and associations that make up civil society. For any tourism strategy to be effective all of these need to be integrated within a comprehensive tourism awareness programme (Burns and Selwyn 2007).

Three Palestinian institutions illustrative of successful local civil society networking are the Alternative Tourism Group (ATG) (Kassis 2008) the oldest alternative tourism operator in Palestine, Kairos Palestine (Kairos 2015), and the recently formed Network for Experimental Palestinian Tourism Organization (NEPTO) which was created during the formation of Abraham's Path (Sa'adeh, 2015) and which is made up of a network of 18 local third sector civil society organizations. Both ATG and NEPTO are deeply anchored in networks of local and international institutions. Both arrange homestays for visitors, encourage experience local cultural activities and meetings with local leaders. One dissertation from the TEMPUS project resulted in the study of Battir (see also Chapter 5 in this volume) that proposed an alternative form of tourism in Palestine which is rural tourism, to complement and add value to the traditional offer based on pilgrimage (Zougbi-Janineh, 2008)

(iii) Knowing/mapping sites

Any professional tourism strategy needs constantly to identify, describe, and map the tourist sites and services on offer. The organizers of the JTC conference emphasized the need to take visitors 'beyond pilgrimage'. This involves extending the visitors' experiences beyond classical holy sites. In Jerusalem this would involve looking beyond the Old City to sites and experiences of interest outside as well as inside the Old City. Is there any reason, for example, why Salah Al-Din Street should not do particularly festive garments at Christmas and Ramadan and invite visitors to take part in these and other festivals?

Festivals (which normally have both sacred and secular aspects) occur throughout the Mediterranean and are not only occasions for local celebration of urban and rural spaces but also as focal points for making visitors welcome (Boissevain 2015). Furthermore, they typically provide opportunities for tourists to meet locals on common ground. Festivals are moments when people may feel disposed to exchange stories about themselves. Experiences of ATG, the Abraham's path, and other alternative tourism initiatives suggest that there is a large and growing market in visitors who want to hear stories about Jerusalemite and/or Bethlehemite families and their modes of life and work, worship, leisure, artistic/musical involvement, schools, hospitality, cuisine, and so on. This is hardly surprising given that at the centre of all tourism everywhere there are stories. In Malta there is a *festa* every weekend throughout the year. All Maltese *festi* include music, food, dressing up, parades, and so on. All welcome tourists to join local expressions of pride of, and identification with, place in tourist. All find their way on to tourist itineraries. One of the studies derived from the EU MA funded programme was by Dabdoub (2008; Dabdoub and Zoughbi-Janineh 2011) entitled 'Star street and the struggle for development in Bethlehem'. If Bethlehem is to develop a sustainable tourism industry that benefits the city in its entirety, it needs a strategic vision that fulfils two aims: exercising more control over tours and tour operators and providing attractions for the visitor that will ensure an extended stay within the city.

In the case of Bethlehem and Jerusalem, world-renowned institutions such as *ARIJ* could provide inspiration in the specialized tourist map making field. The Applied Research Institute (ARIJ) located in Bethlehem and founded in 1990. The Applied Research Institute – Jerusalem (ARIJ)/Society is a non-profit organization devoted to promoting sustainable development in the Palestine occupied territories and the self-reliance of the Palestinian people through greater control over their natural resources. ARIJ works specifically to augment the local stock of scientific and technical knowledge and to introduce and devise more efficient methods of resource utilization and conservation, improved practices, and appropriate technology. ARIJ represents several years of combined organizational experience in the Palestinian territory in the fields of economic, social, natural resources management, water management, sustainable agriculture, and political dynamics of development in the area and plays an active role in the local community as an advocate for greater co-operation among local institutions, as well as international and non-governmental organizations (Applied Research Institute 2015).

(iv) 'Cultural industries' widely defined

At the heart of the tourism offer of any region and/or city lie the 'cultural industries' (Hesmondhaigh 2007). Using this rather loose term as widely as possible, this refers, amongst other things, to all those professions, productive operations, artistic activities, performances, exhibitions, institutions and associations – together (crucially) with the trade(s) with which these are associated – that bear upon the presentation by region and/or city of its history and communal character. In the cultural industries, two dissertations were written one by Sartawi (2008), in which provided a strategy for the Palestinian museums and another on 'Dabke', history development and contemporary possibilities in tourism by Odah (2008).

(v) Hospitality

Hospitality lies at the centre of all tourism and pilgrimage(Selwyn 2000). It is also, arguably and potentially, Bethlehem's and Jerusalem's strongest card in the competitive economy of tourism in historic cities. One central challenge for contemporary Bethlehem, Jerusalem and Palestine more generally is to integrate the accommodation offer (including hotels, hostels, home-stays, couch surfing and airBandB arrangements) with the needs of the 'new' tourists that the emerging Palestinian tourism strategy hopes to attract. The real challenges in this regard are thus not so much how to raise investment for, and to generate financial profits from, five star hotels (such as the PADICO built five star Al Mashtar hotel in Gaza that claims to attract diplomats and other foreign and wealthy local visitors) but investigate how to provide appropriate accommodation for backpackers and other independent tourists who will come to Palestine to walk Abraham's path and the streets of Bethlehem, including Star Street. In this respect the appearance of a new hostel for such tourists in Ramallah is of great interest and importance. A second and equally (or even greater) challenge for future tourism in Bethlehem and Jerusalem lies in the field of gastronomy. The first shoots of innovative Palestinian cookery in Bethlehem (such as *Hosh Jasmin* in Beit Jala) places the role of such cooking in the spotlight. This is also something of considerable potential given the increasing international profile of classical Jerusalem food as a result of the increased profile of the Ottolenghi and Nopi restaurants in London run by the Jerusalem partners Yotam Ottolenghi and Sami Tamimias well as tie-in cookbooks and television series. One of the MA students at Bethlehem University is currently working on a study about hospitality in Palestine, particularly examining the potential for gastronomy tourism in Palestine.

(vi) Crafts

A vigorous craft and souvenir sector is an essential part of any professional tourism offer (Rodwell 2008). In the Palestinian case – whether we are talking of the olive wood crafts of Bethlehem, Hebron glass, Bedouin embroidery, Armenian ceramics, and a host of other examples there is huge potential of a radical expansion of the sector. At this point, as in all others, the issue of the Wall is necessarily raised. Both Jerusalem and Bethlehem cities are cut off from their rural hinterlands by the Wall, thus making it harder for souvenir shops and markets in the Old City to acquire Palestinian crafts from elsewhere in the country. But this does not (nor should not) entirely explain the steady falling away in Bethlehem of the local craft industries and expansion of Chinese imports.

(vii) Tour operators

Many families in Bethlehem and Jerusalem have their own travel businesses as tour operators. One observation we would like to make is that members of several such families attended the conference (there was, by contrast, no representation at all from PADICO). Clearly amongst the tour operating community in Jerusalem (and Bethlehem) several are closely integrated with the ideas and values of the JTC.

(viii) Regional/ international media

We are all aware that one essential component of a professional tourism offer concerns imaginative use of the global media. There is a constant flow of newspaper editorials, TV commercials, brochure publications, as well as exhibitions and shows, such as the annual World Travel Market in London that serve to propel countries' tourism offers into the international sphere. Furthermore, there is enormous potential, arguably virtually untapped in the case of Palestine, to focus on tourist and hospitality offerings. Khoury (2008) for example develop a branding strategy for Palestine under occupation and suggested short/medium and long term recovery strategies and Sahouri (2008) on reconstructing a distorted destination image. Koury recently opened a boutique shop in the star street and instigated an initiative called 'bringing Bethlehem's start street back to life' (This week Palestine 2015).

(ix) Local, regional, international academic networks

Finally, and crucially, there is the educational field. Because (in an ideal world) of their capacities to innovate, move fairly rapidly and flexibly, network internationally, publish, and work with the media, universities can occupy leading positions in tourism – a fact that the EU clearly recognizes since many of their development programmes are based within Higher Education institutions within and just beyond the borders of Europe. The TEMPUS programme was a child (Isaac 2008) of such an EU initiative and, as such, placed Palestinian students and tourism specialists alongside their colleagues in several Mediterranean as well as northern European cities and institutes of higher education. Recently USAID and Bethlehem University launched new hospitality curriculum. USAID invested more than $150,000 and provided technical assistance to the University in order to develop this curriculum which the University's Hospitality School started teaching this spring. The aim is to enhance the training capacity of the tourism service industry and to train graduates to provide high quality services across the hospitality sector and prepare them for the market needs (Bethlehem University 2015).

Conclusion

The first part of this chapter described how the work of skilled staff of BL2000 in the years before the millennium was made redundant by a deal between the investment company, PADICO and Bethlehem Municipality. By opening up Star Street and making the Christmas market into a year-long event, BL2000 had attempted to reform the administration and organization of tourism in Bethlehem in such a way that would have benefited many more of its citizens than the present system does. But, as Dabdoub and Zougbhi (2011: 165) correctly observe 'the tycoons of the Palestinian private sector ... viewed BL2000 and its activities as a simple, quick window of opportunity through which they would jump and reap quick profits. Sustainable and long-term community development ... was not on their agenda'. The Star Street experience highlights the need for a professional civil society run tourism strategy (Sa'adeh 2015; Abu-Dayyeh 2015). The 2015 JTC Jerusalem conference consisted of a range of reports and discussions about tourism and pilgrimage in Jerusalem, Bethlehem and Palestine more widely. There were many papers and reports about initiatives, experiences, theoretical, and practical insights being taken by men, women and civil society institutions active in both public and private sectors in the field. All the evidence from the conference strongly suggested that strategic thinking and practice in the tourism field is actually well established and taking original and creative forms and that its institutional home is indeed within Palestinian civil society itself.

References

Abu-Dayyeh, H. (2015) Verbal presentation at Jerusalem Cluster Conference, entitled Tourism and Palestinian Culture in Jerusalem: Unlimited Opportunities 19–21 May 2015, Jerusalem.

Abu Jaber, L.M. (2008) 'Palestinian tourism law', TEMPUS MA thesis, London Metropolitan University.

Alternative Tourism Group (ATG) (2008) *Palestine and Palestinians,* Beitsahour: ATG.

Applied Research Institute (2010) *Locality profiles and needs assessment in the Bethlehem governorate*, Jerusalem: Applied Research Institute.

Applied Research Institute (2015) About us. Online http://www.arij.org/about-arij/background/historical-background.html [Accessed 12 July, 2015].

Bethlehem University (2015) 'Developing tourism, teaching teachers, testing drinking water', *Bethlehem University News*, 22(2), 7–8.

Boissevain, J. (2015) 'The dynamic festival: ritual, regulation, and play in changing times', *Ethnos: Journal of Anthropology*, London: Routledge.

Burns, P. and Thomas Selwyn, T. (1997). 'Tourism awareness and manpower development'. UNESCO Mission Report. Bethlehem: Palestinian Ministry of Tourism.

Dabdoub, C.S. and Zoughbi-Janineh, C. (2011) 'Contested politics of the Mediterranean: Star Street and the struggle for development in Bethlehem', in M. Kousis, T. Selwyn and D. Clark (eds.) *Contested Mediterranean spaces: ethnographic essays in honour of Charles Tilly*, New York: Berghahn Books.

Daher, Y. (2008) 'Towards the Palestinian tourism board and sustainable tourism in Palestine based on Public/private partnership', TEMPUS MA thesis, London Metropolitan University.

Faulkner, B. (2003) 'Rejuvenating a maturing tourist destination: the case of the Gold Coast', in L. Fredline, L. Jago and C. Cooper (eds.) *Progressing tourism research – Bill Faulkner*, Clevedon: Chanell View Publications.

Hesmondhaigh, D. (2007) *The Cultural Industries*, London: Sage.

Hughes, P. (ed.) (1994) *Planning for sustainable tourism: the ECOMOST Report*, Lewis: International Federation of Tour Operators.

International Centre of Bethlehem (2015) Dar Al-kalema model school. Online http://www.annadwa.org/school/daralkalima.htm [Accessed 24 May, 2015].

International Trade Centre (2013) *The State of Palestine: tourism sector export strategy, 2014–2018*, Switzerland: The International Trade Centre. Online https://www.paltrade.org/upload/multimedia/admin/2014/10/5448e8c6d8011.pdf [Accessed 12 March, 2015].

Isaac, R.K. (2008) 'Master of arts in pilgrimage and tourism', *Tourism and Hospitality Planning & Development*, 5(1): 73–76.

Isaac, R.K. (2013) 'Palestine – tourism under occupation', in R. Butler and W. Suntikul (eds.) *Tourism and war*, London: Routledge.

Isaac, R.K. and Ashworth, G.J. (2012) Moving from pilgrimage to dark tourism: leveraging tourism in Palestine. *Tourism, Culture and Communication* 11(3): 149–164.

Jerusalem Tourism Conference (2015). About us. Online http://www.jerusalemtourismconference.com/AboutUs.html [Accessed 26 June, 2015].

Kairos (2015) About. Online http://www.kairospalestine.ps/about [Accessed 12 July, 2015].

Kassis, R. (2008) 'Alternative tourism in Palestine', TEMPUS MA thesis, London Metropolitan University.

Kershner, I. (2012) UNESCO adds Nativity Church in Bethlehem to heritage list. New York Times, online http://www.nytimes.com/2012/06/30/world/middleeast/unesco-grants-heritage-status-to-nativity-church-in-diplomatic-victory-to-palestinians.html?_r=0 [Accessed 25 June, 2015].

Khoury, S. (2008) 'Tourism development and destination marketing under occupation', TEMPUS MA thesis, London Metropolitan University.

Odeh, M. (2008) 'Palestinian intangible Heritage: Palestinian Dabkeh as a case study' TEMPUS MA thesis, London Metropolitan University.

Revault, P., Santelli, S. and Weill-Rochant, C. (1997) *Maisons de Bethléem*, Paris: Maisonneuve & Larose.

Rodwell, D. (2008) *Conservation and sustainability in historic cities*, Chichester: Wiley.

Sa'adeh, R. (2015) Verbal presentation at Jerusalem Cluster Conference, entitled Tourism and Palestinian Culture in Jerusalem: Unlimited Opportunities 19–21 May 2015, Jerusalem.

Sahouri, J. (2008) 'Bringing Palestine into focus: reconstructing a distorted Destination Image', TEMPUS MA thesis, London Metropolitan University.

Sartawi, A. (2008) 'A strategy for Palestinian museums', TEMPUS MA thesis, London Metropolitan University.

Selwyn, T. (2000) An anthropology of hospitality, in C. Lashley, and A. Morrison (eds.) *In search of hospitality: theoretical perspectives and debates*, Oxford: Butterworth/Heinemann.

Taha, H. (2012) 'World Heritage in Palestine: from inventory to nomination. Online http://thisweekpalestine.com/details.php?id=3349&ed=192&edid=192 [Accessed 26 May 2015].

The Guardian Weekend (2010) Bethlehem, *The Guardian Weekend*, December 18: 36–38.

This week Palestine (2015) Arts and culture. Where to go? Bringing Bethlehem's star street back to life, Online http://thisweekinpalestine.com/wp-content/uploads/2015/06/July-207-2015.pdf

United Nation Office for the Coordination of Humanitarian Affairs Occupied Palestine Territory (UNOCHA) (December 2004) *Costs of the conflict: the changing face of Bethlehem*, Jerusalem: UNOCHA. Online http://www.miftah.org/Doc/Reports/2004/Beth_Rep_Dec04_En.pdf [Accessed 17 May September 2015].

Zoughbi, C. (2008) 'An adventure in the development of Rural Tourism in Palestine: A case study from the Bethlehem District', TEMPUS MA thesis, London Metropolitan University.

15 Envisioning a tourism of peace in the Gaza Strip

Ian S. McIntosh and Jamil Alfaleet

Introduction

The idea that tourism can contribute to peace and positive futures is increasingly gaining currency in the global community (Moufakkir and Kelly 2010). This chapter reports on an initiative which demonstrates the potentials and limitations of such assertions in places of 'hot conflict' such as Palestine. In previous work, the authors were instrumental in setting up a peace incubator through a virtual classroom by linking students from Gaza with students from the United States (see McIntosh and Alfaleet 2014). As a result of these efforts, in 2014 students of Gaza University developed a profound vision for the Gaza Strip in 2050 that identified tourism as the key to a renewed and thriving economy. They envisioned a future distinguished by peace and prosperity. All the problems that currently beset the region were seen as now addressed in 2050 to the satisfaction of the various parties. Additionally, a virtual museum developed by the students in a joint project of Indiana University's Indianapolis campus (IUPUI) and Gaza University, identified 252 sites of touristic potential. These, sites together with the promise of the re-opening of the overland pilgrimage route from Gaza City to Jerusalem (Al Quds) would be center stage in attracting international tourists. Through a process of back casting, the various steps in achieving the vision were under deep consideration by students when the Israel launched its attack 'Operation Protective Edge' on 7 July, 2014, which soon led to widespread loss of Palestinian lives and the destruction of much of the urban landscape of the major cities of Gaza, including a number of the historic and cultural sites just identified as potential tourism assets by the students. The full consequences of this most devastating war is still to be realized but as the authors describe in this chapter, the dream of making Gaza the jewel of the Mediterranean lives on in the minds of those who participated in the visioning exercise.

Envisioning a peaceful and prosperous Gaza

In 2011, leaders of the private and independent Gaza University (formerly the Gaza Women's College) sought to provide opportunities for western style training for their students through a collaboration with US academic institutions. As the

Director of International Partnerships at Indiana University's Indianapolis campus (IUPUI), co-author Ian McIntosh was able to marshal considerable interest in building connections across what was understood to be a profound divide. An introductory internet-based class utilizing Skype in 2012 was taught by McIntosh in cooperation with his counterpart and co-author, Jamil Alfaleet of Gaza University. This initial offering attracted 16 US and 16 Palestinian students, all working together on finding novel solutions to issues of common concern in Palestine and Israel, including borders, refugees, settlements and Jerusalem. While there was considerable discussion with Gaza faculty on the desirability of direct participation by Israeli representatives, the timing was considered inappropriate for the emphasis was to be on local capacity building rather than negotiation (see McIntosh and Alfaleet 2014).

By 2013, over 170 students were enrolled in what was now a Gaza-focused experimental Massive Open Online Course (MOOC) with many faculty sharing their expertise and experiences in peace-building. The Gaza virtual classroom welcomed interested individuals from over 20 countries, including Turkey, Russia, Kenya and Uruguay, who wanted to work hand in hand with Gaza youth on the class topic of identifying a vision of peace and prosperity for 2050, and also the steps for its realization. The prized vision adopted by the class, described in detail later, centered on tourism as the primary driver of development and peace in the region.[1]

The technique of visioning utilized in the Gaza University classes of McIntosh and Alfaleet is best described as both an art and a science: Artistic because adherents compose vivid pictures of an ideal that appeals to all the senses; and scientific because adherents anchor their utopian images so firmly in their minds that when presented with options, only those leading towards the imagined goal will seem viable (Boulding 1990; Kwartler and Longo 2008).

In the visioning exercises from 2012 to 2014, McIntosh and Alfaleet encouraged the students to imagine a Gaza Strip that was both peaceful and prosperous – the jewel of the Mediterranean. The students gathered together the most inspiring array of pictures and words describing what Gaza would look like in 2050. There were dazzling images of vibrant seaports and airports, of bustling high-tech and high-rise shopping and residential facilities, and sports centers, modern and efficient transportation networks, elaborate green spaces and water parks, and most importantly, beautiful, empowered, confident people living a dream life.

A political scientist and head of international programs at Gaza University, Alfaleet described this virtual project of picturing a nonviolent and affluent Gaza Strip as the most popular elective on their campus in 2013. The classroom visioning process was entirely transparent. Lectures were delivered live by McIntosh and colleagues in Indiana and Australia through Skype, then recorded, reviewed by both Alfaleet and the students, and then discussed live and online using a novel new course networking technology developed by engineers at IUPUI called 'the CN', an acronym for course networking. All lectures and reading materials, including the associated online discussion was, and remains, freely available on the web (see www.thecn.com/mooc101).

The target date of 2050 was chosen for the resolution of all issues that divide Israelis and Palestinians because by that time the students would be community leaders and helping to mold the development of their homeland in line with the specifics of their vision. To emphasize this point, in the live sessions McIntosh and Alfaleet would talk of the present only in the past tense. In a very short time period, the students were beginning to feel confident that the power to realize their dream was in their own hands. By making the vision of the future come alive in the students' minds, the teachers temporarily lifted the burden of daily life from their shoulders and provided a safe space for them to think creatively. In 2050, the torment and strife of the Palestinian–Israeli conflict, the Gaza blockade, unemployment and poverty, the sewage and water crisis, the 'imprisonment' and other suffering, would all be a distant memory.

Tourism for Gaza

McIntosh and Alfaleet had investigated with students the various industries that could sustain this wonderful vision, like fishing, strawberry and citrus production, and fresh flower exports. Experts were invited into the virtual classroom to discuss the preconditions for success. It was tourism, however, that attracted the most discussion, and the Spring 2014 semester was dedicated to this topic.

The tourism industry was understood to have the greatest potential for sustainable development outcomes in Gaza. Political and religious interests in the Holy Land have resulted in the greatest density of archaeological sites almost anywhere in the world. While acknowledging that Biblical archaeology was as fraught as the contemporary politics of the region, the question asked of students was how this great archaeological resource would be utilized for the long-term benefit of Palestinians in the Gaza Strip (see Haessly 2010; Higgins-Desbiolles 2008; Pollock and Bernbeck 2005).

Over the course of several months, more than 250 sites of archaeological and touristic merit in the Gaza Strip were identified by Gaza University students, including old churches, mosques, bazaars and the ruins of caravanserai from the old overland Silk Route. For example, one long forgotten site buried in the southern deserts of the Gaza Strip at Deir al Balah was associated with Cleopatra's Egypt. During the reign of Ramesses 2, this was the furthest east of Egypt's garrisoned fortresses. Cypriot, Mycenaean and Minoan artefacts found here speak to Deir al Balah's cosmopolitan past. Many of these precious artefacts, including unique decorated Egyptian coffins, have been looted or removed to art museums in Israel and elsewhere, including by the late Israeli general and amateur archaeologist Moshe Dayan. In the vision of 2050, however, these artefacts had been returned to Gaza's newly constructed museums. Another important site, in northern Gaza, is linked to a bloody siege by Alexander the Great in 332 in which all males were killed and all women and children sold into slavery. This site, known as Anthedon, is one of the oldest Mediterranean ports, but is unfortunately now the scene of a Hamas military training ground. The site has been witness to many Israeli bombings and efforts by local historians and students to have the site protected and the training ground relocated have been ignored. Engagement with such sites reminded the students of the rich history of Gaza and built enthusiasm for the potential for them to serve as vital tourism assets in 2050.

With tourism envisioned as the backbone of the future Palestinian economy, students explored the many dimensions of this industry. They understood that a record number of tourists were now traveling the globe on tour packages, cruises, adventure experiences, and independent itineraries. They acknowledged that all of the visitors and their associated activities generated change in local communities and that these had social, economic and environmental impacts, some of which were positive, some negative, and many unforeseeable. But it was tourism's contribution to community development and poverty reduction, and its ability to spark other economic activities such as agriculture, transportation and handicraft production that inspired the students. As a labor intensive industry which offers low entry barriers for small and medium enterprise, tourism will undoubtedly create opportunities for the vast and growing numbers of unemployed in Gaza (see World Bank 2014).

As the students reviewed Gaza's 250 identified touristic sites, many appreciating their significance for the first time, they experienced a deep sense of pride in the local culture and in the natural environment. They were learning not just about the past, and the past in the present, but also the past's potential as a resource driving a cherished vision of the future.

The subject of pilgrimage was prioritized in the virtual classroom. According to the UN World Tourism Organization (UNWTO) world tourism barometer, religious tourism is among the fastest growing sectors of the global tourism industry (UNWTO 2014), with many hundreds of millions of people undertaking pilgrimages to the major sites in Mecca, Rome, in northern Spain, Shikoku in Japan, and throughout India and Ireland. Pilgrimage (and sacred tourism) was viewed by students as a particularly strong potential driver of economic growth in the Gaza of the future. Jerusalem, or Al-Quds as it is known in Arabic, is the third of Islam's holy sites after Mecca and Medina, and should attract over three million Muslim pilgrims annually. In historic times, the port of Gaza was where many pilgrims would begin their short journey to Haram al Sharif and the Dome of the Rock. It is from this site that the Prophet Mohammed, on his night journey from Mecca, had ascended to heaven bringing back with him vital new religious practices, such as praying five times a day – the second most important of Islam's Five Pillars.

There were two major assignments for students in the virtual tourism class of 2014. Through a SWOT analysis the students were to explore the strengths, weaknesses, opportunities and threats to the future tourism industry. With the vision fulfilled in 2050, students were asked: If three million tourists or pilgrims were to pass through the Gaza Strip and on to Haram Al-Sharif, how would the people of Gaza feed them? Where would they be housed? What forms of entertainment would be available to them, like museums, parks, and cultural activities? A plan of action was to emerge through a process of 'back casting', where each step forward was to be brainstormed, and mapped.

The question of healing the people, both individually and collectively, was understood to be a necessary precondition for realizing this vision. With this in mind, McIntosh and Alfaleet (2014) engaged social workers from IUPUI with strengths in this area of social practice in the virtual classroom. Through singing, sharing, and listening, these educators fostered a real bond between and with the students. From our understanding, healing after generations of suffering and oppression can be defined as having hope in the future. Building both trust and the capacity to do the work of peace was therefore deemed just as important as identifying the specific educational needs of the population (e.g. training historians, archaeologists and hotel managers) and all those who will be fully engaged in the Gaza tourism industry of tomorrow.

Gaza virtual museum

The second assignment for students was to undertake a survey of a major archaeological or historical treasure from the Gaza Strip and then imagine, in a best case scenario, how it would be featured in the ideal vision for Gaza's future. Some students visited old churches and mosques and documented the history and significance of these assets. They were asked to consider how Gazan authorities could best promote such unique examples of Palestinian culture, religion and history. Others visited antique shops to discuss the range of antiquities housed there and try to ascertain their provenance. Additionally the students undertook meetings with government agencies with oversight of tourism, antiquities, and related industries.

In each case, the goal was to have the work of each student or student group uploaded to a virtual museum of the Gaza Strip; a site that was totally constructed by them. This was understood by all to be a prelude to the sort of museum and tourist facility that would become a reality in the Gaza of the future. The virtual museum would be accessible to anyone in the world and it could therefore serve as a marketing tool to attract tourists traveling to the Holy Land to ensure they visited Gaza to not miss such hidden treasures.

The Gaza Virtual Museum would include video footage of student interviews, visits to archaeological sites, analyses of famous artefacts, and so on. The discovery in 2013 of a statue of Apollo that was dredged up by a fisherman from the Mediterranean Sea provided an important case study for the virtual class. McIntosh and Alfaleet, for example, solicited expert advice from expert archaeologists on the sculpture for sharing with the students as they prepared their virtual museum submissions.

An abbreviated entry on Apollo in the Gaza Virtual Museum, for example, would include the following details:

Description: Apollo bronze statue. Age – 2100 years. 450kg weight, 1.75m tall.

Estimated Value: $340US million

Circumstances of Find: Fisherman Jawdat Abu Ghurab found the bronze sculpture 100m offshore at Deir al Balah half buried in the sand in 4m of water. He cut off one finger and took it to the market to see if the metal was gold. There was also an attempt to sell the statue on EBay before it was confiscated by Hamas. The current whereabouts of the sculpture is unknown. Institutions in both France and Switzerland offered to lease and restore the sculpture, given that there are no appropriate museum facilities in Gaza, and especially because there are religious and customary restrictions on the public revelation of the naked male body.

Significance: Rather than a 'true' Apollo (i.e. a divine statue), the Gaza bronze was probably an archaistic figure that served as a 'servant-statue' holding a candelabra or tray and which adorned the houses of rich Hellenized people in the Late Hellenistic/Early Imperial period.

Required Care: A bronze just out of the sea is in danger of 'bronze disease'.

Contact: Gaza Ministry of Tourism

Students were assigned a number of readings, particularly about the work of the non-governmental organization RIWAQ in the West Bank which is dedicated to urban renewal through the preservation of historical treasures (see Riwaq n.d.). The 'archaeology and peace' movement in the Middle East was also examined in detail (see Pollock and Bernbeck 2005). These resources developed the students' appreciation of the ways that a sites' antiquities can enhance community identity and serve as assets for not only tourism but also for global appreciation in the world community.

Museum Studies was a strong focus in the discussion and, in particular, the global Museums of Conscience Movement, part of the International Coalition of Sites of Conscience (see International Coalition of Sites of Conscience n.d.). These 'peace museums' are often the centerpiece of tourism activities in former conflict zones. The Apartheid Museum in Johannesburg, South Africa, or the District 6 Museum in Cape Town, are examples of what one might term activist museums, for they deal with the legacy of injustice and are designed to bring about social transformation. During one class, students were asked to post images of peace monuments online, especially those which are major tourist draw cards. The New York sculpture 'Non-Violence' (also known as 'The Knotted Gun'), which stands outside the United Nations headquarters, was a class favorite. This pro-peace sculpture by Swedish artist Carl Fredrik Reuterswärd depicts a 45-caliber revolver with its barrel knotted into a bullet-blocking twist; a powerful commentary of the desire to end gun-related violence. It has become an essential photo-op for UN visitors.

The students were asked to make an inventory of Gaza sculptures and to imagine what sorts of similar monuments might attract tourists to the Gaza Strip. It is important to note that there is a minimum of statuary in Gaza, given the restrictions imposed by Islam on the representation of the human body. Even the famed Palestinian freedom fighter, Yasser Arafat, is not honored in this manner, despite considerable public pressure to do so. For those budding artists and architects in the class, what the public spaces of Gaza would look like in 2050 was a topic of great interest.

The stage was therefore set for the next stage in the development of the Gaza Virtual Museum with more interviews in the pipeline, and more discoveries of Gaza's rich historical legacy, but then all was to come crashing down in mid-2014 with the Gaza War (Operation Protective Edge). This was the third such war since 'Operation Cast Lead' of 2008 and 'Operation Pillar of Defense' in 2012.

Operation Protective Edge

With control of the Gaza Strip being handed over to the Palestinian Authority in June 2014, and a reconciliation underway between Hamas and Fatah, it seemed that change was at hand. Alfaleet was given the task of helping to lead a social reconciliation committee in Gaza to provide reparations to the families who had lost children in the Hamas-Fatah conflict of 2006. The Palestinian Authority acknowledged Israel's right to exist and renounced violence. While some of the Gaza students had their doubts about the long term viability of the new route to peace, many felt confident that their life-affirming vision was indeed achievable. With this vital first step, it was no longer just a pipe dream. The students had looked deeply into the future and liked what they saw.

The ensuing months, however, were witness to the most appalling destruction and massacre. Of the three wars that Israel had launched against Gaza since 2008, the war of 2014 known by Israelis as 'Operation Protective Edge' was the worst. Over 51 days, more than 2000 Palestinians were killed, and hundreds of thousands were displaced when their homes were destroyed. Industry was targeted, as were schools, power plants, hospitals, media outlets and shopping malls – the entire infrastructure of life in the Gaza Strip.

During the war, Alfaleet, speaking with the aid of his car battery to power Skype calls, spelled out for McIntosh in the USA just how much the vision of the people of Gaza had been perverted by the unceasing and merciless attacks by Israeli soldiers. Usually the most optimistic of people, Alfaleet was now questioning whether Gaza even had a future. The cherished vision of utopia had been forcibly displaced with a new reality of dystopia where there was no longer day or night – all was blurred. Light had been replaced by darkness, and generations of hatred launched. In one telling moment, Alfaleet told McIntosh that he could write a doctorate in psychology on all that he had learned about human nature in his interactions with people who had witnessed atrocities, lost family members, or who were now without hope and little more than the 'walking dead'. Everyone was pulling together though, Alfaleet said. All were in need of counselling but survival was the top priority.

Alfaleet's house was bombed twice and he could not see any reason why he and his family should be singled out in the supposedly 'pin-point missile attacks' on militants. It was illustrative of the use of collective punishment of the entire population of Gaza as Israeli strategy.

During the Skype calls, Alfaleet would ask McIntosh in an excited tone if I could hear the F16s screaming overhead, and the bombs exploding. 'Yes', McIntosh would reply, wondering if Alfaleet would survive that night or even that very moment. With each blast McIntosh could hear the shrieks of the women, for some of the bombs were landing quite close to the school in which Alfaleet and his family had taken refuge (Many people had been corralled there by 'stink bombs' and now there was nowhere else to turn). McIntosh could also hear Alfaleet's eight year old son laughing manically. Apparently he would dance with each explosion and, when a rocket was shot from Gaza towards Israel, he would farewell it on its journey. This was a coping mechanism; a way of dealing with the extreme emotional distress.

While visiting a partially destroyed church shelter where hundreds of displaced people were huddled, including in the toilets, Alfaleet witnessed a scene that he described as 'hell'. A man in total despair was crying out repeatedly 'the dead are the lucky ones'. New mothers with little to sustain their babies pleaded with Alfaleet for help, thinking that he might be a UN aid worker because he was sharing fresh water from his now destroyed farm. Children, some as young as five or six year, were running wild and chanting how they would destroy Israel when they were grown. In this environment, McIntosh and Alfaleet both watched on the Internet as their students in Gaza were transformed from being open and willing to embrace a new formula for peace in the Middle East to being filled with fear and hostility. 'May Allah destroy Israel', some wrote on their Facebook pages.

In one Skype call, McIntosh inquired about the possibility of mass death from disease as a result of so many people living in overcrowded circumstances, and how there was a need for the construction of basic sanitary facilities. Alfaleet laughed and said that no one was talking in such a fashion. Such facilities were a luxury that no one could afford. 'The people need food, water and shelter', he said. 'They need peace. They need their dignity'.

A United Nations report had already declared, prior to the war, that Gaza would be unlivable by 2020 due to problems of pollution, sewage, unsafe drinking water, and other critical shortages (United Nations Country Team in the Occupied Palestinian Territory 2012). This timeframe has surely been brought forward as a result of this latest conflict. Walking around the ruins of once prosperous neighborhoods and bustling industrial zones, Alfaleet described to McIntosh a scene that was worse than what he had witnessed in Turkey following the massive earthquake of 1999. In some parts of Gaza, like Shejaia, you cannot even see where the roads and buildings used to be. 'Nothing shocks us anymore', Alfaleet said. 'We are beyond that. The resolve of the Palestinian people to live a dignified life free from this tyranny has increased one million fold. The infrastructure of life may be gone but not the will of the people for justice and their basic human rights'.

When McIntosh and Alfaleet connected via the Internet, Alfaleet would provide McIntosh with the highlights of the previous 24 hours and the latter would compose Facebook posts – updates for colleagues around the world – on the unfolding situation. Some of these posts described the humanitarian crisis, a new

'Al-Nakbah', and how more bombs had been thrown at Gaza than on Hiroshima in 1945. Some posts described tragic circumstances, for example when a four day old baby was accidentally left behind by parents who had panicked when they received the one minute warning by Israelis to vacate their home prior to it being bombed. Some posts praised Palestinian unity and resilience. Church officials who opened their doors to Muslims seeking refuge, and who were engaged in a 'solidarity' Ramadan, rated special mention. Finally, there was speculation about how only the opening of the borders, both land and sea, could offer hope of a better economy and way of life for all.

When the ceasefire was announced in late August 2014, celebrations rang out all through the Gaza Strip. Victory! But it was more a celebration that the people had survived and that Israel had been forced to the negotiating table. 'Israel's security cannot be secured by force', Alfaleet said. 'If we cannot solve this crisis through negotiations then we are all going to hell. The men of Gaza would rather die an honorable death in fighting the enemy than by the slow choking death of this current endless siege'. But Alfaleet was also pessimistic about the Egypt-brokered peace talks. In his calculation, there had been over 100,000 hours of negotiation between Israelis and Palestinians since the Oslo Accords of 1993. 'All for nothing', he said. He was tired of words.

In trying to rally his spirits, McIntosh told him about the major street demonstrations in support of Gaza in multiple settings around the world. He was heartened by this but he despaired that such gestures could not put a single meal on the table of those who were starving. McIntosh disagreed, and said that the two of them should write an article about the visioning project and try and sway public opinion especially in the USA, the source of the very missiles that were raining down upon his head. 'It will be just words', he said.

In the midst of the crisis, McIntosh had read a news report of a visioning circle held in Israel involving both Jews and Palestinians. Under the banner 'We refuse to be enemies', the visionaries sent a strong message of hope in a future where people were united in a common dream of peace and prosperity (Devaney 2014). Such a sentiment was an essential stepping stone in achieving the vision of Gaza for 2050. McIntosh shared the article with his colleague and Alfaleet identified with the spirit of this message and agreed about the necessity of holding firm to the dream, but the situation was grim. Of the 252 student-identified Gaza tourist sites, for example, it is not known how many of them still exist. Gaza University itself survived the onslaught, but sustained extensive damage. The historic center of old Gaza which was filled with narrow alleys and markets was totally destroyed. Places of worship and historic significance have been lost forever.

Acknowledging that hope was the antidote to trauma, Alfaleet agreed with McIntosh that the world should know more about the dreams and utopian vision of Gaza youth. Even amidst the devastation, the beautiful image of Gaza as a bustling seaport, one of the major trading posts of the Mediterranean, filled with pilgrims and tourists, does not vanish so easily.

Conclusion

The technique of visioning utilized by McIntosh and Alfaleet with their students at Gaza University is employed with a growing frequency as a tool in urban and social planning worldwide. It is a vital approach to assist people in feeling empowered to create the futures they desire. For this work in Gaza students were asked: who did they want to be as a people in 2050, where did they want to be as a state, and how was this to be achieved? Ideally such deliberations are conducted in public with all parties to a conflict present, including interested outsiders. This was the policy that McIntosh and Alfaleet brought to the class when they welcomed participants from many countries. The idea is that when plans for the future become widely known a door is opened for sympathetic outsiders to become active partners in making the vision a reality and for others who may have been unsympathetic, to be less likely to undermine those plans. Gaza students determined that tourism, above all other industries, had the potential to deliver significant and sustainable outcomes of a positive sort for the people of the Gaza Strip by 2050. In the vision of peace and prosperity that they developed, Gaza is a dazzling place, its seaport and airport among the busiest in the Mediterranean. The critical water shortages of the present were a thing of the past and the crippling unemployment problems had been resolved. The 51 day Israeli war on Gaza in 2014 was a devastating setback for the journey to peace and prosperity, but after emerging from the trauma and depression the struggle must continue. By holding firm to the vision they created, both the theory and the practice, the art and the science of envisioning a peaceful and prosperous Gaza through tourism, the students cannot be deterred from the hope they themselves created and will surely achieve their dream.

Note

1   See Ward (2013) for a report by Gaza University student Mohammed H. Al-Aila.

References

Boulding, E. (1990) *Building a global civic culture: education for an interdependent world,* Syracuse: Syracuse Studies on Peace and Conflict Resolution.
Devaney, J. (2014) 'We refuse to be enemies', *The World Post,* 30 July. Online http:// www.huffingtonpost.com/jacob-devaney/we-refuse-to-be-enemies_b_5631661.html [Accessed 15 April 2015].
Haessly, J. (2010) 'Tourism and a culture of peace', in O. Moufakkir and I. Kelly (eds.) *Tourism, progress and peace*, Wallingford: CABI.
Higgins-Desbiolles, F. (2008) 'Tourism and alternative globalization', *Journal of Sustainable Tourism,* 16(3): 345–364.
International Coalition of Sites of Conscience (n.d.). Online http://www.sitesofconscience.org [Accessed 15 April 2015].
Kwartler, M. and Longo G. (2008) *Visioning and visualization. People, pixels, and plans,* Cambridge, MA: Lincoln Institute of Land Policy.

McIntosh, I.S. and Alfaleet, J. (2014) 'The classroom as peace incubator: A US–Gaza case study', *Peace and Conflict Studies,* 21(2): 153–172.

Moufakkir, O. and Kelly, I. (eds) (2010) *Tourism progress and peace,* Wallingford: CABI.

Pollock, S. and Bernbeck, R. (2005) *Archaeologies of the Middle East: critical perspectives,* Malden, MA: Blackwell.

RIWAQ (n.d.). Online www.riwaq.org [Accessed 15 April 2015].

United Nations Country Team in the Occupied Palestinian Territory (2012) *Gaza in 2020. A livable place?* Office of the United Nations Special Coordinator for the Middle East Peace Process, Jerusalem: UNESCO.

United Nations World Tourism Organization (UNWTO) (2014) *World tourism barometer.* Online http://mkt.unwto.org/barometer [Accessed on 15 April 2015].

Ward, E. (ed) (2013) 'Student researcher envisions his role in crafting a brighter future for Gaza', *Research Enterprise, IUPUI.* Online http://research.iupui.edu/enterprise/archive/2013/enterprise-08-19.html#student [Accessed on 15 April 2015].

World Bank (2014) *Palestinian economy in decline and unemployment rising to alarming levels.* Online http://www.worldbank.org/en/news/press-release/2014/09/16/palestinian-economy-in-decline-and-unemployment-rising-to-alarming-levels [Accessed on 15 April 2015].

16 The State of Palestine

The newest country probably with the oldest nation brand in the world

Erdinç Çakmak and Rami K. Isaac

Introduction

State branding is about promoting a state's image, products and resources for tourism, public diplomacy and foreign direct investment (FDI) by means of strategic destination marketing. States, like products, compete with each other for getting competitive advantage in a world of 206 sovereign states (International Olympic Committee 2015). Having a strong state brand means that a country, its products and people, are seen as attractive in the global market place. Such a state potentially attracts tourists, FDI, talented people and its export products find markets easily worldwide. Moreover, when that state speaks in the political realm of international affairs its voice is more likely to be heard. Globalization has made each state aware of itself, its image and reputation worldwide (Van Ham 2001). The lack of a strong state brand potentially means a weakness for countries aspiring to wield political influence in the international political arena.

Although Palestine with Bethlehem and Jerusalem has been an important pilgrimage destination for centuries and probably possesses one of the oldest brands in the world, it suffers from having an unknown state brand. The declared State of Palestine is recognized by 135 UN member states and it has become a member of international organizations such as UNESCO, International Criminal Court, World Health Organization, World Trade Organization, FIFA and International Olympic Committee among others. Nevertheless, two things are clear for the State of Palestine: (i) branding the state of Palestine is no longer a choice but a necessity; (ii) a branding strategy should be performed as an integrated and concerted by all relevant stakeholders like public organizations, private sector, SMEs, residents and diaspora.

Therefore, this chapter aims to serve as an early step of developing the Palestine's state branding strategy. First, it addresses the theory and practice of state branding and its key elements, then continues with an exploration of challenges and opportunities for branding the State of Palestine based on its own unique attributes and circumstances, it concludes with some key suggestions for a state branding management.

Literature review

Sovereign state

Even though there is no academic consensus on the definition of a state, international law uses the declarative theory of statehood as codified at the Montevideo Convention on the Rights and Duties of States in 1933. The first article of this convention states that a state has these essential components '(a) a permanent population, (b) a defined territory, (c) government, and (d) capacity to enter into relations with other States' (Montevideo Convention on the Rights and Duties of States 1933, Article No.1). In this regard, it is possible to take this definition for a point of departure in accepting the contemporary sovereignty of the State of Palestine. The State of Palestine has its own government, a defined territory (according to international law), a permanent population of about four million Palestinians and maintain relations with other states around the world (see Chapter 8).

The independence of the State of Palestine was declared on 15 November, 1988 by the Palestine Liberation Organization (PLO) in Algiers as a government in exile. In 2011 it applied for United Nations membership and in 2012 the status of Palestine was upgraded from 'permanent observer' to 'non-member observer state' by the United Nations General Assembly. As of March 2015, 134 (almost 70 per cent) of the 193 member states of the UN have recognized the new state of Palestine. Today the Palestinian flag is unfurled between other member states' flags at the UN headquarters in New York.

State branding is a difficult task to manage and coordinate even for old and stable states, but it is more proportionally difficult for new states, which are particularly involved in conflict zones such as the case of Palestine. Since the State of Palestine interacts more with other states and international organisations, a state brand strategy may support its sovereignty in the global world.

State branding principles

State branding consists of activities to develop and communicate exclusive multi-dimensional elements of a state to differentiate it from all other competitor states and makes it relevant to its target audiences. A state brand conveys to its audiences not only a name or a flag but also a range of connotations. It builds up a personality that communicates with the whole world how this state contributes to humanity and to the world. Accordingly, crafting a state branding strategy is a major challenge for state governments agencies.

In many cases, states give the responsibility for the development of state brands to Destination Marketing Organizations (DMOs), which mostly operate under national government departments such as national development agencies and tourism boards. This is not an easy task, it requires developing a set of core brand values, which have positive linkages with heritage and proposes a realistic, challenging vision of what can or should be achieved in the future (Hankinson 2007). These core values together with the vision act as precursor of a state's branding strategy. Although there is no consensus on the core elements of state branding principles, some scholars apply basic principles of marketing strategy and branding. Such an approach would likely mean that a strategic plan of a state branding consists of three straightforward steps:

1   Situation analysis (i.e. where are we now?).
2   Strategy framework (i.e. where would we like to be?).
3   Implementation plan (i.e. how do we get there?).

The answers to these questions lead to a long-term direction and scope where states draw strategic conclusions with respect to the formation of their resources and competences to achieve their goals in the areas of FDI, export promotion, tourism and public diplomacy (Dinnie 2008). As Dinnie (2008) suggests, states will rarely be able to excel in all of these competitive domains, each state needs to consider its own state brand direction. Consequently, a state brand needs to be communicated consistently with relevant audiences (e.g. multiple stakeholders, such as tourists, media, residents, and other countries' state and economic agents) through advertising, customer and citizenship relationship management, and diaspora mobilization. The elements of this three part frame are discussed below.

Situation analysis: where is the state brand of Palestine now?

It is necessary to conduct both internal and external analyses first to assess the situation of the state brand Palestine. These analyses evaluate the capabilities and competences of state brand Palestine and focuses on the Palestinian state public diplomacy activities. In the context of Palestine, it is vitally important to highlight its heritage and relationships with the Palestinian people.

As Elias Sanbar (2001: 87), a Palestinian historian and writer, articulates the strange exclusion of the Palestinians from the unfolding of the Palestinian history, particularly in the Western world and thought, in his essay *Out of Place, Out of Time*:

> The contemporary history of the Palestinians turns on a key date: 1948. That year, a country and its people disappeared from maps and dictionaries ... The Palestinian people does not exist, said the new masters, and henceforth the Palestinians would be referred to by general, conveniently vague terms, as either 'refugees' or in the case of a small minority that had managed to escape the generalized expulsion, 'Israeli Arabs'. A long absence was beginning.

The recent history of Palestine is full of catastrophes, sad anniversaries, contradictions, conspiracies and stories of enduring resistance. This history is covered with expressions of the 'biggest', 'longest' and other adjectives, which are worthy of the Guinness Records (Abu Sitta 2008). Reiteration of those adjectives does not in any way diminish their impact and significance. *Al-Nakbah* of 1948 is definitely the most devastating event in Palestine's 5,000 year history compared to any other. The Crusaders came, conquered, butchered people and left. There has been no major dislocation or displacement in the country. The spread of Islam in the seventh century gained adherents and accommodated neighbours who were not strangers to Palestine. The spread of Christianity merely changed the beliefs of the same population from one religion to another. The Jewish Hebrew tribes, meaning *transient* tribes, were very small in number, and their entrance and departure left no physical manifestation of any kind.

Abu Sitta (2008:7) stated in conversation with Uri Avnery, the Israeli peace activist:

> About a million people became refugees in 1948. Their life had suddenly been transformed from a state of tranquillity to a state of utter destitution: families expelled at gunpoint in the middle of night or in the heat of a summer day, screams of help, cries of pain, children lost, mothers clutching pillows instead of their children, thirsty old men shot in the head if they stopped for water in the forced march, a whole family dismembered to pieces by a bomb dropped from a plane while having supper, survivors of massacres walking about in a daze.

In August 1993, Israel and the Palestinian Liberation Organisation (PLO) agreed on the Oslo Accords as a first step of peace process for one of the world's longest-running conflicts. These Accords mean the creation of the PA in the West Bank and the Gaza Strip in 1994 as interim agreement in preparation for a Palestinian State after final negotiations, including issues of return of refugees, and Jerusalem as the capital of the new independent state of Palestine. From this moment, the State of Palestine was, in a way, re-born in the mind of Westerners as a new state. More and more people nowadays are aware of the Palestinians and the Palestinian Authority, as a result of the Peace Process, as well as the sporadic conflicts that is continuing today. Two weeks after the signature of the Peace Accords, a donor conference was organised by the United States, which was attended by forty states and institutions. 2.4 billion dollars in five years were promised to develop the new state of Palestine, economically and socially (Schmid 2006). By 2010, 42 donor countries and 20 UN and other multilateral agencies were involved in peace building activities, and aid rose yearly from US$178.74 million in 1993 to US$2.52 billion by 2010 (Turner 2012).

Accordingly, state branding is becoming inevitable for the state of Palestine in improving its brand image. In other words, what does Palestine want to bring the message to the world or a story that Palestine wants to send?

Tourism in the State of Palestine

Being a landlocked state, Palestine has serious difficulties to compete in primary (i.e. agriculture, forestry, mining and fishing) and secondary (i.e. manufacturing) sectors. Tourism is particularly important for the economic development of country. Tourism has been making an increasing and steady contribution to national wealth since 2005 and currently contributes around 14 per cent of gross domestic product (GDP), an increase of five per cent since 2007. The number of Palestinians employed in the sector is not insignificant, and includes both male and female Palestinians, albeit with genders sometimes dominating distinct subsectors. For example, the accommodation industry is mostly male while the handicraft industry is predominantly female. Approximately 50 per cent of the State of Palestine's tourism revenues come from domestic tourism. Of the other 50 per cent, 85 per cent of those revenues result from international visitors coming for pilgrimage (see Chapter 9 in this volume). Domestic tourism is particularly supported by Palestinians who are living in Israel and sometimes refer themselves as Arab Israel.

Tourism services are growing worldwide. Although it is still difficult to describe the size of the Palestinian tourism services market accurately, estimates by the Ministry of Tourism and Antiquities (MOTA) suggest that tourism revenues have steadily increased since 2005, with possibly a small decrease of between one per cent and two per cent in 2011 before growth returned in 2012 with hotel nights reaching record levels, albeit at a still very low overall occupancy rate of around 30 per cent. Of the 3.5 million visits to Palestinian tourist sites in the first eight months of 2012 (Palestine Trade Center (PalTrade) 2014), a large percentage was made up of Palestinians living in Israel (35 per cent), followed by the Russian Federation (12 per cent), the United States of America (five per cent), Italy (five per cent), Poland (five per cent), Germany (three per cent) and Indonesia (three per cent).

For the tourism sector, perhaps the most significant event in recent history was the establishment of the Palestinian National Authority (PNA) in 1993 and the resulting establishment of Ministry of Tourism and Antiquities (MOTA). Prior to 1993 the State of Palestine did not have control over its tourism policy or marketing strategy. During the Palestine Mandate (1920–1948), there was a Department of Antiquities, responsible for the excavation and preservation of Palestine's cultural sites. Palestine comparative advantage of encompassing Bethlehem, the Birthplace of Jesus; Jericho, the oldest and lowest city in the world, continuously inhabited city in the world; and Jerusalem being home to three monotheistic religions provides a unique tourism offer. Furthermore, there is a diversity of natural attractions as well as cultural activities. From its hospitable people and rich cultural heritage to its beautiful landscape and diverse cuisine, Palestine has lots to offer in addition to its many shrines, Churches and Mosques. Alas, the Palestinian tourism industry has never been given the opportunity or circumstances to show its true potential with, the export performance of tourism service sector being hampered by a range of issues. The perception that the State of Palestine is a dangerous place to visit is one or difficulties of circulation within its territory are other significant obstacles to development.

Export products of the State of Palestine and export promotion

Products from countries with strong image and reputation find relatively easier visibility in markets worldwide. Consumers use country-of-origin cue like a brand name that operates a shortcut in their purchasing decisions in congested and competitive marketplace for products and services. The West Bank has limited natural resources and its economy depends on trade and remittances from jobs in Israel. Since the majority of the West Bank's trade is with Israel, the current restrictive regime is forcing many West Bank Bankers into reliance on aid and worsening the already deteriorating socio-economic conditions. According to the World Bank (cited in United Nations Office for the Coordination of Humanitarian Affairs (UNOCHA) 2008: 1) 'no economy can develop without mobility'.

The Palestinian Reform and Development Plan is built on the assumptions that Israel is willing to take steps to remove administrative and physical barriers to the movement and access of people and goods. Internal closures in the West Bank are imposed by a multifaceted system of physical and bureaucratic obstacles, which control all movements inside the West Bank and onto the roads that are used primarily by Israeli settlers. The term 'external closures' refers to the use of Israeli-controlled crossings that permit movement of goods into and out of the West Bank. Palestinian export trade has been particularly affected by these developments and measures. Goods must first pass the internal closures around urban West Bank centres before exiting the West Bank via one of five Barriers Terminals into Israel or across the King Hussein Bridge into Jordan. As a result, internal and external closures are effectively combined into one system of control of movement of goods (UNOCHA 2008).

In order to better understand the factors driving macroeconomic developments in West Bank and Gaza Strip (WBG), it is important to realise how dependent the Palestinian economy is on Israel. This economic dependency arises from several sources. First, the Israeli labour market has been, and will continue to be, a very important source of employment and income for many Palestinians. Second, Israel is by far the most important trading partner for WBG. Israel accounts for more than 90 per cent of Palestinian exports. And while some imports into WBG originate from outside Israel, virtually all imports come through or from Israel. Third, Israel collects taxes on behalf of the Palestinian Authority (PA), which normally make up about two-thirds of total PA revenues. By affecting these channels, the conflict has had an economic impact on the WBG far beyond the physical destruction of infrastructure.

Exports in Palestine averaged 42.46 USD Million from 2001 until 2014, reaching an all-time high of 85 USD Million in November of 2013 and a record low of 15.92 USD Million in April of 2002 (Trading Economics 2014). Palestine mainly exports cement, base metals, iron and steel, food and beverages, furniture, plastics and dairy products. Palestine's main export partner is Israel. Other export partners include Jordan, the United Arab Emirates, Algeria, Egypt, Saudi Arabia, the Netherlands, Germany, and Canada. A limited volume of goods – less than two per cent of West Bank exports, consisting mainly of uncut stone, is exported across the King Hussein Bridge into Jordan (UNOCHA 2008).

For Gaza, exports are nearly completely banned, and all imports through or from Israel must pass through a single crossing run by the Israeli Ministry of Defense. Gaza also trades informally through underground tunnels between the Gaza Strip and the Egyptian Sinai. However, this illicit trade not formally authorized by Egypt.

It is not a formal trade channel and recently the tunnel trade has reportedly all but stopped. Consequently, the Palestinian territories effectively act as a landlocked country with no effective control over its borders (World Bank 2014).

In 2004, the Palestine Fair Trade Association (PFTA) was founded. It is a national union of fair trade producing cooperatives, processors, and exporters. PFTA's mission is to provide social and economic empowerment of small, marginalized, and excluded Palestinian communities through the concept of fair trade (Palestine Fair Trade 2014). By definition, fair trade is a commercial partnership based on dialogue, transparency, and respect. The goal of fair trade is equity in commerce, which leads to sustained development and safeguards marginalized producers and workers. To that end, fair trade organizations commit to heighten public awareness and form a network committed to campaign for international trade rules and practices, which benefit small and marginalized commercial enterprises worldwide. Small landowner farmers joined together in cooperatives produce a number of fair trade certified products for PFTA. In addition, several cooperatives have been formed by women who prepare traditional products by hand. Some Palestinian products that are promoted and exported include olive oil, almonds, olive oil soap and dried goods such as Za'atar. Za'atar is the signature spice blend of Palestine. Thyme is wild collected from the hills near Jenin, then dried and blended with roasted sesame seeds, ground sumac, and a touch of sea-salt by women-owned cooperatives.

Another Initiative, the so-called Zaytoun CIC, was launched a decade ago as a creative response to the story of Palestinian farmers' loss of land and livelihoods under Israeli occupation. Starting with olive farmers who were selling their oil at a price below the cost of production to Israeli traders, Zaytoun (meaning olive) sought and found a market in the UK which guaranteed producers sales at a fair price. Working with the Fair Trade Foundation to agree on standards for Fair trade olive oil, in 2009 Palestinian producers were the first in the world to sell Fair trade certified oil. Today, Zaytoun's range includes Medjoul dates, almonds, herbs, maftoul and freekeh as well as olive oil soap, and is sold throughout the UK in shops and through a private network of Fair trade enthusiasts and supporters of justice for Palestine (Pawson 2014). Another product that can be promoted as a brand of Palestine is the Taybeh beer. As beer-making businesses go, the Taybeh brewery faces an unusual raft of challenges. It is the only brewery in Palestine, where the population is predominantly Muslims. It operates in bleak economic conditions, with high unemployment and the extra costs and challenges of dealing with the checkpoints and delays that make up Israel's military occupation, and, on top of that, they have to market their Palestinian beer to Israeli customers as main export partner (McCarthy 2009).

Foreign direct investments in the State of Palestine

Political instability, the result of the unresolved conflict and the restrictions on movement and access (Isaac 2010; Isaac and Platenkamp 2012), remains the binding constraint in the Palestinian investment climate, resulting in uncertainty, which elevates the cost of doing business, raises the risk to business operations, and creates uncertainty with respect to investment returns. The uncertainty stems from a multitude of problems related to political instability – the recurrence of incidents and periods of violence; destruction of property; the continues growth of Israeli illegal settlements in the West Bank and their associated infrastructure; continued limitations on access to resources in Area C for Palestinian economic benefit; the fiscal instability of the PA; continued separation and isolation of the Gaza Strip; changes in regulations and restrictions on access to resources and markets; and changes in the nature and degree of restrictions on the movement of people and goods. While there are positive aspects in the investment climate, such as a stable financial sector and low incidence of petty bribery, and firm performance indicates potentially competitive productivity levels, a sustainable economy is still out of reach due primarily to the business constraints and conditions created by political instability (World Bank 2014). Consequently, private investment in the territories of Palestine remains far from sufficient to fuel adequate rates of economic growth to create enough jobs and reduce unemployment.

A number of equity investors, including private equity funds and multinationals, have attracted FDI and launched new investments, a trend that has accelerated in recent years. These success stories tend to have a few common characteristics. Some funds or investors have a specific mandate to invest in the territories of Palestine or in developing countries more broadly. They have a tendency to be large scale and have high visibility, investing in public and government relations. They often have a foreign partner, such as some Gulf Cooperation Council [GCC] sovereign wealth funds), either as an investor or as a financer/ facilitator (such as bilateral or other international development agencies, such as the United States Agency for International Development (USAID), or the Government of the Netherlands). In some cases, these agencies facilitated movement of goods from projects in which they have an investment or interest. Domestic and foreign investments in housing, agri-business, and other sectors appear to be on the rise in comparison to previous years (World Bank 2014). Further, this trend may be aided by increased attention to investment by international and domestic actors, such as the launching of the Initiative for the Palestinian Economy (IPE) developed by the Office of the Quartet Representative, the Palestinian Development and Investment Company Ltd. (PADICO), the Palestine Investment Fund (PIF), and some investors in private equity (PE) funds and the 'Beyond Aid' initiative put forward by the Palestinian private sector through the Portland Trust. Although differing in timeframe (the 'Beyond Aid' initiative has a longer-term perspective) and provenance, they share much of the same structural effort. Investment areas include: agriculture, tourism, construction, energy, information technology and digital entrepreneurship. Both initiatives aim to increase foreign and domestic private and public investment and employment. In addition, a number of large Palestinian Diaspora investors have successfully attracted FDI and launched new private investments. This trend has also accelerated in recent years.

There are three private equity funds and one venture capital fund operating in the territories of Palestine at this time. All of these funds were established since

2011 and have a total committed capital exceeding US$ 206 million, with estimated investments of at least US$ 45 million. In 2006, at the time of the last investment climate assessment study of the World Bank, there were no such funds. Although they are relatively new investments and have had no reported exits to date, the funds are in a growth type and are reportedly actively seeking investments. However, some have reported a small pipeline, with a lack of viable companies and a relatively low flow of deals. Nonetheless, domestic and foreign Palestinian Diasporas' investments in housing, agribusiness, and other sectors appear to be on the rise in comparison to previous years.

In this context, the pipeline should benefit from a recently launched seed fund, Arabreneur (funded by USAID), that will provide financing in the US$ 50,000–US$ 150,000 range, which had been identified as a financing gap for Palestinian start-up companies. Secret remittance flows were estimated to be more than US$ 1.3 billion in 2010, slightly more than total donor assistance channeled through the PA budget totaling $US 1.275 billion in the same year. Remittances are generally considered to be important in contributing to household expenditures and, to some degree, private construction. However, they are not a significant source of business investments.

The regulatory environment under which Palestinian businesses operate is complex. Businesses operating throughout the West Bank and Gaza is subject to Israeli military orders, laws and regulations enforced by the PA in the West Bank, laws and regulations enforced by the de facto Hamas government in Gaza, and Israeli laws and regulations if they operate or do business with partners in East Jerusalem or in Israel. This is in addition to contending with the patchwork of the historical legacy of Ottoman, British Mandate, Jordanian, and Egyptian laws that predate Israeli military orders and current Palestinian law.

Furthermore, in this already complex legal and regulatory environment is the state of legislative paralysis resulting from the lack of a functioning parliament. All legislation passed into law since 2006 has been done exceptionally by presidential decree, which is not an environment encouraging to furthering a legislative reform agenda. The PA has issued a number of laws and amendments to laws by Presidential decree between 2006 and 2013, due to the lack of a functioning Legislative Council.

Public diplomacy of the State of Palestine

Public diplomacy is an informational instrument of state power and concerns how a state manages its image and reputation abroad. For public diplomacy purposes governments carry out various activities abroad and interact not only with their counterparts but also with civil society organizations and individuals to influence public opinion and getting them to understand their position. Deibel (2007) suggests that public diplomacy is used in peacetime by means of informational, cultural, and exchange programs and in wartime through psychological operations and information warfare. Therefore, a peaceful political environment is not necessarily needed to employ public diplomacy. Each state needs to set up a public diplomacy plan to communicate its point of view, builds up long-term relations with others and turn them into favoured partners in the international relations. Leonard, Stead, and Smewing (2002) suggest that public diplomacy can achieve a hierarchy of impacts. First, it can increase target people's awareness towards one's country (e.g. make them think about the country, revising their images, turn their unfavourable opinions). Secondly, it can increase target people's appreciation of one's country (e.g. creating positive attitudes and perceptions). Thirdly, it can engage target people with one's country (e.g. encouraging people to see one's country as an attractive tourism destination, intending to buy products made in one's country, making friends from one's country). Finally, it can influence people (e.g. attracting investors into one's country, making publics to support one's country's political positions). Although the State of Palestine is new, Palestinians employ public diplomacy since almost two decades.

The public diplomacy of the State of Palestine needs to be focused on the countries which are most relevant to Palestinian interests rather than countries, which are likely easy to persuade. Secondly, a proposition is that public diplomacy institutions need to focus on building long-term relationships through cultural exchange programs. For instance, they can open Palestinian House's in target countries' capitals where they can introduce Palestinian cuisine, run music and dance courses, and open exhibitions. For example, Palestinian Kitchen evening events are being organized by the Palestinian Solidarity Campaign in the UK (see www.palestiniancampign.org) and non-traditional public diplomacy such as the UK wide screening of the documentary 'Open Bethlehem' by Laila Sanour (www.openbethlehemcampaign.org), one of the most remarkable and moving documentaries about Bethlehem. The tragedy of the Palestinians encapsulated in the life of one family and one town- Bethlehem. Another possibility is to increase exchange of scholar activities, hosting international conferences such as the International Investment Conference held in Bethlehem, seminars, and continuously staying in tune with foreign media channels.

Increased private investment is needed to reduce Palestinian aid dependency and foster long term sustainable growth and development. Yet many potential investors are unaware of the realities and opportunities available in the Palestinian economy. To address this issue the Palestinian Authority has worked to promote the Palestinian economy as a place to invest. The first Palestine Investment Conference was held in Bethlehem in May 2008. Investment opportunities were presented across a range of sectors including ICT, construction and tourism. Around 2000 people attended the event millions of US dollar deals were announced, including power plant and new housing projects in the West Bank.

Strategy framework: where does the State of Palestine want to be?

Strategic planning involves setting a specific and measureable target for a given time-frame. However, a state has multiple objectives and talks to larger publics in comparison to a business organization. It aims to attract visitors and investors to one's country, boosts export products performance, influences political issues worldwide, and achieves higher value through public diplomacy. In the context of state branding, strategic planning engages with positioning of a state brand. How should the State of Palestine be positioned in the mind of potential tourists, international customers and potential investors? Based upon the results of a situation analysis a positioning strategy needs to be crafted in accordance to the priorities of the State of Palestine. Target markets need to be defined more clearly for incoming tourists and the image of Palestine needs to be analyzed across these tourism markets. Consequently, strategic decisions for the full range of state-brand activities should be identified.

Implementation: what should the State of Palestine do for its brand strategy?

The final, and obviously the most crucial stage in state branding is the implementation phase. How will the chosen strategy for the state brand of Palestine be implemented? It has been suggested that a strategy implementation includes key challenges as ensuring control, managing knowledge, coping with change, designing appropriate structures and processes, and managing internal and external relationships (Johnson, Scholes and Whittington 2005). In the context of Palestine, these key challenges are fine tuned to the following state branding elements, which encompass: state branding advertising, diaspora mobilization, and customer and citizenship relationship management.

State branding advertising

Advertising is seen as the most prominent marketing tool for creating long term effects of a brand. It can deliver multiple benefits to a brand like generating new markets, changing consumer behaviour, rejuvenating a declining brand and boosting rapid sales in short term (Grossman and Shapiro 1984). If some advertising will be bought for the State of Palestine, people procuring the advertising should have basic advertising literacy to avoid some common mistakes. A clear client brief needs to be pitched to an advertising agency and all requirements for an advertising campaign including budgets and timing should be explained in detail. In most cases, an advertising agency creates a creative team for this campaign and offers also to buy media space where the advertising will appear. In an earlier study, conducted by Çakmak and Isaac (2012) suggested that e-word-of-mouth marketing is a powerful tool for Bethlehem, Palestine. Online branding can offer to the state brand of Palestine opportunities to establish itself as a niche brand in a way that would not be possible through using conventional branding techniques. However, advertising absorbs mostly the biggest part of a marketing budget. Dinnie (2008) recommends that if a state has scarce financial resources, it would be better off activating its diaspora rather than placing its hope in mere advertising campaigns.

Diaspora mobilization

Kuznetsov (2006) advises that successful diaspora networks should have three features:

1   Networks bring people together with strong intrinsic motivation.
2   Betwork members contribute directly (e.g. investing in the home country) and indirectly (e.g. intermediating for development projects in the home country) to development of home country.
3   Network members take initiatives to get involved with the home country to transactions (see Chapter 8).

The Palestinian diaspora networks spread across the world epitomize a potentially immense asset for the State of Palestine. By means of the remittances sent by diaspora members, their investments in Palestine, their active home networks engagement with Palestinian issues, and their capacity of state brand's reputation building are diaspora members an essential resource for the new state. Over half of the ten million Palestinians worldwide live outside the Palestinian Territories (Gassner 2008). One should take into account that not every Palestinian living in the diaspora is an exile, and not every exile is a refugee (International Crisis Group 2009). Even if the Israeli–Palestinian conflict must be considered the main cause of the exodus, a sizable diaspora community had already existed previously. Christians especially had been emigrating to Europe and the Americas from the Holy Land since the late eighteenth century. One reason for this was hope of finding better living conditions. Today, several hundred thousand (predominantly Christian) people of Palestinian descent live in Chile alone, more than anywhere else outside the Middle East (Dane and Knocha, 2012). In addition, large Palestinian communities exist in Brazil, El Salvador, Honduras, and Peru. In Peru, both candidates for the March 2004 presidential elections were descendants of Palestinians who had emigrated from Bethlehem in 1912 and 1914 respectively (Gassner 2008).

Throughout Latin America, the descendants of Palestinian immigrants have played and are still playing a defining role in politics, the economy and culture. Presidents of Palestinian descent have held office in both El Salvador and Honduras. While most Palestinians have integrated into their new home countries in the Western world without any problems, they have been prevented from doing so in many cases in the Middle East. For example, Honduras has a thriving Palestinian community, and they are predominantly Christians from the neighborhood of Bethlehem. The first Palestinian migrants came during the Ottomans empire, followed by new groups of Palestinians after the founding of the State of Israel in 1948, the occupied territories of Palestine of the West Bank and Gaza in 1967 and both *Intifadas* (uprisings). According to the Arabic Club (van Lohuizen 2011), housed in a luxury building in Tegucigalpa, Honduras has more than 200,000 residents of Palestinian origin.

Two sisters Carmen and Victoria Selman born in Bethlehem made with their mother a long boat trip to Honduras in 1935. Their father was already there, and he had a shop of Chinese service and linen. They went back three times to Palestine, but as they stated 'our country is gone'. The sisters feel even Palestinians. They have both a Palestinian restaurant and they are planning to open new ones in the country. State branding strategists need to integrate the Palestinian diaspora networks into their overall strategy. Another example is the Palestinian diaspora in Chile that can be also integrated in the overall branding strategy. A team founded by Palestinian immigrants in Chile has not forgotten their origins and are making plenty of signals in solidarity with their country. These are signals that could be used as a brand name. Immigrants to Chile in the nineteenth and early twentieth century helped to form three major footballs clubs in the capital, Santiago. Unió Español were first, followed by Audax Italiano and then in 1920, Palestino. The latter have been the least successful of the trio but they are becoming well known for their gestures of political support for the nation of Palestine. In recent years the club have received attention for their involvement in oases beyond football. During various conflicts between Palestinians and Israelis, including the current one, the club have made no secret of the fact that they fully support Palestine's demand to be recognized as a nation. The club is still run by Chileans with Palestinian roots, the Bank of Palestine are their current sponsors and they have always played in the national colors – red, green, and white striped shirts with black shorts. In 2014, the figure one on the back of the team's shirts was a stylized map of Palestine before the creation of Israel in 1948 (The Half Decent Football Magazine 2014). Also, the Palestinian appearance at the Asia Cup tournament in Australia, where Palestinians hope that footballers can put them on the map.

Customer and citizenship relationship management

Customer relationship management (CRM) refers to a strategic approach that develops appropriate relationships with key customers and customer segments in order to make them loyal to an institute (Payne and Frow 2005). In state branding is the term CRM considered as 'citizen relationship management' (Dinnie 2008). Accordingly, governments need to engage with and respond to their citizens' needs and wishes in which companies do with their customers in a similar way. They need to understand citizens' perceptions of the nation identity and how they feel about the state branding campaign. All the people who are living and working in the State of Palestine must fully comprehend the contributions of new state brand. Recruiting citizens support would be the major desired outcome of a new state branding campaign. If citizens positively perceive the state branding strategy, they may be more willing to communicate with their friends and relatives abroad. In this way they may attract tourists and investors to Palestine, and contribute as a labour pool and customers to the national economy. The new state of Palestine can introduce a citizen ambassador program where citizens become ambassadors of their cities and get engage in the state branding program. International investments as mentioned in this chapter drag thousands of foreign aid workers to various territories of Palestine and that can have various impacts on the local population as well as word-of-mouth to the outside world. Therefore, it becomes clear to observe the relation between international investment and migration of highly skilled foreigners to Palestine (Chaveneau 2013).

Conclusion

This chapter highlights some challenges and many opportunities for state branding of the State of Palestine. As its official recognition grows worldwide, the State of Palestine needs to consider opportunities in promoting itself, its image, products and resources by means of strategic state branding. This chapter outlined the necessity of state branding, however, the branding strategy of the State of Palestine needs to be defined by the Palestinian national organizations. In this respect, the Palestinian Ministry of Planning and Administrative Development would be the most suitable entity in taking these steps forward, in collaboration and consultations with residents, SMEs, private sector as well as public sectors in setting up a strategy for Palestine's state branding. Tourism is a very important sector that can be a starting point for increasing and promoting the image of the State of Palestine. This as a result may also improve the place from a negative to a positive one. Exports products such as olive oil, Palestinian beer, dairy products are all important when it comes to improving the image of the State of Palestine. These can play a signal like a brand name that operate as a quicker way in recognizing a brand and eventually in purchasing decisions. Another crucial element in state branding is the mobilization of diaspora. The Palestinian diaspora around the world could play a very important role and should be integrated in the overall branding strategy.

References

Abu Sitta, S. (2008) 'Reflections on Al-Nakba' in: S. Abu Sitta, N. Sultany, D. Wagner and S, Ali (eds.) *Palestinians and the Jewish State: 60 years of exile and dispossession*, Washington DC: The Palestine Centre.

Çakmak, E. and Isaac, R.K. (2012) 'What destination marketers can learn from their visitors' blogs: an image analysis of Bethlehem, Palestine', *Journal of Destination Marketing and Management*, 1(1–2): 124–133.

Chaveneau, C. (2013) 'Leaving Europe to go to Palestinian territories: looking for work, experience and adventure,' paper presented at the 11th conference of the European Sociology Association, Turino, 28–31 August. RN 35 – Sociology of migration. Distributed paper.

Dan, F. and Knocha, J. (2012) *The Palestinian Diaspora: Palestinian expatriates and their impact on the Middle East conflict*, Ramallah: Konrad-Adenauer-Stiftung (KAS).

Deibel, T.R. (2007) *Foreign affairs strategy logic for American statecraft*, Cambridge: Cambridge University Press.

Dinnie, K. (2008) *Nation branding. Concepts, issues, practice*, 1st ed., Oxford: Butterworth-Heinemann.

Gassner, I.J. (2008) 'Palestinians living in the Diaspora', *This Week in Palestine*, 119. Online http://thisweekinpalestine.com/details.php?id=2402&ed=151&edid=151 [Accessed 16 January 2015].

Grossman, G.M. and Shapiro, C. (1984) 'Informative advertising with differentiated products,' *Review of Economic Studies*, 51(1): 63–81.

Hankinson, G. (2007) 'The management of destination brands: five guiding principles based on recent developments in corporate branding theory,' *Journal of Brand Management*, 14(3): 240–254.

International Crisis Group. (2009) 'Nurturing instability: Lebanon's Palestinian refugee camps', *Crisis Group Middle East Report No. 84* Online http://www.crisisgroup.org/en/regions/middle-east-north-africa/israel-palestine/084-nurturing-instability-lebanons-palestinian-refugee-camps.aspx [Accessed 16 January 2015].

International Olympic Committee (2015). 205 National Olympics Committee. Online http://www.olympic.org/national-olympic-committees [Accessed 1 July 2015].

Isaac, R.K. (2010) 'Moving from pilgrimage to responsible tourism the case of Palestine', *Current Issues in Tourism*, 13(6): 579–590.

Isaac, R.K. and Platenkamp, V. (2012) 'Ethnography of hope in extreme places: Arendt's agora in controversial destinations', *Tourism, Culture and Communication*, 12(2–3): 173–186.

Johnson, G., Scholes, K. and Whittington, R. (2005) *Exploring corporate strategy: text and cases*, 7th edn, London: FT Prentice Hall.

Kuznetsov, Y. (2006) 'Leveraging diasporas of talent: Towards a new policy agenda', in Y. Kuznetsov (ed.) *Diaspora networks and the international migration of skills: how countries can draw on their talent abroad*, WBI Development Studies.

Leonard, M., Stead, C. and Smewing, C. (2002) *Public diplomacy*, London: The Foreign Policy Center.

McCarthy, R. (2009) 'Brewed in the West Bank, drunk in Japan', *The Guardian*. Online http://www.theguardian.com/world/2009/oct/02/taybeh-palestinian-brewery-west-bank [Accessed 17 March, 2015].

Montevideo convention on the rights and duties of states. (1933).Online http://www.cfr.org/sovereignty/montevideo-convention-rights-duties-states/p15897 [Accessed 15 March 2015].

Palestine Fair Trade. (2014) *Palestine fair trade: who we are.* Online http://www.palestinefairtrade.org/index.php?option=com_content&view=article&id=47&Itemid=92 [Accessed 7 March 2015].

Palestine Trade Center (PalTrade). (2014) *The State of Palestine: national export strategy, tourism sector export strategy 2014–2018*, Geneva: European Union, Ministry of National Economy, The International Trade Centre and Paltrade.

Pawson, C. (2014) 'Fair trade: making a real difference to farmers in Palestine', *The Guardian*. Online http://www.theguardian.com/sustainable-business/fairtrade-partner-zone/2014/sep/19/fairtrade-zayoun-palestine [Accessed 17 March, 2015].

Payne, A. and Frow, P. (2005) 'A strategic framework for customer relationship management', *Journal of Marketing*, 69: 167–176.

Sanbar, E. (2001) 'Out of place out of time', *Mediterranean Historical Review*, 16(1), 87–94.

Schmid, D. (2006) 'Palestine: la problématique de l'aide. *Politique étrangère, Automne* 3: 491–503.

The Half Decent Football Magazine. (2014) 'Root pressure', *September Issue*, 331: 39.

Trading Economics. (2014) *Trading economic indicators*. Online http://www.tradingeconomics.com/palestine/imports.

Turner, M. (2012) 'Completing the circle: peace building as colonial practice in the Occupied Palestinian Territory', *International Peacekeeping,* 19(4): 492–507.

United Nations Office for the Coordination of Humanitarian Affairs (UNOCHA). (2008) *Increased need, decreasing access: Tightening control on economic movement. Special Focus.* Online http://www.ochaopt.org/documents/commercial%20crossings%20v5.pdf [Accessed 3 March 2015].

Van Ham. (2001) 'The rise of the brand state: the postmodern politics of image and reputation', *Foreign Affairs*, 8(5): 2–6.

Van Lohuizen, K. (2011) Palestijnse zussen in Honduras, *NRC Handelsblad*, Saturday 12 November.

World Bank. (2014). *West Bank and Gaza investment and climate assessment: fragmentation and uncertainty,* Washington: World Bank.

17 Giving Palestinian tourism(s) a voice

Rami K. Isaac, Vincent Platenkamp,
Freya Higgins-Desbiolles and
C. Michael Hall

The division of space and destruction of place often go parallel with a process of physical and political colonization of land (Isaac and Platenkamp 2012; Isaac *et al*. 2012). In Palestine the colonized are effectively imprisoned behind the Wall and the colonizers occupy the landscape by building more settlements and confiscating more Palestinian land and heritage, such as the case of Rachel's Tomb in Bethlehem (Selwyn 2011; Isaac and Platenkamp 2015). This process and the presence, as well as the form of settlements, signify the domination of one community and culture over the other. In addition, it attempts to legitimize the physical and political presence of the colonizers through the imposition of narratives of (re)interpretation and (re)appropriation of space, landscapes and place of memories (Piqaurd and Swenarton 2011). In other words, a specific Zionist cultural heritage had to be (re)constructed to harmonize with select Jewish and fundamentalist Christian religious narratives that seek to build legitimacy to justify the acquisition and control of Palestinian space in conjunction with an international supportive movement (Ibrahim 2011).

Israel's occupation and annexation of Palestine is not limited to its military elements, but the occupation is too manifested in Israel's use of tourism as a political tool. As Alqasis (2015: 1) commented in an article entitled 'Israel's grip on the Palestinian tourism industry', 'Through a regime of permits, licenses and visas, Israel controls who guides most tourists to the Holy Land, what they are told (through Israeli guides) and where they spend their money'. Tourism is used to strengthen Israel's position as occupying power, to maintain its control and domination of the territories of Palestine and people. In addition, tourism and heritage sites are also used for the dissemination of selective interpretation and, in some cases, outright propaganda to millions of tourists and visitors to the Holy Land, including politicians, community leaders and journalists who sometimes receive free-of-charge first class tours to Israel. These tours are organized in a way that the narrative is crafted though the omission and selected interpretation of crucial information and by ensuring that there is little contact between visitors and local Palestinian communities, the 'living stones' of Palestine. As Rifat Kassis (cited in Alqasis 2015: 1) coordinator of Kairos Palestine, a Palestinian Christian anti-occupation movement, explains: 'millions of tourists come to Bethlehem, Palestine, every year and, without talking to a single Palestinian, return home as enemies of Palestine and ambassadors of Israel'.

In another article in the *Los Angeles Times* Sanders (2011) states that Israel and Palestine compete for Christian pilgrims' business in Bethlehem, where scores of buses arrive each day to visit Jesus' birthplace. The third-generation woodcarver, who sells handmade likenesses of baby Jesus and the Virgin Mary, sees as many as 200 tour buses arrive every day from Israel to visit the Church of Nativity, just a few steps from his store. All tourists are escorted directly from the bus to the church and back again. They are hardly given time to browse the shops nearby and almost never spend the night in Bethlehem (Sanders 2011). Nowadays, Israel has a stranglehold on the flow of international tourists, arriving through Ben-Gurion airport, using Israeli touring buses and Israeli guides. One of the difficulties in the Palestinian tourism industry is that tourists who visit Palestinian cities and towns stay only for a few hours and then return to Israel, where they stay and spend more money, using only Israeli guides and touring buses, merely because Israel has the authority and control over access to Palestinian cities (Isaac 2010). Consequently even when pilgrims visit Palestinian territory, local business do not necessarily profit. The Israeli Ministry of Tourism is nowadays promoting a Christmas Eve alternative to Bethlehem, by inviting pilgrims and foreign diplomats to the Israeli city of Nazareth to enjoy a Christmas market, parade, fireworks display and jolly Santa Claus for the kids (Sanders 2011).

Therefore, it is clear from the facts provided above that Palestinians are finding it hard to have their voices heard and concerted efforts are needed to ensure that Palestinian voices are heard in tourism. Clearly, the relationships between Israel, Palestine and tourism are inherently political. If a critical and informative engagement is to be established then, as in the tourism industry, Palestinian voices need to be heard. If giving voice to Palestinians becomes our main concern, we need a forum to introduce this voice with its justified contribution. For this forum, we use the concept of the 'agora' of Arendt (1958).

The 'agora' and the modes of knowledge in Palestine

Arendt (1958) introduces the agora as a public place, comparable to the Forum Romanum, where individuals present themselves with independent opinions. In this way, a pluralized discussion comes into being that creates the opportunity for individuals to present themselves as human beings and escape the thoughtlessness that dehumanizes our species. On the agora a pluralist discourse can be organized with the originally normative rationality of Habermas (1984), but without its pressure to get to a consensus. This normative discourse will be elaborated as a mode 3 discourse (Kunneman 2005; Platenkamp 2007; Portegies *et al.* 2009), which is related to the earlier developed academic mode 1 and 2 discourses (Gibbons *et al.* 1994; Tribe 1997).

Gibbons *et al.* (1994: 168) state mode 2 knowledge emerges from the 'context of application within its own distinct theoretical structures, research methods and modes of practice which may not be locatable on the prevailing disciplinary map'. In contrast, mode 1 knowledge production remains associated with the more traditional disciplinary academic research, within university structures. Tribe

(1997) and Portegies *et al.* (2009) used this distinction in tourism studies. In addition, Coles *et al.* (2009: 84) describe the distinction as follows: 'mode 1 appears to be the dominant type in higher education these days, as "the traditional center for knowledge production", whereas mode 2 was originally anticipated as taking place outside the university structures'.

Mode 3 knowledge production has been added to the other two modes because of the exclusion of normative and existential questions in this academic (mode 1) and professional (mode 2) research (see Isaac and Platenkamp 2012). In this closing piece, the central focus will be on mode 3 knowledge production. Mode 3 knowledge has been introduced by Kunnenman (2005) in the awareness that in both other modes there has been a long-term tendency to exclude the 'slow questions'. Isaac and Platenkamp state (2012: 174) 'mode 3 knowledge is connected to the 'slow questions' that try to deal with sickness, death, repression, but in addition to the moral virtues, as compassion, inner strengths or wisdom and other sources of existential fulfillments that remain crucial for all generations in various places'.

In a 'global village' there is a need for plural discussions on values and norms. This implies that a plural concerto of various transcendent values and perspectives from all over the globe has to be organized in the tension between self and other. One has to live with differences and try to understand them. Simultaneously there is no escape from them. When hegemonic relations between Israel and Palestine still reign in their power relations, a normative orientation introduces a necessary value-laden discussion on various topics that are produced because of these relations. Through a normative revitalization of the different positions related to these power relations, the actual opinions of all parties involved are being questioned. These discussions have a more philosophical dimension because they are attached to the 'slow questions' (Kunnenman 2005) of life and death. The relation between Israel and Palestine is imbued with normative argumentation. Positions need to be taken here, as in all extreme conditions, and especially respect for the other positions becomes crucial. Each position needs to be seen as an end in itself and, therefore, cannot be manipulated as if it were a means and therefore, this book exemplifies the importance of Palestinian voices as crucial in this process. How to argue in this context remains a relevant question that is also related to possible theoretical ways to bridge gaps between 'selves' and 'others'. In a human world where human plurality dictates the rules and people occupy distinctive, equivalent positions, a normative discourse supports the communicative action (Habermas, 1984) from within the life-worlds of Israelis and Palestinians. This discourse needs a point of anchorage in the contested space of Palestine and the concept of an agora suits this need well. On the agora plural voices present themselves in a serious discussion. These voices can only present themselves if they are included. The Palestinian voice has long been neglected and excluded. Thus, the main aim of this book became to claim this voice in the academia in Palestine, and subsequently, the decision was made to only include contributions for chapters from the Palestinian side.

Hall (2011: 39) stated 'what we do in tourism is inherently political, or has political implications in terms of who gets what, why and where'. Alas, in tourism studies, such questions are hardly asked (Hall 1994, 2007, 2010) and tourism studies to a large extent has remained stubbornly apolitical. Exceptions to this have emerged particularly from scholars aligned closely to the critical tradition. Such scholars have offered challenging political contributions, including: self-reflection in relation to the production of knowledge in the social sciences (e.g. Jamal and Hollinshead 2001; Tribe 1997, 2006); concerns of the marginalized addressed in scholarship (e.g. Higgins-Desbiolles 2007; Wearing et al. 2010); and the issues of human rights, justice and emancipation from oppression (e.g. Higgins-Desbiolles 2008). In this promising context, political analyses of the case of Palestine's tourism has been able to emerge (see the work of Isaac; Blancahrd and Higgins-Desbiolles 2013; Higgins-Desbiolles 2013).

In this closing piece, we call for a revitalization of a critical and humanistic intellectual position (giving voice to the excluded) in the tourism academy (Isaac *et al.* 2012). This revitalization takes the shape of a polyphonic dialogue (Clifford and Marcus 1986) between these different positions. This dialogue concerns not only academic positions but also an intellectual discussion about world-views, politics, economics, media or culture that makes tourism an embedded phenomena. This embeddedness is needed in order to understand tourism not as an isolated phenomenon but as something that is profoundly integrated in society and for which the capacity of voluntary freedom of movement must inherently require an awareness of political action. For this discussion, we promote the polyphonic dialogue on the 'agora'.

In a work such as this, we cannot forget the legacy provided by the public intellectual Edward Said who not only who changed the shape of cultural theory and academic practice with his radical scholarship, but was also a passionate advocate for the Palestinian people. As Giroux (2004: 147) noted: 'a controversial and courageous public intellectual, Said provided a model for what it means to combine scholarship and commitment'. Following Said's dichotomies (2004) of reception-resistance and insider-outsider, the intellectual position in this debate should be organized in the different perspectives that have been taken. Through this implementation, the additional value of the tourism intellectual can have a refreshing and revitalized influence on the paralyzing relativism that often dominates our post-modern discourses.

According to Said (2004), the social world could be conceived as a text. The reader of a text starts with being open to the perspective that has been developed in the text, he/she is receiving the text (reception). The act of reading is 'an act of modest human emancipation and enlightenment that changes and enhances one's knowledge for purposes other than reductiveness, cynicism or fruitless standing aside' (Said 2004: 66). After this account of reading as reception and the concomitant emergence of a horizon of community, Said introduces the second facet of reading, resistance. Reading should also offer alternatives 'now silenced or unavailable through the channels of communication controlled by a tiny number of news organizations' in the face of 'an assault on thought itself, to say nothing of democracy, equality, and the environment, by the dehumanizing forces of globalization' (Said 2004: 66). For Said this resistant facet of reading entails the elaboration of ever widening frameworks of the writer or intellectual in his or her time and of the reader in a complex, overlapping network of institutional and social locations and historical processes. It entails the humanist migrating across such spheres of 'human endeavor as literature, philosophy, history, economics, policy and current events' (2004: 75–76). Resistance, here, becomes the ability to differentiate between what is directly given and what may be suspended or withheld. Does one accept the prevailing horizons and confinements, or does one try as a humanist to challenge them.

To paraphrase Said (2004: 77), in the tourism academy there must be a willingness to be both insider and outsider in the circulating of ideas and values, the circulating of people and the issues that arise within our society or the societies of others and the societies of each in relationship to each other. Such a positioning is vital for tourism that is occurring in an increasingly multicultural milieu, is fraught with tensions and where power is in flux. Such a positioning allows dialogue and engagement which is the only response which will allow us bridge the tensions that are evident in the zones of conflict and allow us to build a future together through our common humanity.

We find this concept of the role of 'insider-outsider' to be crucial to the discussion of the relevance of tourism in the Palestinian–Israeli conflict and other controversial destinations.

References

Alqasis, A. (2015) Israel's grip on the Palestinian tourism industry. Online http://972mag.com/israels-grip-on-the-palestinian-tourism-industry/107445/ [Accessed 10 June].

Arendt, H. (1958) *The human condition*, Chicago: The University of Chicago Press.

Blanchard, L and Higgins-Desbiolles, F. (eds.) (2013) *Peace through tourism: promoting human security through international citizenship*, London: Routledge.

Clifford, J., and Marcus, G. (eds.) (1986) *Writing culture: the poetics and politics of ethnography*, Berkley: University of California Press.

Coles, T., Hall, C.M. and Duval, D.T. (2009) 'Postdisciplinary tourism', in J. Tribe (ed.) *Philosophical issues in tourism*, Bristol: Channel View Publications.

Gibbons, M., Limoges, C., Nowotny, H., Schwartzman, S., Scott, P. and Trow, M. (1994) *The new production of knowledge*, London: Sage.

Giroux, H. (2004) *The terror of neoliberalism: authoritarianism and the eclipse of democracy*. Boulder: Paradigm.

Habermas, J. (1984) *The theory of communicative action*, Cambridge: Polity Press.

Hall, C. M. (1994) *The politics of tourism*, Chichester: John Wiley.

Hall, C. M. (2007) 'Tourism, governance and the (mis-)location of power', in A. Church and T. Coles (eds.), *Tourism, power and space*, London: Routledge.

Hall, C. M. (2010) 'Power and tourism: tourism and power', in D. Macloed and J. Carrier (eds.), *Tourism, power and culture: anthropological insights*, Bristol: Channel View Publications.

Hall, C. M. (2011) 'Researching the political in tourism: where knowledge meets power', in C. M. Hall (ed.), *Fieldwork in tourism methods: issues and reflections*, London: Routledge.

Higgins-Desbiolles, F. (2007) 'Hostile meeting grounds: encounters between the wretched of the earth and the tourist through tourism and terrorism in the 21st century', in P. Burns and M. Novelli (eds.) *Tourism and politics: global frameworks and local realities*, Amsterdam: Elsevier.

Higgins-Desbiolles, F. (2008) 'Justice tourism: a pathway to alternative globalisation', *Journal of Sustainable Tourism*, 16(3): 345–364.

Higgins-Desbiolles, F. (2013) 'Tourism as politics: the case of Palestine', in L. Blanchard and F. Higgins-Desbiolles (eds.). *Peace through tourism: promoting human security through international citizenship*, London: Routledge.

Ibrahim, N. (2011) The politics of heritage in Palestine: A conflict of two narratives. This Week in Palestine, Vol. 155. Online http://www.thisweekinpalestine.com/details. php?id=3358&ed=192&edid=192# [Accessed 15th June, 2015].

Isaac, R.K. (2010) 'Alternative tourism: new forms of tourism in Bethlehem for the Palestinian tourism industry', *Current Issues in Tourism*, 13(1): 21–36.

Isaac, R.K., and Platenkamp, V. (2012) 'Ethnography of hope in extreme places: Arendt's agora in controversial tourism destinations', *Tourism, Culture and Communication*, 12: 173–186.

Isaac, R.K., and Platenkamp, V. (2015) 'Concrete (Dy)Utopia in Bethlehem: a city of two tales', *Journal of Tourism and Cultural Change*, DOI:10.1080/14766825.2015.104 0413.

Isaac, R.K., Platenkamp, V. and Cakmak, E. (2012) 'Message from paradise: critical reflections on the tourism academy in Jerusalem', *Tourism, Culture and Communication*, 12: 159–171.

Jamal, T., and Hollinshead, K. (2001) 'Tourism and the forbidden zone: the underserved power of qualitative inquiry', *Tourism Management*, 22: 63–82.

Kunneman, H. (2005) *Voorbij het dikke-ik*, Amsterdam: B.V. Uitgeverij SWP.

Lasswell, H.D. (1936) *Politics: who gets what, when, how?*, New York: McGraw-Hill.

Piquard, B., and Swenarton, M. (2011) 'Architecture and conflict: Introduction learning from architecture and conflicts', *The Journal of Architecture*, 16(1): 1–13.

Platenkamp, V. (2007) Contexts in tourism and leisure studies. A cross-cultural contribution to the production of knowledge, Wageningen: Wageningen University, unpublished PhD dissertation.

Portegies, A., de Haan, T. and Platenkamp, V. (2009) 'Knowledge production in tourism. The evaluation of contextual learning processes in destination studies', *Tourism Analysis*, 4: 523–536.

Said, E. (2004) *Humanism and democratic criticism*, New York: Palgrave/Macmillan

Sanders, E. (2011) This holy land battle focuses in tourists' wallets. Online http://articles. latimes.com/2011/dec/20/world/la-fg-israel-christians-tourism-20111220 (Accessed 10 June 2015).

Selwyn, T. (2011) 'Tears on the border: the case of Rachel's Tomb, Bethlehem, Palestine," in Maria Kousis, Tom Selwyn, and David Clark, eds., *Contested Mediterranean Spaces: ethnographic essays in honour of Charles Tilly*, Oxford: Berghan Books.

Tribe, J. (1997) 'The indiscipline of tourism', *Annals of Tourism Research*, 24(3): 638–657.

Tribe, J. (2006) 'The truth about tourism', *Annals of Tourism Research*, 33(2): 360–381.

Wearing, S.L., Wearing, M. and McDonald, M. (2010) 'Understanding local power and interactional processes in sustainable tourism: Exploring village–tour operator relations on the Kokoda Track, Papua New Guinea', *Journal of Sustainable Tourism*, 10(1): 61–76.

Appendix

A Code of Conduct for tourism in the Holy Land

A Palestinian initiative

Responsible and just forms of tourism offer communities opportunities to share their cultures, tell their stories, request solidarity and foster tolerance and greater understanding. This is the principle that has shaped this Code of Conduct which has been developed to inform pilgrims and tourists of the reality of Palestine and Palestinians and to seek their support in using tourism to transform contemporary injustices. At the same time, the Code aims to raise awareness amongst Palestinian tourism stakeholders of how tourism in Palestine can be transformed and enhanced to truly benefit both hosts and visitors.

The context of Palestine

The establishment of just and responsible tourism for Palestine and Palestinians requires an understanding of political context and history, for it is these that set the constraints and barriers within which Palestinian tourism has to operate. The Code addresses these directly – and, by doing so, attempts to overcome them.

Palestine is a unique tourist destination – its long history, religious significance and natural beauty make it an amazing place to visit. Palestine's importance derives partly from the fact that it is home to the three monotheistic and Abrahamic religions of Judaism, Christianity, and Islam. Every year it attracts many pilgrims, people of faith and scholars who visit the holy places. Secular tourists come to explore the historical sites, Palestine's vibrant cities, rural life and nature reserves.

However, since the beginning of the 20th century Palestine has seen complicated changes in its political circumstances. These have included the creation of Israel in 1948 and the 1967 war. As a result of the latter, Israel occupied the West Bank, including East Jerusalem and the Gaza Strip. These events have created catastrophic political, economic and social facts which have deeply affected the life of the Palestinian people, most of whom became refugees. In many ways Palestine itself was simply wiped off the map, historic Palestine coming to be known as Israel. In this context tourism became a political tool in the supremacy and domination of the Israeli establishment over land and people, and an instrument for preventing the Palestinians from enjoying the benefits and the fruits of the cultural and human interaction on which tourism thrives. Despite the fact that Israel signed the Oslo Agreements with the PLO in the 1990s and recognised the establishment of the Palestinian Authority to administer some of the Palestinian territories, namely the West Bank and Gaza Strip, many areas of life in those areas are still under Israeli control. For example, Israel controls all access to Palestine (land and sea borders as well as access from the airport), most of the Palestinian water resources, and all movement of people and goods from, to and within Palestine. These facts have significant impacts on the development of tourism in the Palestinian territories and the dissemination of information to tourists. Jerusalem – the heart of tourism in the region – has been illegally annexed to Israel, filled with illegal settlements, besieged, surrounded by checkpoints, and encircled by the Apartheid Wall, all of which has resulted in the city's isolation from its social and geographical surroundings.

Despite all this, the touristic, historic, and holy places found in Israel and the Palestinian territories are united. They cannot be separated from each other. In this regard what we are asking tourists to do is to visit both Israel and Palestine rather than choose to visit just one or the other. This is the route towards more fairness and justice.

Tourism in Palestine provides visitors with a particularly rewarding and enriching experience. Not only may the tourist discover the beauty, spirituality and hospitality of the country but also come to encounter some of the political, economic, and social facts on the ground that shape the daily lives of Palestinians. This is as it should be for much can be gained – both by tourists and by their Palestinian hosts – from a proper relationship between the two. Too often the contact is very slight, consisting of rapid, coach driven visits to the Nativity church in Bethlehem (with a souvenir shop on the way) – a style of tourism that derives from the fact that much of the itinerary is controlled by Israel and the processes of the Israeli tourism industry. Our Code, on the other hand, seeks to contribute to a more general effort to re-engage the tourist with Palestinian land and people in such a way that will benefit local communities, reduce over exploitation of a small number of iconic sites, and also reduce the pollution that results from coach driven mass tourism in the Palestinian towns and cities (especially Bethlehem).

Therefore, we urge you, the tourist, to consider visiting the Palestinian cities, towns and villages and to allow time for encounters with the population living in these places. We believe that in this way, tourism will realise its potential for both you and us. At the same time, we call on the local community to interact positively and in a respectful way with pilgrims and tourists, and to renounce small-mindedness and exploitation of visitors. We should all remember that visits by tourists to the country are an opportunity for cultural, social and human exchange.

The vision of the Palestinian Initiative for Responsible Tourism

The Palestinian Initiative for Responsible Tourism (PIRT) is a network of organisations, associations and public bodies committed to work for responsible tourism to the Holy Land and to act as advocates for this approach to tourism. We are committed to transforming the current tourism patterns in the Holy Land by encouraging pilgrims and tourists to include Palestinian cities, towns and villages in their itineraries in order to achieve a more equal distribution of tourism revenues to all people in this land. Based on our belief that both tourists and hosts can be enriched by human encounters through tourism, we invite travellers to meet the Palestinian people and explore their culture. We strive to create opportunities for local communities to become involved in tourism activities and to earn a fair income from the process. We believe that protecting and preserving the environment is of utmost importance, and thus we are searching for less harmful ways of providing tourism services. We call on all service providers to commit themselves to responsible business practices and to renounce exploitative behaviour. Our objective is to promote a just and responsible tourism in Palestine that benefits the Palestinian people, pilgrims, tourists and all other stakeholders in tourism in the country without harming local communities.

The Code of Conduct

A: travellers to the Holy Land

Preparation

To prepare your trip to Palestine, we encourage you to consider including the following in your preparation:

1   Choose an inclusive and balanced itinerary that allows you to visit and stay in different places.
2   Educate yourself by reading guidebooks, travel accounts and articles about current news and events.
3   Establish contact with Palestinians to get up-to-date information about the current situation, safety, local history, culture and customs.
4   Approach travelling with a desire to learn rather than just observe. Leave prejudices behind.

Your trip

Adopting a considerate attitude towards the people you encounter, the environment, and host communities when travelling in Palestine helps to make sure that your trip is beneficial both for you as a tourist and for the hosts.

1   Your attitude:
    • Respect and learn about the local culture. Although taking pictures is in general welcome, be aware of people's sensitivity about being photographed: always ask first for their approval.
    • Observe local customs. Respect local dress codes and dress modestly.

- Interact and spend time with local people. Be aware that your cultural values may differ from theirs. They may, for example, have different concepts of time, personal space, communication and society. Other values are not wrong or inferior, just different.
2 Your behaviour:
    - Be aware of short-sighted emotional reactions, such as giving money out of compassion. This can be offensive.
    - Make sure that you encounter and engage with the local communities who are struggling for the respect of their dignity.
    - Support communities in a responsible way, without encouraging them to change their customs in order to adopt yours.
    - When visiting holy sites, allow members of the respective religious community to guide you.
3 Your use of natural resources:
    - Co-operate with locals in conserving precious natural resources. Commit yourself to a moderate use when possible.
    - Be open to experience local standards rather than expecting to find the same conditions as in your home town and/or country.
4 Support the local economy:
    - Appreciate local expertise by paying adequately.
    - Buy local products.
    - Contribute to ensuring that tourism has a beneficial outcome for the local community.
    - Use local transportation, guides, accommodation, restaurants and markets to benefit the local economy. Consider giving tips where customary.
5 Remember that the people you encounter have lived under military occupation for many years. Be sensitive when discussing related topics and listen to their points of view.
6 Be inspired by the pilgrim's journey: take your time to live and experience the daily life of the local people.

Returning home

When you return from Palestine do not hesitate to share your experiences with friends and relations. Your Palestinian hosts will be very happy to know that you keep them in your mind and that you tell their and your stories. In this way, you can strengthen the human side of tourism and enhance its benefits to communities and individuals.

7 Share your experience:
    - Think of creating links between your community and the community you visited.
    - Tell the stories of the people you met.

- Discuss and debrief with other members of your group (if you travelled together with others).
- Share with your family; inform your community; write articles.

8   Stick to the commitments you made during your trip:
- Remember the promises you made to the local people you met and honour them.
- Keep the people in your thoughts, pray for them and act when your actions are needed.

9   Allow yourself to be enriched by learning experiences:
- Question your stereotypes/generalisations, both the ones you had before the trip and the ones emerging from your experience abroad.
- Address prejudices and injustice where you meet them.

10 Take action:
- Learn about the involvement and responsibilities of your home country in the Middle East. Expose and confront them when they have been unfair.
- Address statements you do not agree with, such as inaccurate tourism brochures, stereotyped views of Palestine in conversation and inaccurate or biased media portrayals.

B: the Palestinian tourism sector

Whilst Palestine has been a destination for travellers for many centuries, the development of a tourism industry that provides services to a large number of tourists is still rather recent. Indeed, the development has not yet been completed and new capacities are being added. Despite this, we believe that the time has come to work towards a more sustainable development of the sector. Therefore, as representatives of the Ministry of Tourism and Antiquities and private companies, associations and civil society organisations, we call on all tourism stakeholders in Palestine to commit to the practices and policies introduced in this Code of Conduct.

Your behaviour towards tourists: treat them honestly and with respect

1   Respect the religious belief of visitors and the freedom of religious worship. Appreciate cultural diversity. Respect ways of dressing and food preferences of visitors.
2   Tour guides: Provide accurate and useful information to tourists that covers the religious, social and cultural dimensions of Palestine. Do not just tell stories that visitors want to hear and do not repeat stereotypes. Instead of doing this, challenge the visitors by presenting different interpretations. Be aware of your unique role as a tour guide: visitors will draw conclusions about Palestinians from your behaviour.

3 Local communities, tour guides and employees in the tourism sector: Help tourists when they are in need. Be hospitable. Interact with visitors on a human level, do not limit your interactions to economic/financial exchanges.
4 Authority: The tourist police and other official bodies should deal with tourists in a respectful way.
5 Authority and local communities: Undertake efforts to prevent negative and irresponsible behaviour like begging from tourists and exploiting them.

Your responsibility towards local communities. Bear in mind that local businesses have a responsibility towards the people they employ and the communities whose resources they use.

6 Pay fair wages.
7 Distribute the income fairly amongst product producers, providers, sellers and intermediaries.
8 Sell national and local products and handicrafts to tourists. Consider adopting fair trade standards.
9 Develop means of communication and opportunities for interaction between Palestinians and tourists.

Engage in human and cultural exchanges for these can increase the benefits from tourism to Palestinian communities.

10 Create opportunities for local communities to participate in tourism.
11 Increase networking amongst churches and international organisations to explain the Palestinian narrative to complete the picture of people who are familiar with the more well-known Israeli narrative.

Improve Palestinian tourism opportunities by creating new and unique itineraries. In addition, research and develop special Palestinian package tours that can be promoted locally for visitors after they have arrived in the country.

12 Develop the competence of the workforce in the tourism industry and their knowledge of Palestinian identity and history. Further, train tour guides in contemporary issues. Develop the awareness of people interacting with tourists (guides, taxi drivers, host families, etc.).
13 Integrate culture and heritage into tourist programmes. Improve the image of Palestine through organizing festivals, conferences, workshops and use these cultural events to encourage tourists to spend longer periods of time in Palestine.
14 Improve marketing of local handicrafts and national products.
15 Raise awareness that programmes of Palestinian travel agencies should include all different aspects of Palestine, i.e. religion, politics, economics, cultural heritage and leisure.

Our responsibility towards the environment

16 Introduce environment-friendly principles to the operation of hotels, guest houses and restaurants and inform your guests about your standards. Increase the environmental awareness among Palestinians and provide a tourism that respects the environment.

Responsible business practices in the tourism industry

17 Increase transparency in business practices and engage in ethical competition which does not harm the value of tourism.
18 Tourists have the right to fair prices and full enjoyment of their trips.

Establishing the Code of Conduct

The Code of Conduct has been drafted following extensive consultations both locally within Palestine and internationally with those organisations and individuals committed to responsible tourism and justice. It is a living document which invites engagement, comment and feedback for further improvement in achieving its objectives. You can help us to improve it by sending your feedback to pirt@atg.ps.

Organisations which are part of the Palestinian Initiative for Responsible Tourism

- Palestinian Ministry of Tourism and Antiquity
- Alternative Tourism Group
- Arab Hotel Association
- Bethlehem University
- Holy Land Incoming Tour Operator Association
- Holy Land Trust
- International Center of Bethlehem
- Jerusalem Inter-Church Center
- Joint Advocacy Initiative
- Network of Christian Organizations in Bethlehem
- Siraj Center for Holy Land Studies.

Index

Entries in italics indicate titles of documents. Page numbers in italics indicate figures or tables.